PARTIES WITHOUT PARTISANS

COMPARATIVE POLITICS

Comparative Politics is a series for students and teachers of political science that deals with contemporary issues in comparative government and politics. As Comparative European Politics it has produced a series of high quality books since its foundation in 1990, but now takes on a new form and a new title for the new millennium—Comparative Politics. As the process of globalisation proceeds, and as Europe becomes ever more enmeshed in world trends and events, so it is necessary to broaden the scope of the series.

The General Editors are Max Kaase, Professor of Political Science, University of Mannheim and Research Professor Wissenschaftszentrum Berlin, and Kenneth Newton, Professor of Government at Essex University. The series is published in association with the European Consortium for Political Research.

OTHER TITLES IN THE SERIES

Mixed-Member Electoral Systems: The Best of Both Worlds
Edited by Matthew Shugart and Martin P. Wattenberg

Coalition Governments in Western Europe
Edited by Wolfgang C. Müller and Kaare Strøm

Political Institutions: Democracy and Social Change
Josep H. Colomer

Parties without Partisans

Political Change in Advanced Industrial Democracies

Edited by

RUSSELL J. DALTON

and

MARTIN P. WATTENBERG

OXFORD

UNIVERSITY PRESS

OXFORD
UNIVERSITY PRESS

Great Clarendon Street, Oxford OX2 6DP

Oxford University Press is a department of the University of Oxford.
It furthers the University's objective of excellence in research, scholarship,
and education by publishing worldwide in

Oxford New York

Auckland Bangkok Buenos Aires Cape Town Chennai
Dar es Salaam Delhi Hong Kong Istanbul Karachi Kolkata
Kuala Lumpur Madrid Melbourne Mexico City Mumbai Nairobi
São Paulo Shanghai Taipei Tokyo Toronto

Oxford is a registered trade mark of Oxford University Press
in the UK and in certain other countries

Published in the United States
by Oxford University Press Inc., New York

British Library Cataloguing in Publication Data

Data available

Library of Congress Cataloging in Publication Data

Parties without partisans: Political change in advanced industrial democracies/edited by
Russell J. Dalton and Martin P. Wattenberg.
p. cm.
Includes bibliographical references (p.) and index.
1. Political parties. 2. Representative government and representation. 3. Comparative
government. I. Dalton, Russell J. II. Wattenberg, Martin P.
JF2051.P288 2000 324.2—dc21 00–057125
ISBN 0-19-924082-5 (hbk)
ISBN 0-19-925309-9 (pbk)

3 5 7 9 10 8 6 4 2

Typeset in Times by
Cambrian Typesetters, Frimley, Surrey
Printed in Great Britain
on acid-free paper by
T.J. International Ltd
Padstow, Cornwall

Preface

Political parties in advanced industrial democracies are changing in multi-faceted ways. Some scholars write of parties in decline, others of parties in resurgence, and still others of parties as transformed. What accounts for these differing conclusions? We suspected at the outset of this project that the answer stems from the fact that most publications deal with only one of three general areas of work on the subject: parties in the electorate, as organizations, and in government. As demonstrated in this volume, conclusions about changes in parties do indeed vary greatly according to perspective. At the risk of oversimplification, parties in the electorate do appear to be weakening most everywhere, whereas parties in government have largely maintained their functions, and parties as organizations have adapted to a vastly different environment through new methods and procedures. The findings, we believe, signal a considerable change in the nature of democratic politics that are just beginning to be felt.

A prime goal of this work was to bring together scholars who focus on different aspects of parties and get them to address each other's findings and conclusions. We first convened a planning meeting in Laguna Beach, California to discuss how we could best proceed. We agreed to begin from a functional perspective, comparatively examining the various functions that parties are thought to perform in any democracy. The group decided to focus on partisan changes in the established democracies of the Organization of Economic Cooperation and Development (OECD) since 1950. We also settled on trying to get as many of these countries covered in each chapter as possible, relying on archived data, published sources of information, and email queries to various country experts.

After the initial planning meeting, we assembled again during an American Political Science Association meeting at the backroom of a Washington, D.C. restaurant where Newt Gingrich and company reportedly planned out the 'Contract With America.' Although some of us were not particularly impressed with Newt's taste in food, we agreed that most parts of the project were coming along well and that we were ready for a full-fledged conference on changes in party politics. This next meeting took place over two days in March of 1998 in Newport Beach, California, at which time most of the results presented here were discussed. We want to thank Ken Carty, Gary Cox, and Barbara Sinclair for critiquing our findings at this conference, and helping to improve the final product.

Subsequently, many of the contributors took numerous opportunities to get together to discuss substantive details at various conferences and meetings.

(McAllister and Wattenberg even worked out some of the details of Chapter 3 while waiting for the morning sun to melt ice on a 4-seater Cessna plane at the Canberra airport.) Country specialists who authored one chapter often helped to provide data resources for the authors of other chapters; and multiple versions of most chapters were circulated among the project members. It is our hope that the normal coordination problems inherent in any edited volume have been largely minimized by the truly interactive and cooperative nature of this project.

We owe a great debt to the many people around the world who collected data upon which this book relies. It is a testament to modern political science that large scale data collection projects—such as national election studies, the Katz and Mair collection of party data, and the comparative manifesto data—are now available for comparative research. Many of our chapters quite openly build upon these data sources, and we gratefully acknowledge the efforts of others in compiling these data. We also wish to thank the many people around the world who answered the email queries of various contributors to this book and generously shared information with us. The Internet has not only contributed to greater efficiencies in the world economy; it has also facilitated broad comparative scholarly work such as found in this volume.

This communications technology also made it incredibly easy to deal with the fine people at Oxford University Press in the United Kingdom, who readily answered our queries from Oxford while we were sleeping in California. We wish to thank Dominic Byatt for his invaluable support and guidance and to Amanda Watkins for smoothly managing the details of turning a manuscript into a book.

The bulk of the financial support for this project was generously provided by the Center for the Study of Democracy at the UC, Irvine. In addition, the Center for German and European Studies at the University of California, Berkeley provided two grants for research assistants. We are greatly indebted for all this support.

Contents

CONCLUSION

List of Figures

List of Tables

Notes on Contributors

SHAUN BOWLER is Professor of Political Science at the University of California, Riverside. Bowler is co-editor of *Party Discipline and Parliamentary Government* (1999), co-editor of *Electoral Strategies and Political Marketing* (1992), and co-author of *Demanding Choices: Opinions, Voting and Direct Democracy* (1998), which concerns the process of direct democracy. He is currently working on the relationship between direct and representative democracy.

MIKI L. CAUL is a doctoral candidate in political science at the University of California, Irvine, and a research fellow in the Center for the Study of Democracy. Her research interests focus on political parties, participation, and women in politics. Her doctoral research examines the factors facilitating the representation of women in parties within the OECD nations. She has published her research in *Party Politics*, *Comparative Political Studies*, and *Pilipinas*.

RUSSELL J. DALTON is Professor of Political Science and Director of the Center for the Study of Democracy at the University of California, Irvine. His scholarly interests include comparative political behaviour, political parties, social movements, and empirical democratic theory. He is author of *The Green Rainbow: Environmental Interest Groups in Western Europe* (1994), *Citizen Politics*, 2nd edn. (1996), and *Politics in Germany* (1993); he co-authored *Critical Masses: Citizens, Environmental Destruction, and Nuclear Weapons Production in Russia and the United States* (1999), *Germany Transformed* (1981); and he is editor of *Germans Divided* (1996), *The New Germany Votes* (1993), *Challenging the Political Order* (1990), and *Electoral Change* (1984).

DAVID M. FARRELL is Jean Monnet Chair in European politics at the University of Manchester. He is an executive member (from 1998) of the Political Organizations and Parties section of the American Political Science Association, joint editor of *Party Politics*, and author of numerous papers on parties, campaigns, and electoral systems. His recent books include: *Party Discipline and Parliamentary Government* (co-edited, 1999), and *Electoral Systems: A Comparative Introduction* (2000).

MARK M. GRAY is a doctoral candidate in political science at the University of California, Irvine. His research emphases include political participation, the mass media, democratization, and time-series cross-sectional data analysis. His research on explaining declines in voting turnout has appeared in *Comparative Political Studies*.

IAN MCALLISTER is Director of the Research School of Social Sciences at the Australian National University. Previously he held appointments at the University of New South Wales, the University of Strathclyde, and the University of Manchester. He is the author of *Political Behaviour* (1992), *Dimensions of Australian Society* (co-author, 1995), *Russia Votes* (1996, co-author) and *The Australian Political System* (co-author, 1998). His research interests are in the areas of comparative political behaviour, political parties, voters, and electoral systems.

SUSAN E. SCARROW is Associate Professor of Political Science at the University of Houston. Among her main research interests are the development and impact of political parties in established democracies. Her publications include *Parties and their Members* (1996), edited special issues of *European Journal of Political Research* and *Party Politics*, and many journal articles and book chapters on political parties, German politics, electoral systems, and direct democracy.

KAARE STRØM is Professor of Political Science at the University of California, San Diego, and Adjunct Professor of Comparative Politics at the University of Bergen, Norway. His research interests are in the fields of political parties, government coalitions, comparative legislatures, and parliamentary democracy. Strøm's publications include *Minority Government and Majority Rule* (1990), *Challenges to Political Parties: The Case of Norway* (with Lars Svåsand, 1997), *Koalitionsregierungen in Westeuropa* (with Wolfgang Müller, 1997), and numerous articles in journals such as the *American Political Science Review*, the *American Journal of Political Science*, and the *European Journal of Political Research*. In 1994, he received the UNESCO Stein Rokkan Prize in Comparative Social Science Research. Strøm is a Fellow of the Norwegian Academy of Science and Letters.

MICHAEL F. THIES is Assistant Professor of Political Science, University of California, Los Angeles, and 1999–2000 National Fellow at the Hoover Institution, Stanford University. He is currently engaged in research on inter-party delegation in coalition governments and on the electoral foundations of legislative organization. His recent publications include articles on electoral politics and legislative politics in *American Journal of Political Science*, *British Journal of Political Science*, *Legislative Studies Quarterly*, and *Comparative Political Studies*.

MARTIN P. WATTENBERG is Professor of Political Science at the University of California, Irvine. His first regular paying job was with the Washington Redskins, from which he moved on to receive a Ph.D. at the University of Michigan. His research specializes in the study of public opinion and electoral politics in the United States, as well as other advanced industrial democracies. He is the author of *The Decline of American Political Parties* (1998) and *The Rise of Candidate-Centered Politics* (1991).

PAUL WEBB is a Senior Lecturer in Government at Brunel University in London and a former visiting fellow in Social Sciences at Curtin University in Western Australia. Associate Editor of Party Politics, he is the author of *The Modern British Party System* (2000), *Trade Unions and the British Electorate* (1992) and numerous chapters and articles on British and comparative party politics. He is currently editing two comparative volumes on parties in democratic societies for Oxford University Press.

Introduction

1

Unthinkable Democracy

Political Change in Advanced Industrial Democracies

Russell J. Dalton and Martin P. Wattenberg

THE renowned political scientist E. E. Schattschneider (1942: 1) once concluded 'modern democracy is unthinkable save in terms of political parties'. Similarly, James Bryce (1921: 119) stated 'parties are inevitable. No one has shown how representative government could be worked without them.' Joseph Schumpeter emphasized the role of parties, if not the explicit term, in his definition of democracy as 'that institutional arrangement for arriving at political decisions in which individuals acquire the power to decide by means of a competitive struggle for the people's votes' (Schumpeter 1942: 269). These views are shared by many other political scientists and political analysts, ranging from the American Political Science Association's call for more responsible party government in 1950, to a 1999 *Economist* article that examines the role of political parties as the basis of democracy.[1]

Today, mounting evidence points to a declining role for political parties in shaping the politics of advanced industrial democracies. Many established political parties have seen their membership rolls wane, and contemporary publics seem increasingly sceptical about partisan politics. Moreover, the media present images of party scandals and partisan corruptions with apparently increasing regularity. Other signs of partisan change fill the airwaves and the academic journals.

It would be an overstatement to write the parties' political obituary, but a pattern of partisan decline—or at least a transformation in the role played by parties—is increasingly apparent in almost all advanced industrial democracies. At the individual level, there is increased public disenchantment with specific parties and often toward the system of party government itself. Feelings of partisan identification have weakened in many nations. Contemporary publics are apparently more open in expressing their doubts about democratic parties and party systems (Poguntke and Scarrow 1996). The term 'Parteienverdrossenheit'

---

[1] 'Empty Vessels', *The Economist* (24 July 1999), 51–2.

has become a common part of the German political vocabulary. Independence from parties seems widespread in the United States, as exemplified by the Perot candidacy in 1992 and 1996, and support for incipient third party movements (Wattenberg 1998*a*). These discussions have taken on more ominous tones in the 1990s, as satisfaction with the democratic process has dropped notably in many contemporary democracies (Norris 1999; Pharr and Putnam 2000).

Parties are also changing in organizational terms. The proliferation of citizen interest groups and other political intermediaries has provided alternatives to the traditional representational role of political parties (Lawson and Merkl 1988; Dalton and Kuechler 1990). The expansion of the mass media upstages the parties' role as providers of political information. Longitudinal trends frequently document a decline in the number of party members, although scholars debate the political meaning of these data. There are notable cases where party leaderships have even lost some control over internal party decision-making, such as in the selection of candidates or the creation of party programmes.

Finally at the policy level there is mixed evidence regarding the continuing ability of the political parties to structure the policy-making process. Parties still play a dominant role in organizing governments and structuring the policy activities of parliaments, but there are also signs that partisan change is affecting the processes of coalition formation and democratic accountability (Strøm 1997; Bowler et al. 1998). Patterns of increasing party fractionalization and divided government raise the question of whether parties are as effective as they once were in controlling the outputs of government.

Despite the extensive body of literature on political parties, scholars remain divided on the overall pattern of partisan change. At the individual level, some researchers argue that the present period of heightened partisan volatility is not historically distinctive (Bartolini and Mair 1990), or that declines in party attachments are actually slight (Keith et al. 1992; Schmitt and Holmberg 1995). Research on party organizations often highlights how political parties are attempting to adapt to changes in their political environment (Katz and Mair 1995; Ware 1987*a*; Herrnson 1988). The parties' continuing role in the governing process also has been stressed in a variety of recent studies (e.g. Klingemann et al. 1994; Cox and McCubbins 1993). In short, nearly everyone agrees that parties are changing, but whether such change signifies adaptation or decline is controversial.

One reason for the lack of clarity in the literature is that most research has focused on only one nation (or at most a few nations), or only on a single aspect of political parties. When one scholar notes a pattern in one country, another challenges this conclusion with evidence from another nation. One study may address party loyalty among members of parliament, whereas another looks at party loyalty in the electorate. What is missing is a systematic assessment of how the status of parties is changing in advanced industrial democracies, as well as an analysis of the multiple consequences of these partisan trends.

If partisan decline is occurring, such a development holds direct and immediate consequences for contemporary democracies. An altered partisan order would affect the representation of citizen interests, the process by which societal decisions are made, and the process of policy implementation. If democracy without parties is unthinkable, we should be asking what will happen *if* the parties are in decline, and what such a decline portends for the politics of advanced industrial democracies. This is the goal of this book.

A FUNCTIONAL APPROACH TO PARTY POLITICS

A natural starting point for studying partisan change is to consider the functions that parties perform in any democracy. Indeed, the political science literature is replete with lists of party functions. The functions that scholars attribute to political parties in a democratic society are impressive and diverse, reflecting the importance ascribed to them.

Although there are limitations to a functionalist approach, most notably the tendency to rationalize existing patterns of action and ignore other alternatives, the literature has generated a valuable set of criteria by which to study political parties. In any study of partisan change, it is fundamental to begin by asking whether parties continue to perform the roles traditionally attributed to them. We list some of these functions below, using V. O. Key's (1964) tripartite framework: parties in the electorate, parties as political organizations, and parties as governing institutions.[2]

Parties in the Electorate
> Simplifying choices for voters
> Educating citizens
> Generating symbols of identification and loyalty
> Mobilizing people to participate

Parties as Organizations
> Recruiting political leadership and seeking governmental office
> Training political elites
> Articulating political interests
> Aggregating political interests

Parties in Government
> Creating majorities in government
> Organizing the government
> Implementing policy objectives
> Organizing dissent and opposition
> Ensuring responsibility for government actions
> Controlling government administration
> Fostering stability in government

[2] Kaare Strøm and Lars Svåsand (1997: ch. 1) present a complementary discussion of party functions and applies this framework to party change in Norway.

Parties in the Electorate

Political scientists view political parties as peforming vital functions in linking individuals to the democratic process, and thus we begin by discussing the role of parties within the electorate:

1. *Simplifying choices for voters.* Politics is often a complex enterprise. Modern electoral research has demonstrated that the average voter often finds it hard to make sense of all the issues and choices confronting him or her at an election (Campbell et al. 1960; Dalton and Wattenberg 1993). Political parties help to make politics 'user-friendly' for citizens. When the political parties take clear and consistent policy positions, voters are offered valuable information about specific candidates or cues on specific policy issues. The party label thus provides a key informational short-cut concerning how 'people like me' should vote. Once voters know which party usually represents their interests, this single piece of information can act as a perceptual screen (Campbell et al. 1960)—guiding how they view the issues and behave at the polls. From a rational choice perspective, Morris Fiorina (1981) has shown how party identification can be an economizing device for voters faced with complex political decisions. Indeed, a variety of empirical evidence demonstrates how party ties act as a cue in guiding voter opinions and behaviour (Wattenberg 1998*a*; Dalton 1996*a*: ch. 9). Similarly, Schattschneider's early dictum about democratic politics being unthinkable without parties stressed the role that parties play in structuring electoral choice.

2. *Educating citizens.* Besides cutting information costs, political parties also provide people with important political information. Parties educate, inform, and persuade the public. Parties often bring certain issues to the forefront of public attention, and thereby highlight their specific position on these issues. In other instances, parties educate their followers concerning why they should take certain policy stands. In some European party systems, this role is taken one step further. For instance, the German Basic Law mandates that parties should act to inform the public on political matters; the parties receive a generous annual budget from the federal government to pursue these educational responsibilities. In another vein, Samuel Popkin (1991) has described elections as courses in civics education, with political parties as the teachers.

3. *Generating symbols of identification and loyalty.* In a stable political system, voters need a political anchor, and political parties can serve this function. It has long been argued that loyalty to a political party makes citizens less susceptible to being swayed by demagogic leaders and extremist movements (Converse and Dupeux 1962). Converse (1969) also argued that partisan attachments are a conserving and stabilizing force for the democratic polity, creating continuity in voter choices and election outcomes. Furthermore, political parties provide a basis of political identification that is separate from the polity itself, and thus political dissatisfaction with governmental outputs can be directed at specific institutions rather than the state itself.

4. *Mobilizing people to participate.* In nearly all democratic polities, political parties play an important role in getting people to vote and participate in the electoral process (Rosenstone and Hansen 1993; Verba et al. 1978). They perform this function in both direct and indirect ways. The direct process involves the party organization working actively to canvass neighbourhoods to get out the vote. Political parties also mobilize citizens to become involved in the campaign itself, as well as participate in other aspects of the democratic process. Feelings of party attachment or loyalty are a further motivation to vote at elections and become involved in other partisan political activities. Indirectly, the parties' efforts to make politics more 'user-friendly' decrease the costs of voting, and the partisan outcome of electoral activity increases the perceived benefits to the respective party supporters.

Parties as Organizations

A second level involves the functions that parties perform as political organizations, or processes within the organizations themselves:

1. *Recruiting political leadership and seeking governmental offices.* Fundamental to all the classic definitions of a political party is that parties seek to control the governing apparatus by putting forth candidates for political offices (cf. Downs 1957). Thus the party government literature stresses the role of political parties in the recruitment and selection of political elites (Katz 1987*b*; Rose 1974). Parties must actively seek out, screen, and designate candidates who will compete in elections under their label. Many of the parties' internal structures, such as youth groups and internal party offices, are designed to identify and nurture future candidates. In most parliamentary systems, the political parties have developed formal or informal mechanisms to control parliamentary nominations (Norris 1996; Gallagher and Marsh 1988). Because virtually every major office-holder in the countries we are studying was nominated by a political party, this must be considered as one of the most basic functions of any political party.

2. *Training political elites.* The selection of candidates is only part of the parties' role in developing democratic leaders. In most democracies, participation in the political party organization is also an important setting for training prospective elites about the democratic process, the norms of democracy, and the principles of their party. Under the classic party government model, the training may come through a long career in party activism, party office-holding, and then elective office. It is very unusual in strong party systems for individuals to rise to a position of political prominence without a prior career of party service (Aberbach et al. 1981). This socialization function is often considered a vital part of the successful workings of a democratic system.

3. *Articulating political interests.* The structural-functionalist approach holds that a key function of parties is to articulate the interests of their supporters (Almond et al. 1993). Political parties give voice to their supporters' interests by

taking stands on political issues and by expressing the views of their supporters within the governing process. In this sense, parties are no different from special interest groups, which also articulate political interests. However, the centrality of political parties in structuring political campaigns, controlling legislative debates, and directing the actions of politicians gives parties many venues in which to represent the interests of their supporters. The fact that parties and interest groups share this function makes it no less crucial.

4. *Aggregating political interests.* One of the most important differences between interest groups and parties is that parties not only articulate political interests but also aggregate them. In their platform or manifesto, parties traditionally bring the interests of various groups together to form a comprehensive programme for governing (Budge et al. 1987). In disciplined party systems, these programmes provide a basis for governing and an important linkage in the representational process. This linkage mechanism has prompted parties scholars from Giovanni Sartori to Austin Ranney to advocate responsible party government as the basis of democratic representation. The parties' electoral needs also encourage them to bring together a wide variety of interest groups and forge a common programme that these interests can support. Similarly, in governing the political parties must reconcile the diverging interests that they represent (or that are represented within the governing coalition) into a governing programme. Political parties are one of the few political organizations that must combine interest articulation with interest aggregation, thereby distinguishing them from individual politicians, interest groups, and other political actors.

Parties in Government

A final level of analysis involves the role that parties play in managing and structuring the affairs of government. In this area, too, political parties have been identified with numerous key aspects of the democratic process.

1. *Creating majorities in government.* Following an election, the next step of the democratic process is to form a government. In contemporary democracies, it is the responsibility of a political party, or a coalition of parties, to bring together enough elected officials to form a government, or at least to organize each house of the legislature (as in the American case). The literature on government formation uniformly accepts that political parties are the prime actors in this process, and that coalition formation is a partisan activity. Moreover, models of coalition formation indicate that the representation of party policy positions and the distribution of party resources are the key factors in determining which government will form (Laver and Schofield 1990; Laver and Shepsle 1996).

2. *Organizing the government.* Some of the earliest political parties developed as attempts to organize the legislative process (Cox 1987). Political parties provide an efficient mechanism for organizing interests and ensuring cooperation among individual legislators (Budge and Keman 1990). Within legislatures, it is

the responsibility of party organizations in the legislature to maintain party discipline, which is done via a variety of incentive and control mechanisms (Bowler et al. 1998). Parties monitor individual legislators and enforce party discipline. Thus in most parliamentary systems, parties vote as a bloc with few abstentions or deviations. Political parties also usually control the selection of legislative leadership offices (e.g. committee chair positions, and positions in legislative leadership offices) and the distribution of resources to legislators. Democracy without parties might be unthinkable, but large modern legislatures without political parties is almost inconceivable.

3. *Implementing policy objectives.* Once in government, political parties are the central actors in determining government policy outputs, which is one of the key principles of the party government model (Katz 1987*b*). In disciplined party systems, this function is performed by the transformation of the parties' manifesto and campaign promises into law (Klingemann et al. 1994). Even in systems like the United States with weaker party mandates, parties are still the primary agents in negotiating public policy decisions in the legislature. Gary Cox and Mathew McCubbins (1993) have argued that political parties provide a method to solve the collective decision-making problems of legislators by creating an institutional structure by which collective decisions can be made and enforced.

4. *Organizing dissent and opposition.* Of course, not all parties will be in the government. It is therefore up to those parties in the minority to offer an alternative course to what the government is doing (Dahl 1966). The British concept of the Loyal Opposition best represents this point: the opposition party presents a political alternative that acts to limit the present government and offers a potential for change at the next election. As Schattschneider so rightly put it, unless people are aware of a choice between the parties there is no democracy. This choice is regularly manifested in party politics, not only on election day but whenever any piece of major legislation comes up.

5. *Ensuring responsibility for government actions.* A central feature of the party government model is that it provides a mechanism for ensuring political responsibility. With parties controlling the government (alone or in coalition), it is clear who is responsible for the government's action. Responsible party government makes it easier for the public to decide who should get the credit (or blame) for the government's policy choices and outcomes (Powell 2000). Political parties thus provide a mechanism to ensure the responsible action of individual legislators, and the enforcement of judgements about their actions (Cox and McCubbins 1993). If voters are satisfied with the government's actions, they can reward the incumbent parties; if they are dissatisfied, they can vote for the opposition. This creates a strong incentive for party members in the government to work together to deliver the best possible results, because they know their political fortunes will rise and fall as one.

6. *Controlling government administration.* Although the political activities of parties are often focused on the legislative and executive branches, another

important role of parties is to maintain a political presence within the government bureaucracy. At one level, this occurs through the selection of political appointments or ministers to head up executive agencies. In addition, many political systems allow for the assignment of a limited number of administrative positions to political appointments.

7. *Fostering stability in government.* Finally, parties provide the key element of continuity in democratic governance. The specific issues and leaders may well change from one campaign to the next, but the party labels remain. Historic figures like Margaret Thatcher, Charles de Gaulle, and Richard Nixon may well dominate the political scene of a country for a long period of time, but the legacy of such leaders is institutionalized primarily through their ability to effect a lasting influence on their political party. In more specific terms, the stability of governments is directly related to levels of party unity. Stable parties make for stable government.

Taken altogether, the functions that political parties perform can contribute to the good practice of democracy, and quite arguably to the existence of democracy itself—as Schattschneider argued. When these separate functions are interconnected, in the model of responsible party government, a powerful mechanism for representative democracy is provided (Katz 1987*b*; Rose 1974). From a rational choice perspective, political parties are also seen as a potential solution to problems of agency and collective decision-making that arise in representative democracies (Cox and McCubbins 1993; Kiewiet and McCubbins 1991; Cox 1987). As many distinguished scholars have written, political parties are important vehicles for translating mass preferences into policy choices, and for ensuring the efficient functioning of the democratic process. A decline of the ability of parties to perform even some of these functions would be a cause for serious concern.

THE POTENTIAL SOURCES OF PARTISAN CHANGE

Partisan change is a normal element of the political process, and periods of heightened partisan volatility or political ferment dot the political histories of most established democracies. However, we are looking for fundamental and enduring changes that are transforming the role of political parties in advanced industrial democracies. This section briefly outlines some of the forces of political change that have been linked to the partisan changes we examine in this volume. As with party functions, they can be related to micro-, meso-, and macro-level changes in these societies.

Micro-level Changes

The modernization hypothesis begins with assumptions about the changing role of the citizenry in advanced industrial societies. One facet involves the political skills of contemporary electorates. Increasing educational levels have presumably improved the political and cognitive resources of contemporary electorates. With more political information available to a more educated electorate, more citizens now possess the political skills and resources necessary to become self-sufficient in politics (Inglehart 1990: ch. 10; Dalton 1984). These changes mean that contemporary publics are less likely to defer to party elites or to support a party simply out of habit. Instead, people may question elites or resort to non-partisan forms of political expression. These changes erode the affective, habitual partisan bonds that once structured electoral competition in most Western democracies.

The modernization process also transforms the values and interests of contemporary publics. With spreading affluence, the public's interests have broadened to include a range of new post-material issues (Inglehart 1990, 1997). Issues such as environmental quality, lifestyle choices, and consumer rights have expanded the boundaries of politics. These issues often cut across existing partisan alignments, and therefore are not well represented in contemporary party systems. Moreover, the participatory aspects of these values frequently lead post-materialists to eschew the hierarchic and structured nature of partisan politics in favour of methods of direct democracy. Post-material values seem antithetical to the disciplined partisan politics that once were common in many Western democracies.

Another factor contributing to partisan change has been the general erosion of group-based politics in most advanced industrial democracies. Social mobility, geographic mobility, and other modernization forces have weakened the ties between individuals and bounded/bonded communities, such as a working-class milieu or a church community. To the extent that attitudinal attachments to political parties were formed on group-based criteria, then the observed weakening of these social bonds might diminish the strength of partisanship. Recent comparative analyses indicate that the decline in cleavage-based voting has been nearly universal in these societies, and this has led to a corresponding increase in issue-based voting (Franklin et al. 1992). Other recent findings suggest the decline in group mobilization is related to declines in electoral participation (Gray and Caul 2000).

All told, these forces change the relationship between citizens and parties. On one side of the equation, rising levels of education and the process of cognitive mobilization lessen the functional value of party cues to the voter. On the other side, new issue concerns and weakening group ties attenuate the long-term bonds between the public and the parties.

Meso-level Changes

The modernization process in advanced industrial societies involves shifts in the roles of societal actors. In particular, changes in the mass media may contribute to the decline of parties. The mass media are assuming many of the information functions that political parties once controlled. Instead of learning about an election at a campaign rally or from party canvassers, the mass media have become the primary sources of campaign information. Furthermore, the political parties have apparently changed their behaviour in response to the expansion of the mass media. There has been a tendency for political parties to decrease their invest-ments in neighbourhood canvassing, rallies, and other direct contact activities, and devote more attention to campaigning through the media.

Other research suggests that the political content of the mass media has changed to downplay the importance of political parties. Martin Wattenberg (1998*a*) has shown that the American media have shifted their campaign focus away from the political parties toward the candidates. A similar personalization of campaign coverage can be seen for some European democracies (Swanson and Mancini 1996*b*).

Just as the media have pre-empted part of the parties' role in delivering polit-ical information, a myriad of special-interest groups and single-issue lobbies have assumed some of the parties' role in representing public interests. The prolifera-tion of such groups is part of the modernization process, both in the increasing diversity of citizen interests and the public's tendency to engage in independent political action. Like traditional interest groups, these groups can work with polit-ical parties. However, the new wave of public interest groups often press their interests without relying on partisan channels (Dalton 1994: ch. 9).

Another set of changes are occurring within the parties themselves. Several studies have discussed a trend of increasing professionalization and institutional-ization within contemporary political parties (Katz and Mair 1995; Farrell 1994; Scarrow 1996). These changes are partly in response to other changes in the polit-ical process, such as the increased reliance on the mass media during election campaigns and the declining mass memberships of many parties. Once initiated, however, they tend to reinforce the transformation of parties as political institu-tions. For instance, increasing professionalization may further marginalize the value of party membership to the organization; hiring campaign consultants may shift even more resources to media-centred campaigning.

Macro-level Changes

An additional set of forces have been working at the system level, creating a dynamic of diffusion across political parties. One set of such developments involves changes in the technology of politics. For instance, the development of relatively low-cost public opinion polls has created a new tool for campaigners. This has given the parties greater insight into the minds of voters, and created a potential for political marketing and changes in election strategies.

A related technological change is the growth of the mass media as an infor-mation source. In one sense, the media have been a rival to political parties in providing citizens with information about political and political cues to guide their decisions. In addition, the media have also become a new tool of parties.

Where private media advertising is allowed, this has become an important (if not central) part of election campaigns. More generally, the different format of television reporting has changed the style of the campaign to more visually appealing and candidate-centred activities.

New campaign technologies have also transformed the cost structure of elections. Public opinion polls and media advertising shifts campaigning from a labour-intensive style (rallies, door-to-door contacting) to a capital-intensive style of mass marketing. Political parties have increasingly sought public funding of their activities in response to these demands. These reinforcing developments have many implications for the organization and operation of political parties.

Another institutional change involves methods of candidate selection. A growing number of individual parties, or entire party systems, have accepted primaries or other methods of candidate selection that actually weaken their role in selecting candidates. The most advanced example is the United States, where the expansion of open primaries and non-partisan elections has undermined the parties' hold on recruitment. Within the British Labour Party there has been a shift in nomination power away from the party in parliament to party conventions and local constituency groups. In 1992, the German SPD selected its chancellor candidate through a mail ballot of its members. These and other developments lessen the importance of parties in the political process and therefore reinforce the dealignment process begun by other social forces.

Finally, a number of scholars have described partisan decline as part of a general crisis of contemporary democracies. In its various forms, this performance explanation argues that the multiple and conflicting policy demands being placed on contemporary democracies exceed their ability to perform (Crozier et al. 1975; Huntington 1981). As agents of the democratic process, parties suffer as a consequence of the government's performance deficit.

In summary, we have described a process of political change that is very broad and diffuse. Some of these factors might influence the functions of parties as organizations, others might influence the role of parties in the electorate, and still others affect the functions of parties in government. It would be unrealistic to view this as a deterministic process. Current research on political parties emphasizes their adaptation to many of the trends we described above. This interplay of changes and reactions will determine the future of partisan politics in advanced industrial democracies.

Nevertheless, we can observe elements of partisan change—or partisan decline—in most advanced industrial democracies. Changes in a single nation in the role or status of parties might be linked to the specific trials and tribulations of the parties. The collapse of the Italian and Japanese party systems in the early 1990s, for instance, was directly linked to the specific corruption scandals in these two nations. The weakening of American parties was at least partially due to the impact of political crises from Vietnam to Watergate. Yet, when a pattern appears across a wide variety of nations, it suggests that the causes are common to advanced industrial societies. The relative simultaneity of changes in the behaviour of parties leads us to look for such a broad transformative force that might affect a large set of nations.

If one agrees with Schattschneider and many other political analysts that political parties are the central institutions of democratic governance, then a modernization process that changes the role of political parties deserves our attention. This is the case whether one is interested in electoral politics, the procedures for elite selection, mass representation, legislative politics, or the implementation of policy.

METHODOLOGY OF THE STUDY

This is an ambitious project, and one that could not have been done by a single individual. Indeed, it is only possible because it draws upon existing research on political parties—integrating this work in an initial stage, and then building in additional data collection and analysis. This task is even more demanding because we must go beyond past research based on single nations or a single portion of the thesis of partisan decline. To be convincing, further research must be comprehensive in both thematic and cross-national terms.

In terms of cross-national coverage, we begin with the set of large, continuously democratic OECD-member nations as our core.[3] This set of nations provides the most reasonable approximation of 'advanced industrial democracies'. In addition, these nations offer substantial variation in their party systems, electoral experiences, and other political factors that are embedded in our two theoretical models. Finally, we are most likely to identify existing empirical data sources for this set of nations because of the well-developed state of social science research in many of them.

Core nations included in this study are: Australia, Austria, Belgium, Britain, Canada, Denmark, Finland, France, Germany, Ireland, Italy, Japan, Netherlands, New Zealand, Norway, Sweden, Switzerland, and the United States.

Because we are interested in large-scale social and political changes in advanced industrial societies, it is important to track political change over a relatively long period of time. The political party literature often discussions the model of responsible party government in terms of the political systems of the 1950s or early 1960s. The changing nature of politics in advanced industrial societies first became apparent during the late 1960s and the 1970s. These trends have continued into the 1980s and 1990s. Therefore, we have adopted a longitudinal research design, tracking political change over the second half of this century.

---

[3] We excluded Spain, Portugal, and Greece from our analyses because of their relatively recent transitions to democracy, and their lower level of economic development compared to most other OECD nations. We have excluded Iceland and Luxembourg because of their small size, although when data are available for these nations it is reported in some chapters.

OUR RESEARCH FRAMEWORK

From the outset our goal was to assemble a team of scholars to examine the theme of party change from multiple perspectives. We have chosen to follow V .O. Key's model of party in the electorate, party organizations, and party-in-government. The analyses at each level were often facilitated by the existence of large-scale data collections, such as the national election study series or the Katz and Mair (1992) study of party organizations. The project was organized into three teams to examine each aspect of partisan change, and this defines the structure of this volume.

Part I studies partisan change at the individual level. It is widely argued that partisan identification, or equivalent long-term affective party ties, is a central concept in understanding individual political behaviour. Chapter 2 by Russell Dalton examines whether these partisan ties are weakening in advanced industrial democracies. He argues that a pattern of dealignment is eroding partisanship in most nations, and this trend is linked to processes of cognitive mobilization and modernity. Dalton, Ian McAllister, and Martin Wattenberg (Chapter 3) demonstrate how eroding partisanship is altering the electoral behaviour of contemporary publics. Because fewer voters now approach each election with standing partisan predispositions, electoral volatility has generally increased and decisions are being made on the issues and candidates of the election. In addition, fewer citizens are being mobilized into partisan and campaign activity. In Chapter 4 Martin Wattenberg examines whether these trends have affected turnout in elections, thereby diminishing participation in this central act of the democratic process.

Part II examines several important areas of potential change regarding parties as political organizations. Susan Scarrow's analysis in Chapter 5 demonstrates that party membership is continuing to decline in most party systems, as political parties shift away from the mass party model that previously predominated. Chapter 6 by David Farrell and Paul Webb outlines changes in the nature of election campaigning by parties. They show how these changes have had important consequences for how parties operate as organizations. In Chapter 7, Susan Scarrow, Paul Webb, and David Farrell turn to an analysis of change in the internal distribution of power within party organizations. They find a general pattern of democratization in decision-making regarding leadership selection and party manifestos.

Part III focuses on parties-in-government. In Chapter 8 Shawn Bowler examines the role of parties within the legislative arena. Running counter to the dealignment theme, he finds that institutional rules continue to enshrine parties as the key actors in the legislative process, and he demonstrates there is little systematic empirical evidence that the influence of party is declining in legislative decision-making. Chapter 9 by Kaare Strøm examines the role of party within the governing structure of modern democracies. Strøm considers whether party control over the selection of legislative candidates or government cabinet members has changed over time, and whether direct forms of democracy are simultaneously rising. Chapter 10 considers the potentially ultimate influence of political parties—on the policy outcomes of government. Miki Caul and Mark Gray find that parties have responded to the more dynamic aspects of election campaigns by becoming more flexible (adaptive) in their campaign programmes. This chapter also examines the changing influence of party control of government and policy outputs. Michael Thies reviews this evidence in Chapter 11, arguing that parties are an inevitable structuring force in democratic politics.

In the end, our analyses attempt to marshal the evidence from a number of large-scale research projects to provide a comprehensive assessment of how political parties are changing in contemporary democracies. By assembling this evidence in a single volume, and for nearly all advanced industrial democracies, we hope to provide a systematic assessment of the present role of political parties in the democratic process.

CONCLUSION

It has become a reoccurring fashion in political science research to proclaim that parties are in decline—just as there is a counter-reaction arguing that these claims are overstated.[4] Let us be clear, we do not expect to see political parties become extinct in our lifetime. Political parties play important roles in the democratic process, and the value of parties to democracy will ensure their continued survival. At the same time, the political process can change—and advanced industrial democracies have witnessed substantial social and political trends over the past generation that are altering the context in which political parties function. And even more important, if parties change then this may have important implications for how the democratic process functions.

This book asks the reader to think the unthinkable: is there evidence that parties are generally in decline in advanced industrial societies? And if so, what are the implications of these developments for contemporary democracies? At a minimum, the evidence presented here demonstrates that parties are adapting to these societal changes, altering how they connect to voters, organize themselves internally, manage electoral campaigns, and perhaps the way they govern. In broader terms, these trends may also change how democracy itself functions.

---

[4] This clearly has been a well-developed cottage industry in American political research. See, for example, Broder (1972) or Lawson and Merkl (1988) on the side of partisan decline. On the other side, a number of works have discussed the continuing strength or even the reinvigoration of American political parties (e.g. Abramowitz et al. (1983) and Beck et al. (1997)).

PART I

Parties in the Electorate

2

The Decline of Party Identifications

Russell J. Dalton

ONE of the most important measures of the nature of party-based democracy is public attachment to political parties. In a recent essay on the state of political parties in America, John Coleman (1996) argues that the key question of partisan politics is whether parties are able to mobilize and integrate the mass public into the democratic process. Parties should not be measured by their organizational activities alone—although these are important measures of partisan politics—but by the goals of this activity. An important measure of the nature of party politics is the public's identification with political parties and the system of party government.

This chapter approaches the study of partisan change with an individualist emphasis for two reasons. First, public ties to political parties measure both the vitality of party government and provide a context within which parties, candidates, and other political actors operate. The number of campaign rallies organized by a party, the election mailers and brochures, and the party contact with voters are means toward an end—developing public support for the party, and indirectly legitimacy for a system of party-based democracy. Second, the processes of political modernization outlined in Chapter 1 often lead to changes in the citizen's relationship to politics. For example, rising educational levels and changing communication patterns should alter how citizens relate to politics. Thus many of the changes in the functional bases of party politics should first appear in public attitudes and behaviours.

This chapter begins by discussing the importance of partisanship as a concept in electoral research. The analyses review the evidence of change in partisan attachments for a broad set of advanced industrial societies. Despite the extensive work that has been done on partisanship, scholars remain divided on the extent of

This research was supported by a grant from the German Marshall Fund of the United States and from the Center for German and European Studies, University of California, Berkeley. I want to thank a number of colleagues for assisting us with the collection of national data series and providing advice on this paper: Atle Alyheim, Clive Bean, Harold Clarke, Olafur Th. Hardarsson, Michael Lewis-Beck, Helmut Prochart, Bradley Richardson, Risto Sänkiaho and Peter Ulram. Mark Gray provided invaluable assistance with the empirical data in this paper.

partisan decline (e.g. Keith et al. 1992; Zelle 1995; Schmitt and Holmberg 1995). By expanding the cross-national scope and cross-temporal range of the evidence, these analyses provide a more definitive answer on whether partisanship is generally changing in contemporary democracies. Intertwined with this research is a consideration of what factors might be prompting systematic change in party attachments. The results provide a basis for understanding other aspects of party government in contemporary democracies.

THE FUNCTIONAL IMPORTANCE OF PARTY IDENTIFICATION

A strong case can be made that the concept of partisan identification is the most important development in modern electoral behaviour research. The early analyses of the Michigan election studies demonstrated how partisanship was a central element in political identities (Campbell et al. 1960, 1966). Gradually, the concept of party identification was exported to other democratic party systems (Butler and Stokes 1969; Baker et al. 1981). Debate often followed this American export (e.g. Budge et al. 1976; Richardson 1991), as researchers noted that other party systems lacked some of the features that gave partisan identification its analytic power and conceptual basis in the United States. Nevertheless, electoral researchers have generally accepted that the concept could be usefully applied in most democratic systems. Most voters approach elections with a standing set of party predispositions, even if the conceptualization and measurement of these predispositions differ according to the political and electoral context.

The concept of party identification has reached such a prominent position in electoral research because these orientations are seen as key determinants of many different aspects of political behaviour. The developers of the concept stressed its functional importance:

The present analysis of party identification is based on the assumption that the . . . parties serve as standard-setting groups for a significant proportion of the people in this country. In other words, it is assumed that many people associate themselves psychologically with one or the other of the parties, and that this identification has predictable relationships with their perceptions, evaluations, and actions. (Campbell et al. 1954: 90)

One key function for partisan identities is that they serve as an organizing device for the voters' political evaluations and judgements (Borre and Katz 1973; Wattenberg 1998a: ch. 2; Miller 1976). For instance, once an individual becomes psychologically attached to a party, he or she tends to see politics from a partisan perspective. Being a social democratic identifier makes one more likely to be sympathetic to social democratic leaders and the policies they advocate, and sceptical of the leaders and policies of the opposing parties. Faced by a new issue or political controversy, the knowledge of what position is favoured by one's own party is a valuable cue in developing one's own position. Indeed, the authors of

The American Voter described partisanship as a 'perceptual screen'—through it one sees what is favourable to one's partisan orientation and filters out dissonant information. The stronger the party bond, the stronger are the selection and distortion processes.

Moreover, in comparison to social-group cues, such as class or religion, party attachments are relevant to a much broader range of political phenomena because parties are more central to the political process. Issues and events frequently are presented to the public in partisan terms, and nearly all politicians are affiliated with a political party. Furthermore, as researchers have focused attention on the information short-cuts that voters use to orient themselves to politics, partisanship has emerged as the ultimate cost-saving device (Fiorina 1990). Partisan cues are an efficient decisional short-cut, because they enable citizens to use their partisan identities to decide what policies to support and oppose.

This cue-giving function of partisanship is strongest for voting behaviour, because it is here that citizens make explicit partisan choices. For the unsophistic-ated voter, a long-term partisan loyalty and repeated experience with one's preferred party provides a clear and low-cost cue for voting. Even for the sophis-ticated citizen, a candidate's party affiliation normally signifies a policy programme that can serve as the basis for reasonable electoral choice. Similarly, partisanship gives party leaders an expected base of popular support which gener-ally (within limits) views their actions in a favourable light and supports them at the next election. Most established political parties enter elections with a stand-ing commitment from their past supporters, and partisan ties encourage a stabil-ity and continuity in electoral results. Electoral change normally occurs at the margins of these partisan coalitions.

Partisan ties also perform a mobilizing function. Just like sports loyalties, attachment to a political party draws an individual into the political process to support his or her side. Participation in campaign activities is generally higher among strong partisan identifiers (Verba et al. 1978). Partisans are more easily mobilized by political parties to turn out at the polls, and feel a stronger sense of personal motivation to support their preferred parties and candidates.

Finally, partisanship encompasses a variety of normative attitudes regarding the role that political parties should play in the democratic system. Herbert Weis-berg (1980) expressed the formal theory for this view, arguing that party identifi-cation is multidimensional—tapping evaluations of specific parties, independence from parties, and support for the *institution* of the party system in general (also see Gluchowski 1983).

In summary, feelings of partisanship tap the popular vitality of representative democracy. Partisan ties bind individuals to their preferred political party, as well as the system of party democracy. Partisan ties also help orient the individual to the complexities of politics, and provide a framework for assimilating political information, understanding political issues, and making political judgements. Furthermore, partisan ties mobilize individuals to participate in parties, elections, and the processes of representative government. Thus, the extent of partisanship is an important political variable, and changes in these feelings over time provide us with a measure of the functioning of party-based democracy.

PATTERNS OF PARTISAN DEALIGNMENT

Given the importance of partisanship in the electoral behaviour literature, the first signs of weakening partisan attachments in the American public came as a surprise to many electoral scholars (Burnham 1970; Nie et al. 1976; Converse 1976). The decline in US partisanship was often linked to exceptional political crises: the civil rights conflict, Vietnam, and urban unrest. However, a similar trend soon appeared in Britain and other European party systems (Dalton et al. 1984; Crewe and Denver 1985).

Weakened partisan attachments in a single nation (or a few nations) might be explained by the particular political circumstances of the nation. Declining British partisanship, for instance, was often traced to the economic struggles of the 1970s and the parties' ineffectual response to these challenges. However, if these patterns are replicated across a wider variety of nations, it forces us to examine broader social changes that are influencing a wide range of contemporary democracies. The individual evidence of party decline eventually was generalized into a hypothesis of *partisan dealignment* in advanced industrial societies (Dalton et al. 1984; Dalton 1984; Inglehart 1990: ch. 10). The dealignment thesis holds that party ties were generally eroding as a consequence of social and political modernization, and thus most advanced industrial societies should experience a dealignment trend.

The dealignment thesis argues that this trend has developed because of a combination of individual and systemic factors that are transforming contemporary advanced industrial democracies (see discussion in Chapter 1). For instance, increasing educational levels have improved the average citizen's political and cognitive resources. With more political information available to a more educated electorate, more people now possess the level of political skills and resources necessary to become self-sufficient in politics. In addition, other systemic changes have diminished the political role of parties within the democratic process. For instance, the growth of the mass media and the proliferation of public interests groups have impinged on the interest articulation and informational functions of the political parties. There is evidence that the mass media are both replacing parties as sources of political information and possibly diminishing the partisan content of this information.[1] As will be discussed in later chapters of this book

---

[1] Just as the media have assumed an information role, a myriad of special-interest groups and single-issue lobbies have assumed some of the parties' roles in representing public interests. These groups can work with political parties as has been the past pattern of labour, business, and other economic interest groups. However, public interest groups and single-issue groups often press their interests without relying on partisan channels.

(Chapters 6 and 7), the parties themselves were also changing, adopting new institutional forms and new methods or running campaigns that decreased reliance on party members and decreased the direct personal contact with the citizenry.

In summary, these social trends lead to a general process of partisan dealignment that we believe is occurring in most advanced industrial democracies. Moreover, this dealignment hypothesis differs in fundamental ways from explanations based primarily on party performance (e.g., Zelle 1995). The dealignment thesis implies that we are witnessing a *broad and ongoing decline in the role of political parties for contemporary publics*—not a temporary downturn in public satisfaction with parties as others have argued. Dealignment also suggests that new forms of democratic politics—such as the expansion of direct democracy, the opening of administrative processes to public input, and the expanding use of the courts by citizen groups—will develop as citizens shift to non-partisan forms of action. The result of these processes should be a general erosion of partisanship in among contemporary publics.

MEASURING CHANGE IN PARTISANSHIP

Numerous country studies have tracked changes in party attachments over time, and there is an extensive literature on partisanship in democracies with established national election studies. Often this evidence varies in the time frame or breadth of nations, which makes generalization difficult. Even in single nations, scholars sometimes disagree on whether partisan ties are weakening.

The most extensive attempt to measure trends in partisanship is Hermann Schmitt and Sören Holmberg's research (1995). They used data from the national election studies and Eurobarometer (EB) surveys for several West European nations. In total, they tracked partisanship for fourteen European nations and the United States. Their findings support the theme of partisan dealignment, although they offer the following ambiguous conclusion: 'If there is an overall tendency in Western European partisanship it is of loosening party bonds. But specific developments, by country and by party, are so varied that any general "overall" view disguises more than it discloses' (1995: 121).

Schmitt and Holmberg marshal an impressive array of data, which is nevertheless limited in several ways. One limitation is their emphasis on empirical analysis rather than theory testing. The dealignment thesis holds that long-term societal changes have at least partially undermined the political and cognitive basis of party identification in advanced industrial democracies. The test of this hypothesis should focus on long-term partisanship data for a set of stable advanced industrial democracies. Schmitt and Holmberg present data series from a diverse set of nations (including relatively new democracies, and less affluent societies), often with very short time spans. Our goal is to find data more directly appropriate to testing the dealignment theory.

Another set of problems with the Schmitt and Holmberg work is methodological. They rely on the Eurobarometers as an exclusive data source for eight nations; the EB data series only begins in mid-1970s or later and there have been significant changes in the wording of the partisanship question. Schmitt and Holmberg also did not devote sufficient attention to specific national conditions that might interact with dealigning forces. In 'new' democracies, party attachments might initially grow until dealigning forces counteract the partisan learning model (Converse 1976).[2] For example, research on German partisanship stressed the development of party attachments in the immediate post-war decades (Baker et al. 1981; Norpoth 1983); but then the dealigning process eroded these ties (Dalton and Rohrschneider 1990). The same pattern might apply to new party systems such as Spain, Portugal, and Greece. Furthermore, the newer democracies display fewer of the advanced industrial characteristics that might encourage dealignment. The most fertile field for uncovering partisan dealignment is in the established party systems that might have been described as 'frozen' around stable cleavages in the 1960s and 1970s.

Finally, Schmitt and Holmberg are overly cautious in interpreting their own empirical evidence. Of the 21 regression coefficients they present for the percentage of strong identifiers, 19 are negative. Of the 21 coefficients for the overall percentage of identifiers, 14 are negative. Admittedly, many of these negative coefficients are not statistically significant, but the number of survey timepoints is often quite small and they do not consider the confounding factors we noted above (see Appendix on statistical methodology in Chapter 3). Thus, an assessment that 'The Trend is Down in Many Countries, *but* . . . [italics added]' (1995: 101) appears to be an understatement. A general theory that works 80 per cent of the time in a mixed set of test cases seems fairly potent.

This chapter improves and expands upon the Schmitt/Holmberg analyses. First, the list of nations now includes all of the advanced industrial democracies for which partisanship data are available. Second, the new democracies of Southern Europe (Greece, Spain, and Portugal) are excluded on the grounds that they have relatively new democratic systems and their socio-economic development trails the advanced industrial democracies. Third, whenever possible national election study data are used because they represent the most valid data source for each nation.[3] The national election studies normally have a better sampling procedure,

---

[2] Schmitt and Holmberg (1995) are sensitive to these points and discuss them in the methodological appendix, but these important issues are not considered within the text of their analyses and do not seem to influence their conclusions.

[3] In practical terms, this means using national election survey data instead of the Eurobarometers for several European nations. The greatest problem in Eurobarometer time-series analysis is a change in the party identification question across surveys (e.g. Katz 1985; Schmitt 1989). By using national election studies this problem is minimized, though not completely resolved. Most of the national election studies also have a longer time series than the Eurobarometers. For comparison, we update the Schmitt/Holmberg Eurobarometer results for these nations in n. 7.

TABLE 2.1 *Trends in Party Identification over Time*

Nation	% with PID	% Identifiers b	sig.	% Strong Identifiers b	sig.	Period	(N) Time-points
Australia	92	−0.179	0.19	−0.593	0.00	1967–98	(8)
Austria	67	−1.120	0.00	−0.777	0.00	1969–94	(9)
Belgium*	50	0.039	0.85	−0.286	0.05	1975–96	(21)
Britain	93	−0.189	0.01	−0.929	0.00	1964–97	(9)
Canada	90	−0.386	0.05	−0.150	0.17	1965–97	(9)
Denmark	52	0.001	0.95	−0.207	0.36	1971–98	(9)
Finland	57	−0.293	0.49	−0.147	0.61	1975–91	(4)
France*	59	−0.670	0.00	−0.316	0.04	1975–96	(21)
Germany	78	−0.572	0.00	−0.573	0.00	1972–98	(8)
Iceland	80	−0.750	0.08	−0.350	0.06	1983–95	(4)
Ireland*	61	−1.700	0.00	−0.807	0.00	1978–96	(18)
Italy*	78	−1.300	0.00	−0.968	0.00	1978–96	(18)
Luxembourg*	61	−0.580	0.02	−0.386	0.00	1975–96	(21)
Japan	70	−0.386	0.06	—	—	1962–95	(7)
Netherlands	38	−0.329	0.13	−0.129	0.36	1971–98	(9)
New Zealand	87	−0.476	0.01	−0.750	0.01	1975–93	(7)
Norway	66	−0.220	0.34	−0.280	0.18	1965–93	(8)
Sweden	64	−0.690	0.00	−0.473	0.01	1968–94	(10)
United States	77	−0.366	0.00	−0.190	0.05	1952–96	(11)

Note: The % with party identification in column 1 is the average of the percentage expressing an identification in the first two surveys in each series.

Source: Nations marked with an asterisk (*) are based on the Eurobarometer surveys; other nations are based on the respective National Election Studies.

often use in-person interviews, have standardized party identification questions, and their collection is coordinated with the timing of national elections. Fourth, when only Eurobarometer data are available for an established European democracy, the analyses are extended further into the 1990s.

Table 2.1 employs the Schmitt/Holmberg methodology of regressing the year of the survey on two measures of partisanship: the trend in the *total number of identifiers* as well as the trend in *strong partisans* over time for the nineteen nations with relatively complete data series.[4] To our knowledge, this represents the universe of longitudinal data on partisanship for these nations.[5]

[4] Each nation uses a different question tapping partisan attachments, and therefore the statistics in Table 2.1 should not be used to make direct comparison of the level and rates of change in partisanship across nations.

[5] There are a series of Swiss national surveys, but the format of the partisanship question changes over time and thus limits comparability (Nabholz 1998; Longchamp 1991). The Japanese election studies also varied the partisanship question over time; therefore we use data from the Yomuri Poll. The empirical evidence for France is, perhaps, in greatest dispute. Changes in the format of the partisanship question have produced widely differing results (see Pierce 1995:

The second and third columns of Table 2.1 display the time trends for the percentage of party identifiers in each nation. Seventeen of the nineteen trends are negative; thirteen of these coefficients are significant at the 0.10 level, even though the number of data points is quite small.[6] For example, the –0.366 coefficient for the United States means that the percentage of partisans decreased by about 16 per cent over the 44 years from 1952 to 1996 (–0.366 * 40 = 16). The next two columns display the time trends for the percentage of strong partisans. All of the strength coefficients are negative, albeit of different magnitude and statistical significance. The decrease in American, British, and Swedish partisanship has long been observed in the literature, but now these nations are joined by most other advanced industrial democracies.[7]

A visual sense of these changes can be drawn from Figure 2.1. The figure plots the distribution of party attachments in a pooled European sample from 1976 until 1992.[8] Although this time period is relatively brief, the overall downward trend is unmistakable. And in nations where there is a longer time series available from election studies, such as in Britain, the evidence of decline is normally stronger (and in the British case occurs before the EB series starts). The percentage of non-partisans in the pooled European analyses increases from 30 per cent in 1976 to over 40 per cent in the 1990s.

The evidence of dealignment shown in Table 2.1 is stronger than Schmitt and Holmberg's results partially due to the inclusion of seven nations that they did not examine, where partisanship is clearly weakening (Australia, Austria, Canada,

---

ch. 3; Lewis-Beck, 1984; Haegel 1993). If one attempts to synthesize these conflicting pieces of evidence, it appears that partisanship strengthened during the initial years of the Fifth Republic, and then has eroded over the past two decades. But because of the changes in question wording in the national election surveys, we have used the Eurobarometer data for France.

[6] Schmitt and Holmberg follow a common methodology of computing statistical significance based only on the number of survey timepoints. We follow their methodology to be consistent in replicating their analyses. An alternative approach is to pool surveys and use the combined samples to estimate whether changes are statistically significant over time. Obviously, such pooled results more easily yield significant trends; when differences between timepoints average 3 or 5 per cent this is statistically significant ($p<0.05$) with large sample surveys. See a discussion of this point in the Appendix to Chapter 3.

[7] For comparative purposes, we updated the Eurobarometer results presented in Schmitt and Holmberg (1995) to include 1993–6 timepoints. Below we present the results (unstandardized b) for overall party identification and strong identifiers for the Eurobarometer nations in Table 2.1 that were based on national election study.

Nation	% ID	Strong ID
Britain (1978–96)	–0.583	0.111
Denmark (1976–96)	–0.094	–0.093
Germany (1975–96)	–0.666	–0.400
Netherlands (1975–96)	0.004	–0.358

[8] Figure 2.1 is based on the weighted sample pooling the nine nations for which data exist for this full period: Belgium, France, the Netherlands, Germany, Italy, Luxembourg, Denmark, Ireland, and Britain.

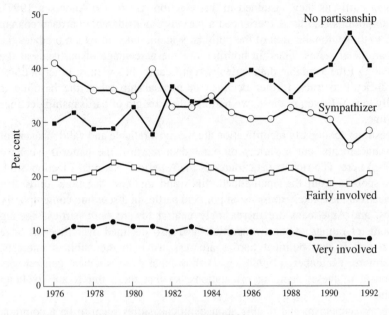

FIG. 2.1. Partisan Attachment in Europe, 1976–1992

Source: 1972–96 Eurobarometer cumulative file.

Finland, Iceland, Japan, and New Zealand). In addition, the passage of additional time has strengthened the dealignment trend in several nations. For example, German partisanship dropped off more clearly in the elections of the 1990s, although initial signs of dealignment could be seen in earlier elections (Dalton 1996*b*; Dalton and Rohrschneider 1990). The collapse of the Tories in the 1993 Canadian elections similarly accentuated a dealignment trend in Canadian politics (Clarke and Kornberg 1993, 1996). The dealignment trend in Austria also accelerated in the 1990s (Plasser et al. 1996). The downturn in Australia, New Zealand, and Japan also became evident in the 1990s (Bean 1996; Tanaka 1998). In summary, the consistency of the results is now much stronger than the Schmitt and Holmberg findings.

A discussion of the apparent anomalies also might help us understand the breadth of the dealignment process. Denmark and Belgium display the weakest evidence of dealignment over time. In both nations we may be beginning our research too late in the dealigning process to study earlier periods of more stable partisanship. Strong class-based voting existed in the Danish elections of the 1950s and early 1960s, and these alignments were weakening over time. The second Danish timepoint is the 1973 realigning election (often called the 'earthquake election'); since then the Danish parties have worked to recover from the losses in partisans they sustained in this election (Borre and Andersen 1997). Belgian politics also has experienced a period of considerable partisan change linked to the regionalization of the political system, much of which predates the Eurobarometer series. Thus, in both nations the percentage of partisans at the beginning of the available data series is significantly below most other nations; it is difficult to track further declines in partisanship when the baseline is initially low. Yet, even in these two nations, the strength of partisanship declines over time.

Questions about party identification are the most reliable and valid measure of party attachments, but a variety of other data reaffirm the patterns we have described here. The richest data source is the American National Election Studies. Responses from the open-ended 'likes and dislikes' questions finds that Americans are less likely to focus on political parties in discussing contemporary politics, and Americans are increasingly neutral toward *both* parties. Feeling thermometer ratings of the two parties have also declined over time, as have general beliefs that political parties are responsive to the public's interests. Furthermore, Wattenberg (1998a: ch. 7) shows that there is a clear generational component to these changing orientations, so that these trends are likely to continue.

Greater scepticism and doubts about political parties seem to be a common development in other advanced industrial democracies. A Gallup question traces a decline from 30 per cent of Canadians who expressed quite a lot of confidence in political parties in general in 1979 to only 11 per cent in 1996. Enmid surveys show that the percentage of Germans who express confidence in the political parties has decreased from 43 per cent in 1979 to only 26 per cent in 1993 (Rieger 1994: 462). Surveys in both Germany and Austria find that public confidence in political parties rates at the bottom of a list of diverse social and political institutions (IPOS 1995; Plasser and Ulram 1996). The recent restructuring of the party and electoral systems in Italy, Japan, and New Zealand were all accompanied by feelings of antipathy toward the political parties (Bardi 1996; Tanaka 1998; Vowles and Aimer 1994). Similarly, the British public has become significantly less trusting of political parties and politicians (Webb 1996; Curtice and Jowell 1995). There is also evidence of extensive public dissatisfaction with Norwegian and Swedish political parties (Strøm and Svåsand 1997; Miller and Listhaug 1990). Indeed, very few scholars have recently claimed that public support for political parties and the structure of party government is increasing in their nation of specialization.

It is certainly possible that these trends may reverse in the future, or that partisanship might increase in a recent election survey. As politicians become cognizant of these trends, they may react with policies and activities designed to renew the ties of their former partisans; in other instances, an engaging political leader or an intense political controversy may mobilize partisan attachments. Despite these possible perturbations, we suspect that the general downward trend reflects long-term and enduring characteristics of advanced industrial societies that encourage their continuance.

If party identification is the most important attitude in electoral behaviour research, then the breadth of these dealignment patterns should have major implications for these polities. Moreover, the cross-national breadth of dealignment suggests that more than a series of coincidental political crises lie behind these trends. Despite the wide variation in the electoral histories, governmental records, and institutional structures of these nations, the consistency of these findings is striking. Dealignment is not primarily a result of Vietnam and Watergate in the USA, frustrations with the Social Democrats in Sweden, or coalitional politics in Austria. The similarity in trends for so many nations forces us to look beyond specific and idiosyncratic explanations for these patterns. For public opinion trends to be consistent across so many nations, something broader and deeper must be occurring.

IDENTIFYING SOURCES OF DEALIGNMENT

Many factors have undoubtedly contributed to the spreading patterns of partisan dealignment (see Chapter 1). The declining role of parties as political institutions certainly has played an important part in this process. A myriad of special-interest groups and single issue lobbies have assumed many of the parties' interest articulation functions. The mass media are also assuming many of the information functions that political parties once controlled.

At the individual level, however, there are two broad theories to explain the dealigning trends we have observed. One approach focuses on changes in the nature of contemporary electorates that might be identified with the modernization process of advanced industrial societies. Rising educational levels and the growing availability of political information has increased the skills and resources of contemporary electorates. More individuals are thus able to manage the complexities of politics on their own, without recourse to the political cues that partisanship provides (Dalton 1984). Furthermore, public values are shifting to emphasize individualism and lessen deference to external sources of political cues, such as political parties.

A contrasting explanation, and the most common explanation in nation-specific studies of dealignment, is to link these trends to specific dissatisfaction with the performance of parties and the democratic process. Dealignment in the United States, for example, is traced back to Vietnam and the political scandals beginning with Watergate; in Austria it is linked to the collapse of the post-war consensus and popular dissatisfaction as represented by the Freedom Party; British dealignment is thought to stem from the steady erosion of Britain's status in the world and the end to the post-war collectivist consensus. Thus political dissatisfaction and the failure of parties are the root causes of these dealigning trends according to some scholars (e.g., Lawson and Merkl 1988; Zelle 1995).

It is difficult to test these alternative theories directly with the data at hand. However, we can examine the implications of the two rival theories for the patterns of partisan change, and thus marshal indirect evidence on the sources of change and the likely permanence of partisan dealignment.

Generational Patterns

Philip Converse's (1969) partisan learning model maintained that the strength of partisanship should increase with age (or more precisely, with a history of continued support of one's preferred party). At the same time, American and British partisanship display a distinct generational element to dealignment (Converse 1976; Alt 1984). In these nations the decrease in partisanship was linked to the influx of young voters unattached to political parties. And low levels of youthful partisanship carried over to the adult years. These results suggested that new political forces were impeding partisan learning among the young. The fact that dealignment patterns have persisted for nearly a generation is evidence of ongoing social and political change rather than short-term responses to specific political scandals.

To test for a generational pattern of dealignment we paired together election studies from the beginning and end of the time-series in Table 2.1 (when we had access to the individual survey data). For each nation we modelled the strength of partisanship as a combination of three factors: age, the year of the survey, and an interaction term combining age and the year of the survey. A positive relationship between age and the strength of partisanship is expected in each nation. The overall dealignment trend should produce a negative coefficient for the time variable. Finally, if the decrease in partisanship is concentrated among the young, the age*time interaction coefficient should be positive, indicating that the age gradient in the latter survey is steeper because partisanship in the young at the second timepoint is weaker than in the first survey.[9]

Table 2.2 displays the regression analyses from nine nations. The results generally confirm the theoretical expectations. For example, in the United States the age relationship (in 1952) is 0.0063; this value is very close to Converse's pooled results for the 'stable state' period of the 1950s and early 1960s (Converse 1976). The negative coefficient for time (b=–0.4156) signifies the decrease in the average strength in partisanship by 1992. The positive coefficient for the interaction term

---

[9] In more precise terms, we coded year of the survey 0 for the first timepoint and 1 for the second timepoint. We then created an interaction term that multiplies age (in years) by this dummy variable. Thus the equation can be interpreted as two separate models. First survey: $a+b1$ (age); the other variables have a value of 0 in this year. Second survey: $(a+b3) + (b1+b2)$ (age); $b3$ is from the interaction term and is the decrease in the intercept between timepoints, and $b2$ is the adjustment of the age slope for the second timepoint.

TABLE 2.2 *Age and Partisanship Relationships over Time*

Nation	Intercept	Age	Time	Interaction	R/N	Period
Belgium*	3.039	0.0063*	−0.4291*	−0.0006	R=0.20	
		(0.0001)	(0.1169)	(0.0020)	N=3023	1978–92
Britain	2.626	0.0034*	−0.2342*	0.0003	R=0.18	
		(0.0016)	(0.0841)	(0.0017)	N=4170	1964–92
Denmark*	2.809	−0.0150	−0.4578*	0.0002	R=0.16	
		(0.0109)	(0.0968)	(0.0001)	N=2988	1978–92
France*	3.182	0.0075*	−0.3504*	0.0020	R=0.19	
		(0.0012)	(0.0974)	(0.0021)	N=3142	1978–92
Germany	3.347	0.0167*	−0.8510*	0.0650*	R= 0.16	
		(0.0070)	(0.0630)	(0.0090)	N=20,316	1977–95
Italy*	2.737	0.0029*	−0.2476*	0.0012	R=0.13	
		(0.0014)	(0.1071)	(0.0023)	N=3271	1978–92
Ireland*	3.167	0.0065*	−0.7691*	0.0062*	R=0.26	
		(0.0013)	(0.1035)	(0.0022)	N=3007	1978–92
Luxembourg*	3.106	0.0040	−0.0238	0.0017)	R=0.11	
		(0.0026)	(0.1797)	(0.0030)	N=1114	1978–92
Netherlands	2.183	0.0070*	−0.1556*	0.0017	R=0.17	
		(0.0010)	(0.0691)	(0.0014)	N=4182	1971–94
Norway	1.595	0.0106*	−0.1930*	−0.0003	R=0.25	
		(0.0010)	(0.0820)	(0.0020)	N=3725	1965–93
United States	2.724	0.0063*	−0.4156*	0.0039*	R=0.19	
		(0.0015)	(0.0889)	(0.0019)	N=4232	1956–92

Source: See Table 2.1; nations marked by an asterisk are based on Eurobarometer data; Germany is based on the pooled 1977 and 1995 Politbarometers. Table entries are unstandardized regression coefficients; standard errors are in parentheses. Coefficients significant at the 0.05 level are denoted by an asterisk.

(0.0039) means that the age gradient had steepened by 1992. Expressing these relationships in simple percentage terms: 30 per cent of young people (under age 30) were strong partisans in 1952, but only 21 per cent had strong ties in 1992.

All told, there is a statistically significant positive relationship between age and partisanship in most nations as well as a positive interaction effect, albeit of differing strengths. In most cases the interaction effect produces a change in the age relationship that is a considerable proportion of the baseline relationship. For instance, the interaction effect in Italy is roughly half the basic age coefficient, even if the interaction term is not statistically significant. In short, the decrease of partisanship in advanced industrial democracies has been disproportionately concentrated among the young.

Cognitive Mobilization and Dealignment

The early literature on partisanship held a negative view of non-partisans. Non-partisans were at the margins of the electoral process; they were uninvolved in elections and unsophisticated about politics. As Angus Campbell and his colleagues described them (1960: 143): 'Independents tend as a group to be somewhat less involved in politics. They have somewhat poorer knowledge of the issues, their image of the candidates is fainter, their interest in the campaign is less, their concern over the outcome is relatively slight.' If the growth of independents meant growing numbers of uninvolved citizens, it would be a negative development for contemporary democratic politics.

Part of the dealignment thesis, however, holds that advanced democracies are producing a new type of independent. A starting point for this thesis is W. Phillips Shively's (1979) research on the functional basis of partisanship. Shively suggested that voters develop party identifications as a short-cut to help them handle difficult and often confusing political decisions. Relying on cues coming from a party identification can lessen the costs of political involvement.

The modernization of advanced industrial societies may have changed this functional calculus. The expansion of education has increased voters' political skills and resources. At the same time, the growing availability of political information through the media reduces the costs of acquiring information. Contemporary publics in most nations are also more interested in politics (see Table 3.9 in Chapter 3). In short, the process of cognitive mobilization has *increased* voters' political sophistication and their ability to deal with the complexity of politics— and this may have *decreased* the functional need for partisanship among many better-educated and politically involved citizens.

There is already some evidence to support the cognitive mobilization thesis. Dalton (1996a: 219) found that the percentage of cognitively sophisticated non-partisans in the USA increased from 10 per cent in 1952 to 18 per cent in 1992, while the number of unsophisticated non-partisans increased by only 3 per cent. Dalton and Rohrschneider (1990) showed that the decrease in German partisanship from 1972 to 1987 was concentrated among the politically interested, rather than the apathetic.

We tested for the impact of cognitive mobilization with a methodology similar to the generational analyses. We assume that non-partisans were initially concentrated among the less educated and those scoring low on cognitive mobilization. Over time, the proportion of new, educated 'apartisans' should grow, adding to the number of traditional non-partisans. To sort out the combination of these two groups of non-partisans, the analyses determine whether the relationship between cognitive measures and partisanship has weakened (or reversed) over time as new apartisans develop.

Table 2.3 presents a series of regression analyses linking education to partisanship. The USA typifies the expected pattern. In 1952 there was a slight tendency for partisanship to be stronger among the better educated ($b=0.033$), but the interaction term in 1992 ($b=-0.055$) indicates that this relationship had reversed by the later timepoint. In other words, in 1992 non-partisans were slightly more common among the better educated. This pattern is also found in most of the other nations in the table, although most of these analyses are based

TABLE 2.3 *Education and Partisanship Relationships over Time*

Nation	Intercept	Educ.	Time	Interaction	R
Belgium*	1.963	−0.006	−0.222	−0.013	R=0.09
		(0.007)	(0.059)	(0.011)	
Denmark*	2.278	0.043	−0.027	−0.018	R=0.10
		(0.008)	(0.071)	(0.012)	
France*	2.147	0.019*	−0.304*	−0.007	R=0.16
		(0.006)	(0.053)	(0.009)	
Germany	3.417	0.087*	−0.412*	−0.042	R=0.13
		(0.021)	(0.054)	(0.029)	
Italy*	2.296	−0.005	−0.286*	−0.004	R=0.14
		(0.007)	(0.052)	(0.010)	
Ireland*	2.060	0.028*	−0.290*	−0.003	R=0.16
		(0.009)	(0.057)	(0.013)	
Norway	2.166	−0.036*	−0.192*	0.006	R=0.17
		(0.012)	(0.052)	(0.014)	
United States	2.948	0.033	−0.128	−0.055	R=0.12

Source: See Table 2.1; nations marked by an asterisk are based on Eurobarometer data; Germany is based on the pooled 1977 and 1995 Politbarometers. Table entries are unstandardized regression coefficients; standard errors are in parentheses. Coefficients significant at the 0.05 level are denoted by an asterisk.

on the shorter and less reliable Eurobarometer series.[10] Six of the seven Eurobarometer nations show a negative interaction term, implying that the growth of non-partisanship has occurred disproportionately among the better educated.

The Eurobarometers include a separate measure of 'cognitive mobilization' which represents the combination of political skills (as measured by educational level) and political engagement (as measured by the frequency of political discussion). Table 2.4 documents a general positive relationship between political engagement and partisanship—the pattern that led to the characterization of non-partisans as the politically uninvolved and ill-informed. Even over the relatively short time period of the Eurobarometer series, there is an erosion of this relationship in each nation as demonstrated by the negative sign for most interaction terms. The size of the effects is admittedly small, but it is consistent. If the relationship between cognitive mobilization and partisanship had remained constant over time, then the level partisanship should have increased because the levels of education and cognitive mobilization have increased. But just the opposite has occurred because the more cognitively sophisticated have decreased their partisan attachments.

---

[10] Norway presents an interesting deviation that may fit other class-structured European polities. In the 1965 Norwegian Election Study partisanship was actually stronger among the less educated, because leftist and agrarian parties mobilized these social strata. By 1993 this relationship had weakened but not reversed.

TABLE 2.4 *Cognitive Mobilization and Partisanship Relationships over Time*

Nation	Intercept	Cogn.	Time	Interaction	R
Belgium	1.640	0.152*	−0.121	−0.037	R=0.17
		(0.021)	(0.110)	(0.037)	
Britain	1.519	0.190*	0.170	−0.029	R=0.20
		(0.021)	(0.099)	(0.037)	
Denmark	2.017	0.005	0.002	−0.004	R=0.06
		(0.022)	(0.139)	(0.041)	
France	1.775	0.106*	−0.319*	−0.007	R=0.21
		(0.017)	(0.099)	(0.033)	
Germany	1.502	0.219*	−0.013	−0.071	R=0.21
		(0.024)	(0.114)	(0.039)	
Italy	1.841	0.203*	−0.370*	−0.019	R=0.27
		(0.018)	(0.102)	(0.036)	
Ireland	1.530	0.190*	−0.221	−0.005	R=0.22
		(0.022)	(0.107)	(0.039)	
Netherlands	1.938	0.150*	−0.145	−0.043	R=0.20
		(0.018)	(0.109)	(0.035)	

Source: 1978 and 1992 Eurobarometer surveys. Table entries are unstandardized regression coefficients; standard errors are in parentheses. Coefficients significant at the 0.05 level are denoted by an asterisk.

Cognitive mobilization has important cumulative effects. This can be seen more clearly in analyses that Inglehart (1990: 366) presented. He classified partisans and non-partisans into two groups, those who are cognitively mobilized and those who are not—the latter group presumably uses partisanship as a source of political cues because they lack the resources to follow politics on their own. He found that the percentage of sophisticated non-partisans in Europe had increased significantly over a single decade. Furthermore, there are more of these sophisticated non-partisans among younger generations. In summary, an increase in non-partisanship among the politically sophisticated has been a significant force in promoting partisan dealignment.

Performance and Dealignment

In contrast to social modernization explanations of partisan dealignment, another approach emphasizes performance criteria as an explanatory variable. Carsten Zelle (1995), for instance, argued that German dealignment was based on a negative public reaction to the mounting policy problems facing Germany, and growing evidence of scandals and corruption within the German parties. Many of the individual national studies of partisan trends link dealignment to poor performance by the political parties. If governments have difficulty meeting public expectations, political parties serve as an intermediary political institution that absorbs some of the dissatisfaction. Clarke, Dutt, and Kornberg (1993) used time-series models to demonstrate the link between performance and partisanship for a set of West European nations. Indeed, the performance model is integral to the democratic process.

Table 2.5 tests the performance model using the same procedures applied in our previous analyses. The Eurobarometers include a measure of satisfaction with the way democracy is functioning in the respondent's nation. This measure is regressed against partisanship at the beginning of the time period, and an interaction term measures whether this relationship has changed over time. The results indicate that there is only a weak relationship between political satisfaction and the strength of partisanship, and even the direction of this relationship varies across nations. Moreover, there was not a generalized change in this relationship over time, as seen in the varied results for the interaction terms. Dealignment was not generally concentrated among the satisfied or among the dissatisfied, but appears to be relatively independent of political support.

We would argue there is a practical flaw in the performance model. By its nature, performance cannot provide an explanation of general dealignment trends unless we believe that all governments are performing worse than in the past. Most analysts would agree that over the past few decades some governments have performed relatively well, and others have performed poorly (Bok 1997; Pharr and Putnam 2000). And the unclear polarity of satisfaction effects raises further doubts about whether the performance model can explain broad trends of dealignment.

TABLE 2.5 *Satisfaction with Democracy and Partisanship Relationships over Time*

Nation	Intercept	Satisfaction	Time	Interaction	R
Belgium	1.961	0.024	−0.156	−0.008	R=0.09
		(0.027)	(0.103)	(0.038)	
Britain	1.832	0.011	0.192*	0.021	R=0.13
		(0.027)	(0.092)	(0.036)	
Denmark	2.122	0.022	−0.185	0.023	R=0.04
		(0.028)	(0.122)	(0.042)	
France	2.235	−0.113*	−0.276*	0.039	R=0.14
		(0.021)	(0.081)	(0.033)	
Germany	2.052	0.050	−0.512*	0.090*	R=0.16
		(0.028)	(0.116)	(0.041)	
Italy	2.329	−0.027	−0.483*	0.112*	R=0.14
		(0.030)	(0.084)	(0.043)	
Ireland	1.661	0.043	−0.089	−0.010	R=0.06
		(0.023)	(0.090)	(0.033)	
Netherlands	2.299	−0.023	−0.373*	0.096*	R=0.06
		(0.027)	(0.116)	(0.041)	

Source: 1976 and 1992 Eurobarometer surveys. Table entries are unstandardized regression coefficients; standard errors are in parentheses. Coefficients significant at the 0.05 level are denoted by an asterisk.

PARTISAN DEALIGNMENT AND POLITICAL CHANGE

What is stunning about partisan dealignment is the commonality of trends across a wide variety of advanced industrial democracies. In a single nation such developments might be linked to the specific trials and tribulations of the parties. When a pattern appears across a wide variety of nations, however, it suggests that a common set of forces are affecting these nations.

At least in part, dealignment can be traced to political changes that have eroded the role of parties as political institutions. Even more important, the citizenry is changing. As a result, political parties are not developing new attachments among the young, as they must to maintain previous levels of partisanship. The new non-partisans are more often drawn from the better educated and the politically sophisticated. Policy performance undoubtedly plays some role in declining partisanship, but it is significant that the dealignment trends have been most apparent among a new generation of political sophisticates.

It is inevitable that weakening party bonds will have broad consequences for individual political behaviour. Several of these consequences will be examined in subsequent chapters. To the extent that party identification performed important functions of structuring political attitudes, guiding voting preferences, and mobilizing partisans to participation in the political process, then the decay of partisan ties should have equivalent effects on these other aspects of political behaviour. Chapter 3 examines several of these hypotheses.

I would suggest that dealignment trends may hold even broader implications for the nature of democratic politics (a topic we will consider at greater length in the concluding chapter). If dealignment is a continuing development for contemporary publics, then this poses a challenge to the process of representative democracy. Because as voters distance themselves from political parties, this weakens the causal chain of the party government model. Without a reliable electoral base, parties must change their campaign strategies and their methods of mobilizing political support. Without stable partisan constituencies, the representation of public preferences within the political process becomes more complex. The full implications of dealignment, of course, depend on what we uncover for the performance of parties in other stages of the political process. But the erosion of party attachments across the advanced industrial democracies has implications that reach beyond the nature of elections.

3

The Consequences of Partisan Dealignment

Russell J. Dalton, Ian McAllister and
Martin P. Wattenberg

THE preceding chapter provided striking evidence that party identifications are weakening in most advanced industrial democracies. Because party identification has been central to theories of mass political behaviour for four decades, its decline should have fundamental implications for the nature of citizen politics. As noted in Chapter 2, partisanship provides a highly effective method of organizing political information, evaluating political stimuli, guiding electoral choices, and providing political stability. Partisanship is seen as the glue that binds together diverse political beliefs, guides behaviour, and serves as a stabilizing force within political systems. Therefore, we should expect that weakening party bonds will have broad consequences for individual political behaviour.

There are, however, many scholars who question whether there has been real change in partisan behaviour. Stefano Bartolini and Peter Mair argue that evidence of partisan change is illusionary: 'Not withstanding the seductive imagery of transformation which permeates many of the prevailing interpretations of contemporary Western European politics, it is clear that, in the long term, the bounds which tie the electorates into a set of political identities and alignments have demonstrated their resilience' (Bartolini and Mair 1990: 287). Mair has continued this theme in his more recent writings, arguing that the evidence of electoral change is a 'myth' (1993; 1997). In a recent review of the anti-party literature, Thomas Poguntke similarly concludes 'the data I have analyzed do not support generalizations about a general decline of parties and the rise of anti-party sentiment in Western democracies' (Poguntke 1996: 338). Others have argued that even the evidence of weakening parties is an apparition (e.g. Keith et al. 1992; Widfeldt 1995).

This chapter assembles a variety of evidence on the changing nature of citizen politics that should be expected as a consequence of weakening partisanship. We begin by examining the electoral impact of dealignment. Aggregate election statistics describe the long-term trends. In addition, we assemble individual-level survey data from the national election studies in several nations. For instance, as the long-term bonds between voters and parties erode, this creates the potential for greater volatility in results from election to election, increased split-ticket voting and other electoral consequences. Another section examines the relationship between partisan and candidate images. Finally, we examine whether participation in various forms of partisan activity has diminished as a consequence of weakened partisanship. In short, our goal is to demonstrate that partisan dealignment is transforming the relationship between citizens and parties in advanced industrial democracies.

ELECTORAL BEHAVIOUR

The most obvious and direct impact of partisanship is on electoral behaviour. Partisanship provides a standing predisposition that guides voter preferences; barring other information, partisans vote for 'their' party in the belief that the party and its candidates generally best represent their interests. Survey research has repeatedly demonstrated a close relationship between partisanship and voting behaviour in most democratic elections. In parliamentary systems the relationship is typically very strong (Holmberg 1994) because of the limited number of elected offices and the high levels of party cohesion. In electoral systems with multiple offices and diverse voting choices, like the United States and Switzerland, partisanship can be of even greater value in guiding a wide variety of voting choices (Wattenberg 1998a).

On the national level, strong partisan ties can act as a stabilizing influence on electoral politics. Philip Converse and Georges Dupeux (1962) argued that the potential for voters to be attracted to new parties and demagogic leaders is considerably lessened if citizens identify with one of the established parties. Indeed, American elections generally demonstrate that significant third party presidential candidates disproportionately draw their support from the ranks of independents, regardless of the candidate's political ideology. In Britain, support for the Liberals and their successors has been disproportionately drawn from previously unmobilized voters lacking partisan attachments (Crewe and King 1995). More generally, the existence of widespread partisan ties dampens the impact of short-term political events on election outcomes and limits the potential electoral appeal of new parties and political personalities. Extensive partisanship among the electorate thus works to stabilize party alignments and lessen electoral change.

Aggregate Data Patterns of Volatility

One of the first signs of dealignment should be a weakening of partisan consistency at both the micro and the macro levels. Our analyses begin by examining aggregate electoral statistics for the established OECD democracies, and then turn to a wide range of available survey data.

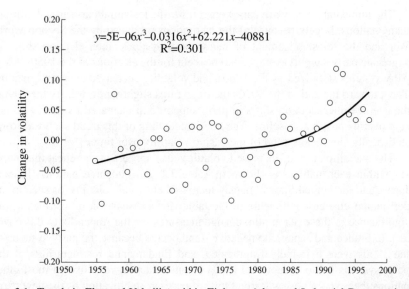

$$y=5E–06x^3–0.0316x^2+62.221x–40881$$
$$R^2=0.301$$

FIG. 3.1. Trends in Electoral Volatility within Eighteen Advanced Industrial Democracies, 1950–1997

Note: The results are based on all legislative elections for our 18 core advanced industrial democracies, from the second post-war election until 1997. The figure plots the change in volatility from the average of the first two elections within each nation. The figure pools the national data by year and then plots the best-fit trend line produced by Curve Expert 1.3.

Source: Mackie and Rose 1991; *Electoral Studies* 1992–7.

The simplest measure of electoral change is the volatility of party vote shares between elections—the average change in party vote shares between adjacent elections.[1] Previous research has found some evidence of growing volatility in party vote shares by the late 1970s (Dalton et al. 1984; Crewe and Denver 1985; Pedersen 1979).[2] Figure 3.1 presents the pattern of aggregate volatility for eighteen advanced industrial democracies over the entire post-war period. In order to best illustrate the trend over time, each data point represents the average volatility score for all elections held in our set of countries that year. Volatility scores are standardized by measuring the change from the average volatility in the first two post-war legislative elections for each individual country.

[1] The volatility index is calculated as the total percentage point gains for all the parties between the two adjacent elections, divided by 2 (see Pedersen 1979).
[2] Bartolini and Mair (1990) have pointed out that volatility was greater in the inter-war period than during the more stable years of the post-war era. While we do not dispute this finding, it does not address our basic question of whether party systems have changed from their post-war patterns. In addition, we believe that Bartolini and Mair's calculation of 'inter-bloc' volatility significantly underestimates the degree of historical and contemporary electoral change.

The immediate post-war years were a time of substantial partisan volatility in many nations, largely because of the disruptions produced by the Second World War and the re-establishment of many party systems. Inter-election shifts in aggregate party support averaged 9.0 per cent for the elections of the 1950s. Most party systems stabilized by the 1960s, and volatility decreased in several nations. Then, toward the end of the 1970s the trend turns slightly upward. By the 1990s, the average inter-election shifts in party support had increased by nearly 10 per cent over its post-war baseline. The linear modelling of this trend shows a strong statistically significant trend of increasing volatility over time.[3]

The overall pattern of increased volatility also appears if we repeat the analyses within each nation, as shown in Table 3.1. All but three nations (France, Japan, and the United States) display increased electoral volatility, as seen in the per annum change coefficients in the table (for a discussion on estimating the significance of these per annum change measures see the Appendix to this chapter). In France and Japan, the negative trend occurs because the party systems of the 1950s were extremely fragmented, and fundamental restructurings of the party systems led to exceptional levels of inter-election volatility. In most other nations there was a post-war trend toward partisan stabilization as the new party system took root, but then volatility increased by the 1990s just as partisanship began to erode. By the 1990s, the average volatility score (12.6 per cent) was larger by half than for the 1950s.

Because partisanship binds voters to their preferred party, dealignment also should free more voters to shift their party support to other contenders. Established parties may fragment, as a more fluid electorate opens these voters to new appeals. For example, Canada's Progressive Conservative Party saw its status in parliament decimated when the Reform Party emerged and captured many of its supporters. After having won the majority of seats in the House of Commons in 1984 and 1988, it suddenly found itself reduced to a mere two seats after the 1993 election. New Zealand's Labour Party suffered a similar fate in 1990, following a period of unprecedented economic reform. The party plunged from 56 to 29 parliamentary seats, presaging a period of intense fragmentation in the New Zealand party system (Vowles and Aimer 1993).

In addition, new political challengers may enter the fray. Ross Perot's candidacy in the 1992 election illustrated how a candidate without either prior political experience or the support of a party apparatus could garner 19 per cent of the US presidential vote. The rise of other new parties, such as Silvio Berlusconi's Forza Italia, Pauline Hanson's One Nation Party in Australia in 1998, or the New Zealand First Party led by the charismatic Winston Peters are additional indicators of political volatility today. In the past two decades most democratic party

---

[3] The simple linear regression shows a positive slope over time, and the R squared (0.245) is close to the value of the curvilinear model presented in Figure 3.1.

TABLE 3.1 *National Trends in Electoral Volatility, 1950s–1990s*

Nation	1950s	1990s	Per annum change	Period	(N Time-points)
Australia	0.05	0.08	0.086	1953–95	(14)
Austria	0.03	0.08	0.045	1951–96	(19)
Belgium	0.09	0.10	0.002	1950–95	(15)
Britain	0.06	0.04	0.005	1950–97	(14)
Canada	0.07	0.25	0.230	1953–97	(15)
Denmark	0.07	0.11	0.120	1950–98	(19)
Finland	0.04	0.12	0.180*	1951–95	(13)
France	0.20	0.10	–0.170	1975–93	(13)
Germany	0.10	0.07	0.210*	1953–94	(12)
Ireland	0.14	0.15	0.009	1951–92	(14)
Italy	0.10	0.40	0.540	1953–96	(12)
Japan	0.41	0.11	–0.007	1952–96	(17)
Netherlands	0.05	0.14	0.220*	1952–94	(11)
New Zealand	0.05	0.16	0.330*	1951–96	(16)
Norway	0.04	0.16	0.280*	1953–97	(14)
Sweden	0.03	0.13	0.200*	1952–94	(15)
Switzerland	0.03	0.08	0.160*	1951–95	(12)
United States	0.05	0.04	–0.070	1950–94	(12)

Source: Calculated from national legislative results. The 1950s column is the average volatility for the first two elections in the 1950s; the 1990s column is the average of the most recent two elections in the 1990s. The regression coefficients are multiplied times 100 for ease of presentation; coefficients significant at the p<0.05 level are marked by an asterisk.

systems have experienced new political challenges from Green parties on the left and nationalist or neo-liberal parties on the right.

Figure 3.2 presents the trends in the effective number of parties for our set of democracies.[4] The effective number of parties—and thus the fragmentation of these party systems—is generally increasing in advanced industrial democracies. The upward slope was modest until the end of the 1970s, but has accelerated over the past two decades. By the mid-1990s the effective number of parties had increased by more than 150 per cent on average.

National patterns in the effective number of parties fill in the details of this general picture (Table 3.2). In every nation but one (the Netherlands) the effective number of parties has increased in the post-war era. There are several cases such as Belgium, Italy, and Japan where turbulence and fragmentation of the party system have been obvious; but in most nations this same process of increasing partisan diversity has been occurring, albeit less dramatically. Moreover, even though we have only a dozen or so elections to establish these trend lines within each nation, most of the per annum change coefficients are statistically significant.

---

[4] For the calculation of this measure see Laakso and Taagepera (1979).

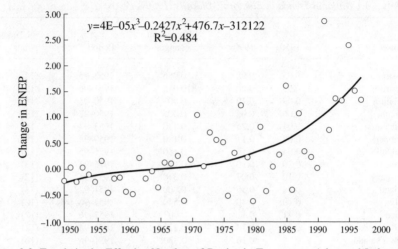

FIG. 3.2. Trends in the Effective Number of Parties in Twenty-one Advanced Industrial Democracies, 1945–1997

Note: Change represents any observation subtracted from the mean of that nation's first two post-war lower house elections. These scores were then pooled and averaged by year and plotted. Best-fit trend line produced by Curve Expert 1.3.

Source: Mackie and Rose 1991; *Electoral Studies* 1992–7.

Often, electoral analysts focus on the patterns of a single nation, or the short-term trends in party fortunes. A significant shift in party fortunes, such as the collapse of the Tories in Canada or the rise of New Left or New Right parties in Europe are normally explained in terms of the idiosyncratic political forces of the nation. In contrast, we have described a pattern that represents a general development of advanced industrial democracies, and this pattern has grown stronger and more apparent since it was first detected (Dalton et al. 1984; Crewe and Denver 1985; Franklin et al. 1992). The 'frozen' democratic party systems that Seymour Lipset and Stein Rokkan (1967) once observed have become more fluid political environments where new parties are forming and electoral change is increasing over time.

Individual-Level Behaviour

Aggregate electoral statistics are particularly useful for mapping the broad contours of electoral change because they are available over time for all our nations. Beneath these aggregate statistics, however, the *gross* shifts in voters between parties can be much greater than the *net* shift of party vote shares. More precise measures of changes in electoral behaviour come from interviewing the voters themselves. Long-term survey data series are less prevalent than electoral

TABLE 3.2 *National Trends in Effective Number of Parties, 1950s–1990s*

Nation	1950s	1990s	Per annum change	Elections	(N)
Australia	2.5	3.0	0.008*	1951–96	(19)
Austria	2.6	2.7	0.023*	1953–95	(14)
Belgium	2.8	9.9	0.185*	1950–95	(15)
Britain	2.3	3.6	0.022*	1951–97	(13)
Canada	2.9	3.7	0.016*	1953–93	(14)
Denmark	4.0	4.7	0.041*	1950–94	(18)
Finland	5.0	5.9	0.020*	1951–95	(13)
France	5.8	7.9	0.023	1951–97	(13)
Germany	3.9	5.6	0.034	1953–94	(12)
Iceland	3.9	5.0	0.036*	1953–87	(11)
Ireland	3.3	3.7	0.005	1951–92	(13)
Italy	4.0	7.6	0.077*	1953–96	(12)
Japan	4.0	4.5	0.018	1952–96	(17)
Luxembourg	3.1	4.1	0.038*	1954–90	(8)
Netherlands	4.6	4.8	−0.011	1952–94	(12)
Norway	3.4	4.9	0.033*	1952–97	(12)
New Zealand	2.2	4.0	0.030*	1951–96	(16)
Sweden	3.3	4.1	0.018*	1953–94	(15)
Switzerland	5.0	7.1	0.052*	1952–95	(12)
United States	2.1	2.1	0.001	1950–96	(23)

Source: Calculated from national legislative results. Table entries for per annum change are the unstandardized regression coefficients of time on the effective number of parties; coefficients significant at the 0.05 level are marked by an asterisk. The first two columns are the averages for the first two elections of the 1950s and the last two elections of the 1990s.

statistics, and comparable trends do not exist for all nations, but more than enough data exist to demonstrate the profound changes in individual-level behaviour that have occurred in many countries.

Party identifiers approach each election with standing predispositions that structure their perceptions of the candidates and issues of the campaign. The 'yellow dog' Democrats of American politics, the *Stamwähler* of German elections, or the 'blue ribbon' Australian Liberals are all illustrations of the habitual loyalties of partisan voters. Thus research has routinely shown that partisans are more likely to support the same party in succeeding elections, and cast a straight party vote in each election. Therefore, the weakening of partisan ties should produce a concomitant decline in the partisan consistency of voters from election to election. Table 3.3 presents the long-term trends for several different measures of individual-level voting consistency from the respective national election studies. The self-reported consistency of voting in adjacent elections is denoted as 'switched between elections'; other questions tap an attitudinal willingness to vote for another party (e.g. 'thought of voting for other party').

TABLE 3.3 *Survey-Based Measures of Volatility*

Nation	Per annum change	Period	(N time points)
Australia			
Switched between elections	0.383	1967–98	(9)
Britain			
Switched between elections	0.114	1964–97	(8)
Switched between elections (non-voting)	0.043	1964–97	(8)
Thought of voting for other party	0.159	1964–92	(8)
Canada			
Switched between elections	1.056	1974–93	(5)
Denmark			
Switched between elections	0.254	1971–98	(7)
Finland			
Considered different party	1.250	1983–91	(3)
Germany			
Switched between elections	0.318	1961–98	(10)
Switch voters (KAS surveys)	0.764	1980–96	(15)
Italy			
Switched between elections	1.325	1972–96	(5)
Netherlands			
Switched between elections	0.194	1971–98	(9)
Sometimes voted for other party	1.319	1971–98	(7)
New Zealand			
Switched between elections	0.803	1963–96	(6)
Norway			
Switched between elections	0.616	1969–93	(7)
Sweden			
Switched between elections	0.563	1956–94	(13)
Switched during election	0.301	1956–94	(12)
Switzerland			
Switched between elections	0.464	1971–95	(4)
United States			
Switched between elections	0.229	1952–96	(11)
Vote for different party	0.731	1952–96	(8)

Source: Respective national election studies; 1996 US vote for different party variable is from the Roper Poll. Per annum change is calculated with an unstandardized regression coefficient.

Although the degree of change varies across nations, the direction of change is clearly uniform. There is an increasing tendency for voters to report that they shifted their votes between elections, especially in nations where the declines in partisan attachments have been greater. In Sweden, for example, only 7 per cent of the electorate said they changed their vote between the 1956 and 1960 elections, but vote switching grew to 29 per cent in the 1994 election (Holmberg 1994). Moreover, attitudinal questions show that the reported willingness of voters to shift votes between elections has increased in every nation for which time-series data are available. For instance, even after the turbulence of the Dutch party system in the late 1960s, only a fifth of the Dutch public in 1971 said they sometimes voted for different parties; in the 1998 election more than two-thirds of the electorate reported such changing preferences. Similarly, in Australia almost three-quarters of voters in 1987 said that they had always voted for the same party in national elections; by 1998 that had declined to just under half of all voters.

Some researchers have pointed out the limitations of the type of recall data used in Table 3.3 to measure votes in adjacent elections (Niemi et al. 1980).[5] There is a tendency for survey respondents to over-report consistency in describing their present and past voting patterns, either for conscious or unconscious reasons. Thus, measures of consistency based on recall vote probably underestimate the true degree of partisan change. Yet this measurement problem should be relatively constant over time, and should not create the systematic effects observed in our time trends.

The evidence on increasing partisan volatility is bolstered by an examination of panel studies that can track the actual consistency of reported voting behaviour across time. Figure 3.3 summarizes the results of these panel comparisons for the United States, Britain, Canada, and Germany.[6] Party identification, by definition, should be a relatively stable political orientation, and this shows in the relatively small number of individuals who switch partisan ties between adjacent elections. At the same time, the size of these switchers is slowly increasing. For instance, between the 1964 and 1966 elections in Britain, only 17.9 per cent of the respondents shifted their partisanship; between the 1992 and 1997 elections this had increased to 31 per cent.

Evidence of partisan dealignment also emerges from other aspects of voter choices. For instance, the electoral system in several nations gives voters the opportunity to divide their votes between parties within the same election. Indeed, this is one of the reasons that researchers initially stressed the functional value of partisanship: the American voter 'has to cope simultaneously with a vast collection of

---

[5] There are considerable difficulties in calculating exactly comparable change statistics using recall data, and the statistics in Table 3.3 should therefore be considered as approximate trends. Besides the fallibility of voters' memories, various methodological factors affect recall consistency. For instance, some surveys ask for current and present vote in the same survey wave whereas others ask for previous vote in the pre-election survey and current vote in the post-election study. Again, however, these methodological artefacts are unlikely to vary systematically over time and thus produce the general trends we observe.

[6] One should not compare the absolute levels across nations because different time lags are involved in each case. For example, the Canadian surveys normally span 4–5 years; the German panels are pre-post election surveys of a few months duration. See Clarke and Stewart (1998) for additional panel comparisons over time. Our methodology differs from Clarke and Stewart's in that we focus on comparisons across panels of relatively equal time duration in both time-points. We do this because there is a general pattern for partisan consistency to decrease over longer time periods, presumably because more exogenous factors change shift party preferences. Thus, a four-year panel would show greater partisan change than a two-year panel, all else being equal.

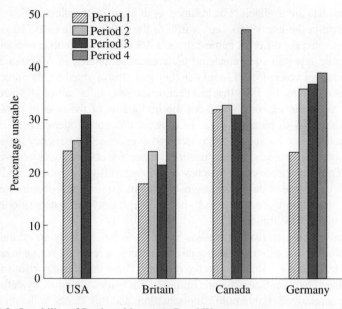

FIG. 3.3. Instability of Partisanship across Panel Waves

Note: The figure entries are the percentage who changed partisanship between panel waves. United States: Period 1 is 1956–60, Period 2 is 1972–6, Period 3 is 1992–6 (using the two-year panels yielded similar results); Britain; Period 1 is 1964–6, Period 2 is 1966–70, Period 3 is 1974–9, and Period 4 is 1983–7; Canada: Period 1 is 1974–9, Period 2 is 1980–4, Period 3 is 1984–8, and Period 4 is 1988–93; German data are from pre-post election panels: Period 1 is 1972 panel, Period 2 is 1983 panel, Period 3 is 1987 panel, Period 4 is 1990 panel.

Source: Respective national election studies.

partisan candidates seeking a variety of offices at federal, state and local levels; it is small wonder that he becomes conscious of a generalized belief about his ties to a party' (Butler and Stokes 1969: 43). To a more limited degree, vote splitting is possible in other nations. Australians can divide their votes between different parties in House and Senate elections; Germans can cast a first vote for a candidate of one party and a second vote for a different party; Swedes can cast different votes at the national and sub-national levels.

In those nations where we have been able to track such split-ticket voting over time, voters are now more likely to divide their ballots among different parties (Table 3.4). For instance, less than a sixth of Americans split their ballots between a presidential candidate of one party and a congressional candidate of another in the 1960s. By the 1990s, this had risen to between a quarter and a third of the electorate. Similarly, up until the late 1970s, less than 10 per cent of all German voters split their first and second votes.[7] In 1990, 16 per cent of West Germans

[7] One distinct feature of the German statistics is that they are based on a large sample of

TABLE 3.4 *Split-Ticket Voting*

Nation	Per annum change	Period	(N timepoints)
Australia			
House/Senate votes	0.174	1969–98	(8)
Canada			
Split federal/provincial partisanship	0.600	1974–88	(4)
Germany			
1st/2nd vote	0.221	1957–90	(9)
Sweden			
Parliament/county	0.611	1970–94	(9)
Parliament/local	0.672	1970–94	(9)
United States			
President/House	0.240	1952–96	(12)
House/Senate	0.471	1952–92	(11)
State and local	1.324	1952–80	(7)

Source: Respective national election studies. Per annum change is calculated with an unstandardized regression coefficient.

split their two votes between different parties. Similar patterns of increased split-ticket voting are found in Australia and Sweden.

It is worth noting that these patterns in voting behaviour are also apparent in an increasing tendency for divided government. The incidence of split party control has dramatically increased at both the federal and state levels in the United States (Fiorina 1992). As of early 1997, only nineteen states had one party in control of the governorship as well as both legislative Houses. Most visible, of course, is the regular division in partisan control of the presidency and the Congress since 1955 to the point where Wattenberg (1998a) has labelled the current state of American party politics as 'the era of divided party government'. A comparable pattern can be found in the Federal Republic of Germany. For the first twenty years of the FRG's history, the same party coalition controlled the Bundestag and the Bundesrat. From 1976 until 1996, partisan control of these two Houses has been divided for about one-third of this period. In the seven Australian elections between 1949 and 1964, the government had a majority in the Senate in all but one; in the thirteen elections between 1967 and 1998 the government achieved a Senate majority in only two.

One additional measure of relevant electoral behaviour is generally available from national election studies: the timing of one's voting decision. Voters with partisan identities enter election campaigns with standing partisan predispositions;

actual ballots analysed by the election office, and not public opinion survey results. Unfortunately, this practice ended in 1990 because of concerns about voter confidentiality.

TABLE 3.5 *Late Timing of Electoral Decision*

Nation	Per annum change	Period	(N timepoints)
Australia			
During election	1.470	1987–98	(5)
Britain			
During election	0.450	1964–97	(9)
Canada			
Election day	0.270	1965–93	(5)
Denmark			
During election	–0.035	1971–94	(11)
Finland			
Last few days	1.125	1983–91	(3)
Germany			
Last few weeks	0.157	1965–90	(5)
Netherlands			
During election	0.953	1970–98	(9)
Last days	0.636	1971–98	(8)
New Zealand			
During campaign	0.539	1963–93	(5)
Norway			
During election	0.897	1957–93	(7)
Sweden			
During campaign	1.038	1964–94	(11)
Switzerland			
Shortly before	0.496	1971–95	(6)
United States			
On election day	0.976	1952–96	(12)

Source: Respective national election studies. Per annum change is calculated with an unstandardized regression coefficient.

election campaigns acted to mobilize these partisan ties. Partisan dealignment implies that fewer voters begin the election cycle with such predispositions, and this makes them more susceptible to the short-term issues and themes of the campaign. If this is correct, fewer voters will say that they decided how to vote before the campaign, and more will claim that they decided during the campaign, or even on election day itself.

Table 3.5 tests our expectations about changes in the timing of electoral decisions. The specific question wording varies across the nations, but the overall pattern is unmistakable. These electorates display a consistent pattern of delaying their choice until later stages of the campaign. For instance, 27 per cent of the Australian voters said they made their voting decision during the campaign in 1987; by 1998 the late deciders had increased to 51 per cent. There may be specific circumstances in one election or another that affects the voters' uncertainty, such as changes in party leaders across elections or the issues of the campaign. But even allowing for such idiosyncrasies the trend is clear: contemporary voters are less likely to enter elections with standing partisan predispositions.

In summary, the evidence in this section illustrates the behavioural manifestations of declining partisan loyalties. The stabilizing and conserving force of partisan attachments has generally weakened in advanced industrial democracies, resulting in real and apparent consequences for electoral politics and the patterns of partisan control.

CANDIDATES AND PARTIES

As partisanship in the electorate has weakened, it stands to reason that voters would have to substitute other factors in their decision-making process. One such factor that has drawn considerable scholarly attention is the role of the politicians themselves in affecting electoral outcomes. In the United States, this phenomenon is frequently termed 'candidate-centred politics'. This term reflects the fact that Americans typically vote for many offices all at the same time, some of which are even specified by law as non-partisan offices. For example, in November 1998 voters in Orange County, California, were asked to select people for thirty-two offices, twenty-one of which were officially non-partisan. Each of these candidates, like most office-seekers in the United States, raised most of their campaign funds on their own and assembled their own personal campaign organization. Thus, it can be said that the relative lack of partisanship in American elections has led to a system of candidates, for candidates, and by candidates.

The development of the American candidate-centred system has its origins in the progressive movement of the early twentieth century. Progressives put into place primary elections to select each party's candidates, thereby denying the party organizations a major role in the crucial nomination function. Until recently, primaries were a unique American political innovation. As part of a general wave of democratization, allowing the people at large—or at least dues-paying members—to select a party's leader and/or candidates has recently started to spread. Half of the countries covered by this study have now had at least one major party conduct some form of primary—the United States, Canada, Japan, Denmark, Finland, Britain, Australia, Ireland, and Belgium (Carty and Blake 1999). In emerging Latin American democracies, such as Mexico, Argentina, Chile, and Uruguay, the spread of primary elections has been a fast-spreading development. And Israeli parties have institutionalized primaries to select candidates for the position of directly elected prime minister, as well as to determine placements on party lists—a practice that Hazan (1997) believes has seriously undermined Israeli political parties.

Although American political parties were immediately weakened by the adoption of primary elections, it was not until the advent of television campaigning that candidate-centred politics was fully realized. Primaries made it possible to obtain a party nomination on one's own, but for decades most candidates still required the support of the party organization to get their message out for the general election. Television has freed candidates from such reliance on the party, thereby allowing campaigns to be run independently of party affiliation. As a result, American candidates came to stress their own personal qualities and issue stands, and citizens naturally came to view the major issues through the perspective of the candidates rather than parties (see Wattenberg 1998*a*, ch. 5).

A comparison of the nomination acceptance speeches given by Harry Truman in 1948 and Bill Clinton in 1996 illustrate how American leaders have come to de-emphasize partisanship. In both elections, the incumbent president faced a similar situation of overcoming a seemingly devastating victory for the Republicans in the preceding congressional elections. Whereas Truman adopted a strategy of frontally attacking the Republicans, Clinton shied away from mentioning partisanship at all—referring to one party or the other just twice in a marathon sixty-six-minute speech. By contrast, in his twenty-four minute address to the 1948 Democratic Convention, Truman made twenty-seven direct references to the Democrats or Republicans. In particular, he argued that the Republican Congress had proved disastrous, ending on the following dramatic note:

I must have your help! You must get in and push and win this election. The country can't afford another Republican Congress!

The only portion of Clinton's acceptance speech that suggested the need for a change of partisan control of the Congress was indirect. In discussing the budget confrontation with the Congress, he stated:

I could never allow cuts that devastate education for our children, that pollute our environment, that end the guarantee of health care for those who are served under Medicaid, that end our duty or violate our duty to our parents through Medicare. . . . We didn't let it happen before. We won't let it happen again. Of course, there is a better answer to this dilemma. We could have the right kind of a balanced budget with a new Congress—a Democratic Congress.

With such a lack of partisan-laced rhetoric it is no wonder that ticket splitting was sufficient in 1996 for the Republicans to retain control of the US Congress, as opposed to the severe losses they suffered in the Democrats' 1948 sweep.

Whether the weakening of partisanship in the electorate will ever lead to this sort of candidate-centred issue message in established parliamentary systems remains to be seen. Because the candidates for prime minister appear on the ballot in only one constituency in district-based systems, and typically not at all in party list systems, we suspect the answer will be 'no'. The case of Britain's Tony Blair provides a telling example. Blair has been widely portrayed as a leader who personifies his party, having reshaped its policy direction in his own image. Yet, in his two key speeches of the 1997 general election campaign, a rhetorical emphasis on the party as a whole can clearly be seen. Blair mentioned one of the parties by name roughly once a minute,[8] much like Harry Truman in 1948. Typical of Blair's partisan-laced rhetoric is the following excerpt:

The manifestos of new Labour and the Conservative Party have now been published. They represent a real choice. Between the future and the past. Between a party for the many and party for the few. Between leadership and drift. I urge the British people to study what both parties are offering. . . . I am confident they will choose new Labour.

Although Blair may have reshaped the party into 'new' Labour, the key point for our purposes is that partisanship was still heavily emphasized.

One way to assess whether there has been an increasing focus on leaders versus parties is through content analysis of print coverage of campaigns over time. Wattenberg (1998a) found that the ratio of mentions of candidates compared to parties in campaign articles increased dramatically in the United States from 1952 to 1980. These data are presented and updated in Table 3.6. In addition, comparable statistics have now been collected based on content analysis over time of major newspapers or magazines in Canada, Britain, Austria, and France (see Gordon 1999; Prochart 1996). In each case, the media's attention to leaders has increased over time. The most recent data point for each country shows that the media are now referring to the leaders more frequently than the parties. The results suggest a clear distinction between presidential and parliamentary systems. In the American and French presidential systems, the candidate–party ratio has been over 5 : 1 over the last decade, whereas in the parliamentary systems the highest ratio recorded was 2 : 1 in Canada in 1974. Thus, we believe that the presence of parliamentary systems in most advanced industrial democracies will probably slow any trend towards candidate-centred politics due to the decline of party identification. In a parliamentary system, even voters who are no longer committed to a party still face a structural situation where the crucial choice is between parties rather than the personal stands and qualities of prime ministerial candidates. Unlike presidential systems, accountability and stability within a parliamentary system are based on the legislature; it is thus essential for a prime minister to retain the confidence of his party colleagues (McAllister 1996: 284–5).

This contrast between presidential and parliamentary systems can be shown by comparing the patterns of party and candidate preferences and behaviour of major party voters in a variety of countries where two parties dominate.[9] In each case we measure voters' preferences by comparing their ratings on interval scales (e.g. 0 to 100 scales or 0 to 10 scales). Our interest here lies merely in the patterns of

[8] This analysis is based on an analysis of transcripts of Blair's speeches of 1 and 3 April 1997, which launched his manifesto and slogan, respectively. Because we had transcripts rather than tapes of these speeches, we had to estimate how long it took to deliver these speeches based on our own reading of them aloud.

[9] Major party voters are those who voted for the Democrats or Republicans in the USA, RPR or Socialists in France, Liberals or Conservatives in Canada, Labour or Liberal/National coalition in Australia, and SPD or CDU/CSU in Germany.

TABLE 3.6 *Ratio of Candidate and Party Mentions in Election Stories*

USA 1952	1.7	UK 1959	0.7
USA 1956	2.0	UK 1966	0.8
USA 1960	3.0	UK 1974	0.9
USA 1964	3.0	UK 1983	1.3
USA 1968	3.6	UK 1987	1.1
USA 1972	3.6	UK 1992	1.1
USA 1976	4.5	UK 1997	1.3
USA 1980	5.2		
USA 1988	5.2	Canada 1957	1.2
USA 1996	5.6	Canada 1968	1.7
		Canada 1974	2.0
France 1965	4.3	Canada 1984	1.1
France 1974	4.4	Canada 1997	1.6
France 1981	3.7		
France 1988	5.4	Austria 1966	0.4
France 1995	5.6	Austria 1975	0.4
		Austria 1986	1.0
		Austria 1995	1.3

Source: Content analysis of the *Chicago Tribune* by Wattenberg (1998a) for 1952–80 and Gordon (1999) for 1988 and 1996; *Le Monde*, *The Times* (London), and *Toronto Globe and Mail* by Gordon (1999); and *Umfang und Plazrerung* by Prochart (1996).

party and candidate preferences—not their degree. Thus, a German voter who rates Schroeder at 0, Kohl at 0, the SPD at +2, and the CDU at –2 is classified simply as having no candidate preference and a party preference for the SPD. As some combinations do not contain very many cases in any single survey, we have combined data from a number of surveys in Tables 3.7 and 3.8 where there is little difference in the findings for the years involved.

Table 3.7 shows that in the USA, Canada, Australia, and Germany, the most common pattern is for major party voters to have consistent party and candidate preferences. This was most prevalent among Germans[10] in the 1970s and 1980s, where an average of 86 per cent of SPD and CDU/CDU voters preferred the candidate of the party they ranked highest. Canada's major party voters were the least consistent, perhaps stemming from the conflicts many face between their regional and federal political loyalties (see Clarke et al. 2000). This increases the likelihood that one might feel closer to one of the parties but not like a particular candidate because of where he or she was from. In Canada, the USA, and Germany of the 1990s, the pattern of preferring a candidate but being neutral between the parties was more common than vice versa. However, this is clearly most common in the United States—as would be expected given the advanced state of candidate-centred politics in its presidential system.

---

[10] Only data from the Western part of Germany are used for the 1990s in order to provide a true comparison to the earlier period when Germany was divided between the democratic West and communist East.

TABLE 3.7 *Patterns of Party and Candidate Preferences (major two-party voters only)*

	USA 1980–96	France 1988	Australia 1993–8	Canada 1974–9	Canada 1988–93	Germany 1972–87	Germany 1990–98
Consistent candidate and party preference	75	83	79	78	73	86	79
Prefer a party/ no candidate preference	4	5	7	5	7	5	6
Prefer a candidate/ no party preference	12	5	5	7	8	2	8
Inconsistent candidate and party preference	5	4	4	7	9	5	8
No candidate or party preference	4	3	5	3	4	2	2
TOTAL	100 (N=5,633)	100 (N=848)	100 (N=4,625)	100 (N=3,405)	100 (N=2,553)	100 (N=4,815)	100 (N=1,914)

Source: Various national election studies for these five countries. Data have been averaged for years as indicated.

TABLE 3.8 *Voting Behaviour by Patterns of Party and Candidate Preferences (major two-party voters only)*

	USA 1980–96	France 1988	Canada 1974–9	Canada 1988–93	Germany 1972–87	Germany 1990–8	Australia 1993–8
% voting with candidate preference							
Consistent candidate and party preference	97	99	96	89	98	97	98
Prefer a candidate/ no party preference	89	83	78	68	59	75	70
Inconsistent candidate and party preference	77	84	32	39	15	37	24
% voting with party preference							
Prefer a party/ no candidate preference	79	73	80	79	93	75	93

Source: Various national election studies for these five countries. Data have been averaged for years as indicated.

As Table 3.8 shows, voters with conflicting candidate and party preferences behave much differently in the presidential systems of France and the United States from voters faced with a similar decisional dilemma in the three parliamentary systems. Both American and French presidential voters who faced this situation opted for their candidate preference over three-quarters of the time compared to less than two-fifths for voters in the other countries, the low being a mere 15 per cent for German voters of the 1970s and 1980s. We can also show the relative lack of a candidate focus for voters in parliamentary systems by examining the behaviour of those with a candidate preference but no party preference. American and French voters were the most likely to vote with their candidate preference in this situation, and once again German voters of the 1970s and 1980s were the least candidate oriented.

Although we can conduct this type of analysis in two separate time periods only in Germany and Canada, these data do indicate that there has been a movement towards candidate-centred politics even within a parliamentary system as partisanship has declined. This finding with regard to Germany is consistent with Anderson and Zelle's (1995) argument that the correlation between candidate preference and vote has risen over time in the Federal Republic. Nevertheless, it should be noted that even the German data from the 1990s fail to display anything close to the degree of dominance of candidates over parties that clearly exists in presidential systems. Our review of media content analysis data similarly shows that parties are not being squeezed out of the picture in parliamentary systems to nearly the same degree as in American and French presidential systems. Therefore, the trend toward greater participation of citizens in party affairs through primaries and other means may not weaken parties in a parliamentary system in the manner they have in the United States.

PARTICIPATION AND ELECTION CAMPAIGNS

Partisan dealignment might also affect citizen involvement in election campaigns. Campaigns are first and foremost party affairs in parliamentary systems. Parties organize and structure the activities that take place during parliamentary elections, from local meetings addressed by constituency candidates to nationally televised public events, such as debates between major party leaders. With fewer identifiers and dues-paying members (see Chapter 5), parties may lack the resources for traditional grass-roots campaigning, such as canvassing and mail drops. Furthermore, a smaller party membership has significant implications for the types of candidates that are selected, how they manage their campaigns, and for elite recruitment generally.[11]

---

[11] This has given rise, it is argued, to the phenomenon of the 'career politician' (Norris 1997a; Riddell 1996).

Election campaigning has also changed considerably over the past half-century (see Chapters 6 and 7 below). Election campaigns are now highly professional affairs, involving public relations consultants and media specialists; the party is less an entity with a history and established platform and more like a political product that must be marketed to its best advantage (O'Shaughnessy 1990).[12] The growth of the electronic media, particularly television, has tended to diminish the role of the party. The electronic media also make it is easier to communicate events and issues through personalities, and voters themselves find it easier to hold an individual leader accountable than an institution such as a party (McAllister 1996). Overall, the modernization of political communications may have contributed to an increasing personalization of politics, regardless of whether the system is presidential or parliamentary (see previous section; Swanson and Mancini 1996*b*).[13]

At the same time, there are reasons to expect that the growing political skills and abilities of contemporary publics should stimulate political involvement (Teixeira 1992; Topf 1995*b*; Dalton 1984; Inglehart 1990). As education levels have risen in virtually all Western democracies, more individuals now possess the ability to participate in politics. The expansion of the mass media and the explosion of available information on current political events should stimulate political involvement. Because campaigns and parties are the prime instruments of democracy, we might expect campaign participation to increase over time, *ceteris paribus*.

In contrast, some scholars have questioned the assumption that social modernization should stimulate political involvement. Robert Putnam (1995, 2000) recently has drawn attention to the potential atomizing influences of the modernization process. Putnam suggests that some of these same modernizing forces, such as television and changing employment patterns, have demobilized Americans and led to decreasing involvement in social and political groups in America. Similarly, American electoral research has highlighted the 'puzzle of political participation' (Brody 1978), that is, voting turnout is going down while education is rising.

In short, the question of whether the social and economic forces of advanced industrial societies are stimulating or retarding general political involvement remains unresolved. We begin by examining whether there are general trends in the level of political interest in advanced industrial societies. Then we focus our attention on actual participation in elections. Election research has identified two main dimensions of election campaign activity: the act of voting itself, and

---

[12] As former Senator Herman Talmadge put it in 1986: 'They take some fellow, dress him up in their fashion, teach him to read from some idiot board for 20 seconds. You can't separate the men from the boys' (quoted in Luntz 1988: 229).

[13] In Britain, Butler and Stokes (1974: 367–8) trace the change to the 1960s, when they estimated that the party leaders had a significant impact on party fortunes. In the United States, the change is usually traced to the 1964 presidential election, when Johnson's victory over Barry Goldwater was attributed to his greater personal popularity (Nie et al. 1976: 307 ff).

involvement in various aspects of the campaign (Verba and Nie 1972; Verba et al. 1978). Because of its theoretical and political importance, we devote the next chapter to the act of voting. This chapter examines other forms of campaign involvement, such as working for a party or displaying campaign advertising.

Interest in Politics and Election Campaigns

The modernization process in advanced industrial democracy has created tremendous changes in society and politics over the past two generations. Yet, it is unclear whether this has systematically affected citizen interest in the political process. To be sure, politics remains a secondary topic behind more immediate life concerns, such as work, family, and one's living conditions. At the same time, the government's impact on these life concerns has grown over time, as well as the potential political skills and resources of contemporary publics.

We can track changes in public involvement in politics in general, or elections in particular, by drawing together trends from the various national election study series (see Table 3.9). In some nations the series taps general political interest, in some nations the standard election study question taps interest in elections, and in other nations both types of questions are available. Political interest often shows considerable fluctuation across elections; some campaigns occur in a time of crisis, or involve issues and/or candidates that stimulate public interest. For instance, Americans' political interest peaked during the late 1960s and early 1970s as a result of the Vietnam War and the political unrest of the decade. In the three presidential elections of the 1960s the proportion of Americans who said that they were 'very interested' averaged 39 per cent; the same figure for the three elections of the 1980s was 10 points lower. Similarly, political interest in Australia increased following the 1975 constitutional crisis and the dismissal of the Whitlam Labour government, which focused attention on the role of the head of state.

At the same time, the per annum change coefficients in Table 3.9 show that political interest is generally increasing over time. In almost every nation, the level of interest in the two most recent elections averages higher than in the first two elections. The one inconsistent case is the United States, where the trends in political interest and campaign interest are both downward because of the high politicization levels of the turbulent late 1960s and early 1970s.

In summary, political interest is generally increasing in the advanced industrial democracies. We should expect short-term perturbations from this trend, but the trend itself is clear. Contemporary publics are more interested in political matters, and to the extent that trend data are available, they are also more interested in election campaigns, and even more likely to care about the outcome of elections.[14]

---

[14] Trends from the American and British election studies show that the proportion of the public that cares about the election outcome has increased in both nations: United States: $b=0.155$, 1952–96 (12); Britain: $b=0.262$, 1963–97 (11).

TABLE 3.9 *Interest in Politics and Elections*

Type of campaign activity	Per annum change	Period	(N time points)
Australia			
Political interest	0.655	1967–98	(5)
Austria			
Political interest	0.873	1975–96	(5)
Canada			
Election interest	0.497	1974–93	(4)
Denmark			
Political interest	0.042	1971–81	(6)
France			
Political interest	0.561	1953–95	(5)
Germany			
Political interest	0.589	1952–90	(11)
Italy			
Political interest	0.753	1968–96	(5)
Netherlands			
Political interest	0.920	1971–98	(9)
Norway			
Political interest	2.338	1985–93	(3)
Sweden			
Political interest	0.310	1960–94	(12)
Switzerland			
Political interest	0.895	1975–95	(6)
United States			
Election interest	−0.156	1952–96	(12)
Follow politics	−0.404	1964–96	(9)

Source: Respective national election studies; Longchamp (1991) for Switzerland; Plasser and Ulram (1997) for Austria; Segatti, Bellucci, and Maraffi (1999) for Italy. Allensbach data for Germany. Per annum change is calculated with an unstandardized regression coefficient.

Campaign Activity

Although interest in campaigns provides a broad measure of political engagement, our primary question is whether actual involvement in election campaigns has also changed over time. Democracy is not just a spectator sport—it requires the active involvement of its citizens.

The American National Election Study again has a long series of campaign activity measures (see Table 3.10), showing a general decrease over the period. One of the sharpest downward trends involves displaying bumper stickers; such activity peaked at 21 per cent of the electorate in 1960, but has not exceeded 11 per cent since the early 1970s. Most other trends show a slight downward movement. The one increasing activity involves talking to people to influence their vote. The overall index of campaign activity indicates a steady downward trend.

TABLE 3.10 *Trends in American Campaign Activity*

Activity	1952	1956	1960	1964	1968	1972	1976	1980	1984	1988	1992	1996
Work for a party or candidate	3	3	6	5	6	5	4	4	4	3	3	2
Go to a meeting	7	7	8	8	9	9	6	8	8	7	8	5
Give money	4	10	12	11	9	10	16	8	8	9	7	7
Wear a badge or have a bumper sticker	—	16	21	17	15	14	8	7	9	9	11	10
Persuade others how to vote	28	28	34	31	33	32	37	36	32	29	38	27

Source: American National Election Study, 1952–96.

Earlier analyses of participation in America mirror the findings presented here. When Sidney Verba and his colleagues (Verba et al. 1995: 72) tracked participation patterns from 1967 until 1987 they found little evidence of increasing campaign involvement. Persuading others how to vote, attending a political meeting, and working for a party or candidate changed very little. Only financial contributions significantly increased over these two decades, reflecting the growing importance of chequebook participation in increasingly expensive American elections. Similarly, Steven Rosenstone and John Hansen (1993) used an extensive series of Roper Polls to track a general decline in participation in government. They found that the percentage of Americans who wrote a letter to their representatives or who participated in community meetings had also decreased from 1973 to 1990.

Declining campaign involvement is not a distinctly American phenomenon. Trends in campaign activity from outside the United States display similar trends (Table 3.11). For instance, the proportion of British voters who have attended a party meeting declined from 8 per cent in 1964 to just 4 per cent in 1987. The trends for participation in party meetings or campaign rallies are down in virtually every nation. This is a clear indication of how elections have shifted from mass-based participation to vicarious viewing of the campaign on television.[15]

Perhaps the most direct measure of partisan engagement in campaigns is the declining percentage who have worked for a party or candidate. In all but one nation (Austria) the long-term trend is downward. More generally, almost regardless of the form of election campaign activity, fewer citizens today actually participate in election campaigns. Of the 28 coefficients in the table, 23 are negative. Although the coefficients vary in magnitude, the direction of change is clear. Contemporary electorates are becoming less likely to participate in elections, and they are becoming more likely to be spectators.

TABLE 3.11 *Cross-national Trends in Election Campaign Activity (%)*

Type of campaign activity	Per annum change	Period	(N time points)
Australia			
Attended political meeting	−0.153	1993–8	(3)
Worked for party or candidate	−0.205	1993–8	(3)
Talked to friends about vote	−1.658	1993–8	(3)
Contributed money	−0.176	1993–8	(3)
Austria			
Attended political meeting	−0.212	1974–96	(3)
Worked for party or candidate	0.028	1974–96	(3)
Talked to friends about vote	−0.244	1974–96	(3)
Britain			
Attended indoor party meeting	−0.183	1964–87	(8)
Worked for party or candidate	−0.143	1964–87	(8)
Canvassed	−0.013	1964–87	(8)
Read electoral address	0.091	1964–87	(8)
Canada			
Attended meeting	−0.465	1974–93	(5)
Work for party	−0.246	1974–93	(5)
Tried to convince others	−0.044	1974–93	(5)
Germany			
Attended political meeting	−0.087	1974–89	(4)
Worked for a party or candidate	−0.183	1974–89	(4)
Talked to friends about vote	−0.175	1974–89	(4)
Netherlands			
Number of campaign activities	0.001	1972–89	(6)
Norway			
Attended party nominating meeting	−0.045	1969–93	(5)
Switzerland			
Attended political meeting	−0.357	1975–89	(2)
Worked for party or candidate	−0.357	1975–89	(2)
Tried to convince others on vote	0.143	1975–89	(2)
United States			
Attended political meetings	−0.024	1952–96	(12)
Worked for party or candidate	−0.028	1952–96	(12)
Talked to others about how to vote	0.068	1952–96	(12)
Displayed campaign badge/ car sticker	−0.257	1956–96	(11)
Donated money	−0.003	1952–96	(12)
Index of campaign activity	−0.014	1956–96	(11)

Sources: Respective national election studies in most nations; Austria: 1974 Political Action Survey, 1989 Political Culture Comparison Survey, 1996 Political Culture Change in Austria Survey; Britain: Gallup Poll 1997 British Election Study; Germany: 1974 Political Action Survey; 1980 Political Action Survey; 1985 Citizen Expectations Survey; 1989 Political Culture Comparison Survey; Switzerland, 1975 Political Action Study and 1989 Political Culture Comparison Study.

CONCLUSION

Just as Schattschneider argued that parties were essential to the democratic process, electoral research has argued that partisanship was essential to the public. Partisanship, or feelings of party identification, provides a framework for evaluating and interpreting political information; partisanship provides a cue for making political choices; and partisanship stimulates involvement in the institutions and processes of representative democracy.

The cumulative evidence of Chapters 1 and 2 suggest that dealignment has weakened the partisan ties of contemporary publics, and this is having corresponding effects on patterns of political behaviour. We recognize that partisan trends are seldom linear, and specific campaigns may accentuate or attenuate feelings of partisan affiliation. Similarly, a specific election might stimulate political interest or diminish the public's attention to the campaign. Such short-term electoral forces also can produce election-specific patterns of volatility. Given these vagaries of electoral politics, the long-term electoral trends described in these analyses are all the more striking. The unique effects of specific elections appear to be perturbations around long-term trends that are transforming electoral behaviour in systematic ways.

Fewer voters now come to elections with standing partisan predispositions. Even if they have loyalties to a party, these loyalties are weaker; more voters now make their electoral choices based on the campaign issues and candidates. As a result, election volatility is increasing. Much as has been shown for group-based voting cleavages (Franklin et al. 1992), there has been a shift from long-term sources of electoral choice to more short-term influences on the vote. Furthermore, citizens are now less likely to participate in the campaign process. Without emotional ties to their preferred party, fewer voters work for their party at election time or visibly demonstrate their party support during elections.

The implications of our findings for the democratic process remain unclear. Millions of citizens are still voting, even if they are not relying on party cues or early-learned partisanship to the degree they once did. On the one hand, this might encourage the public to judge candidates and parties on their policies and governmental performance—producing a deliberative public that more closely approximates the classic democratic ideal (Franklin et al. 1992: ch. 15). This development may be more likely because the new independents tend to be young, better educated, and cognitively mobilized. The result may be an electorate that comes closer to the model of rational and deliberate choice enshrined in democratic theory, but often lacking in democratic reality.

On the other hand, the lack of long-standing partisan loyalties may also make electorates more vulnerable to manipulation and demagogic appeals (Holmberg 1994: 113–14). Many individuals may find campaigns illuminating, but it is also possible that extraneous events may temporarily cloud serious political debate. The preoccupation with 'Jennifer's ear' in the 1992 British election or the machinations of Perot in the 1992 American presidential election are recent examples of where narrow topics at least temporarily overshadowed serious debate about the future of the nation. The attraction of personalistic leaders, including demagogic politicians such as Haider and LePen, may be another consequence of dealigned politics. Partisan dealignment has the potential to yield both positive and negative consequences for electoral politics, depending on how party systems and voters react in this new context.

Dealignment has also pushed some citizens away from partisan activity, such as participation in elections. Whereas once parties mobilized 'their' voters to participate in elections and cast a ballot at election time, these bonds to a preferred party are now weaker. Rosenstone and Hansen (1993) argued that as parties shifted away from direct personal-contact activities, such as door-to-door campaigning and campaign rallies, and toward a media-centred campaign, this lessened the opportunities for individual citizens to become involved in party work and other campaign activities. This is a pattern that is developing in most advanced industrial democracies (see Chapters 5 and 6 below), and thus Rosenstone and Hansen's conclusion may apply generally to other democracies. As the public was leaving the parties, the parties were also abandoning a reliance on the public at large to carry out some of their key functions.

A possible implication of declining participation in election campaigns is the shift in overall political involvement toward other forms of political action. Whereas elections were once seen as the focal point of political activity, it is often argued that elections are being displaced by unconventional forms of participation, such as petitions, protests, and demonstrations (Barnes, Kaase et al. 1979; Jennings and van Deth 1989). These new forms of participation have emerged as a result of value change among the young, the rise of new social movements and new issue concerns, and increasing cognitive mobilization within the electorates of the advanced societies (Inglehart 1990; Dalton and Kuechler 1990). Indeed, there is ample evidence that the incidence of unconventional forms of political protest have increased across the electorates of many advanced societies (Inglehart 1997: 312–15). Unconventional political participation may have attracted some citizens to participate in democracy through protests or citizen initiatives, but we would also argue that changes in the nature of party politics have led to declining electoral-based participation.

The prospects of these trends for contemporary democracies is uncertain—in part it depends on how the political parties and other elements of the democratic system respond. These are themes that are addressed in subsequent chapters of this study, and will lead to a consideration of the future nature of electoral politics. It is clear, however, that these trends are changing democratic politics in a way that Schattschneider and earlier electoral researchers never envisioned.

Appendix

Measuring Significance

This appendix discusses how to measure the significance of changes in public opinion over time. Two methodologies have been used in the public opinion literature. The *time-series* approach uses each survey result as a single point in a time series, and assesses the statistical significance of changes based on trends across surveys with the N equal to the number of separate national samples. This methodology was used to measure trends in partisanship in Chapter 2, as well as some of the aggregate statistics on party change in Chapter 3. It is equivalent to analyses of aggregate economic statistics or other national characteristics over time.

In contrast, the *survey* approach focuses on the raw survey data, measuring whether the differences in opinions over two or more surveys are statistically significant. Because these comparisons are based on large survey samples, the N for these comparisons is quite large—usually several thousand or more.

Employing these two techniques on the same cross-sectional data will yield dramatic=ally different estimates of statistical significance because of the large differences in the N used in calculating probability statistics. A brief example based on changes in American party identification can illustrate the effects of the two approaches. Between 1964 and 1970 the percentage of Americans identifying with a political party declined by a sizeable amount:

1964	1966	1968	1970
75.3	69.8	69.4	67.9

Using the time-series technique, one gets the following *in*significant results:

$b = -1.13$, se = 0.38, sig = 0.099, N=4

In contrast, if one analyses the cumulative file of surveys from these four years, and calculates a regression model predicting identification with a party (coded 0,1) by year of interview, the following results are revealed:

$b = -1.15$, se=0.003, sig = 0.0000, N=5,925

The two methodologies thus give nearly identical estimates of the per annum changes because they are measuring the same trend over time. The time-series analysis is not statistically significant because of the small number of surveys upon which it is based. In contrast, the analysis based on individual data has a much greater N—being based upon individual interviews rather than timepoints—and thus the results are very highly significant.

Some recent research on comparative public opinion trends has used the time-series method (e.g. Klingemann and Fuchs 1995). If one had access to the raw survey data, we believe that it would be more appropriate to base the statistical analysis on the survey methodology. Unfortunately, we often did not have access to the raw data from all the national surveys analysed in this volume. In such a case, Benjamin Page and Robert Shapiro (1992: 44–5) suggest another alternative. They note that with large sample sizes of approximately 1,500, a difference between two surveys of at least six percentage points would be statistically significant. We suggest this as a reasonable rule of thumb in judging the statistical significance of the trends discussed in this chapter and in other survey trends presented in this volume. In terms of the per annum change measures we present, a 6 per cent trend for two surveys over this period would be equivalent to a 0.300 per annum change coefficient over the typical time-series span we present from the 1970s to the 1990s. In general, the longer the time series and the more observations it is based upon, the less the per annum change has to be in order to reach significance. We therefore offer this reference standard as a general guideline for readers to take into account when assessing significance in the absence of the best available data. The analyses in this chapter will focus on the direction of the trends and not try to formalize significance level.

4

The Decline of Party Mobilization

Martin P. Wattenberg

WHEN E. E. Schattschneider wrote that 'political parties created democracy' he was primarily referring to their historical role in expanding citizen participation. In the era prior to the development of parties, voting was typically the purview of a small percentage of the populace. Political parties both fought for an expansion of suffrage and mobilized the newly enfranchised to go to the polls. Conversely, throughout history when parties have failed to perform their functions, electoral participation has declined. In sum, the saga of electoral participation in advanced industrialized countries is one in which the state of political parties, and the party system more generally, has played a critical role.

The United States presents an important case study of the relationship between party system development and electoral mobilization. The very first party system in the world appeared in the USA in the late eighteenth century and historians generally credit the emergence of parties with significantly increasing the levels of turnout. William Chambers (1963: 32) writes that turnout figures from this period 'show voting participation increasing as party development and rivalry advanced'. These nascent parties served to stir up interest in political questions and to provide a vehicle through which to channel popular participation.

Most of the leaders of America's first party system did not consider themselves professional politicians, however, and the idea of a regularized party opposition had not yet been conceptualized (Hofstadter 1972). Party leaders who lost their bids for office often withdrew completely from the political arena rather than try to mobilize voters for political change. In particular, the Federalists were poorly organized, and after repeated defeats they no longer even bothered to offer up a presidential candidate by 1820. As this first party system crumbled, it is notable that turnout fell off dramatically—in many states by as much as half (McCormick 1975: 95–6).

The rise of professional politicians in America's second party system led to the development of party organizations as a means by which to regularly mobilize the electorate. The sharp rise in voting turnout from 27 per cent of white adult males in the multi-factional US presidential election of 1824 to 80 per cent in 1840 is often attributed to the development of keen nationwide party competition. As

Chambers (1975: 13) writes, 'A strong sense of identification with or loyalty to the party and its symbols, an attachment which had never developed in any significant measure in the first party system, became the order of the day.' Getting to the polls to support one's party came to be seen as a social duty to be performed regularly.

In sum, as Robert Dahl (1961: 22–3) states in his classic study of politics in New Haven, 'Before the extensive development of political parties more or less in their modern form, voting turnout was sporadic.' Sometimes burning issues would get nearly half of the eligible electorate of New Haven out to vote, but other times the turnout could drop below 10 per cent. The establishment of highly developed grass-roots party organizations led to a great surge in turnout and a stabilization of participation rates, according to Dahl.

The American experience can be generalized to other democracies. As modernization proceeded in other countries that today make up the OECD, turnout increased hand in hand with the development of stable and well-organized political parties. Leon Epstein (1967: 127) writes that, 'Whenever a nation extended the right to vote to relatively large numbers, parties developed in evident response if they did not already exist.' Epstein further explains that the parties' function of regularized labelling became indispensable when candidates could no longer expect much of the electorate to know them personally and hence be able to assess their qualifications.

Bingham Powell's (1982) study of twenty-nine democracies in the 1960s and 1970s argues that modernization is associated with higher turnout because it leads to party systems that are firmly linked to demographic factors such as class, religion, and ethnic identity. The fact that modern party systems reinforce social cleavages makes it possible to mobilize citizens based on their group identifications. In contrast, Powell maintains that in traditional pre-modern societies, parties are often little more than coalitions of local notables that rely on personal appeals. His empirical analysis clearly demonstrates that such pre-modern political systems have lower turnout rates than systems with modern political parties (see Powell 1982: 120–1).

However, because of the recent multifaceted changes in party systems which are documented throughout this book, there is good reason to believe that the parties of the late twentieth century have entered into a new historical era. Many of these changes have transformed parties into institutions that are less likely to be effective in getting voters to the polls than they once were. This chapter presents evidence for the proposition that political parties are no longer performing their function of electoral mobilization as effectively as in the past.

PARTISAN CHANGE AND TURNOUT DECLINE

The word *campaign* is part of today's international political vocabulary, but it was not always so. The term was originally a military one: commanders mounted campaigns, using their armies to achieve strategic objectives. The functional equivalent of an army for political parties is its mass membership. Parties have traditionally relied upon their members to stand in the political front lines, carrying their message out to the electorate at large. Party members put up signs and pass out leaflets during the campaign. On election day, they man the phone banks and knock on doors to get out the vote. Taken together, these membership activities undoubtedly serve to stimulate turnout. Thus, it is reasonable to hypothesize that as party membership has declined since the 1950s (see Chapter 5) voter participation should have fallen off as well.

Even in the United States, where the practice of formal dues-paying members never existed, grass-roots organizations were prominent on the political scene for over a century. Such organizations quickly began to wither during the early years of television. Banfield and Wilson (1963: 122) were among the first to note the impact of technology on parties when they ascribed to television the weakening of the importance of an American precinct captain's visits: 'The precinct captain who visits in the evening interrupts a television program and must either stay and watch in silence or else excuse himself quickly and move on.'

As voters have come to experience campaigns through television rather than through personal contact with members of party organizations, voting has become less of a social act and more of a civic duty. No longer do voters go to the polls because they have been urged to do so by their friends, relatives, and neighbours. Rather, those who decide to vote do so largely to express their opinions.

The fact that party loyalty has generally declined, as demonstrated in Chapter 2, has set more potential voters adrift in a complicated political world without crucial guidance to help them translate their opinions into voting actions. As noted in Chapter 1, parties help to simplify the political world for the average citizen. Without this 'user-friendly' method for making political choices, turnout should be expected to decline.

Even for those who continue to have an identification with a political party, there is reason to postulate that this identification is less likely to mobilize people as in the past. When partisanship was closely tied to class and religion, the conjoint of social and political identifications provided a very strong incentive for party identifiers to turn out. These linkages, however, have been considerably withered in recent years, as demonstrated by Franklin et al. (1992). Following the logic laid out by Powell (1982), as the bond between political parties and social groups declines, so should voter participation.

The decline of class-based politics, in particular, has meant that traditional socialist workers parties have been transformed. What Kirchheimer (1966) termed the 'catch-all' party, has spread throughout most of the OECD nations. With the major exception of the United States (where no viable socialist alternative ever existed in the first place), most advanced industrialized party systems have seen a substantial lessening of ideological differences between the major political parties. Whereas going to the polls once involved choosing between a socialist versus a non-socialist government, today's partisan choices are rarely so stark. This long-term trend was accelerated by the discrediting of the socialist model when communism collapsed throughout Eastern Europe.

The weakening of social cleavages has also opened the way for the development of post-material cleavages in many advanced industrialized party systems (Inglehart 1997). The rise of a new issue dimension would ordinarily be expected to stimulate turnout because it would make party systems more relevant to current societal concerns. However, post-materialism emphasizes the importance of political participation *outside* the political arena. Therefore, as Inglehart (1997: 43) has noted, 'In Postmodern society the emphasis is shifting from voting, to more active and issue-specific forms of mass participation.'

Whereas leftist post-materialist parties have deliberately eschewed strong leadership, new parties on the right have emerged around charismatic personalities such as Jean Marie LePen in France, Joerg Haider in Austria, and Silvio Berlusconi in Italy. Although the personalization of electoral competition has appeared most prominently on the new right, it is a trend that is occurring widely throughout established democracies (see Swanson and Mancini 1996*b*). In a sense, the recent personalization of party politics harks back to the pre-modern factions that Powell attributed the low turnout of lesser developed democracies to. As the basis for political mobilization, personalized politics is transitory and fragile, and is therefore another factor that should lead to turnout decline.

Finally, the incentive for citizens to vote for elected officials has been lessened in many OECD countries because of the extension of direct democracy. More referenda were held in Western Europe (excluding Switzerland, which has long practised them) in the 1980s than in any previous decade (Butler and Ranney 1994: 5), and this trend has continued in the 1990s. National referenda have included such controversial topics as membership in the European Union (various countries), divorce (Ireland), abortion (Italy), nuclear power (Austria), electoral reform (New Zealand and Italy), and whether to abandon the monarchy (Australia). When such issues are removed from the arena of party politics, the policy consequences of voting for national offices are lessened. For example, British turnout would probably not have fallen to a new post-war low in 1997 had Labour been expected to make decisions on a common currency, electoral reform, and devolution rather than calling referenda on these subjects.

In sum, there is ample reason to hypothesize a generalized decline in turnout in the OECD nations based on recent changes involving parties in the electorate, parties as organizations, and parties in government. Perhaps the only aspect of recent partisan change that might be expected to stimulate turnout is the process of realignment that has been clearly present in such countries as Italy, Japan, and Canada. The cyclical theories of Burnham (1970) and Beck (1974) posit that realignments make the party system more relevant to a new generation of voters and therefore stimulate turnout. As will be seen near the end of this chapter, realignment has certainly not served this purpose as of yet.

DEMOGRAPHIC FACTORS AND TURNOUT

Beyond realignment in some countries, there are various changes in the composition of electorates that might be expected to lead to an increase in turnout in recent decades. Seymour Martin Lipset's 1959 classic entitled *Political Man* argued that '(p)atterns of voting participation are strikingly the same in various countries.' Among the patterns he noted were that '(m)en vote more than women; the better educated, more than the less educated; urban residents more than rural' (Lipset 1963: 187). In the interim years since Lipset drew these generalizations, these three variables have all changed such as to lead to higher turnout, *ceteris paribus*.

According to Lipset's summary of the then existent literature, women's lower turnout rate was due to the fact that so many were housewives. 'The sheer demands on a housewife and mother mean that she has little opportunity or need to gain politically relevant experiences,' wrote Lipset (1963: 206). Since the early 1960s, however, there has been a vast influx of women into the workforce in advanced industrialized societies.[1] Furthermore, issues specifically affecting women have entered the political arena, thereby politicizing many women who are not employed. New value-laden gender issues such as abortion and equal rights have had an impact on all women, regardless of their employment status. Thus, one no longer sees reference to women having a lower turnout rate in the literature. The development of gender equality with respect to participation in elections should therefore have served as a force increasing overall levels of turnout since the 1950s.

Another revolutionary social change in recent decades has been the explosion of higher education in OECD nations. Contemporary electorates are clearly the most educated in the long history of democracies. As Philip Converse (1972: 324) has stated, in analysing 'engagement in any of a variety of political activities from party work to vote turnout itself: education is everywhere the universal solvent, and the relationship is always in the same direction.' Unlike the diminished relationship between gender and turnout, the education–turnout nexus remains substantial (Lijphart 1997: 3). Indeed, in the United States, the turnout gap between the better and lesser educated has actually increased in recent decades (Wattenberg 1998*b*). All else being equal, rising educational levels should contribute to increasing turnout rates in advanced industrialized democracies.

The third variable listed by Lipset concerning the low turnout of rural voters is hardly likely to be a factor drawing down national participation rates today. Lipset wrote that the principal reason for this pattern was the social and political

---

[1] For example, in the United States in 1960 only 38% of women were in the workforce compared to 83 per cent among men; by 1996, 59% of women were working compared to 75% of men.

isolation of rural electorates. However, the development of television has left scarcely anyone isolated from political news, and a much smaller percentage of people in advanced democracies now live in rural areas anyway.

Yet, not every demographic factor that has long been known to be related to turnout around the world has changed such as to spur higher electoral participation. The young have always had the lowest levels of participation, even in new democracies (Niemi and Barkan 1987), and most OECD countries have expanded the franchise to 18–20-year-olds since the 1950s. Married people have slightly higher turnout rates than the unmarried, and marriage rates have declined throughout advanced societies in recent decades. Union membership has fallen in most of these countries as well, a development that has reduced the stimulus for working people to vote (see Gray and Caul 2000).

These changes in the age composition, marriage rates, and union density of OECD electorates, however, are scarcely as revolutionary—or as likely to impact turnout—as the boom in higher education, the movement toward gender equality, or the ending of the isolation of rural electorates. Overall, based solely on demographic changes since the 1950s, electoral participation should be expected to show a generalized increase.

MEASURING TURNOUT

Before presenting the data, a discussion of several definitional considerations in measuring turnout is in order. First, any analysis of turnout requires a specification of the denominator to be employed in the calculations. The choice involves whether to use the figures for the voting age population (VAP) of each country or the actual number of registered voters. Each has its advantages and disadvantages. VAP data offer the advantage of ensuring that all those who are eligible are counted, but have the disadvantage of including non-citizens and felons who are usually ineligible to vote.[2] In contrast, registration lists offer the advantage of excluding ineligible members of the population but have the disadvantage that some who are able to vote may not be on the registration rolls.

Although neither choice is optimal, the drawbacks associated with voting age population are more likely to be fairly constant over time whereas the problems with registration lists are clearly increasing in some countries. The United States has recently experienced a notable increase in the proportion of resident non-citizens in recent decades, but if they are removed from the VAP numbers the

---

[2] It should be noted that non-citizens have not always been excluded from voting. For example, in America it was once common for the party machines to take people right from the immigrant boats to the polling places. The disenfranchisement of non-citizens was in many ways a method of curtailing the power of the party machines in early twentieth-century America. Yet, non-citizens continue to be counted by the US Census and their numbers play a significant role in decennial reapportionment and redistricting.

turnout percentages are only marginally affected.[3] In any event, one would certainly not want to use registered voters as the denominator in American turnout calculations because of the voluntary nature of the registration process, as well as changes in registration laws over time.

Outside the United States, virtually all eligible voters were on the registration rolls in the 1950s, but this is no longer the case in a number of countries. For example, in Canada the percentage of the VAP on the electoral list has fallen from 96 per cent in 1953 to 89 per cent in 1997. In the 1999 election in New Zealand, about 9 per cent of the eligible voters were not registered compared to just 1 per cent in 1951 (Vowles, personal communication, 2000). In Great Britain, *The Economist* (3 April 1997) reported that the percentage of people missing from the electoral register had nearly doubled over the last thirty years because mobility rates have risen, and the poor have vanished to avoid first the poll tax and then the council tax. Although French citizens are required to register, as in the USA the burden for doing so falls entirely on the individual, and the percentage of the VAP on the rolls declined from 92 to 86 per cent from 1958 to 1993. Therefore, this study follows the example of Powell (1986) and the recent IDEA (1997) global participation report by employing VAP as the denominator in estimates of turnout.

A second definitional consideration regards the numerator. Most nations use the number of people who actually show up at the polls for their official turnout report. However, a substantial percentage of voters in some countries spoil their ballot. (In the OECD since 1950, the highest figure for spoiled ballots was 8.4 per cent in Belgium in 1978.) Given that these people have not cast a vote in support of a political party or its candidates, it seems appropriate to exclude them from this analysis because they clearly have not been mobilized by the parties. Over-all, this decision has little impact on the results over time, as the percentage of spoiled ballots has increased only marginally from an average of 1.7 per cent in the 1950s to 2.3 per cent in the 1990s.

Finally, it must be noted which elections have been selected for analysis. As a general rule, the turnout numbers reported here are from elections for the lower house of the national parliament—for these contests usually decide who will form a government. In the presidential systems of the United States and France, it is unclear whether presidential or legislative elections are most crucial. The Ameri-can electorate certainly believes that presidential elections are more important, as demonstrated by their higher participation rates in these contests. Thus, an excep-tion to the general rule is made for the USA by incorporating presidential

---

[3] In 1960, just 2.1% of the US population were non-citizens, whereas by 1996 this had increased to 7.1%. Adjusting the turnout figures in 1960 for non-citizens raises the turnout rate from 62.8% to 64.1%. A similar adjustment for 1996 increases the turnout estimate from 49.1% to 52.8%. Thus, among citizens the decline of turnout was just 11.3% compared to 13.7% for the entire voting age population.

turnout.[4] Such an argument could also be made in the case of France. However, French citizens could only vote for president directly starting in 1965. As this book is concerned with partisan changes since 1945, French legislative election data will have to be used instead.[5] Finally, because of the unsettled nature of democracy in many countries immediately after the Second World War, the time-series analysis begins in 1950 and continues through the Danish election of March 1998.

EVIDENCE FOR NEARLY UNIVERSAL TURNOUT DECLINE IN THE OECD NATIONS

The preceding sections have set up a crucial question to be answered: which is more important in causing more or fewer people to go to the polls, partisan or demographic changes? If the functions of parties are indeed crucial to mobilizing voters, then it should be found that turnout has declined even in the face of largely countervailing demographic factors.

Table 4.1 compares the average turnout in the first two elections of the 1950s with turnout in the two most recent elections for the nineteen established democracies of the OECD states. The results provide striking support for the conclusion that turnout has declined in advanced industrialized democracies. In seventeen out of these nineteen countries, recent turnout figures have been lower than those of the early 1950s. It is rare within comparative politics to find a trend that is so widely generalizable.

The median change from the 1950s has been a 10 per cent decline in turnout. To put this in perspective, these democracies currently have a total voting age population of 589 million people and a median turnout rate of 70 per cent. If turnout rates were 10 per cent higher (i.e. 77 per cent), an additional 41 million people could be expected to vote in national elections—a number almost equal to the entire voting age population of France.

Party systems that are notoriously weak have seen the most pronounced drops in electoral participation, whereas the presence of strong political parties appears to have dampened the decline of turnout. Turnout has fallen the most in Switzerland, where political parties hardly perform their usual functions because of the nation's reliance on referenda to decide any important policy question (Kobach

---

[4] An additional reason not to use congressional turnout in the USA is that in some districts where there is an uncontested race no actual ballots are cast for the House of Representatives. This has frequently been the case in Louisiana, where any candidate who wins the primary with over 50% of the vote is automatically elected; it was also the case in the majority of congressional districts in Florida in 1998. In any event, an examination of turnout trends in congressional and presidential elections reveals very similar trends.

[5] A comparison of the trends in turnout for French legislative and presidential elections reveals a very similar decline for each.

TABLE 4.1 *Change in Turnout Since the 1950s Among the Voting Age Population*

	First two 1950s elections	Two most recent elections[a]	Percentage change
Switzerland	60.8	36.9	−39
France	69.7	56.4	−19
New Zealand	92.6	75.0	−19
United States	61.7	52.2	−15
Japan	73.0	62.7	−14
Austria	87.8	75.9	−14
United Kingdom	81.5	72.3	−11
Germany	81.1	72.0	−11
Netherlands	85.2	76.4	−10
Canada	65.9	60.5	−9
Ireland	73.8	67.8	−9
Italy	89.5	82.0	−8
Finland	76.8	71.1	−7
Belgium	82.7	78.1	−6
Iceland	90.3	86.7	−4
Norway	77.9	75.5	−3
Australia	81.1	80.4	−1
Denmark	77.5	81.0	+5
Sweden	76.9	81.1	+5

[a]As of March 1998.

Note: Entries are based on elections for the lower House of the national legislature, with the exception of the United States, where they represent presidential election turnout. Percentage change is calculated as the ratio of the two columns, not as an absolute difference.

1994). In the candidate-centred presidential systems of France and the United States (see Chapter 3) very substantial turnout declines are also apparent. And in Japan, where political loyalties revolve around ties to leaders of internal party factions rather than to the party itself (Flanagan et al. 1991), turnout has also declined markedly. In contrast, in Scandinavia, where political parties that mobilize the working classes have traditionally been strong, recent turnout rates compare fairly well with those of the early 1950s. Sweden and Denmark are the two countries in which turnout has actually increased. Finland, Iceland, and Norway are all near the bottom of the list in terms of participation decline—along with Australia and Belgium, both of which have had compulsory voting throughout this period.

Yet, even in Scandinavia, a sizeable decline in turnout can be found if one takes the 1960s as the starting point rather than the early 1950s. The Scandinavian countries are unusual in that turnout actually increased from the 1950s to the 1960s. This difference between Scandinavia and the rest of the OECD is demonstrated by the standardized turnout numbers presented in Table 4.2. For each country, the average turnout for the first two elections of the 1950s serves as a

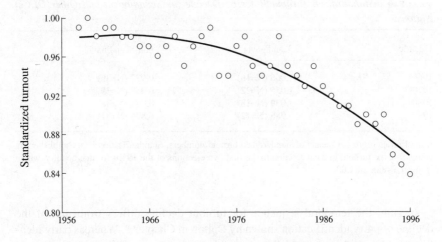

FIG. 4.1. Turnout Decline in the OECD Nations (excluding Scandinavia)

Note: Entries represent a three-year moving average of standardized turnout numbers, with the average turnout in the first two elections of the 1950s serving as a baseline for each country.

baseline from which to standardize all subsequent turnout figures. For example, if turnout had averaged 60 per cent in 1952 and 1956 and then risen to 66 per cent in 1960, the standardized turnout for 1960 would be 1.10. Thus, the figures in Table 4.2 demonstrate that on average turnout increased by 7 per cent in Scandinavia in the 1960s while falling by about 2 per cent in the other advanced democracies. Since the 1960s, however, Scandinavian turnout has fallen at roughly the same rate as found for the 1950s to the 1990s in the rest of the OECD.

Perhaps most important to note from Table 4.2 is that turnout decline has not proceeded in a linear fashion in either Scandinavia or the other countries. Only slight declines are found through the 1980s, followed by substantial drop-offs in participation during the 1990s. By calculating a three-year moving average of the standardized turnout numbers, a more precise view of the trend can be displayed for the non-Scandinavian countries. (There are not enough cases for such an analysis of Scandinavian turnout.) Figure 4.1 pinpoints the decline of turnout as being a continuous phenomenon from the late 1980s to the present. As late as 1985 the moving average had never fallen below 0.95 without rising up to that level again soon afterwards. After 1985, standardized turnout never again reached the 0.95 level, and by 1996 had dipped to an all-time low of 0.84. In other words, turnout in these countries had been within a narrow band from the 1950s to the mid-1980s, with at most a decline of 5 per cent. Since the mid-1980s, there has been a rapid decline in electoral participation of another 10 per cent.

TABLE 4.2 *Standardized Turnout Rates by Decade for Scandinavia and Other OECD Nations*

Decade	Scandinavia	non-Scandinavia
1960s	1.066 (N=16)	0.977 (N=39)
1970s	1.055 (N=22)	0.958 (N=39)
1980s	1.039 (N=18)	0.941 (N=38)
1990s	0.986 (N=12)	0.876 (N=31)

Note: Entries represent means of standardized turnout numbers. Standardization is accomplished by comparing the turnout in each election to the first two elections of the 1950s for that country, which is given a value of 1.00.

In sum, the temporal sequence for turnout decline differs from that of the decline of party identification shown by Dalton in Chapter 2. Whereas party identification has withered gradually, turnout decline as a general feature of advanced industrialized societies is mostly a phenomenon of the last dozen years. This difference may simply reflect the fact that party identification is an attitude whereas turnout is a behaviour. It is common for mass attitudes to shift gradually over time, but it takes a major shock, or what Carmines and Stimson (1989) label a 'punctuated equilibrium' to impact a habitual behaviour like participation in elections. There is little doubt that shake-ups in the party systems of the OECD democracies have provided the necessary jolt to send turnout plummeting.

An examination of the timing of turnout decline in the G7 nations will serve to illustrate this point, as a discussion of turnout decline in each of the OECD nations would be unwieldy. In most of these countries, it is possible to identify an election in which turnout fell more than 5 per cent below the average for the first two 1950s elections and has never since risen back above this threshold. The commonalities in these elections are readily apparent. Turnout first began to decline markedly when the party systems of these countries experienced a major upheaval. Though the nature of partisan change differs, in each case the decline in the relevance of long-standing party cleavages—or the major parties themselves—led to a smaller percentage of the population being mobilized to go to the polls. A chronological review of these critical points in the decline of turnout in the G7 will serve to flush out this key point.

The first of the G7 countries to experience significant turnout decline was the United States, beginning in 1972. A portion of this decline was no doubt due to the expansion of the franchise to 18–20-year-olds in that year. However, 1972 also marked a serious splintering of the Democratic Party. As Miller et al. (1976) wrote, the majority Democratic Party was in 'disarray', and hence unable to mobilize the electorate as effectively as before. On the other side, Nixon won what many analysts termed a 'lonely landslide' by running a candidate-centred campaign. The personalization of politics that was evident in this year marked the beginning of a sea-change in American politics which resulted in a long-term dealignment (see Wattenberg 1998*a*).

Other countries in the G7 did not begin to follow the American pattern of dealignment and declining turnout for quite some time. It was not until 1987 in West Germany that turnout decline was apparent for another of the largest democracies. This election marked the first campaign since the historic events of 1982–3 in which the Free Democrats' change of coalition partners led to a turn (*die Wende*) from a socialist to a non-socialist government. After this shift had itself played out, the consequences of whether the CDU or SPD held power probably seemed far less to many citizens, thus reducing incentives to vote in the future.

A very similar argument can be made for France, where the key date for turnout decline was 1988. In 1986, right-wing parties won control of the legislative assembly, thereby forcing President Mitterand, a Socialist, into a power-sharing arrangement (*cohabitation*) for the first time in the Fifth Republic. After two years of cooperation between the left and right, the parties could no longer as effectively call their supporters to the polls based on fears of letting the other ideological *tendance* have power.

In the early 1990s, Canada, Japan, and Italy all crossed the threshold of noteworthy turnout decline as their traditional party systems collapsed. In Canada, the governing Progressive Conservative Party was reduced to a mere two seats in the historic 1993 election. Despite the emergence of Reform and the Bloc Québecois as new major players in the party system, turnout fell sharply and continued to slide in 1997. Similarly, in Japan turnout dropped off dramatically in 1993 when the Liberal Democrats lost their majority for the first time since 1955 and the Socialists began to wither away. The development of various new parties, including one actually called 'New Party', did little to spur turnout, and by 1996 Japanese turnout had hit a post-war low. In Italy, the corruption scandals of the early 1990s led to the disintegration of the governing Christian Democratic Party, and to a reshaping of the left-wing parties as well. Candidate-centred politics emerged with full force in Silvio Berlusconi's Forza Italia (see Swanson and Mancini 1996*b*) in the 1994 election, which marked the key downward turning point for turnout in Italy.

In contrast to the other G7 countries, the decline of turnout in the United Kingdom has preceded in a linear fashion ($p < 0.01$). Nevertheless, it is noteworthy that the largest drop in British turnout from one election to the next was recorded from 1992 to 1997. During this period, the Labour Party was transformed into a party much less tied to the union movement and socialist beliefs. Tony Blair repeatedly referred to the party as 'New Labour'. One cynical journalist asked Blair in 1997 whether he was going to officially change the party's name accordingly, or perhaps get rid of 'Labour' entirely and call it the 'New Party'. Although easily laughed off by all at the campaign press conference, this question nicely summed up the widely held view that Labour was no longer just the party of unions and the working class. As such a reconstituted party, it was far more successful in gaining a large vote share while at the same time less able to bring citizens of low socio-economic status to the polls.

Significant shifts in party fortunes and the development of new parties have long been thought to be associated with increases in turnout (see Burnham 1970; Beck 1974). The fact that these partisan changes have occurred at the same time that turnout has plummeted in a number of countries suggests that dealignment rather than realignment is occurring. As Abramson et al. (1998: 260) have recently written about the United States, it is 'difficult to consider any alignment as stable' when turnout is so low.

CONCLUSION: THE DECLINING MARKET FOR THE PARTIES' PRODUCT

Given that the decline of turnout in OECD nations has been a relatively recent phenomenon, one can only speculate as to whether we are witnessing a long-term trend or merely a momentary aberration. Perhaps as new parties and patterns of competition become institutionalized, turnout rates will recover. On the other hand, if turnout decline is indeed due to changes in the nature of political parties, then we can expect today's low voting rates to continue, and possibly worsen. The candidate-centred mass media campaign is clearly here to stay, as are most of the other partisan changes this chapter has postulated as being responsible for declining turnout.

As individual office-seeking organizations, there is unfortunately little reason for parties to be concerned about poor turnout levels. In fact, it is more efficient for a party to win an office with fewer votes. This would be akin to General Motors making just as much money with the sale of fewer cars.

Yet, for the party system as a whole, lower turnout spells trouble just as a decline in overall car sales would for car manufacturers. In the political world, party leaders are the functional equivalent of CEOs, members of parliament function as upper-level management, and party members perform essential roles akin to assembly line workers. On the other side of the supply and demand equation, party identifiers are like loyal customers, and those who vote represent the total consumer base for the product. If the CEOs, management, and workers of the auto companies were working more efficiently, but nevertheless selling fewer cars, industry analysts would no doubt conclude that the car business was in dire straits. The fact that voter turnout has declined indicates that there is less of a market for the parties' product and that party systems around the advanced industrialized world have fallen upon hard times.

PART II

Parties as Political Organizations

5

Parties without Members?

Party Organization in a Changing Electoral Environment

Susan E. Scarrow

THE mass party was an enduring and influential invention of the late nineteenth century, but by the end of the twentieth century it seemed like an increasingly imperilled form. As Maurice Duverger's (1963) classic portrayal tells us, in many countries political life was once transformed by the creation of such parties. They constructed nationally networked membership associations which cultivated political identities and mobilized newly enfranchised populations. This organizational style originally most appealed to the left, but the mass party's successful techniques soon were emulated and adapted by parties across the political spectrum. Because mass parties emphasized enrolment and political education, and because they encouraged citizens to extend their political involvement beyond merely voting, they broadened the realm of citizen politics and provided concrete links between politicians and those they claimed to represent.

Although Duverger's account of mass parties has been widely accepted as a description of political developments during the first half of the twentieth century, other scholars soon questioned Duverger's assessment that the mass party was becoming the dominant organizational form. As early as the 1960s, Otto Kirchheimer (1966) and Leon Epstein (1980) argued that the popularity of this organizing style had begun to wane, sidelined by changes in society and technology. Subsequent developments have only strengthened the case against Duverger's prediction of mass party dominance. They have not, however, settled the question of how party organizations will change, and in particular, of how parties that once pursued large enrolments will treat the remnants of these organizations. At the extreme, some predict an 'Americanization' of party life that will spell the

Some of the information used in this chapter was supplied by Andrew Appleton, Luciano Bardi, Lars Bille, R K. Carty, Kris Deschouwer, David Farrell, Andrew Knapp, Ruud Koole, Andreas Ladner, Ian McAllister, Wolfgang Müller, Thomas Poguntke, Patrick Seyd, Jan Sundberg, Lars Svåsand, Michael Thies, and Paul Webb. Their generous assistance is gratefully acknowledged. Thanks are also due to Michael Bruter and Miki Caul for their research assistance.

complete end of locally rooted, membership-based, organizing. Less extreme predictions foresee that parties will retain their membership organizations, but that enrolment will become a less meaningful act as local party life stagnates, and as members lose rights which once gave them influence over party decisions. In either case, there is agreement that shifts away from the mass party model are likely to affect the wider texture of political life, since they are likely to reduce the extent to which parties function as outlets for, and stimulants to, civic participation.

This chapter takes up questions raised by this volume's exploration of possible party decline by examining parties as membership-based organizations, asking how this aspect of the mass party model has fared over the past half-century. In keeping with the plan of this book, and in contrast to many previous assessments of party development, the focus here is not exclusively European, but encompasses the eighteen OECD member states which have been continuously democratic since 1945. In addition, the analysis will consider party organizational development over a relatively long time span, evaluating recent developments in light of various baselines. As will become clear, these broad perspectives provide ample confirmation of recent reports of widespread drops in party membership. However, they also offer clear warnings against exaggerating either the rise, or the demise, of membership-based organization.

PARTY ORGANIZATIONS IN DECLINE:
THE PERENNIAL DIAGNOSIS

The diagnosis of party decline in an organizational sense predates the notion of declining party attachments by almost three-quarters of a century. For more than 100 years a string of notable scholars have announced in decidedly pessimistic tones that social and technological forces are ineluctably altering the ways that parties link citizens with arenas of state power. What has changed in these diagnoses is the understanding of what constitutes 'decline' in an organizational sense, an understanding that has shifted along with prevailing attitudes about the desirability of parties as well-organized popular associations. At the beginning of the twentieth century the verdict of decline often was infused with a moral sensibility by those who feared the *growing* capacity of extra-legislative party organizations. In contrast, later analysts were more likely to equate decline with *waning* organizational capacity. A quick review of these shifting assumptions about the drawbacks and advantages of strong, locally rooted, parties provides a useful context for understanding current suppositions about the implications of mass party decline.

In the first half of the nineteenth century, British and American debates about political parties focused primarily on the behaviour of parties in legislatures and in elections. However, as later observers began to accept parties as inevitable features of the legislative landscape, reflections on party governance began to pay closer attention to party activities outside legislatures. Many commentators were worried by what they saw, and warned that increasingly strong extra-legislative parties threatened good government, or even democracy itself. As one of the fiercest critics of permanent party organizations put it, 'The more perfect the organization at the disposal of party convention is, . . . the more it demoralizes the party and lowers public life' (Ostrogorski 1982: ii. 347).

While Ostrogorski's denunciations of 'machines' and 'caucuses' were dismissed as extreme by some, many of his contemporaries shared his view that strong party organization was undesirable, because it enabled political elites (often described as 'the wirepullers') to manipulate the masses. Ostrogorski and other scholars of the pre-First World War era often backed their party criticisms with examples drawn from the United States, which at this point was generally acknowledged to be the country which had seen 'the most complete development' of party organizations (Bryce 1982: lxx; on late nineteenth-century party criticism see Epstein 1986 and Quagliariello 1996). Defenders as well as critics of party-based democracy decried the abuses of the American municipal patronage machines, and lamented that such parties were likely to produce bad policies, poor citizens, and inadequate leaders (Belloc and Chesterton 1911; Bryce 1889; Hasbach 1912; Maine 1886; Ostrogorski 1982; Smith 1892). Central to many of these attacks on strong party organization was a belief that the people are basically sensible but are easily deceived about their own best interests. These arguments about the dangers of strong parties were echoed and amplified by American Populists and Progressives, who successfully promoted reforms (such as the introduction of primary elections, referendums, and recall procedures) which were intended to undermine or suppress dominant local party structures (Beard 1910; Cree 1892; Croly 1914; Stickney 1906; Weyl 1912). The resulting changes helped to weaken the American municipal machines, and contributed to the rise of American candidate-centred political organizing.

Paradoxically, just as the era of the American machine party was beginning to wane, some scholars began to re-evaluate its contributions to political life. These new assessments displayed less distrust of political leaders, and also less confidence in the judgements of 'the people'. For instance, while not denying the corruption and other abuses associated with the party machines, some analysts presented more sympathetic portrayals of their efforts to integrate new populations into the political life of a nation of immigrants. They depicted patronage-based organization as a routine element of politics in some situations (Bone 1949: ch. 17; Herring 1940: 154–5). At the same time, even US political scientists began to note the civic benefits provided by national parties with strong local roots. Such parties were held capable of counteracting the anomie of mass society by constructing legitimating links between citizens and their governors (APSA 1950).

This idea of organized parties as vehicles for integrating the political masses was most famously articulated by Sigmund Neumann (1965; 1956). Neumann's experience of the collapse of Weimar democracy led him to argue that modern democracies could not survive unless democratic parties provided the kind of organizational integration offered by their non-democratic rivals. By Neumann's time it was European Social Democratic parties, not US municipal machines, which served as models for strong democratic party organization. It was on such parties that Duverger bestowed the 'mass party' label. Duverger praised the emergence of mass parties as a positive step in democratic evolution, precisely because their locally articulated structures ensured a 'closer and more faithful contact between the mass of the people and their ruling elites' (1963: 427). Functionalist-inspired discussions of the 1950s and 1960s likewise assigned parties the tasks of political 'integration' and 'mobilization'—jobs that were to be at least partially accomplished by their nationwide local networks (cf. Rokkan 1966a; Weiner and LaPalombara 1966). These and other authors were haunted by the inter-war collapse of European democracies, and were worried by the many threats to newly established democracies. For many mid-century analysts, the question of whether strongly organized parties could promote regime stability thus became more important than earlier concerns that strong party organization placed public welfare in the hands of party 'wirepullers'. From this perspective, mass parties' local networks could make an important contribution to the success of electoral democracy by fostering political integration.

Ironically, just as scholars began highlighting the virtues of parties with strong local structures, researchers began questioning the extent to which parties could or would maintain grass-roots organizations. Since the 1960s a growing chorus has proclaimed the demise of parties as community-based agents of political socialization and mobilization. This purported demise has been a central feature of such diagnoses as organizational 'contagion from the right' (Epstein 1980: 257–60), the spread of the 'catch-all party' (Kirchheimer 1966), the rise of the 'rational-efficient' party organization (Wright 1971), the advent of the 'electoral-professional party' (Panebianco 1988), the end of the 'generative' phase of pluralism (Pissorno 1981: 272), party 'cartelization' (Katz and Mair 1995), the 'crisis of the mass parties', and even 'party failure' (Lawson and Merkl 1988).

These various diagnoses share two important features. First, they all pronounce the obsolescence of hierarchical mass parties, particularly of the active local units which provided social and political identities for enrolled supporters, and legitimacy and electoral loyalty for party leaders. Second, all point to similar sociological and technological changes as contributing to the seemingly inevitable downfall of local party organization. These changes include the erosion of traditional social milieux, the associated weakening of political loyalties, and the shift towards expensive mass media campaigning. Such changes are said to reduce the supply of potential party members, and at the same time to make parties less interested in formally enrolling their supporters.

As many researchers note, the declining appeal of the mass party model does not necessarily imply that party organizations will become less able to accomplish basic electoral tasks. Indeed, centralized, professional parties may prove to be better campaigners and fund-raisers than more locally rooted associations. Thus contemporary reflections on the implications of mass party decline are not so much about parties' electioneering capacities as about their capacity to generate political integration and political legitimacy ('linkage').

PARTIES AS MEMBERSHIP ORGANIZATIONS: WHAT DIFFERENCE DO MEMBERS MAKE?

Those who predict the demise of parties as membership organizations usually link this trend to a simultaneous reduction in parties' demand for members, and in the supply of citizens who might be persuaded to enrol. Demand-side arguments emphasize that electorally oriented parties have become more professional and more media-dependent since the 1950s, and therefore no longer need the kinds of services once provided by member volunteers. Supply-side arguments emphasize shifts in citizens' lifestyles and political preferences (e.g. post-materialism, new leisure opportunities, declining political attachments), contending that these developments have made it ever more difficult for parties to recruit formal membership support. Of course, neither demand-side nor supply-side changes necessarily spell the complete end of membership-based party organizations. Professionalized parties may well continue to seek members because they value them for something besides their volunteer contributions, and even post-materialists might view some types of party organizations as rewarding outlets for individual political energies. However, if at least some of the above-named forces are at work, they could significantly depress the success of party enrolment efforts, and could alter party strategies for organizing those who do enrol.

Formally enlisting supporters has been a standard device of party organizers since the advent of mass suffrage, but this technique has not been universally adopted—many parties have flourished without this kind of organized base. Nor is membership-based party organization a prerequisite for stable representative democracy or enduring party systems, as the American example clearly demonstrates. Thus, one should not overdramatize the possible consequences should parties cease to function as grass-roots membership organizations. Yet it also might be a mistake to suggest that the impact of such a shift would be confined to the affected parties. If parties appear to be abandoning or failing in attempts to formally organize supporters this may lead to fundamental changes in the ways that parties link citizens to their political elites. These expectations of change derive from our understanding of the ways in which members can aid their parties, and of the concessions party leaders often make in hopes of attracting and retaining members.

At a general level, the main reason for parties to enrol supporters is the assumption that members can help them achieve their political goals. At a more specific level, however, party organizers may hold widely varying expectations regarding why it is helpful to have members, and about what (if anything) members should do to make themselves useful. In many cases, the answer to the latter question may be nothing: some parties may highly value even enrollees who are entirely passive. Having a roster of party members (particularly a growing roster) conveys a message of popular legitimacy and enables a party to claim that it has strong ties to 'ordinary citizens'. Members who are inactive within their party can provide their party with a stable voting base that is relatively easy to mobilize because it is registered with the party. However, many parties expect that at least some members will do more than merely publicly register their support and show up on election day. Parties often look to members to provide more concrete types of aid, such as donating money or time to campaign efforts. Parties may also view their membership bases as essential reservoirs out of which to draw candidates for local, and perhaps even national, offices.

The best way for parties to attract members to perform any of these services is to offer supporters incentives for getting involved. They typically encourage enlistment by offering non-political benefits, such as opportunities for socializing (making the local party branch into either a formal or *de facto* social club), or enhanced access to jobs or education. Parties also may offer members political privileges, such as promising easier access to public officials, or giving them a role in party decision-making. Parties also can attract some members by making membership and participation in local party life a standard pathway to, or even a prerequisite for, candidacy and elective office.

Whether parties attract members with selective or collective benefits, they are bound to have a more general impact on civic life. Parties with locally organized members are more likely than others to reach out to citizens individually, urging existing members to use their own social networks to recruit new members and mobilize electoral support. Even when such contacts do not create the kind of social integration envisage by Neumann (1956), they may be much more effective than centralized media campaigns in building ties to citizens, and in conveying the impression that a party is more than just an enterprise of the political elite. Parties that offer members social benefits may foster attachments to political sub-communities, and may thereby combat declining party identification. In addition, local parties can serve as good training grounds for citizens to become active in politics. They may also mobilize members in ways that counteract some of the biases towards social inequality seen in other, more individualistic, modes of political participation (Verba et al. 1978; Parry et al. 1992; Togeby 1992). Although membership-based parties will not necessarily produce any of the results listed above, such effects are absent where parties do not even attempt to enrol members. Therefore, one important reason to evaluate the extent of the decline of parties as membership organizations is that such a shift seems likely to hasten (not just to be caused by) the weakening of bonds between citizens and public officials.

One way to assess the nature of parties' organizational links with their supporters is to examine parties' membership figures. These numbers—or their absence—provide useful clues about parties' organizational aims and their impact. At one extreme, parties which eschew formal membership obviously do not aspire to the mass party form. In other words, the unavailability of membership numbers may be quite revealing, something that could be all too easily forgotten in examinations that exclude countries and parties for which membership data is lacking. For example, it is instructive to note that there are no firm figures on long-term changes in North American party enrolment because for most of the twentieth century national parties in the United States and Canada did not attempt to cultivate centrally coordinated membership organizations.[1] Therefore, these two countries are absent from some of the tables and discussions which follow, but that does not mean that they will be excluded from the broader search for trends in party organizational development.

The quality of available enrolment figures is sometimes almost as revealing as the numbers themselves. For instance, parties which lack precise enrolment figures probably lack tight direct links of communication between individual members and the central party, as the central organization obviously does not possess the address files it would need to send individual members either mailings or ballots.[2] Similarly, when central parties begin to more closely monitor their membership (for instance, by centralizing dues collection procedures) they may begin to issue more accurate membership counts, though the figures are likely to show an initial decline as a result of such newfound accuracy. Such patterns occurred when the British Labour Party changed its affiliation requirements for local parties in the late 1970s, and when the German Social Democratic Party began rigorously purging its rolls of non-paying members in the 1980s.[3] In these and other parties, centralization and computerization have had similar modestly deflationary effects on membership figures (on the Netherlands, Koole 1994: 287; on Ireland, Farrell 1994: 225). Knowing what produced these drops alerts us that they should be viewed more as indications of the increasing efficiency of central party organizations than of waning interest in party enrolment.

As this discussion suggests, one of the perennial problems of comparative research into party membership trends is the great variation in the extent to which parties attempt to gather accurate enrolment figures. Whereas some national parties keep central records listing each individual member, others make do with

---

[1] In the 1990s Canada's larger national parties made greater attempts to construct nationally organized membership bases. Some regional parties, such as the Parti Québecois and the New Democrats, have a longer tradition of membership-based organizing (Carty 1991).

[2] Of course, in some cases researchers may be forced to rely on rough estimates simply because central party organizers chose not to share information about their members.

[3] Whereas the SPD's 1980 membership figures included almost 100,000 people who failed to pay annual dues, fifteen years later this had been reduced to 22,000 (SPD 1995).

estimates of their locally enlisted supporters. Further complicating matters is the fact that many parties' practices in this regard have changed over time. Thus a broad examination of party membership trends almost inevitably winds up comparing figures which are not gathered in comparable ways. These imprecisions are less problematic, however, when the intent is to investigate long-term and very general developments, as this chapter sets out to do. Blips produced by party accounting methods and fluctuations related to electoral cycles should be smoothed out when examining long-term developments instead of yearly shifts.

Finally, even where accurate enrolment data is available, researchers have to make decisions about how these figures should be tallied. The general practice, and the one that will be followed here, is to examine individual enrolment numbers whenever these are available. Given the questions raised in this chapter, these figures are preferable to tallies which include indirect membership because they most accurately reflect the extent to which parties use their organizations as vehicles for political mobilization and integration. In parties with indirect membership, it is the affiliated organizations (trade unions, church-related organizations, agricultural associations, etc.), which usually take responsibility for transmitting political identities and mobilizing supporters. As a result, while shifts in indirect membership may be a good indicator of the strength of party links to particular social sectors—they reveal much less about the strength of parties as locally rooted conduits for citizen participation and mobilization.

The following sections examine long-term trends in aggregate enrolment across a large group of countries. Wherever possible, the analysis will rely on enrolment totals provided by the parties themselves. Elsewhere, figures are taken from estimates provided by national experts. In order to calculate aggregate totals it has sometimes been necessary to fill in missing data for specific parties by extrapolating from the surrounding known points. Thus, the nature of the data, and procedures for treating missing data, have almost certainly introduced some imprecision into the numbers examined below. Although such inaccuracies make it problematic to conduct detailed year-on-year statistical analysis with this data, they are unlikely to obscure (or falsify) long-term trends.

THE DEVELOPMENT OF MEMBERSHIP PARTIES: THE BROAD PICTURE

Is party enrolment declining, and if so, how unprecedented is this drop? These questions were posed repeatedly during the last quarter of the twentieth century as researchers have sought to distinguish the fortunes of individual parties from the fate of this particular mode of citizen participation in politics. Answers to these questions have varied in part as a result of three main variables in the analysis: whether membership is measured in absolute or standardized terms, which cases are examined, and which baseline is chosen.

Different measures of membership development may produce varying conclusions about whether enrolments are stable or declining. Membership figures can be expressed in raw numbers (M), or they can be standardized in terms of each party's vote (M/V), or of the overall electorate (M/E). Some authors have dismissed the first two measures as unsatisfactory because they do not take adequate account of the context of party development and the relationship between organizational and electoral success (Katz and Mair et al. 1992: 331). Yet, the appropriateness of each measure partially depends on the reasons why party size is of interest. If the aim is to assess the extent to which parties provide outlets for citizen political participation, it makes sense to standardize party membership in terms of the total electorate. However, if the aim is to compare particular parties' success in providing supporters with an organizational home, it makes sense to standardize membership in terms of party vote. In contrast, absolute membership figures may be best for judging the aggregate strength and political capacity of grass-roots party organizations, showing whether parties have sufficient supporters to maintain some kind of presence at the local level. While each of these measures may be useful, each may lead to different conclusions about organizational trends, particularly in periods where the size of the overall electorate (or of a particular party's support) shifts rapidly.

The consequences of the choice of measures are apparent in the varied interpretations of developments in European parties from the 1960s to the 1980s. In absolute terms, overall party enrolment did not decline in every country during this period. However, because electorates were expanding in these years (partially as a result of a reduced voting age), when figures are standardized in terms of eligible voters they paint a much more convincing picture of general organizational decline (Bartolini 1983; Katz 1988; Katz and Mair, et al. 1992; Mair 1994: 4; Widfeldt 1995: 138).

Another important variable in assessments of party change is the choice of cases. Most recent examinations of trends in party enrolment have looked exclusively at European parties. But there is no need to confine our attention to Europe when assessing broad trends in party organization. As stated in Chapter 1, the social and technological changes generally linked to party transformation have been present in all advanced industrial democracies, so posited organizational changes should be visible in all of them. Thus, a more comprehensive and conclusive picture of trends in party development should emerge when examining this book's subset of OECD countries rather than looking at European experiences alone.

Opting for this broader universe of countries does not completely answer the question of which parties to examine. Although the intent here is to investigate the fortunes of 'mass' or 'membership' parties, reference to an ideal type provides little guidance about which parties to include in the assessment. Nor can the choice be made according to size alone, since Duverger long ago warned that mass parties—parties of the masses—are not distinguished by their size, but by such structural features as permanent organization between elections, and formal enrolment of dues-paying individual members (1963: 63–7). As Duverger himself noted, however, even these structural characteristics do not provide a definitive basis for classification, since they may be shared by parties that have little interest in organizing grass-roots support. It is because of such ambiguity that the present investigation includes as many national-level parties as possible.

Table 5.1 presents the trends in total party membership from the 1950s until the present. Table 5.2 presents the ratio of party members to the electorate (M/E) over time. Taking a broad sample of countries and parties from the 1960s to the mid-1990s yields a picture of post-war membership decline whichever membership measure is chosen.[4] Of the fourteen countries for which membership data are available over a long time span, only five saw an increase in absolute enrolments from the 1960s to the 1990s (Belgium, Germany, Ireland, Japan, and Switzerland). Of these, only Germany and Japan experienced an increase in standardized enrolments. Moreover, when evidence from these four countries is examined more closely, it becomes clear that none of them exhibits patterns that strongly contradict the conclusion of generalized party organizational decline. German, Belgian, and Irish parties saw memberships expand after the early 1960s, but since then have witnessed declining enrolments.[5] In Japan, the reports of membership growth reflect a development that is not strictly comparable to membership change elsewhere, as much of the reported enrolment is in fairly decentralized associations organized to support local candidates.

In short, this broad examination yields a fairly general picture of party memberships in decline by the 1990s, whether membership is measured in absolute or standardized terms. This picture of generalized decline remains whether the early 1950s or the early 1960s serves as the baseline. To the extent that complete records are available from the 1950s they also show higher enrolments compared to the mid-1990s (see Table 5.1). As noted above, some of this downward trend may reflect a general improvement in record-keeping rather than a real change in enrolment practices. In addition, it should be noted that the two cases excluded from Tables 5.1 and 5.2 (the United States and Canada) do not support the picture of 'decline', though they do match the picture of contemporary parties as lacking strong membership bases. While experiences in these two countries do not entirely fit the picture of a trend for citizens to disengage from one sort of tie with political parties, overall the decline is too general, and in many cases too steep, to dismiss as either an administrative artefact or as the product of country-specific effects.

---

[4] In comparison, all but one of ten European countries which were included in the Katz/Mair study registered a drop in relative enrolments since the 1960s, while all but two showed a decline in absolute enrolments: this was a much more uniform pattern of absolute and relative decline than was visible at the end of the 1980s (Katz, Mair, et al. 1992).

[5] Ireland, where membership estimates for some parties reach back only to the end of the 1960s, shows a similar picture of enrolment growth followed by more recent decline.

TABLE 5.1 *Aggregate Party Enrolment*

	1950	1960	1970	1980	1990s
Australia	—	—	265,000	234,000	174,000 (1996)
Austria	1,041,000	1,262,000	1,308,000	1,321,000	990,000 (1994)
Belgium	—	478,000	495,000	615,000	485,000 (1995)
Denmark	597,000	599,000	489,000	276,000	202,000 (1995)
Finland	396,000	485,000	531,000	579,000	428,000 (1995)
France	1,259,000	589,000	644,000	1,089,000	582,000 (1995)
Germany	1,126,845	1,018,000	1,299,000	1,954,000	1,852,000 (1996)
Ireland	—	59,000	82,000	98,000	93,000 (1997)
Italy	3,698,000	4,280,000	4,620,000	4,078,000	1,867,000 (1996)
Japan	205,000	404,500	741,500	2,175,000	3,648,000 (1989)
Netherlands	630,000	730,000	369,000	523,000	229,000 (1996)
New Zealand	288,000	264,000	228,000	167,000	50,000 (1993)
Norway	—	324,00	399,000	456,000	276,000 (1997)
Sweden	1,110,000	1,092,000	1,104,000	1,429,000	376,000 (1997)
Switzerland	—	367,000	357,000	367,000	391,000 (1994)
United Kingdom	3,436,000	3,065,000	2,424,000	615,000	820,000 (1997)

Note: Beginning data for Australia was 1972; Austria 1956; Ireland 1967, and 1980 is 1986; New Zealand 1954

Sources: Multiple countries: Daalder 1987; Daalder and Mair 1983; Henig and Pinder 1969; Henig 1979; Jacobs 1989; Katz and Mair 1992; Kirchner 1988; Lane and Ersson 1987; Paterson and Thomas 1977. Australia: Aitkin et al. 1996; Jupp 1964; Jupp 1982; Mayer 1973; Galliganet al. 1998. Austria: Dachs et al. 1997; Maderthaner and Müller 1996. Belgium: personal communication, Kris Deschouwer. Britain: personal communication, Pat Seyd. Denmark: personal communication, Lars Bille. Finland: Allardt and Pesonen 1960; Sundberg 1996. France: Ysmal 1994; Meny and Knapp 1998; MacRae 1967. Germany: Frye 1985; Morsey 1966; Stöss 1983; personal communications from party headquarters. Ireland: Chubb 1970; personal communication, David Farrell. Italy: Bardi and Rhodes 1998; Farneti 1985; Galli and Prandi 1970. Japan: Berton 1991; Cole et al. 1966; Day and Degenhardt 1980; Richardson 1997. New Zealand: Chapman et al. 1962; Levine 1979; Milne 1966; Mulgan 1994. Netherlands: personal communication, Ruud Koole. Norway: Rokkan and Campbell 1960; Valen and Katz 1964; personal communication, Lars Svåsand. Sweden: Widfeldt 1999. Switzerland: Geser 1991; Geser et al. 1994; Gruner 1975.

Parties' reports of generally falling enrolments are reinforced by responses from public opinion surveys about party membership (Table 5.3). National election studies and other surveys from ten of the fifteen relevant countries provide a long-term record of self-reported membership levels (and in two additional countries comparable responses are available over a shorter period). In eight of these countries membership levels dropped between the 1960s and 1970s and the 1980s or 1990s. Italy, one of the two countries where self-reported membership increased at the end of the 1980s, undoubtedly would show a steep decline if comparable figures were available for the late 1990s. Thus, self-reports largely confirm that enrolment within a political party is becoming a much less popular outlet for political participation.

TABLE 5.2 *Member/Electorate Ratio (%)*

	1950s	1960s	1970s	1980s	1990s	Change 1960s to 1990s	Change 1950s to 1990s
Australia	—	—	3.7	2.6	1.5	—	—
Austria	23.9	26.2	25.9	24.2	17.1	−9.1	−6.8
Belgium	—	9.8	10.0	9.1	7.6	−2.2	—
Denmark	15.7	14.3	14.0	7.5	3.1	−11.2	−12.6
Finland	16.4	19.1	17.2	14.4	10.5	−8.6	−5.9
France	7.5	2.2	1.9	3.1	1.5	−0.7	−6.0
Germany	2.9	2.7	3.7	4.5	3.2	+0.5	+0.3
Ireland	—	—	4.6	4.5	3.4	—	—
Italy	13.9	12.7	12.8	7.1	3.2	−9.5	−10.7
Japan	0.3	0.7	1.1	2.7	4.2	+3.5	+3.9
Netherlands	11.4	9.5	4.4	4.1	2.2	−7.3	−9.2
New Zealand	23.8	20.2	14.6	7.8	2.1	−18.1	−21.7
Norway	—	16.0	12.8	13.4	7.9	−8.1	—
Sweden	23.4	22.0	19.6	23.7	7.1	−14.9	−16.3
Switzerland	—	23.4	10.4	9.1	8.7	−14.7	—
United Kingdom	10.0	9.0	6.2	3.8	1.9	−7.1	−8.1

Note: Table entries are party members as a percentage of the electorate within each party.

For first election of 1950s–1980s, except Austria, 1956, Ireland 1987, New Zealand 1954. For latest election of 1990s for which membership data are available, as follows: 1990 Japan; 1991 Belgium, Switzerland; 1993 Denmark, New Zealand; 1994 Austria, Germany, Italy, Netherlands, Sweden; 1995 Finland; 1996 Australia, Ireland; 1997 France, United Kingdom.

Before assessing the implications of these findings of falling membership since the 1960s, it is worth stepping back to put the figures into a broader historical perspective. This investigation, like most similar ones, has evaluated recent organizational developments in light of mid-twentieth century norms. What the examined evidence does not settle is the question of when the decline set in—do the enrolments of the 1950s and 1960s represent the apogee of party-building efforts, or were party memberships already in decline by this point? This question of choosing the appropriate baseline for evaluating current trends is one of the least examined features of party decline debates. Recent investigations of party change usually take the 1950s or the 1960s as their starting point. When the question of party decline focuses on citizens' expressed political attachments, this choice of starting point is sometimes dictated by the availability of survey evidence. Investigations of organizational change tend to follow suit, even though they are not constrained by the same rigid cut-offs on data availability. However, as the next section explains, viewing mid-century parties as the organizational norm may unduly stack the deck in favour of finding a decline.

TABLE 5.3 *Self-Reported Party Membership (% of respondents)*

	1960-1	1962-3	1964-5	1966-7	1968-9	1970-1	1972-3	1974-5	1976-7	1978-9	1980-1	1982-3	1984-5	1986-7	1988-9	1990-1	1991-2	1992-3	1994-5	1996-7	Changes 1960/70s to 1980/90s
Austria					24					22		24	23		18				15		(−)
Belgium												05		07	09						(−)
Denmark						17				12	11	05		10	13						(−)
Finland							19					16	19	14		11					
France												04			04						
Ireland												04			04						
Italy					07							07			09						(+)
Japan							08	06	14	20	15	16		18	18	18		16			(+)
Netherlands						12	09		08		09	08		08	08						(−)
New Zealand							20	18		21	19			08	08	14			06	04	(−)
Norway			14	14		14		13		14			14	12			11			(−)	
Sweden	18		17	16	12				15	11		16	12	12	09						
Switzerland													18	14	14	13					
United Kingdom						10	03	08				07		09	14					(−)	
United States	03		04		03						03									04	(−)

Note: Table entries are % of the public that say they are a member of a political party.

Sources: Austria, Italy, Netherlands, Norway, Switzerland, United Kingdom, United States national election studies, various years; Others: Widfeldt (1995), plus Denmark, Togeby (1992); Japan, Richardson (1997); New Zealand, Levine and Roberts (1992).

DECLINE FROM WHAT?

Since the 1960s a great deal of scholarly effort has been devoted to refuting Duverger's thesis about the 'modernity' of the mass party by documenting how changes in local and national party organizations are leading parties away from the mass party form. However, much less effort has been made to document the extent to which mass parties *ever* represented the dominant pattern of local party activity. It is a useful corrective to return to Duverger's time to establish the extent to which strong local party organizations of the democratic left and right were normal or new in the 1950s. Taking a broader temporal view makes it possible to more fairly evaluate the extent to which the shrinking party memberships of the 1980s and 1990s mark the end of long-established patterns. In other words, we can ask which is more unusual for the twentieth century—parties' organizational successes of the early 1960s, or the subsequent drops in their memberships?

A review of the data provides the salutary reminder that only a limited number of democratic parties succeeded in establishing mass-style organizations prior to the Second World War. In the inter-war period four of the eighteen countries examined here lacked any democratic parties which could lay claim to the mass party label (see Table 5.4). Italy lacked contested elections for most of this period. Japan held elections, but for a legislature which held only limited powers, and in this country legal restrictions hindered the free development of party organizations. In the United States and Canada the national parties of the 1920s and 1930s were not constructing nationwide networks of permanently active local membership associations.[6] The main Belgian parties of the left and right had only indirect memberships, and relied on other organizations to conduct partisan education and mobilization. In three other countries during this period (Austria, Netherlands, Switzerland) only the parties of the left relied on membership-based organizations, while in Ireland a non-left party (Fianna Fáil) constructed a network of active local associations with loose membership affiliations.

Thus, prior to 1945 only nine of the eighteen OECD democracies examined here could claim to have democratic parties on different ends of the political spectrum which were constructing membership-based party organizations. Moreover, in several of these countries the efforts of the democratic right were only modestly successful. The German Catholic Centre Party was Weimar's one non-left democratic party which tried to consolidate its electoral position by building up a membership-based organization. This party enjoyed some early success, but both its membership and electoral support plummeted as the 1920s progressed (Morsey 1966).[7] In France, the Radicals were the only non-left party that tried to

---

[6] In Canada, the regionally important CCF did embrace mass style organization, as did the NDP and several other small parties in the second part of the century

[7] Of course, by the beginning of the 1930s a party of the non-democratic right, the National Social Democratic Workers' Party—the Nazi Party—enjoyed considerable success in organizing its membership base.

TABLE 5.4 *Democratic Parties with Membership-Based Organization Prior to the Second World War*

Country	Electoral democracy	Democratic parties with membership-based organization	
		Left	Non-left
Italy			
Japan			
Belgium	xx		
Canada	xx		
United States	xx		
Austria	xx	xx	
Ireland	xx		xx
Netherlands	xx	xx	
Switzerland	xx	xx	
France	xx	xx	xx (weak)
Finland	xx	xx (weak)	xx (weak)
Germany	xx	xx	xx (weak)
New Zealand	xx	xx	xx (weak)
Australia	xx	xx	xx
Denmark	xx	xx	xx
Norway	xx	xx	xx
Sweden	xx	xx	xx
United Kingdom	xx	xx	xx

Note: 'xx' indicates the presence of electoral democracy or one or more democratic mass-membership oriented parties during the inter-war period.

enrol supporters during the inter-war period. But its membership requirements remained very loose, and its primary organizational support continued to be supplied by notables rather than by party members (Bardonnet 1960). Non-Socialist parties in Finland had only weak, loosely defined memberships prior to the Second World War (Nousiainen 1971: 55–6). In New Zealand, the National Party only began its efforts to establish a mass-style organization after 1936, when this centre-right party was created out of the union of two cadre-style parties (Milne 1966: 164). In short, only five of the eighteen countries (Australia, Denmark, Norway, Sweden, and Great Britain) could claim well-established, democratic, membership-based parties of both the left and the right prior to the Second World War.

A more traditional way of summarizing these data is to portray the rise of mass-style organization in the first half of the twentieth century as largely a phenomenon of the left. Yet, even on the left, parties were not uniformly strong during the inter-war period (Bartolini 1983); nor were they necessarily stronger than their post-1945 counterparts. Membership figures for the 1920s and 1930s are available for Socialist, Social Democratic, and Labour parties from ten of the eighteen countries examined in this project.[8] All but two of these parties (the Austrian and German) had larger real enrolments in 1950 than in 1930, and all but one (the German) had larger real enrolments in 1960 than in 1930.[9] Thus, for many of the parties of the left, and for all of the non-left parties, the decade or two after the end of the Second World War brought organizational growth which was not just a return to pre-war norms.

This assessment of the full history of democratic membership-based parties in the twentieth century gives a clearer idea of the context within which Duverger pronounced mass parties to be the most modern form of democratic political organization. When Duverger published the French edition of his book in the early 1950s, parties around the world—particularly non-left parties—were initiating or reviving their efforts to incorporate supporters in formal organizations. In some countries, including France, Britain, and Finland, citizens responded particularly enthusiastically to these efforts. Elsewhere, including Belgium, Germany, Ireland, the Netherlands, and Switzerland membership did not surge until the 1960s, when non-left parties began to put more emphasis on formally enrolling supporters. Similarly, in Canada it was not until the 1960s that the nationwide parties became more active in their pursuit of individual enrolment, and even then the idea was slow to catch on (Carty 1991). Political enrolment in Japan did not swell until the mid-1980s, when new campaign finance laws gave candidates incentives to enlist their supporters. In other words, Duverger's 1951 prediction of 'contagion from the left' needs to be understood as just that—a prediction of things to come, not a description of the state of party organizations during the first half of the century.

Both the ascendancy and decline of the democratic membership party occurred in the decades after the Second World War. It was only in the 1950s and 1960s that many countries had parties of both the left and the right successfully pursuing mass enrolment strategies. Before and after this period, parties exhibited an uneven pattern of commitment to, and success in, enlisting supporters in permanent organizations. While membership figures like those in Tables 5.1 and 5.2 undoubtedly show a widespread drop in absolute and relative party membership in the last quarter of the century, it should be stressed that the high enrolments of the third quarter of the century were unusual in their own way. Not only are mass enrolment parties not a prerequisite for democracy; they were not even a norm for most of the twentieth century. To say this is not to discount the real changes that have been occurring; it is merely to call for more care in interpreting these shifts. The next section continues this task of interpretation, examining what difference these drops have made to parties' presence in society. To what

---

[8] For Austria, Denmark, France, Germany, the Netherlands, New Zealand, Norway, Sweden, Switzerland, and the United Kingdom

[9] The exception here, the German Social Democrats, were necessarily organizing in a much smaller country after Germany's post-war division.

extent have declining memberships impaired parties' ability to use their organizations to construct links with society?

MEMBERSHIP DECLINE AND PARTY CAPACITY: THE CONTRIBUTIONS OF GRASS-ROOTS ORGANIZATION

Although the recent drops in absolute and relative party membership almost certainly represent a decline in parties' capacity to promote social integration, they have not necessarily diminished the ability of local organizations to support party goals in other ways. Given that the number of active members is unlikely to move in linear proportion to aggregate party size, membership drops may not even result in a large decline in the extent of some kinds of party activity. We know that most party members are not active; studies from many countries estimate that only 10 to 45 per cent of members participate regularly in the activities of their local branches (cf. Heidar 1994; Müller 1996: 270; Seyd and Whiteley 1992; Falke 1982: 75; Becker et al. 1983: 80; Veen and Neu 1995: 11–12). Within this range, however, activism levels may well increase as branch size decreases, as parties' labour needs are often fixed (i.e. local parties need a specific number of branch officers and local government candidates, etc.). In line with this, one survey of local parties in Germany found that the absolute number of members involved in the local campaigns was only slightly affected by party size (Scarrow 1993).[10] If activism levels are affected by branch size, declining aggregate party enrolments may or may not imply decreasing levels of individual involvement within parties, or of overall party activity. This caveat is reinforced by suggestive evidence from the World Values Study, which shows that in seven out of thirteen countries in the set considered here, aggregate levels of party membership and the degree of activity among party members moved in opposite directions during the 1980s (see Table 5.5).

Another way to explore the extent to which enrolment fluctuations have weakened parties' roots in local communities is to investigate changes in what parties are doing at the local level. There is, unfortunately, little systematic longitudinal evidence in this area. However, thinking about party strength in terms of the tasks to be accomplished suggests two indicators of how locally organized partisans can affect community life: (1) the extent to which parties organize local government; and (2) the geographical spread of parties' local organizations. An examination of these indicators reinforces the warning against overstating the verdict of party decline at the grass roots.

In many countries the role of parties in local political arenas has been affected

---

[10] This does not contradict the finding by Seyd and Whitely that overall levels of constituency campaigning increased along with party size (1992: 184).

TABLE 5.5 *Self-Reported Party Participation Rates*

	1981 members	1990 members	Change 1981–1990 members	1981 activists/ members	1990 activists/ members	Change 1981–1990 activists/ members
Belgium	2.5	5.8	+3.3	0.56	0.27	−0.29
Canada	5.3	7.3	+2.0	0.62	0.52	−0.10
Finland	3.0	13.6	+10.6	0.16	0.50	+0.34
France	2.5	2.7	+0.2	0.72	0.59	−0.13
Germany (western)	8.1	7.5	−0.6	0.47	0.39	−0.06
Ireland	4.1	3.8	−0.3	0.39	0.58	+0.19
Italy	6.4	5.0	−1.4	0.79	0.70	−0.09
Japan	2.6	2.0	−0.6	0.81	0.70	−0.11
Netherlands	7.6	9.4	+1.8	0.21	0.24	+0.03
Norway	13.3	13.9	+0.6	0.29	0.26	−0.03
Sweden	13.5	10.1	−3.4	0.16	0.40	+0.34
United Kingdom	4.6	4.9	+0.3	0.33	0.31	−0.02
United States	11.3	14.5	+3.2	0.27	0.32	+0.05

Note: Table presents data on party membership in the first three columns and data on the ratio of members to activists in the second three columns.

Sources: World Values Study 1981 and 1990.

since the 1960s by local government consolidation, and by the increasing dominance of partisan candidates. Two-thirds of the countries examined here have carried out at least modest reductions in the number of basic units of government over the last few decades.[11] Most of the countries where such reforms were instituted were ones in which parties were involved in local governance in at least some jurisdictions. Local government consolidation tended to strengthen parties' role by eliminating the smaller and generally more rural government units where non-party candidates were more likely to succeed. Thus, local government reform often gave parties an increased role in decision-making and personnel gate-keeping, thereby giving them expanded opportunities to structure voters' choices. Some examples of the impact of local government reform come from Scandinavia, where support for non-partisan candidates in Norwegian local elections fell from 18 to 7 per cent between 1945 and 1985 (Selle and Svåsand 1991: 472), and where the proportion of Danish local councillors elected under a national party label rose from 60 to 85 per cent after reforms were implemented (Pedersen 1987: 43). Similar shifts to partisan local government were recorded in Britain and Germany (HMSO 1986; Gunlicks 1986), and may have occurred elsewhere as well.

Increasing partisan competition at the local level probably led to a concomitant expansion of local parties' campaign efforts. Because local government

[11] Exceptions were Canada, Ireland Italy, Japan, Switzerland, and the United States

campaigning styles are much less documented than national efforts, it is imposs- ible to draw firm conclusions about the implications for local parties. Given the scarcity of professional party employees at the local level, the limited reach of local media outlets, and the general absence of public funds for local government campaigns, local candidates clearly have a limited ability to replace volunteer campaigners with money. Therefore, expanding partisan competition in local government may well have boosted the activities of locally organized members in at least one domain.

Another measure of a party's grass-roots strength is the extent of its organ- ization throughout all parts of the country. In places where a party has no local branches, citizens have few opportunities to meet party activists, vote for party candidates for local government elections, or be directly recruited to the party (Selle and Svåsand 1983: 215). The importance of considering local party strength in geographic terms becomes particularly clear when examining some of the strongest Social Democratic parties of the 1920s. For instance, in the inter-war era the Austrian Social Democrats (SDAP) were stronger than their post-war counterparts (the SPÖ) in terms of such indicators as members per branch or the ratio of members to voters. Yet in terms of organizational coverage, the Social Democrats were actually weaker in the earlier period, concentrating their organizational and electoral efforts in urban areas, and failing to compete in large areas of the country. In the 1920s, they had branches in fewer than 40 per cent of local government units, whereas by the 1960s this figure had risen to over 80 per cent as the party expanded its reach well beyond the limits of 'Red Vienna' (Holtmann 1996: 148–51; Müller 1996: 229). Analysts report that such patterns of geographic expansion occurred elsewhere in the post-war period, as parties on both the left and the right began to organize outside their traditional areas of electoral strength (cf. Selle and Svåsand 1991: 473).

This phenomenon of expanding organizational coverage seems to be quite widespread. Comprehensive long-term data on the number of party branches are available for eight of the eighteen countries in this study. If we look at the parties in these countries that were electorally most successful, we find that between the beginning of the 1960s and the end of the 1980s almost all of them (91 per cent) expanded their local organizational coverage in terms of party units per local government units (see Table 5.6). In Austria, for instance, the SPÖ had only 0.82 local party branches relative to the number of local governments in 1959, but by 1989 this ratio had increased to 1.41. Although increases like these partly reflect the above-mentioned local government consolidation, they should not therefore be dismissed as merely a mathematical artefact. The incorporation of outlying villages and suburbs into urban areas also increased the real reach of party pol- itics, thereby giving existing party branches organizational responsibility for broader areas. In most cases, the expanding organizational coverage also reflects the efforts of increasingly catch-all parties to push their appeal beyond traditional urban or rural strongholds.

TABLE 5.6 *Organizational Density by Party*[a]

| | Basic Party Units per Local Government Unit | | |
	1959	1989	Change
Austria			
SPÖ	0.82	1.41	+0.59
ÖVP	1.49	1.79	+0.30
FPÖ	0.45	0.62	+0.17
Denmark			
SD	0.92	2.42	+1.50
V	1.15	3.39	+2.24
KF	0.39	1.19	+0.80
Finland			
KESK	4.86	7.87	+3.01
SKDL/VAS	3.68	2.62	−1.08
SDP	2.66	3.12	+0.46
Germany			
CDU	0.25	1.09	+0.84
SPD	0.36	1.17	+0.81
CSU	0.10	0.33	+0.23
Italy			
DC	1.57	1.63	+0.06
PCI	5.26	1.42	−3.84
PSI	n/a	1.03	n/a
Netherlands			
KVP/CDA	0.83	1.04	+0.21
PvdA	0.94	1.03	+0.09
VVD	0.41	0.84	+0.43
Norway			
DNA	3.22	5.13	+1.91
H	0.78	1.37	+0.59
KRF	0.70	1.03	+0.33
Sweden			
S	n/a	10.46	n/a
FP	1.26	2.21	+0.95
M	2.20	5.94	+3.74

[a] For each country, table shows three parties which won most votes in first national election after Jan. 1960.

Sources: Katz and Mair 1992; Humes and Martin 1961: exhibit 2; Norton 1994: 40.

These indications of expanded organizational coverage and increased involvement in local government are a reminder that membership figures alone do not provide a complete picture of parties' local organizational strengths. Although drops in membership are very visible and relatively easy to track, it is much more difficult to form an accurate assessment of how these reductions have affected intra-party life and inter-party competition. Clearly, membership decline and grass-roots organizational decline are not one and the same.

THE MYTHS (AND REALITIES) OF MASS PARTY DECLINE

Over the past half-century, students of party politics have embraced and embellished Duverger's natural history of party evolution. They routinely have invoked a periodic view of party organizational development that spans from the cadre, to the mass, to the catch-all and beyond. Though these ideal types undoubtedly help in summarizing general tendencies, it is risky to accept them uncritically. Political scientists have tended to focus on the progression from one model to the next, often neglecting the early parts of this chain. Such neglect makes it all too easy to cling to unexamined myths about mass party dominance and to draw incorrect inferences about the extent and implications of recent mass party decline. Thus, one way to summarize this chapter's exploration of the changing strength of parties as membership organizations is to confront three myths of party organizational decline.

> Myth 1: The heyday of the democratic mass party was during the first half of the twentieth century.

Some mass parties did flourish in this period, but the above discussion makes it clear that they were atypical. For parties on the right, and even for some parties on the left, membership-based organizing only became a reality during the third quarter of the century.

> Myth 2: Membership decline should always be equated with the decline of party organizational strength.

This chapter opened with a discussion of the varied ways in which members may boost their parties' electoral fortunes. The figures presented above suggest that parties may be doing better in deriving some of these benefits than others. The dimension on which most parties are almost certainly doing the worst is the one which involves deriving legitimacy from the public endorsement supporters make when they enrol in a party. Most party leaders cannot invoke enrolment figures as indicators of their party's, or of their own, popularity. However, parties may be doing better in winning other types of support from their shrinking memberships. Many of them seem to have voluntary organizations that are much stronger than they were a generation ago in terms of geographic coverage, and in terms of direct involvement in local politics. In addition, new systems of centralized enrolment and dues collection may make it easier for central party organizers to communicate messages to and through members, and to tap the membership base as a source of funds.

In other words, although parties which were able to enrol large proportions of their voters may have been strong in terms of their ability to pursue a strategy of social encapsulation, they may have been comparatively weak in terms of their ability of contest elections in volatile electoral markets. Because of this, party strength does not necessarily decrease along with absolute, and particularly with relative, drops in enrolment. This is true not only because the increased efficiency of professional organization can compensate for declining membership, but also because large memberships are not necessarily efficiently organized to carry out political tasks. To accurately assess a party's organizational strength, we need to have a clear understanding of the tasks the party needs to accomplish, and of the resources it possesses for accomplishing them.

Myth 3: There are few countervailing pressures to offset the well-known incentives for parties to abandon membership-based organizing.

In fact, a variety of factors push parties and their leaders to set some value on their membership bases. Even if members provided no help in electoral competition between parties, they might still play an important role in intra-party battles. Members' support can be useful in struggles between, as well as within, parties. The latter is particularly true when party rules or national laws give members direct or indirect control over important party decisions. In these circumstances, would-be candidates always have reason to try to enlist their supporters into the ranks of voting members. Countries such as Norway, Finland, Germany, and New Zealand all have laws which stipulate or encourage a direct or indirect role for members in the candidate-selection process. Such laws are likely to help sustain membership-based organization. Even where such a role is not legally mandated, party leaders may want to delegate candidate selection to members because of the mantle of legitimacy such procedures confer. For example, in the 1990s the opposition British Labour Party enacted a series of reforms aimed at expanding its role and giving the appearance of increased membership control. In the wake of its disastrous 1997 defeat, the British Conservative Party began centralizing and formalizing membership enrolment procedures and delegating new powers to members. The Japanese and German laws on party finance have also given parties good reasons to enrol supporters. Although these types of enrolment incentives may not entirely counter-balance the pressures for parties to abandon membership-based structures, the fact that some institutional and social changes seem to bolster the perceived utility of party members should stop over-hasty conclusions about party organizational decline.

SMALLER MEMBERSHIPS, STRONGER MEMBERS?

This chapter provides a warning against overstating either the rise or obsolescence of membership-based party organizing. It is true that membership parties are not what they once were, but it is also the case that strong membership parties were never as widespread as some accounts suggest.

To say this is not to deny the evident changes in party organizations, and in parties' organizational ambitions. Few of today's membership parties are striving to be 'mass' parties in the sense that Duverger or Neumann described (i.e., parties which attempt to solidify their political support by enlisting supporters from a particular class into a party-linked social and cultural network). On the other hand, parties' enrolment losses do not necessarily signal that members have ceased to contribute to party success. Indeed, they may make those who remain on the rolls even more important. As a result, parties may even increase their efforts to attract and retain enlisted supporters. This conclusion will be examined in more detail in Chapter 7, which asks whether party leaders are responding to membership losses by showing increasing willingness to share some decision-making responsibilities with members. As will be shown there, in recent years a wide range of parties have elevated the decision-making roles of individual members. Some parties have also restructured their internal links to increase contacts between central party organs and individual members. Such changes suggest that party leaders are often unwilling to forgo the support that members can provide. Whether these efforts will succeed remains to be seen, but they are a reminder that the ongoing process of party transformation is not inevitably destined to continue until membership bases disappear altogether.

6

Political Parties as Campaign Organizations

David M. Farrell and Paul Webb

ELECTIONS lie at the heart of the relationship between parties and democracy. Just as it is impossible to conceive of a definition of representative democracy which does not place elections centre-stage, so it is also difficult to conceive of a definition of parties which does not stress their electoral function. This latter point is shown by Sartori (1976: 64) in his famous 'minimal definition' of a party as 'any political group that presents at elections, and is capable of placing through elections, candidates for public office'. Given this symbiotic relationship between parties and elections, it is important to have a clear idea of how parties operate in elections and elections affect parties.

There is already an extensive literature on the professionalization of campaigning, which in part deals with the interface between election campaigning and political parties (for overviews see Bowler and Farrell 1992; Butler and Ranney 1992; Farrell 1996; Swanson and Mancini 1996*b*). This issue tends to be dealt with in terms of the general debate over party decline; thus far there has been little attention to the internal, organizational consequences of changing campaign techniques for parties. Both issues are considered in this chapter.

This chapter will show party organizations as highly adaptive, investing heavily in time and resources in the new campaign technologies, professionalizing and centralizing their organizations (particularly around their top leaderships), and paying far more attention to image and specific campaign issues as opposed to traditional ideological standpoints. The increasing tendency is less one of selling themselves to voters, but rather one of designing an appropriate product to match voter needs. In sum, these changes amount to a situation where the contemporary political party has successfully repositioned itself to survive the uncertainties of

The drafting of this chapter has benefited hugely from extensive feedback received from the editors and from the other project participants at the several meetings held in Irvine. In addition, we are grateful to the following colleagues for their very helpful guidance on trends in their country of expertise: Luciano Bardi, Clive Bean, R. K. Carty, Kris Deschouwer, Michael Holmes, Wolfgang Müller, Jon Pierre, Thomas Poguntke, Jan Sundberg, Lars Svåsand, Anders Widfeldt, and Colette Ysmal. The usual disclaimer applies.

operating as representative institutions in the increasingly participatory age of the end of the millennium.

The chapter proceeds in two main parts. The first section outlines the main aspects of change in the nature of election campaigning, focusing on how parties have been affected. The second section offers a more detailed examination of those aspects of campaign change which appear to have most fundamental consequences for how parties operate internally, as well as for their general role in the political system.

THREE STAGES IN THE PROFESSIONALIZATION OF CAMPAIGNING

Two points are worth stressing at the outset. First, we recognize that developments in campaigning and party professionalization are mediated by cultural and institutional circumstances, both at a systemic and at a party level (see below, and Part I of this volume). Second, we want to avoid placing undue stress on the technological aspects of campaign change, as this can lead to a tendency to focus only on the mechanics of campaigning and to give insufficient attention to campaign messages.[1] A common criticism political marketing specialists make of political science treatments of campaign professionalization (e.g. *European Journal of Marketing*, 30: 10/11 (1966); O'Shaughnessy 1990; Scammell 1995) is that the analysis of campaign change tends to be unfocused and incomplete. It is largely for this reason that the extent to which campaigns really have been changing is often disputed.[2] The political marketing literature places great stress on the need to develop an all-encompassing model of campaigning, particularly one which recognizes the central importance of the campaign message.

At the risk of oversimplification, the professionalization of election campaigning can be broken down into three main stages, which are dealt with in more detail elsewhere (Farrell 1996). In this chapter, we divide the analysis into three main areas where campaign changes have most clearly affected parties: technical, resources, and thematic developments. Table 6.1 provides a rough summary of these three areas of campaign change over time.[3]

---

[1] If anything, it would probably be most accurate to characterize the approach being adopted here as 'soft technological determinism' (Smith and Marx 1994)

[2] It is not all that difficult to find examples of 'new' campaign practices in elections earlier in the century (a point stressed by such authors as Bartels 1992; Dionne 1976). According to a political marketing approach, however, it is a mistake to treat certain aspects of campaign change in isolation; the campaign and its message have to be looked at in their entirety.

[3] For the original version of this Table, which refers to the three stages as 'premodern', 'television revolution', and 'telecommunications revolution', see Farrell (1996) In her adaptation, Pippa Norris (1996) refers to them as 'premodern', 'modern', and 'postmodern'. To some extent, these three stages could be said to coincide with Katz and Mair's (1995) distinction between 'mass', 'catch-all', and 'cartel' parties.

TABLE 6.1. *Three Stages in the Development of Election Campaigning*

	Stage 1	Stage 2	Stage 3
Technical developments			
Campaign preparations	Short-term; *ad hoc*	Long-term; specialist committee established 1-2 years in advance of election	'Permanent campaign': establishment of specialist campaign departments
Use of media	'Direct' & 'indirect' Direct=party press, newspaper ads, billboards Indirect=newspaper coverage	Emphasis on 'indirect' Direct=ad campaigns Indirect=public relations, media training, press conferences	Emphasis on 'direct' Direct=targeted ads, direct mail, videomail, cable TV, internet Indirect=as before
Resource developments			
Campaign organization	Decentralized Local party organization Little standardization Staffing: party/candidate-based, voluntary	Nationalization, centralization Staffing: party-based, salaried professional	Decentralization of operation with central scrutiny Staffing: party/candidate-based, professional, contract work; growth of leader's office
Agencies, consultants	Minimal use; 'generalist' role Politicians in charge	Growing prominence of 'specialist' consultants Politicians still in charge	Consultants as campaign personalities International links 'Who is in charge'?
Sources of feedback	Impressionistic, 'feel' Important role of canvassers, group leaders	Large-scale opinion polls More scientific	Greater range of polling techniques Interactive capabilities of cable and internet
Thematic developments			
Campaign events	Public meetings Whistle-stop tours	TV debates; press conferences 'Pseudo-events'	As before; events targeted more locally
Targeting of voters	Social class support base Maintain vote of specific social categories	Catch-all Trying to mobilize voters across all categories	Market segmentation Targeting of specific categories of voters
Campaign communication	Propaganda	Selling concept	Marketing concept

The first stage of campaigning was characterized by the following aspects. First, in the case of technical features of campaigning, there was little or sporadic preparation, and communication tended to be through party press, posters, mass rallies, and canvassing. Second, in terms of resources, there was a heavy use of traditional party bureaucracies and volunteer activists, a focus on the local campaign with little centralization or coordination, and more value was placed on intuition than on objective feedback. Third, in terms of themes, events were staged around the use of the party leader in public rallies and whistlestop tours to boost the campaign efforts of the local politicians. The target audience was made up of fixed social categories, resulting in a greater emphasis on mobilization than persuasion. Campaign communications consisted primarily of propaganda, described by Wring as 'a one-directional communication process in which passive audiences found themselves subjected to the sometimes manipulative appeals of political elites' (1996*b*: 102; also Shama 1976; Wring 1996*a*).

The second stage of campaign professionalization was primarily characterized by the arrival of television. First, careful campaign preparation centred around the role of specialist campaign committees established long in advance of the election. There was an emphasis on television as a major means of communication, with leaders and candidates being media-trained, and substantial resources devoted to public relations. Great weight was attached to indirect modes of communication. Second, there was a professionalization of party bureaucracies (Panebianco 1988), bringing in media and marketing specialists. The use of campaign consultants and agencies coincided with a nationalization of campaigning in which power and resources were concentrated at the centre. Third, there was an increasing emphasis on the party leader, and a focus on nationwide standardization and broadcasting of a single campaign message. The parties were now seeking to catch votes from all social categories, and therefore placed less emphasis on target audiences, or what Kirchheimer (1966) would refer to as the *class gardée*. Campaign communications involved selling, where some effort was made to test the market, but where ultimately the 'product was sacrosanct'; the key guiding belief was that public opinion was malleable (Scammell 1995: 9).[4]

The third main stage of campaign professionalization coincides with the arrival of new telecommunications technology (e.g. cable and satellite technology, and the explosion of the internet) and its gradual incorporation into the machinery of campaigning. The suggestion is that the USA started to enter this stage from about 1988 onwards (e.g. Abramson et al. 1988); arguably some European countries are only just entering this stage today. Its characteristics—as might

---

[4] This aspect is given prime importance in the political marketing literature, in which it is seen as *the* factor which marks out a professional 'marketing' campaign. For discussion of why the British Labour Party's 1987 campaign—viewed generally as the most 'professional' of the campaigns in that election (e.g. Butler and Kavanagh 1988; Webb 1992)—might be classified as *less* 'professional' than the Conservatives' campaign on the grounds that greater stress was placed on 'selling' than on 'marketing', see O'Shaughnessy (1990); Scammell (1995).

be described in the context of a European (still party-centric) election—include the following features. First, there is the arrival of the permanent campaign, with campaign preparations centred around well-established campaign departments. Greater weight is attached to more direct modes of communication, particularly those offered by cable TV and the internet. Second, the campaign organization is staffed by campaign professionals. There is also an extensive use of campaign consultants and agencies, in some instances sidelining established party apparatus in favour of the development and resourcing of a leader's office, resulting in questions over who is 'in charge'. Third, there is greater attention to targeted campaign messages, often known as 'narrowcasting', which involves making greater use of feedback and then adapting of the message to suit the audience. A full panoply of alternative communication devices is used to direct targeted campaign messages at specific categories of voters. As Wring (1996a, 1996b) and others (Scammell 1995; Shama 1976) point out, campaign communications in this stage are much more consumer-oriented; now it is the *product* which is malleable. This seems to imply a model of party competition that is overwhelmingly preference-accommo-dating rather than preference-shaping, though it should be said that there are necessarily some limits to this malleability. For party policy appeals to remain credible, programmatic adaptation should remain within the bounds of enduring party policy reputations (Laver 1997: 136), or such pledges are likely to be discounted by sceptical voters. This development in itself raises a concern of some interest to students of party decline, for if the parties should lose all sense of persisting policy reputation, then they might be regarded as fundamentally oppor-tunistic and vacuous by electors, thereby exacerbating the risk of anti-party senti-ment (Poguntke and Scarrow 1996; see also Deschouwer 1996).

A summary such as this risks being dismissed as an oversimplification. It is important, therefore, to set out two main qualifications. First, it is clearly a distor-tion to summarize the professionalization of campaigning in terms of three rather fixed stages, as real life does not work like this. Strictly speaking, each row in Table 6.1 should more accurately be seen as a continuum along which campaign organizations are moving—from a pre-modern pole to an advanced-modern pole. Not all the changes are occurring at the same time (e.g. the telecommunications revolution has gone through a number of stages, most recently centred around the internet). Furthermore, not all countries or campaign organizations fit the staged pattern of change implied by Table 6.1. This point is best seen in the case of new European democracies, many of which skipped much of stage 1 (Jakubowicz 1996; Mickiewicz and Richter 1996; Rospir 1996); it is also shown by the cases of some newly emerging democracies in Latin America which appear to have advanced faster and further into stage 2 than many western European democra-cies (Angell et al. 1992). Our threefold typological continuum is therefore essen-tially a heuristic device, a classificatory scheme of ideal types which serves to aid our understanding of campaign change.

A second point of qualification is the need to take into account the crucial

TABLE 6.2. *The Campaign 'Environment'*

	TV spots	Leaders' 'debates'[a]	Restrictions on TV access[b]	Other campaign restrictions	Campaign finance
Australia	Yes	Yes	Proportionate		Yes
Austria	Yes	Yes	Proportionate		Yes
Belgium	No	Yes	n/a		No
Canada	Yes	Yes	n/a	limits on expend.; 48-hour ban on polls	Yes
Denmark	No	Yes	Equal		No
Finland	No	Yes	Equal		No
France	No	Yes	Equal	limits on expend.; 7-day ban on polls	Yes (for Pres.)
Germany	Yes	Yes	Proportionate		Yes
Ireland	No	Yes	Proportionate	limits on expend. (since 1998)	Yes (since 1998)
Italy	Yes	No	No	7-day ban on polls	Yes
Japan	Yes	Yes	Proportionate	limits on expend.; candidate restrictions[c]	Yes (since 1995)
Netherlands	Yes	Yes	No		No
New Zealand	Yes	Yes	Proportionate	limits on candidates' expend.	No
Norway	No	Yes	No		Yes
Sweden	No	Yes	Equal		No
Switzerland	No	No	n/a		No
U.K.	No	No	Proportionate	limits on local expend.	No
U.S.	Yes	Yes	No	limits on Pres. expend.	Yes (for Pres.)

[a] In some cases (notably Scandinavia), there is little actual debate between the candidates, who are instead quizzed by a panel of journalists.

[b] In some cases by law, in others, rules set by broadcasters.

[c] Most of the restrictions are focused on candidates (not parties), among them: ban on campaigning until final 15 days; no doorstep canvassing; restrictions on speech-making and on distribution of written materials.

importance of the environment in which campaigning occurs. Many institutional and cultural factors will affect the nature of campaigning and how it is changing (cf. Farrell 1996; Swanson and Mancini 1996*a*). This point is particularly pertinent in the case of US campaigning which is unique in many respects. Given the fact that the US is a candidate-centred system, where parties have been said to be in decline for forty years or more (although there has been some recent 'revisionism' in this debate), and where there are few significant limitations on how to campaign (e.g. total freedom on the purchase and airing of TV spots), it is clear that many parliamentary democracies are unlikely to follow some common US campaign practices. Therefore some of the cells in stage 3 of Table 6.1 may never apply in certain cases. Japan and several of the other countries being considered in this volume (e.g. the polling restrictions imposed in Canada, France, and Italy) stand out in this respect, as revealed in Table 6.2's summary overview of the key environmental features under which political parties have to operate. Furthermore, given the lack of a party-centred tradition in the USA, there are also a number of areas where US practice is bound to differ from the parliamentary norm, thereby making it difficult to locate the US case in all the cells of Table 6.1.[5]

CAMPAIGN PROFESSIONALIZATION AND PARTIES

The previous section stressed that the relationship between parties and elections was complex, and ever-changing. In this section, we elaborate on the three main areas of campaign change—technical, resource, and thematic—each of which has had consequences for the parties. The influences on parties of campaign change are twofold, affecting their internal organizational structure, as well as their external role in the political system. Clearly the two effects are related; indeed, it might be argued that the former precedes the latter.

Technical Changes

The two principal technical changes have of course been the development of television, and then new communications technologies. Given that the full effect of TV has now been felt and covered extensively in the literature, there is little need to speculate about it. Table 6.2 summarizes the state of play regarding access to and use of television in our range of countries. The most important symbol of the

---

[5] This discussion puts a somewhat different gloss on the debate about whether campaign professionalization should be seen as little more than a process of 'Americanization,' implying that other countries are simply copying fashions set in the USA (for discussion, see Swanson and Mancini 1996*a*; Negrine and Papathanassopoulos 1996). If, in a number of respects, the evidence points to 'American exceptionalism', then it is difficult to see how the US case can so easily be said to be setting the trends for others to follow.

TV age, the leaders' debate, is now a common occurrence in most cases. In his review of the evidence at the start of the 1980s, Anthony Smith (1981: 174–5) showed how leaders' debates were already a common occurrence in OECD countries. As Table 6.2 reveals, only Italy, Switzerland, and the UK now remain as exceptions.[6] The process of broadcasting deregulation and the emergence of new stations has had one further consequence of relevance here—namely the relaxation of rules on campaign advertising, which have allowed parties to broadcast their own TV spots (Kaid and Holtz-Bacha 1995). According to Anthony Smith's evidence (1981: 174–5), at the start of the 1980s the only countries in our sample which permitted private TV spots were Australia, Canada, Japan, and the USA. As Table 6.2 shows, these have since been joined by Austria, Germany, Italy, Netherlands, New Zealand, and Sweden.

More recent developments in new communications technologies are of even greater interest; in this chapter we will seek to emphasize a number of points which bear upon their effects on parties in the campaign process. To assess campaign technical change in western European parties at the start of the 1990s, a questionnaire was circulated to the authors of chapters in the Bowler and Farrell (1992) volume. Responses to these questionnaires reveal a variety of important points about the role of technology in contemporary election campaigns. Much use is now made of opinion polls and other survey data by parties, both in preparing and coordinating their campaigns. In cases where there are no or few polls, this is generally due to a lack of funds. Green parties tend to have some form of ideological objection to the use of surveys (though the fact that these parties are small and relatively under-resourced must also be a factor). Danish parties also tend to make relatively little use of opinion polls, consistent with the comments of Bille and his colleagues (1992: 79) that 'Danish parties are reluctant to make use of many of the paraphernalia of contemporary campaigns'; as well as with the relatively low levels of campaign spending compared to countries of similar size (Table 6.3).

In his classic study of campaign rationality, Rose (1967) stresses the distinction between the commissioning of polls and their actual use. Our questionnaire returns provide some evidence of campaigns being altered as the result of poll findings. For the most part, this phenomenon tends to occur in the right-of-centre parties,[7] consistent with the view that a shift towards new campaign styles is

---

[6] In the UK, this is not for want of trying by the TV companies. In the past it was the incumbent prime ministers who refused to debate with their counterparts, usually on the grounds that it would only serve to help increase their credibility as 'prime ministers in waiting'. The tables were turned in 1997, when because of very unfavourable poll trends, the outgoing prime minister, John Major, challenged the far more popular Labour leader, Tony Blair, to a TV debate.

[7] In Finland, the Social Democrats and the Left-Wing Alliance also appear to have adapted campaign strategies in the light of poll trends. It is interesting to note that most of the Finnish parties share the same polling agency, Finnish Gallup (Sundberg and Högnabba 1992).

easier for parties that are less burdened by ideological baggage. Of course, in cases where the campaign did not appear adaptable, it may be that the poll evidence did not suggest the need for campaign change, or that there was insufficient time to make adjustments.

There is no readily discernible pattern on the use of direct mailing and targeted advertising, a feature of the third stage of campaigning (though here we are relying on somewhat dated evidence from the early 1990s). In general, parties in Austria, Britain, and Germany make use of both; there is more sporadic use of these techniques in Denmark and Ireland; in Finland at the start of the decade parties used direct mail but not targeted advertisements, while in the Netherlands parties used targeted advertisements but not direct mail.

The Television Age ushered in nationalized campaigning, with an emphasis on the broadcasting of single coordinated nationwide messages. In sharp contrast, the Digital Age appears to be shifting the culture of campaigning back towards more focused, localized, targeted communication. The name of the game will now be narrowcasting, or what Bonchek (1997) refers to as 'netcasting'. A number of interrelated communications technologies are involved, each contributing to the same effect. These include cable and satellite technology, the digital revolution, and the internet (Abramson et al. 1988). It is the latter development (particularly what it offers through e-mail and the World Wide Web) which currently is attracting most interest. Of course, the limited penetration of these new technologies to date represents a constraint on movement towards the stage 3 model of campaigning. In the UK, for instance, a majority of citizens do not presently have either cable or satellite TV; even if they do, the quality of local or regional news programmes is unlikely to induce many to rely on these over the established national networks. Similarly, initial research suggests that the internet made a very limited impact on the first UK general election campaign in which the parties consciously sought to exploit its possibilities (Gibson and Ward 1998). Nevertheless, the potential of these new technologies to impact significantly on the future of political campaigns cannot be overlooked.

We only need to look at the use of websites by the US presidential candidates in the 1996 election to obtain a sense of the potential of this medium; in particular, Bob Dole made a concerted effort to use his website as a means of countering his image as too old and doddery (though this initiative was perhaps not helped by his inability to remember the correct address). Research showed that Dole's website was accessed more than 3 million times in the first six months of its operation (Corrado 1996). Phil Gramm's website was accessed almost 200,000 times—at a set-up cost of just $8,000. Gramm claimed that he made eight times as many contacts with the public by way of the web as he could have made with first-class mail (Just 1997). Two years later, in a *Campaigns & Elections* survey of campaign organizations during the US midterm elections, Ron Faucheux (1998) found clear evidence of a growing reliance on the internet as part of a campaign's 'media mix'. Having a website has become *the* important new political campaign tool for any self-respecting candidate.[8] Today, well over 100 million people are estimated to be connected to the internet, at least half of these in the USA. According to Westen (1996: 59), 1995 marks the start of the 'Digital Age', when for the first time 'personal computers outsold television sets; the number of E-mail messages surpassed surface mail messages; and data traffic over telephone networks . . . exceeded voice traffic'.

The fastest growing part of the internet is the World Wide Web, with the number of websites doubling every three months. A study by the Pew Research Center (1996) during the 1996 campaign revealed the following: 12 per cent of the voting age population obtained political or policy news from the internet during the year, and about 4 per cent sought information specifically on the presidential campaign. Post-election research found that 3 per cent of voters said the internet was their principal election news source. Clearly this is one prominent area where US campaigns are far in advance of the situation in most other countries, though not Sweden where 35.3 per cent have internet access. The figures on internet access in other countries are not quite so dramatic: Australia 17.9 per cent, UK 12.3 per cent, Germany 7.5 per cent, France 6.6 per cent (see *Netpulse* 2(19) 1998). Although virtually all parties today have their own websites, we have yet to see the kind of use being made of them during election campaigns that has been evident in the USA. But this can only be a matter of time. In the 1997 UK election, for instance, all the parties had websites, and the Labour Party's site received 100,000 hits. The picture is pretty similar for most parties across our sample countries.[9] On the basis of their review of the British evidence, Gibson and Ward (1998: 33) speculate that '[g]iven the speed of developments during the last five years, . . . it is not unreasonable to assume that over the next decade party communication and campaigning on the Internet will have moved from the fringe toward the mainstream'.

The internet fills a communications gap, and if nothing else it will provide a new link between politicians and voters. In his review of the different families of media, Bonchek (1997) finds that the internet is a distinctive communications medium, most notably in that it is so cheap to access and relatively cheap to use as a communications tool. Furthermore, it combines the role of personal, group, and broadcast modes of communication. Neuman's (1991) research suggests one area where the internet could make a significant contribution to political communications. He distinguishes between two extreme areas of communications: interpersonal, and national communication, and he suggests that one area where we are likely to see further developments is in 'mini-communication'. His principal point is that the new media technology will not replace existing forms of communication but rather will supplement them.

---

[8] On this point, see the discussion in *Campaigns & Elections* July 1996, and September 1998; see also *Netpulse on* http://www.politicsonline.com/news.

[9] For useful listings of party web sites, see http://homeluna.nl/~benne/politics/parties.html. See also the discussion in *ECPR News* 10(1) 1998: 6–11.

It is possible to paint a picture of a future campaign in 'cyberworld' where the plethora of websites, listservs, and news groups and the extensive e-mail exchange between interested voters provides an incredible array of available information to voters. Just such a picture is painted by a number of authors (e.g. see the speculative pieces in Corrado and Firestone 1996). And we believe it is not out of the question. If we accept this scenario, what consequences does it have for the election campaign? It could be that yet more people become turned off from politics as there are so many other more interesting things available; on the other hand, it is at least as likely that it would further enhance the 'cognitive mobilization' of citizens (Barnes, Kaase et al. 1979; Dalton 1996a). If the results are positive, one likely by-product should be a rise in feelings of political efficacy and demands for further participatory opportunities. Such a development would probably test the agenda-setting capacity of political parties even further than has already been the case in the TV age, and if parties are unable to respond effectively there is always the potential for growing popular dissatisfaction. Of course, this discussion must remain speculative, but even so, it is hard not to be struck by the potential for significant change inherent within the new media.

Nevertheless, there are some scholarly arguments that suggest the web may not prove to be as revolutionary for political parties as many others assume. Research by Margolis et al. (1997) on the use of the web by mainstream candidates in 1996 showed clearly how cyberspace is replicating the real world, i.e. things appear to be settling into a new equilibrium with the established parties still in control. It may be easy enough for a small party to establish its own website, but unless it has sufficient resources and expertise it is unlikely to be able to develop as interesting and innovative websites as larger, better resourced parties (though for an alternative view, based on British evidence, see Gibson and Ward 1998). Russell Neuman (1991) has developed this point more generally. His thesis is that the expansionary tensions provoked by the communications revolution have to contend with the dampening down pressures of the 'psychology of the mass audience' (principally its habitual low interest in politics), and the economies of scale and concentration of ownership, which ensure that the media equilibrium is maintained. In this context, the conclusion may well be that little really changes.

The Margolis and Neuman reservations aside, it is hard to escape the conclusion that the internet will have major implications for the nature of campaign discourse. Given that the internet is based on text retrieval and dissemination, its significance must lie primarily as an informational resource which can potentially enhance the cognitive political awareness of citizens. This tends to imply a prominent place for issues and serious image questions related to the credibility and trustworthiness of parties and candidates (see below).

The internet might also play an important role in developing more targeted debates. The centralizing tendencies of television and the modern campaign led to a reduced emphasis on local issues and more attention to national matters. The internet tends to eschew geographically focused communication, bringing people together on the basis of particular issues rather than the locale or district where they happen to be living. The actual evidence of this to date is pretty limited; if anything, parties are prone to focus on one-way downward communication, rather than on trying to encourage two-way communication (Faucheux 1998; Gibson and Ward 1998). One interesting exception is a 1997 experiment in the Swedish Left Party, which developed a new 'female politics charter' on the basis of comments and feedback through its internet discussion group. The novel feature here was that comments were invited from the public at large and given equal prominence to those from dues-paying party members. Karl Löfgren comments: 'Whether this radical, and probably controversial, tendency will actually become more widespread within parties is still uncertain. But, if so, it will inevitably challenge our current understanding of the "membership party" ' (1998: 11; see also Chapter 7 below).

A final area warranting attention is how technical change has affected parties' bank balances. Technological development does not come cheaply; the contemporary campaign is an expensive business. There is plenty of evidence from single-case studies of the amount of money being spent today by parties on their election campaigns. For instance, official expenditure (seen as an underestimate) by candidates in the 1995 French presidential election totaled 427 million francs (Machin 1996: 46); in the 1997 UK election the Conservative Party spent more than £28 million (all the more impressive given that until a short time hitherto the party was still paying off an accumulated debt of nearly £20 million (Neill 1998: Table 3.7)). The gathering of comparative data on campaign finance is fraught with many difficulties, not least the fact that, unless required by law, the parties are often extremely unwilling to volunteer information. In the Katz/Mair party organization project some effort was made to try and gather this information, and warning notes were occasionally attached by the country authors (Katz and Mair 1992). With this in mind, Table 6.3 makes some effort to explore the trends.

A few clear trends are evident in Table 6.3. First, in virtually all cases, campaign expenditures rose through to the late 1980s. When we look at the percentage changes from the 1970s to the 1980s, the (partial) exceptions are Italy, Austria, and Sweden. However, the latter two cases ended the period overall with higher campaign expenditures. The Italian case with respect to campaign finance is difficult to assess. The scholars (Bardi and Morlino 1994) who gathered the data doubted their accuracy (a doubt which was dramatically soon confirmed by the Tangentopoli scandal). Second, it is interesting to note that the two cases which show the fastest growth—the UK and Ireland—were also the only cases where political parties did not receive state funding.[10] Third, a closer examination of the underlying trends indicates that the largest fluctuations in campaign expenditure seem to occur in the 1960s and 1970s, suggestive of a general process of

---

[10] This is no longer true for Ireland, as will be discussed later in this chapter.

TABLE 6.3. *Party Election Campaign Expenditure in Western European Countries, 1960s–1990s*

Country	No. of parties	Total average party expenditure per decade				% change 1970s–80s
		1960s	1970s	1980s	1990s	
Austria	3	18.7 (3)[a]	21.8 (4)	18.1 (2)	21.3 (1)	−17.0
Belgium	8		19.5 (1)	20.3 (2)		4.1
Denmark	4		1.8 (3)[b]	2.2 (4)		22.2
Finland	3		1.5 (3)	1.7 (2)		13.3
Ireland	3		1.3 (1)	3.4 (5)		161.5
Italy	7		34.5 (2)	31.7 (2)		−8.1
Netherlands	4[c]	1.8 (1)	2.5 (2)	2.5 (4)		0.0
Norway	5		3.6 (1)	3.8 (3)		5.6
Sweden	3	5.6 (3)	8.1 (4)	6.6 (3)		−18.5
United Kingdom	2	13.4 (2)	10.0 (4)	16.7 (2)		67.0

[a] includes 1959

[b] SF 1979 expenditure not available; have used 1978 figures instead

[c] prior to 1977, we are aggregating the figures for ARP, CHU, and KVP.

Notes: Figures in parentheses are the numbers of elections making up the decennial averages. The data have been standardized using cost of living deflators (base year of 1987), and have been converted to US$ at the average 1987 exchange rate.

Sources: Katz and Mair (eds.) 1992; *International Financial Statistics Yearbook* 1979; World Bank, *World Tables* 1992.

stage 2 campaign professionalization which was occurring in these years (see Bowler and Farrell 1992; Butler and Ranney 1992).

In general, the trends in the Katz/Mair data set, buttressed by more recent information provided by country experts, present a staged pattern of increase, often characterized by an initial surge in the amount of money being spent, followed by some reining-back of expenditure, followed in turn by another surge. For instance, after the large increases in expenditures during the 1970s, there was a 'steady-state' period in the early 1980s, with expenditure levels rising only gradually. Towards the end of the 1980s and into the 1990s, levels of campaign expenditure tended to jump again, perhaps as a result of further developments in campaign professionalization.

Information provided by country experts on campaign expenditure in the 1990s suggests quite a mixed picture recently.[11] Countries where campaign expenditure appears to continue to be on the rise include Britain, Canada, Germany, Sweden, and the USA. For the most part, these increases reflect the

[11] The following experts provided useful background information: Luciano Bardi (Italy), Clive Bean (Australia), R. K. Carty (Canada), Kris Deschouwer (Belgium), Michael Holmes (Ireland), Wolfgang Müller (Austria), Jon Pierre (Sweden), Thomas Poguntke (Germany), Jan Sundberg (Finland), Lars Svåsand (Norway), Anders Widfeldt (Sweden), and Colette Ysmal (France).

growing expense of the modern campaign. But in at least some cases the increase is simply due to state finance laws which have built-in inflators to take account of cost of living increases or population growth.[12] By contrast, there are a number of countries where campaign expenditure appears to have either stabilized (Australia, France, Ireland) or decreased (Belgium, Finland, Italy). Again, a number of factors are behind these varying patterns. For instance, the Australian and Irish trends reflect a period of retrenchment by overstretched party organizations, and also a degree of more targeted spending (e.g, Irish parties have shifted away from expensive newspaper advertising towards greater use of outdoor billboard advertising). French campaigns costs have plateaued since the 1980s when legislation was passed restricting the use of new campaign technology. In Finland, an economic crisis forced the parties to cut back on their campaign expenditures. In Italy the retrenchment was forced on the parties by the removal of state funding. Similarly, in Belgium (which, like Italy, went through its own party funding scandal) the expenditure reductions were the direct result of new legislation designed to force the parties to spend less—a policy which has proven quite popular for voters and parties alike.

There is some reason to believe that a trend may be developing toward the limitation of campaign spending, either directly or indirectly. For instance, Ireland passed new legislation introducing extensive public funding of parties in 1998. The legislation also sets a ceiling on national campaign expenditure which is likely to constrain the campaign activities of the larger, better-endowed parties, causing one set of commentators to predict that this 'will change the nature of Irish political campaigning' (Laver and Marsh 1999: 159). It also seems certain that Britain will adopt new legislation setting financial limits on parties' national campaign expenditure following a government-commissioned inquiry into party funding (Neill 1998).

Resource and Personnel Changes

New technology requires new technicians. As we know from the well-documented US experience, political consultancy has been a major growth industry. In the more party-centred west European and Australasian systems, however, we can expect somewhat different patterns (Farrell 1998; Farrell et al. 1998). In western Europe, there have been three particularly notable developments. The first of these is a growing strength of central party organizations, as revealed by a quantitative examination of the resources available to parties. To this we can add two parallel changes of a more qualitative nature, incorporating the emergence of party leaders' offices and the growing professionalization of campaign staff.

---

[12] The German case is interesting here because a recent reform of the state funding laws has linked state funding to the numbers of paid-up members. This change has hurt the Green Party in particular, given its fluid organizational structure.

These qualitative trends further enhance the capacity of central party elites to coordinate and control campaign activities. We shall consider each of the developments in turn.

Quantitative trends in party resourcing

Our survey of quantitative trends takes in both the funding and the personnel available to political parties. It is far from easy to obtain reliable comparative longitudinal data on some of these variables (especially staffing levels), but again the Katz/Mair handbook (1992) provides us with a reasonably good source. These data cover forty-two parties from nine west European democracies, although we do not have information for every variable for each party.[13] In running from the 1960s to 1990, the data cover the first two stages of campaign development and, in the case of some countries, arguably the beginning of the third. We have selected five key indicators of party resourcing, for which the national trends are summarized in Table 6.4, and presented by party in the appendix. This table incorporates information about the changing number of staff employed at three different levels of party organization—the central party, the sub-national party, and the parliamentary party—and about changes in the overall level of income and state funding available to central parties.

Focusing on staffing levels first, it is clear from Table 6.4 that the majority of parties considered have increased their staff, especially at the central and parliamentary levels. Indeed, just five out of forty-one parties shed staff from their central headquarters, and of these only the Dutch Christian Democratic Appeal did so to a notable extent (see Appendix). At the parliamentary level the upward trend is even more clear-cut; only the Norwegian Socialist People's Party appears

[13] The gaps which exist in the data mean that we are reduced to: 41 parties (in all 9 countries) for which we have central staff time-series data, 25 parties (across 7 countries) for which we have sub-national data, 35 parties (in 8 countries) for which we have parliamentary staff data, 35 parties (in 9 countries) for which we have time-series data on overall central party income, and 29 parties (in 8 countries) for data on central party income derived from state subsidies. For the most part, the data are based on five-yearly averages between 1960 and 1989. The figures for Norway and Denmark are based on four-year averages that correspond more closely with the electoral cycles of these countries.

Calculations for parties in Italy and the USA have not been included here. In the Italian case, no time trend data are available for the three main parties covered by the period (the Socialists, Communists and Christian Democrats, the latter two of which were almost certainly among the best resourced of any European political parties during the three decades following 1960); given that this is the case, the available data can only provide a highly misleading impression of the overall situation in this country. The US data are fraught with rather different problems. There are often difficulties in comparing US parties with their European counterparts, of course; in this context, the question arises as to which elements of the respective party organizations might constitute the 'central' and 'parliamentary' parties. Overall, it is hard to disagree with the view of Kolodny and Katz, who argue that party staffing in the USA is 'extraordinarily hard to estimate' for a variety of reasons, including: 'widespread sharing or loaning of employees . . . idiosyncratic and highly variable decisions about whom to include in staff lists, and . . . the time of the year or point in the election cycle at which the estimate is made' (1992: 888).

TABLE 6.4. *Average Changes in the Resources of West European Political Parties*

	Central staff	Sub-national staff	Parliamentary staff	Central party income	Subsidies to central party
Austria	+15.6 (36%)	−15.0 (11%)	+16.6 (217%)	+8,865,863 (192%)	+3,866,260 (369%)
Denmark	+2.9 (33%)	+0.8 (42%)	+14.6 (352%)	+559,789 (66%)	+261,978[a]
Finland	+11.2 (91%)	+3.2 (17.8%)	+3.8 (279%)	−748,045 (13%)	−595,414 (13%)
W.Germany	+20.0 (8.6%)	−6.0 (2%)	+696.6 (525%)	−9,265,034 (22%)	−1,487,199 (6%)
Ireland	+13.7 (216%)	n/a	+42.0 (105%)	+383,487 (91%)	76,079 (88%)
Netherlands	+8.5 (61%)	n/a	+4.3 (11%)	+1,216,551 (90%)	+5,346 (43%)
Norway	+6.5 (59%)	−2.5 (16%)	+4.6 (139%)	−378,351 (16%)	+296,249 (23%)
Sweden	+11.5 (39%)	−10.2 (16%)	+6.8 (83%)	−1,340,686 (17%)	−1,534,682 (32%)
U.K.	+10.0 (18%)	−169.0 (56%)	n/a	+2,375,070 (42%)	n/a

a It is not possible to calculate the percentage change this represents given that growth is from no subsidy at all.

Notes: This shows the mean rate of change in terms of both raw units and percentages. The parties included in the national averages and the periods of comparison are detailed in the Appendix. Only parties which can be compared across the specified period are included in the calculations. The financial comparisons are restricted to years in which general elections took place. Figures for income and subsidies refer to net changes in real value terms, with prices standardized at 1987 levels and expressed in US dollars. Cost of living deflators are taken from the *International Statistics Yearbook*, 1979, and the World Bank's World Tables, 1992. Exchange rates are those used for December 1987, as reported in *The Times*.

Sources: Same as for Table 6.3.

to have lost staff at all, and these losses are far from notable. However, at the sub-national level the picture is different; just nine out of twenty-five parties show net growth over time and the three British parties have clearly undergone dramatic local staffing reductions. In sum, all the countries featured in the Katz/Mair data set have seen growth in central and parliamentary staffing, and there are few distinctive national developments, although the Federal Republic of Germany appears to be in a league of its own, experiencing a massive growth of its parliamentary parties.[14] By contrast, not one of the countries for which we have been able to calculate national averages shows decisive growth in sub-national staffing, although the Nordic countries come closest to achieving this; all other systems show staff shrinkage at the local level, the UK massively so. Allowing for the relative paucity of data at the sub-national level, these data suggest that this is the one area which parties have neglected (or been unable) to develop in terms of the deployment of personnel. Allied to the almost universal decline of party membership numbers since the 1960s (Katz, Mair, et al. 1992; see Chapter 5 in this volume), this finding points to a general decline of local party organizations in Western countries.

We asked our country experts for information on recent staffing trends in the 1990s. Few of them reported any significant changes from the general picture presented so far. For the most part, the numbers of staff are related specifically to the level of state funding received by the party, which in turn is affected by the party's electoral fortunes (determining how much funding the party is entitled to). As this funding method is employed throughout most of continental western Europe, this suggests little by way of dramatic shifts in the numbers of staff employed by these parties. There are, however, a few exceptions. For instance, in Italy, the tangentopoli scandal led to considerable changes in the party system and the scrapping of state party funding, and thus resulted in dramatic reductions in the numbers of party staff. By contrast, in Belgium the recent federalization of the country has seen the rise of a range of new regional governments and the need for extra party staff to service these. This factor, along with the introduction of state funding since 1989 (increased in 1993), has resulted in a period of staffing expansion for the parties. Trends in Britain, where parties receive no state funding, and Ireland, where until very recently the level of funding was small by international standards, suggest a more fluid staffing policy, with evidence of the parties being prepared to build up quite large staff numbers in the lead-up to an election, only to downsize once the election is over.

The overall picture of continuing growth of the national party is confirmed by reference to the data on financial resources. Twenty-one of the thirty-five parties, and five out of nine countries for which we have time-series data, show financial growth in real terms from the mid-1970s to late 1980s. Again, the Nordic area

---

[14] An important caveat must be issued regarding the German data, since they incorporate part-time employees whereas data from other countries do not.

and—more surprisingly—West Germany stand out against the tendency of central party real incomes to grow. To set this in context, however, we should note that German, Swedish, and Finnish parties were among the richest in Europe at the beginning of the period analysed and remained relatively wealthy at the end (see Table 6.5). They have hardly, therefore, become impoverished.

The data on subsidies to central parties are interesting in so far as they bear directly on one of the most widely discussed concepts in the recent literature on Western political parties, namely Katz and Mair's 'cartel party' (1995). The growing organizational strength (measured in central party staffing and funding) that so many parties display may seem paradoxical, for it is widely observed that Western parties are losing their capacity to penetrate society and mobilize the loyal support of citizens. The huge literature on such features of modern political behaviour as electoral volatility, partisan dealignment, and membership decline are testament to this development (see Chapters 2–5 of this volume). How can parties continue to thrive organizationally *in spite* of their declining basis of social support? One obvious explanation for the paradox is provided by the cartel party thesis, which contends that established parties exploit the state itself as an alternative source of organizational resources:

In short, the state, which is invaded by the parties and the rules of which are determined by the parties, becomes a fount of resources through which these parties not only help to ensure their own survival, but through which they can also enhance their capacity to resist challenges from newly mobilized alternatives. The state, in this sense, becomes an institutionalized structure of support, sustaining insiders while excluding outsiders (Katz and Mair 1995: 16).

The final column in Table 6.4 (and Appendix) bears upon this point in that it reports the changing quantities of state subvention flowing to party central offices. The real value of such funds increased for seventeen of the twenty-nine parties analysed, while the average state subsidy increased in real terms for five of the eight countries. Again, the countries where the real value of subsidies fell are those which headed the European league of subventions at the start of the time series (Germany, Sweden, and Finland), and again they remained high in the rankings at the end. Interestingly, the extent to which parties depend on the state for central office income has tended to grow in recent years. Only in the case of Sweden was there a notable reduction in the level of financial dependency on the state; elsewhere it either increased or remained virtually static (see Table 6.5).

Qualitative developments in party resourcing

The qualitative developments which have affected the resourcing of European parties as campaign organizations are more recent in origin. Of particular note are: (1) the increasing reliance on specialist campaign agencies and political consultants, and in a number of prominent cases, (2) the gradual emergence of the party leader's office staffed by handpicked campaign, media, and policy specialists working directly with the party leader. Together, these trends constitute what

TABLE 6.5. *Average Central Party Incomes and Subsidies in Western Europe*

Country	Average income at beginning of period	Average income at end of period	Average subsidy at beginning of period	Average subsidy at end of period	Subsidy as % of overall income at beginning of period	Subsidy as a % of overall income at end of period
Austria	4,627,266	13,113,105	1,047,266	3,866,257	22.6	29.5
Denmark	843,318	1,403,107	n/a	261,980	n.a.	18.7
Finland	5,998,872	5,250,827	4,497,790	3,902,376	75.0	74.3
Germany	42,105,303	32,840,272	24,587,309	23,099,993	58.4	70.3
Ireland	423,375	806,862	86,730	162,809	20.5	20.2
Netherlands	1,357,352	2,575,403	12,359	17,705	9.1	6.9
Norway	2,308,032	1,929,681	1,317,906	1,614,155	57.1	83.6
Sweden	7,722,020	6,381,342	4,860,640	3,325,958	62.9	52.1
United Kingdom	5,656,539	8,031,609	n/a	n/a	n/a	n/a

Note: All figures expressed in US dollars, standardized at 1987 price levels (see Table 6.3).

Source: As for Table 6.3.

is often referred to as 'the professionalization of party campaigning' (as in Panebianco's 'electoral-professional' ideal-type (1988)). As always, there is some national variation based on particular circumstances: e.g. it is far easier for Tony Blair as *the* leader of the British Labour Party to establish a personal office than it is for, say, Gerhard Schröder at the German SPD.[15] Some attempt was made to explore these developments in the Bowler and Farrell (1992) survey of national experts in the early 1990s. For the most part, the parties were still using *ad hoc* campaign bodies rather than permanent standing committees or departments. The few exceptions were the Danish Christian People's Party and three left-of-centre parties (British Labour, the Danish Social-Liberals, and the Left-Wing Alliance in Finland). It should be noted however, that in many of the cases where *ad hoc* bodies ran campaigns, preparations were arranged by permanent or semi-permanent bodies made up of teams of experts and campaign specialists. The numbers actually involved in campaign coordination were typically very small, averaging about eight people based around the party leadership.[16]

Apart from the ubiquitous advertising agencies, there is rather mixed evidence about the use of outside agencies and consultants. In the early 1990s, none of the parties made use of them in Denmark, the Netherlands, or Germany. In Britain only the Conservatives appeared to use such expertise, though by the end of the decade Labour was following suit, even to the extent of importing one or two individuals from Bill Clinton's team in the run-up to the 1997 general election. In Germany (and hitherto in the British Labour Party) this seems to reflect the fact that the parties have tended to employ their own specialists 'in house'. This practice is also true to some extent of the other cases, though it possibly also reflects a degree of reluctance to make full use of the service of specialists in general (Farrell 1998). Of the few cases where parties included outside experts in their campaign coordination, only in Austria (and to an extent in the Irish Fine Gael party) were these consultants incorporated on a formal basis; in other words, only in those cases can one talk of outside consultants and agencies having a potentially very significant role in campaign decision-making.

As writers like Panebianco (1988) and Katz and Mair (1995) have shown in their discussions of the electoral-professional and cartel party models, these changes in campaign personnel reflect a general shift in the internal power relations within parties, with the parliamentary face—and especially that part of it intimately associated with the party leadership—emerging as the main power house. What this may amount to, at its most extreme, is a change in the culture of political parties away from their mass traditions, particularly in the case of the left-of-centre parties. In its place emerges a new role for parties as campaign

---

[15] As the UK campaign histories show, Tony Blair's hold over his party is a relatively recent luxury for Labour leaders (Kavanagh 1995; Scammell 1995).

[16] Inevitably, the Finnish Left-Wing Alliance, as a new party with a rather decentralized structure (Sundberg and Högnabba 1992), had a much larger number of people involved in campaign coordination.

machines operating in support of the principal candidates—a role which the US parties appear to play today (Herrnson 1988; Katz and Kolodny 1994).

Thematic Changes

Changes in campaign theme have been of two main forms: 'presidentialization', and shifts in what the political marketing specialists would call 'campaign communication'. The first point is virtually incontrovertible. Across western Europe (to say nothing, for instance, of the presidential political systems of Latin America) there has been a distinct shift in campaign focus, with much greater attention focused on the party leader (Bowler and Farrell 1992; Farrell 1996; Swanson and Mancini 1996a). To a large degree this process has been fed by television and its requirements. We saw above how parties have been concentrating their resources at the centre, largely based around the party leadership. This trend reflects a power-shift within political parties, but it also is suggestive of a change in the nature of campaign discourse, with image and style increasingly pushing policies and substance aside. Clearly, there may be a number of factors determining whether the party leader is not a dominant, but rather a major theme, not least the issue of his or her personal popularity and/or tendency to tread on banana skins. The relevant distinction for our purposes is whether the leader is merely a minor theme. Today, it is very hard to find any examples among the main parties of a national election campaign where the party leader is consigned to a minor role. In short, there is little disputing the fact that campaigns have become 'presidentialized' (Mughan 1993; 1995).

Related to the emphasis on image in campaigns has been a general shift in the nature of campaign communications, which is usefully encapsulated by the political marketing literature as a shift from selling to marketing. As the means of accumulating feedback has become more sophisticated, and the desire to test opinion more ever-present, there has been a perceptible shift in the politician's psyche from treating politics as an art to treating it instead as a science. The initial standpoint used to be one of setting the product (usually based on some predetermined ideology) and seeking to steer public opinion in this direction. Saliency theory (Budge and Farlie 1983) argued that certain types of parties 'owned' certain types of policies (e.g. defence for the right, and health policy for the left) around which they centred their campaigns.

Today, political strategy increasingly appears to centre on finding out what the public wants to hear and marketing the product accordingly. In the context of centralized party resources which facilitate carefully coordinated campaigns, this enhances the strategic autonomy and flexibility of leaderships. Such policy movements may enhance the responsiveness of parties to popular demands, but they may also render enduring policy reputations harder to identify; in the UK, for instance, the New Labour party of Tony Blair (which seems to exemplify the marketing approach) leap-frogged the Liberal Democrats in order to dominate the ideological centre-ground (Budge 1999: 5–6); similar tendencies were noted in Germany before its 1998 election. This trend seems destined to continue as the traditional party hierarchies are replaced by brash new professionals whose primary loyalty is to the leader rather than to an ideology or a party tradition.

CONCLUSION

Political parties have invested heavily in election campaigning, making full use of new technologies, adapting their organizations and employing specialist agencies and consultants. As a result, the party of today and the way it operates in the context of electioneering, is a significantly different creature from what it was twenty years ago. This chapter has pointed to three major developments in parties as campaign organizations: first, parties have tended to become more centralized and professionalized; second, they have become more cognizant of citizen opinion and demands; and third, party and (especially) leader image has come to assume a prominent thematic role in campaigning. From each of these we might derive speculative insights into the nature of democratic change.

From the centralization of parties and the decline of local party organizations which seem implicit in contemporary formulations such as the electoral-professional and cartel party models, we might conclude that the nature of citizen participation is changing. Fewer individuals now take on political roles as loyal party members, perhaps preferring to participate via non-partisan single-issue groups. Moreover, if the new media technologies have even half the effects currently being predicted for them, this tendency may only be reinforced. At its most extreme, some have foreseen a trend toward some form of direct democracy centred around the communication capabilities of the new media (Abramson et al. 1988; Grossman 1995). It is hard to see what kind of role there will be for political parties in such a scenario.

However, it would be unrealistic to be carried away by these visions at this stage. More likely is the survival of both parties and representative democracy, albeit in adapted forms. Thus, for example, we might expect greater use of referendums and public initiatives, far greater attention to the accumulation of citizen feedback, and possibly moves towards 'more complex, two-way electronic interactions on individual issues' (Budge 1996: 132). Parties have proven adaptable and resilient entities up to now, and may well adapt again to this new environment; after all, they are still likely to remain the principal conduit for political recruitment, demand aggregation, and control of government. Moreover, notwithstanding the compelling evidence of local organizational atrophy, it should not be assumed that parties have concluded that individual memberships are an entirely irrelevant anachronism, nor that local members lack any significant impact on the policy process or electoral outcomes; the persuasive evidence of authors such as Scarrow (1996) and Seyd and Whiteley (1991; Whiteley et al. 1994) suggest that party members are still important in a number of respects (see also Chapters 5 and 7 in this volume).[17]

From the evidence of the growing sophistication of party efforts to tap public opinion, it might also be tempting to conclude that parties are in decline in another sense, i.e. that they are increasingly unprincipled, opportunistic power-seekers who will fail to offer voters clear or meaningful choices. Again, however, caution is in order. The bold transformations of European social democracy inherent in the projects of Blair and Schröder should not obscure the painstaking efforts of political scientists who have demonstrated repeatedly that parties 'almost always maintain the same ideological positions in relation to each other and in fact change policy remarkably little' (Budge 1996: 131). Furthermore, it would be unwise to assume that parties never seek to mould, rather than simply follow, voter preferences—especially once they are in power. Dunleavy and Ward (1981), for instance, demonstrate that there are a number of ways in which parties controlling the levers of government (and a few in which parties in opposition) can decisively shape the policy demands of citizens. In short, parties can and do still lead as well as follow public opinion, though a shift in emphasis may be underway.

Finally, from the growing thematic emphasis of so many campaigns on party and leader image, it is tempting to conclude that political competition is increasingly trivialized and insubstantial in Western democracies (e.g. Jones 1996; Lawson and Ysmal 1992; Patterson 1994). However, caution should be exercised in rushing to judgements of this nature. We should at least ask what kinds of images are promoted by campaigns, for some are far from trivial or insubstantial. If, for instance, one thinks of the standard models of party competition devised by Western political scientists, it is readily apparent that these place primary emphasis on the policy packages which parties put before the electorate. Yet implicit in such models are reputational factors which have nothing to do with the intrinsic (de)merits of the policies alone. The rational and serious-minded voter must assess the credibility of a policy pledge, as well as its innate character, and considerations of credibility turn in part on perceptions of the competence and veracity of politicians. Thus, it is one thing to think that a politician has a good policy for alleviating unemployment, but it is quite another to believe that he or she is likely to (*a*) keep their word if returned to office, or (*b*) prove competent to follow through on the promised intent of the policy. Therefore, it is rational and important for any organization campaigning for office to concentrate part of its efforts on fostering a reputation for integrity, veracity, and competence. These are essentially matters of image-building, which may relate to either the leadership or the party in general. To give one example, the British Conservative Party's sudden and dramatic loss of its long-cherished reputation for economic competence on

[17] Though, it is worth noting that 'virtual' parties have arrived. See, for example, the website of the new Italian party, Nuovo Movimento (http://www.nuovo-movimento.com).

the occasion of the Exchange Rate Mechanism crisis of 16 September 1992 undermined its subsequent economic policy initiatives and contributed substantially to Labour's electoral landslide in May 1997 (King 1997: 186). Labour lost no opportunity during the intervening period to launch attacks aimed at reminding voters that the Tories could no longer be trusted to run the economy in a competent manner.

In short, parties and their organizations have shown many signs of change as they have sought to adapt to the altered political, social, and technological environments in which they find themselves, and they undoubtedly will have further adaptations to negotiate in the future. They remain stubbornly persistent entities with important roles to play at the heart of the contemporary democratic process.

Appendix

Quantitative Changes in the Resourcing of West European Political Parties

	Central staff	Sub-national staff	Parliamentary staff	Central party income	Subsidies to central party
Austria	*(1966–90)*	*(1966–90)*	*(1966–90)*	*(1975–90)*	*(1975–90)*
SPÖ	+ 9 (12%)	–15 (11%)	+ 25 (278%)	+ 17,709,495 (210%)	+ 5,989,741 (384%)
ÖVP	+ 30 (60%)	–	+ 16 (178%)	+ 8,318,058 (248%)	+ 4,939,119 (358%)
FPÖ	+ 8 (160%)	–	+ 9 (180%)	570,035 (27%)	+ 669,911 (328%)
Denmark	*(1972–89)*	*(1972–89)*	*(1972–89)*	*(1975–88)*	*(1975–88)*
SF	+ 7 (+350%)	–1.0 (100%)	0.0 (0%)	+ 978,121 (316%)	+ 306,549
SD	– 2 (9%)	+ 4.0 (133%)	+ 43.0 (1433%)	+ 1,372,784 (46%)	+ 688,988
RV	+ 4.0 (80%)	–	–	+ 304,615 (60%)	+ 146,119
KRF	+ 5.0 (500%)	0.0 (0%)	+ 3.0 (100%)	+ 113,545 (36%)	+ 55,673
CD	+ 2.0 (200%)	0.0 (0%)	+ 2.0 (18%)	+ 29,878 (24%)	+ 112,563
V	+ 6.0 (75%)	0.0 (0%)	+ 18.0 (360%)	–	–
KF	+ 7.0 (64%)	0.0 (0%)	+ 19.0 (+317%)	–	–
Finland	*(1960–89)*	*(1965–89)*	*(1965–89)*	*(1975–87)*	*(1975–87)*
SKDL	– 0.6 (4%)	–1.0 (6%)	+2.2 (220%)	–2,017,001 (37%)	–2,463,762 (51%)
SDP	+ 16.8 (+191%)	–1.6 (–10%)	+ 7.0 (700%)	–1,936,205 (18%)	–980,540 (13%)
KESK	+ 6.8 (42%)	+ 22.0 (105%)	+ 5.2 (520%)	–608,901 (11%)	–399,314 (8%)
SFP	+ 3.8 (40%)	+ 2.0 (44%)	+ 1.0 (100%)	+ 167,428 (12%)	+ 275,173 (32%)
KOK	+ 29.0 (220%)	+ 21.8 (436%)	+ 5.4 (540%)	+ 654,454 (10%)	+ 591,374 (13%)

W. Germany

	(1972–89)	*(1972–89)*	*(1969–89)*	*(1972–87)*	*(1972–87)*
SPD	+ 22 (40%)	−6 (2%)	+735 (443%)	−20,061,287 (34%)	−10,233,702 (28%)
CDU[a]	+ 43 (28%)	—	+1102 (532%)	−6,921,906 (12%)	+ 3,330,164 (11%)
FDP	—	—	+253 (1012%)	−811,910 (7%)	+ 2,441,941 (34%)

Ireland

	(1965–89)	*(1975–89)*	*(1977–89)*	*(1972–87)*	*(1972–87)*
LAB	+ 6 (200%)	—	+ 11 (1100%)	+ 252,196 (151%)	—
FG	+ 17 (213%)	—	+ 52 (1300%)	+ 710,823 (219%)	+ 76,079 (88%)
FF	+ 20 (333%)	—	+ 63 (900%)	+ 187,441 (24%)	—

Netherlands

	(1970–89)	*(1980–89)*	*(1973–86)*	*(1973–86)*	*(1973–86)*
PvdA	+ 26.6 (73%)	—	+ 14.4 (+17%)	+ 2,152,238 (58%)	+ 7,818 (71%)
PSP	+ 1.0 (33%)	—	+ 2.5 (71%)	—	—
PPR	+ 8.0 (400%)	—	+ 6.0 (600%)	+ 158,723 (66%)	+ 9,724 (109%)
CDA[b]	− 35.5 (103%)	—	+ 17.7 (23%)	+ 2,325,865 (212%)	−5,998 (29%)
D'66	+ 3.0 (75%)	—	+ 8.3 (237%)	+ 229,378 (56%)	+ 9,841 (114%)
VVD	+ 1.0 (+6%)	—	+ 9.0 (22%)	—	—

Norway

	(1965–89)	*(1973–89)*	*(1973–89)*	*(1973–89)*	*(1973–89)*
SF/SV	+ 5 (100%)	0 (0%)	−2 (40%)	−66,857 (8%)	+ 118,251 (5%)
DNA	+ 10 (37%)	+ 5 (22%)	+ 15 (500%)	−1,491,643 (35%)	—
SP	+ 6 (120%)	+ 2 (11%)	+ 5 (250%)	—	—
KRF	+ 5 (50%)	+ 10 (100%)	+ 2 (40%)	—	—
V	+ 2 (40%)	+ 1 (20%)	+ 1 (50%)	+ 295,196 (76%)	−9,979 (4%)
H	−5 (24%)	−3 (4%)	+ 10 (250%)	−250,100 (7%)	+ 780,475 (7%)
FRP	+ 3 (150%)	0 (0%)	+ 1 (50%)	—	—

	Central staff	Sub-national staff	Parliamentary staff	Central party income	Subsidies to central party
Sweden	*(1965–89)*	*(1965–89)*	*(1970–89)*	*(1976–88)*	*(1976–88)*
SAP	+ 48.0 (149%)	–	–	–1,715,623 (10%)	–2,817,515 (31%)
VPK	+ 12.4 (248%)	–	–	–920,805 (33%)	–958,983 (42%)
C	+ 11.2 (86%)	–	+ 6.8 (74%)	–1,913,091 (29%)	–2,950,800 (53%)
FP	+ 10.4 (69%)	+ 16.2 (27%)	+ 6.8 (94%)	–492,303 (12%)	–1,022,595 (30%)
MOD	–4.2 (7%)	–6.0 (16%)	–	–1,661,606 (20%)	+ 76,483 (2%)
U.K.	*(1960–89)*	*(1960–89)*	*(1974–87)*		
CON	+ 3 (3%)	–289 (50%)	–	+ 4,122,996 (44%)	–
LAB	+ 21 (42%)	–153 (62%)	–	+ 1,984,059 (30%)	–
LIB	+ 6 (32%)	–66 (89%)	–	+ 1,018,206 (133%)	–

[a] These figures are for the CDU and CSU combined.

[b] CDA figures are calculated by aggregating data for the CHU, KVP, and ARP for the earlier time point in the comparison.

Notes: The precise period analysed varies according to data availability, but is generally from the earliest possible date in the 1960s through to the late 1980s for staff and from the mid-1970s to late 1980s for finance. Financial comparisons are restricted to election years. Figures for income and subsidies refer to net changes in real value terms, with prices standardized at 1987 levels and expressed in US dollars. Exchange rates used are those for December 1987, as reported in *The Times.*

Sources: As for Table 6.3.

7

From Social Integration to Electoral Contestation

The Changing Distribution of Power within Political Parties

Susan E. Scarrow, Paul Webb, and David M. Farrell

CHAPTERS 5 and 6 dealt with a central theme in the Western literature on post-war party change—the decline of the party of mass integration and its gradual replacement by the party of electoral contestation. There are a number of well-known models of party transformation which share this broad perspective and highlight processes of change. The earliest of these are more than three decades old now, going back to Otto Kirchheimer's (1966) catch-all prophecy, and to Leon Epstein's (1967) account of 'contagion from the right'. Both Kirchheimer and Epstein foresaw the growing dominance of electorally driven parties which had only shallow ideological commitments. Such changes were perceived to follow from social transformations which weakened both social group identities and the role of parties as articulators of specific group interests. In place of its traditional role as an agent of social and political integration, the modern political party came to be regarded as a highly professional machine motivated primarily by the desire for electoral success. The implications of this for patterns of party competition in certain party systems quickly became well known: electoralism of this sort would most likely lead to policy convergence in pursuit of the median voter, meaning that citizens would be offered fewer real policy choices, and would have to make electoral choices based on such factors as short-term issues, managerial competence, and candidate personality. Subsequent studies have largely confirmed these predictions, finding that the declining electoral salience of established political cleavages encourages parties to de-emphasize long-term positions in favour of more ephemeral issues and personalities (Franklin et al. 1992).

We are grateful to the following colleagues for their very helpful guidance on trends in their country of expertise: Luciano Bardi, Clive Bean, R. K. Carty, Kris Deschouwer, Michael Holmes, Andreas Ladner, Wolfgang Müller, Jon Pierre, Thomas Poguntke, Jan Sundberg, Lars Svåsand, Michael Thies, Anders Widfelt, and Colette Ysmal. The usual disclaimer applies.

The transformation thesis extends beyond matters of ideology and party competition, however. Processes of change are also thought to affect parties' internal structures. To begin with, a modern electoralist party is not expected to have the same need of a mass membership as the old party of mass integration (the subject of Scarrow's Chapter 5). Furthermore, disciples of Kirchheimer such as Angelo Panebianco (1988) argued that parties' increasing sensitivities to electoral markets have combined with technological advances to forge important changes in campaign style; instead of relying on volunteers to mobilize cleavage-based support, the parties are increasingly expected to employ professional advertisers and marketing consultants in order to reach out to voters (the focus of Farrell and Webb's chapter). Underlying each of these subjects is a matter of considerable importance to any assessment of the nature and extent of party organizational change—the internal distribution of power. This is the question to which we turn in this chapter.

DEMOCRACY AND THE STRUCTURES OF POLITICAL PARTIES

Investigations of power relations within parties inevitably touch on more far-reaching questions about the roles parties play in the realization of democratic systems of governance. Assessments of the state of parties' internal structures tend to reflect preferred models of democracy, resting on distinct assumptions about what parties should do as mechanisms for linking citizens with their governors. For instance, intra-party democracy is most valued as an end in itself by those who emphasize participatory aspects of democracy. According to this perspective, parties' decision-making structures are important because they provide opportunities for citizens to influence the choices voters are offered, as well as broad opportunities for expanding civic skills. According to more elitist models of democracy, competitive elections are the most vital component of the linkage mechanism, and parties' most essential contribution is to offer voters clear electoral choices. For those who emphasize this representative aspect of modern democracies, the ways in which parties arrive at these choices has much less normative importance than the fact that distinct choices are offered. This view was most succinctly summarized by E. E. Schattschneider, who argued that 'Democracy is not to be found *in* the parties but *between* the parties' (1942: 60, emphasis in original). Indeed, from this perspective it is less interesting to ask whether parties' internal structures are democratic than whether they help or hinder parties in choosing policies and personnel which reflect the preferences of their broader electorates.

Throughout the past century politicians and political analysts have suspected that there is a trade-off between intra-party democracy and electoral democracy. This suspicion rests on the assumption, famously voiced by Roberto Michels (1959), that party leaders have different motivations from the broader party membership, and that these motives predispose them to be more sensitive to voters' preferences. This assumption informs the main models of post-war party transformation, which assert that the role and influence of the ordinary members have been reduced as parties have begun paying more attention to the process of courting voters; meanwhile, the autonomy of the leadership has grown correspondingly (Kirchheimer 1966). Thus, the classic literature has tended to emphasize how members may hamper the efforts of an electoralist leadership. For instance, Leon Epstein's well-known diagnosis of 'contagion from the right' noted that one of the advantages enjoyed by parties with few active members was that it was 'easier to impose a central and efficient direction of campaigns by professionals' (1980: 258). Similarly, Panebianco's electoral-professional party requires maximum strategic autonomy for the leadership so that it can play the game of party competition unhindered by the demands of party members.

Some of the more recent literature on party change invokes John May's 'law of curvilinear disparity' to explain why the influence of the membership might be regarded as so pernicious by electorally motivated party leaders. The law of curvilinear disparity is premissed on the notion that leaders are driven by vote-maximizing imperatives, whereas activists (or 'sub-leaders') are motivated by purposive incentives, such as the desire for influence over party policy or candidate selection. Thus, while leaders can be expected to seek out policy positions which approximate those of the median voter as nearly as possible, sub-leaders among the activist membership are more likely to be concerned about maintaining ideologically 'pure' (which is to say radical) positions (May 1973). This scenario creates the obvious prospect of intra-party tension and difficulties of party management.

The assumption that May codified has proved remarkably enduring, even though research into the question of May's law has failed to produce a consensus on the extent to which it actually operates. For instance, accounts of factional struggle in the British Labour Party have sometimes pointed to the role played by radical extra-parliamentary activists (Kogan and Kogan 1982). Similarly, Herbert Kitschelt's account of Social Democratic Parties in Austria, Germany, and the United Kingdom in the 1980s argued that structures of party democracy empowered activists who were further to the left than more 'electoralist' leaders, and thereby hampered the parties' ability to adapt effectively to changing electoral environments (Kitschelt 1994: 244–52). On the other hand, in one of the more systematic efforts to test May's law, Pippa Norris uncovered evidence suggesting that the parliamentary elite is generally the most radical party stratum in Britain, with party voters the most moderate and active members falling between the two ideologically. In view of this, we might feel justified in renaming May's 'law' one of *linear* disparity, at least in so far as major parties in Britain are concerned (Norris 1995*a*). Research into the ideological profiles of party strata in the USA has produced similarly unclear conclusions (Miller and Jennings 1986; Hauss and Maisel 1986).

In some respects the evidence about this phenomenon is beside the point for arguments about organizational transformation, as there is little doubt that perceptions of grass-roots radicalism are widespread among politicians, journalists, and academic commentators alike. Moreover, even if leaders were convinced that members would reach the 'right' decisions in the end, they still might want to increase their own flexibility and control over the timing of strategic decisions, instead of needing to wait the approval of party conferences or party plebiscites. In short, whether or not May's 'law' is operative, there are good reasons to think that an electoralist party leadership will desire to keep the internal powers of the membership as limited as possible—especially with regard to policy-making.

That said, the literature on intra-party power does not necessarily lead us to expect party leaders to approach the task of 'taming' their grass roots by crudely stripping members of their democratic rights. In most cases this might be politically very difficult and damaging for party legitimacy, given that the cognitive mobilization of Western publics has shifted in favour of participatory democracy, something which is especially evident on the part of the most politically aware and active citizens in post-industrial societies (Barnes, Kaase, et al. 1979; Dalton 1996a; Budge 1996; Chapter 1 of this volume). In addition, such a strategy would also likely be seen as unnecessarily damaging to a party's electoral prospects, given that party planners have various reasons to view members as vote-winning assets (Scarrow 1996). Indeed, in an era where many debates have populist overtones, legitimacy—the image of being 'of the people'—may be one of the least substitutable of the benefits which members can corporately confer. How much legitimacy members provide may be intimately linked to intra-party decision-making processes, and in particular to the extent to which party leaders can claim that they and their policies have a mandate from the membership.

Because even electoralist parties have incentives to attract and retain members, we would expect them to balance upward power shifts with attentiveness to members' political privileges. Parties need to provide reasons for supporters to enroll, and political rights may become an increasingly important enticement as ongoing social changes force parties to alter their mix of enrolment incentives. In particular, where cleavage-based politics erodes, parties may be forced to rely more on selective than on solidary incentives to attract members. Political rights within the party are among the least costly of the selective incentives which parties are able to provide.

Another reason for expecting to see changes in the internal distribution of power is the changing nature of parties' links with associated collateral organizations. The notion that the party of electoral contestation will be prepared to sacrifice exclusive links with collateral organizations is explicit in Kirchheimer's model of catch-all transformation (1966: 363–4). More recently, Thomas Poguntke has demonstrated empirically that such linkages have typically eroded across European parties as the electoral value of close ties with specific interest organizations has diminished. Thus, as social change has weakened the capacity of collateral organizations such as trade unions to aggregate and deliver votes, parties have become less interested in according them representation in party forums such as national executive committees (Poguntke 1998: 176). What Kirchheimer failed to anticipate was that the erosion of collateral organization rights within the party might coincide with the extension of individual membership rights. However, it seems likely that such a shift will create wider opportunities for rebalancing the distribution of political rights within party structures.

Thus, modern electoralist parties are challenged to find ways of responding to growing internal and external demands for extending grass-roots participatory rights. Yet today's parties also are subject to increasing pressures to retain or enhance their strategic autonomy in order to compete effectively in an increasingly volatile electoral market (see Chapter 4). Though these trends may affect all parties in democratic societies, the task of adjusting to them becomes more difficult the greater a party's electoral ambitions, and the less defined its 'natural' constituency. As a result, the effects of these trends may be most visible in parties that are relatively large, and relatively centrist.

One way parties may achieve a balance between leadership autonomy and procedural democracy is to pursue models of intra-party democratization which effectively dilute the influence of the most ideologically radical members by increasing the impact of the less active, and supposedly more moderate, members. In his account of the 'paradoxical role of party members' in contemporary parties, Peter Mair (1994: 16) has described this approach thus:

[I]t is not the party congress or the middle-level elite, or the activists, who are being empowered, but rather the 'ordinary' members, who are at once more docile and more likely to endorse the policies (and candidates) proposed by the party leadership . . . [T]he activist layer inside the party, the traditionally more troublesome layer, becomes marginalized . . . [I]n contrast to the activists, these ordinary and often disaggregated members are not very likely to mount a serious challenge against the positions adopted by the leadership.

This view of party change is often buttressed with references to the British Labour Party, whose leaders pursued precisely this kind of strategy as they sought to wrest control of the party from the radical activists who were briefly ascendant during the early 1980s (Webb 2000: ch. 7). This case, which provides strong anecdotal support for the view that party leaders may be turning to a kind of democratization to suit their own ends, is doubly influential because British examples have traditionally held a prominent place in theories about party organizational development. However, up to now there has been little effort to organize systematically the expectations that seem confirmed by developments in the British Labour Party, or to examine the extent to which these patterns are being replicated by parties elsewhere. These are the tasks which we will pursue in this chapter. In brief, we believe that the view of party transformation outlined above generates a number of expectations concerning three key areas of potential membership influence within parties: candidate selection, leadership selection, and policy-making. It is these hypotheses which we shall be investigating during the course of this chapter.

HYPOTHESES

In this section we offer generic hypotheses derived from common descriptions of the transformations which are often said to be occurring in large parties throughout the OECD democracies. We concede, however, that party changes are influenced by specific institutional contexts, such as systems of government and electoral rules. Given that the majority of our cases are unitary parliamentary democracies, our general hypotheses will initially be framed in terms of such systems, though we shall allude to alternative possibilities where different institutional contexts apply.

Candidate Selection

In terms of the selection of candidates for national legislatures we would not expect to find evidence of a simple diminution in the power of ordinary party members. Indeed, Kirchheimer (1966: 198–9) predicted that the future of the political party was to provide political integration by giving citizens opportunities to participate in the selection of political personnel. As noted above, in parties which are more oriented towards electoral contestation than mass integration it is important to provide grass-roots members with selective incentives to join and participate in certain activities. Opportunities to influence candidate-selection are one of the most politically significant of the selective benefits which parties are able to offer their members. On the other hand, from the perspective of party leaders increasing members' influence over candidate selection may prove costly. Typically, electorally oriented leaders will prefer legislators who are generally of a similar ideological profile to themselves; this should help ensure a cohesive legislative party, which fosters easy party management in the short run, and enhances prospects of re-election in the long run. In addition, party leaders have good reasons to prefer selection rules which give them leverage over sitting legislators by enabling them to prevent incumbent reselection. Leaders lack such leverage in heavily decentralized systems, such as in the United States. As a result, as long as party leaders share May's assumptions about the different priorities of activists and ordinary members, we would expect to find evidence that they have tried to reduce the costs that may result from implementing more inclusive candidate-selection processes. They may do this by implementing rules which give relatively inactive members, rather than local party elites or activists, the decisive say in choosing candidates. We expect that leaders will promote these types of change using the language of democratization, emphasizing that they represent a transfer of privileges from party officials to the party grass roots. Thus, they will favour procedures which maximize access and recognize members' formal equality. Our main hypotheses about candidate selection are, therefore, as follows:

C1. *Where it did not already exist, right of final selection will have shifted towards the mass membership.* Typically, this will be achieved at the expense of local or regional party elites (through the introduction of membership ballots, for instance). This expectation holds for both parliamentary and presidential candidates.

C2. *National electoral party elites will retain (or assume) a veto over local membership candidate-selection decisions.* This safeguard will be adopted by an electoralist leadership which fears that local selection procedures might occasionally produce undesirable candidates. 'Electoral party elites' refer to those leaders who have a direct vested interest in electoral success, i.e. those who are, or expect to be, candidates for national executive office and who therefore desire maximum autonomy over their party's policy. Generally, this will be the parliamentary leaderships of parties in parliamentary democracies. In presidential and semi-presidential systems, however, the constitutional separation of executive and legislative elections makes it less likely that a president or presidential candidate will hold such veto power over the selection of legislative candidates.

Leadership Selection

With respect to leadership selection, we expect that an electoralist leadership would prefer to retain control within the legislative party itself in order to stave off challenges from party 'sub-leaders' (for instance, congress delegates and local activists) who are not driven primarily by electoral motivations. Such challenges are far less likely to materialize when the selectorate is known to be sympathetic to the leadership. However, balancing this instinct for central elite control against the growing demands for participation means that such matters may not be straightforward. It may be important to stable party management and to the leader's legitimacy that his or her selection be broadly endorsed. In this case, the overriding imperative is to avoid control of leadership selection falling into the hands of the radical activists. Consequently, the main hypotheses that we propose here are:

L1. *Selection of the electoral party leader will generally rest either in the hands of the members of the parliamentary party, or will have passed to the mass membership in some form or other* (typically a membership ballot). Because party congresses are the institutional fora in which sub-leaders typically have most influence, an electoralist party would be unlikely to want the power of selection to remain there.

L2. Where the electoral party leader is selected by an electoral college of some kind, party rules will ensure that the majority of the vote is accounted for by the parliamentary elites and/or the mass membership. Logically, given the previous hypotheses, the leadership can be expected to want to ensure that the sub-leader groups within the party do not control a majority of the votes in the college.

Policy-Making

Finally, it is in the area of party policy-making that the electoralist party leadership has the most obvious need to retain control, for this activity bears directly upon the core party goal of effective party competition. Thus, the leadership has a particular need to maximize its strategic autonomy over the policy-making domain. Once again, however, it may have to balance this instinct against demands for democratic control of the party and its programme. Indeed, many of the old parties of mass integration had traditions of formal sovereignty of party congresses over the programme. However, our concern lies with the core of the party programme, that which is incorporated in an official election manifesto or statement. Naturally, whatever the manner in which such statements are adopted, leaders can attempt to increase their post-election autonomy by reducing the specificity of these pre-election pledges, and by running campaigns that focus more on personalities than on policies. Nevertheless, we posit that wherever parties still produce official election manifestos, party leaders will be most concerned to retain direct control over their production. Thus, our hypotheses about policy-making are:

P1. Control of the manifesto remains in, or passes into, the hands of the electoral party leadership. The logic is similar to that expressed in C2; those leaders who have a direct vested interest in electoral success desire maximum autonomy over party policy in order to better position their parties.

P2. In the name of democracy, the leadership may seek grass-roots legitimation of the manifesto by a formalized process of consulting the mass membership. Again, one way to achieve this is to hold a membership ballot, though parties may develop other mechanisms to incorporate members into the process while conferring minimal control over the outcome. These processes will go some way towards meeting demands of democratization without severely restricting the autonomy of the leadership; indeed, they may prove an ideal way of weakening the influence of a radical strata of sub-leaders who might have entrenched representation rights in a party congress or on a party executive.

P3. In general, electoral leaderships will seek to curtail the power of party congresses over policy by reducing the frequency with which they are held. In fact, there are a number of ways in which we might expect leaderships to use procedural devices in order to limit the power of party congresses in which sub-leader groups typically have most sway. However, for practical reasons we are limiting this aspect of our investigation to something which can readily be measured—the frequency of party congresses. Although we are not suggesting that this is likely to be a strong correlate of sub-leaders' general power, if the frequency were reduced from, say, an annual to a biennial meeting, we would certainly expect this to reflect on their significance in the policy-making process.

The propositions presented above predict that parties' decision-making processes will display movement towards what Ranney (1981: 82–5) described as greater centralization *and* greater inclusiveness. Though it might seem that centralization and inclusiveness should vary inversely, in fact these options are not incompatible. Our expectation is that decision processes are becoming more centralized in that national (or in federal parties, regional) leaders are tightening their control over the ultimate outcomes. At the same time, these processes are becoming more inclusive in that they are being opened up to allow more individuals a direct—though not necessarily determinative—say in the decisions.

It may be useful to envisage a continuum of inclusiveness in party decision-making. Occupying the end of least inclusiveness are three alternative sets of protagonists who would generally be regarded as elements of a party elite: the leaders of the legislative party, the legislative party at large, and the party's extra-legislative national committee. 'National committee' itself is a term which could cover a variety of bodies with differing names, size, memberships, functions, and powers, but we can safely argue that such a body is unlikely to number more than 200 or so at most, and it is clearly distinct from a full party congress. Decision-making responsibility might be further broadened through delegation to sub-national elites, such as the leaders of provincial or local party units. The national party congress is the fifth point on our continuum of inclusiveness. As such bodies usually consist of delegates from various party levels, and often from various interests which are organized within the party, decision-making by a party congress represents a significant step towards greater inclusiveness; nevertheless, it is often also a key forum in which sub-leaders and activists can exert influence.[1] More inclusive still are those parties which give a direct voting role to their dues-paying memberships, but the furthest point along the continuum of inclusiveness belongs to those organizations which offer a decisive role to party voters and sympathizers in the electorate at large.

In practice, placing party decisions along this continuum of inclusiveness is likely to be an inexact science, in part because formal procedures often involve several of these layers of decision-makers. Thus, placements are necessarily rough averages that attempt to take account of which individuals or bodies hold powers of suggestion or veto that are primarily symbolic, and which ones exercise decisive influence.

---

[1] Here 'party congress' may refer to a regular conference with a broad remit, or a special electoral convention or college whose main purpose is the selection or endorsement of party leaders, candidates, or manifestos. Such a congress will usually number a minimum of several hundred delegates and could easily run into thousands in the larger parties.

In framing the preceding propositions we have tried to be as general as possible, given that the social and technological forces said to be driving these changes have affected all the established electoral democracies. Our aim is to draw conclusions about the extent to which parties in these varied political systems are manifesting similar patterns of organizational development. In the sections that follow we examine evidence of the distribution of internal party power in twenty democracies. The major difficulty in trying to assess the validity of these predictions is that formal rules and actual practices do not always coincide, nor do they necessarily change at the same rate. Sometimes rules may change to catch up with actual practices; in other cases, new rules may introduce processes that are ignored in practice. The emphasis here will be on party rules, because such changes are easiest to document; nevertheless, we will not overlook changes in political practice, because how rules are applied clearly matters. As will be seen, while the evidence provides some indication that the predicted patterns are indeed apparent, such transformations have not been universal, nor have all recent changes been in a single direction.

SELECTING CANDIDATES

Selecting candidates is widely recognized as one of the most consequential functions parties perform in representative democracies. By extension, then, access to the candidate-selection process is a crucial indicator of power distribution within a party. It is also a promising area for observing changes in this power distribution, in part because parties vary widely in the way they make selection choices.

In most countries parties' selection processes remain largely unregulated by the laws which carefully govern aspects of public elections. There are a few notable exceptions to this rule. One is the United States, where states began imposing very detailed regulations about candidate selection at the beginning of the twentieth century. In addition, in countries such as Finland (since 1970), Germany (since 1967), and Norway (since 1921) laws have less specifically encouraged parties to adopt relatively open and democratic candidate-selection practices. Elsewhere, however, parties have been legally free to choose their candidates as they please, though their chosen procedures are likely to be shaped by what Czudnowski (1975: 220) labelled the 'institutional infrastructure of politics and government'. Key components of this infrastructure are governmental and territorial divisions, and the system of electoral laws. Thus, regional party units and regional party leaders seem to have greater control over candidate-selection processes in federal systems (Gallagher 1988: 256; von Beyme 1985: 239). Similarly, electoral systems shape party selection rules by defining whether parties need to find individual candidates for single member districts, or to prepare a candidate slate for one or more multi-member districts. While Gallagher (1988: 258–60) has shown that electoral rules alone do not determine

TABLE 7.1 *Candidate Selection for National Legislatures*[a]

	Can non-members participate in selection process[b]	Do statutes give option of member vote on selection? (+ more inclusive since 1960)	Do local or regional delegates vote on or ratify selection?	Can national party leaders impose or veto selections, and/or change list order
Australia	no	Lab in some states	Lab, Lib, Natl	Lab
Austria	ÖVP sometimes	+Gru, +ÖVP, +SPÖ	all parties	FPÖ, ÖVP, SPÖ
Belgium	no	AGA, ECO, PVV	CVP, PVV,VU	AGA, CVP, VU
Canada	Can sometimes	all parties	no	yes
Denmark	no	+CD, +KF, +KRF, RV, +SD, +SF, +V	V	CD, KRF, SF, SD
Finland	no	+all parties	all parties	all parties
France	no	+PS	UDF, PC, PS, RPR	PS, PC, RPR, UDF
Germany	no	+CDU, +Gr, +SPD	CDU, CSU, SPD	All except FDP & Gr: limited non-binding veto
Ireland	no	+FG, +Gr	FF, FG, Lab, PD	FF, FG, Gr, Lab
Italy	no	no	all parties	all parties
Japan	no	no	no	all parties
Netherlands	no	D'66	CDA, D66, A Greenleft, Pvd	CDA, D66, PvdA, VVD
New Zealand	no	+Lab	Lab, Nat'l	Lab, Nat'l
Norway	no	no	DNA, H, KRF, SP, SV, V	no
Sweden	no	S, C sometimes	FP, M, S, VPK, C, MP	no
Switzerland	no	no	most parties, most regions	SD
United Kingdom	no	Con, +Lab, +LibDem		Con, Lab, LibDem
United States	all parties	no	no	no

[a] Party abbreviations follow Katz and Mair 1992.
[b] Dues-paying members

Sources: Aitkin et al. 1996; Arian 1998; Carty n.d.; Carty 1991; Erickson 1997; Fukui 1997; Haegel 1998; Helander 1997; Katz and Mair 1992; Katz and Mair 1994; Jaensch 1994; Jupp 1964; Overacker 1952; Sheppard 1998; Simms 1996, and various national country experts referred to in the chapter acknowledgements.

the comparative centralization or inclusiveness of candidate-selection systems, such rules do set important constraints on parties' decision processes. Nevertheless, parties retain a great deal of freedom when working within these general frameworks. As a result, there is no reason to believe that system-specific constraints completely obscure more general patterns of organizational development.

The first prediction about likely shifts in candidate-selection processes (C1) states an expectation of increasing inclusiveness. Of course, what it means to 'shift' depends on the nature of prior selection rules, and where parties originally stood on the inclusiveness continuum. In practice, by the 1960s almost all parties outside the far-left and far-right used selection rules which were inclusive enough to involve local party leaders in at least a consultative capacity. Many also included local or regional party delegates in the process. As a result, for most parties to move towards greater inclusiveness would mean to grant individual members opportunities for directly influencing selection decisions.

In eight of the eighteen countries examined here, rule changes in at least some parties since the 1960s do conform to the prediction that electoralist parties will make selection processes more inclusive. In Denmark in the late 1960s and early 1970s, four parties introduced the option of member ballots to decide candidate selection. In the 1970s a new electoral law required Finnish parties to begin holding intra-party primaries for selecting candidates. In 1979 the New Zealand Labour Party adopted a new requirement to hold advisory polls of members who attended selection meetings (Sheppard 1998). In the 1980s and 1990s possibilities for members directly to participate in selection processes were introduced (or in the case of the ÖVP, revived) by the traditionally major Austrian parties (ÖVP, SPÖ), the major German parties (CDU, SPD), the British Labour Party, and by Fine Gael in Ireland. In addition, in Canada, a country where members traditionally have voted in local selection meetings, at least one party experimented in the 1990s with opening these votes to non-members (Carty n.d.).

These changes match the expectations outlined above. Still, it is important to note that there have also been a few moves in the opposite direction. From the 1970s onward several Belgium parties phased out or abolished use of membership balloting as part of the candidate-selection process. In the 1980s and 1990s most Dutch parties (except D'66) eliminated options of balloting local party members. The Australian Labor and Liberal parties began shifting away from membership 'primaries' as early as the 1950s. In addition, there are the many parties in which selection processes have continued to rely on delegates to make selection decisions. Similarly, the United States' procedures cannot be said to have become more inclusive because at the beginning of the period under consideration the parties' selection processes (mainly primary elections) were already very inclusive in comparative terms.

In sum, this broad survey of inclusiveness in candidate-selection provides only limited support for the expectations laid out at the beginning of this chapter: in eight of the eighteen countries some or most parties have changed in the predicted direction. However, this pattern has not been universal. Indeed, three of the countries in which parties began the 1960s with relatively inclusive procedures have seen some parties eliminate earlier opportunities for members to have a direct say in candidate-selection processes. Moreover, changes in formal rules have not been matched by similar changes in actual selection processes. For instance, in the early 1990s both the Austrian ÖVP and SPÖ changed their statutes to recognize membership primaries as a candidate-selection mechanism. Both parties used these new procedures in 1994, but failed to use them in the subsequent two national elections (Müller et al. 1999: 209–11). Thus, while there is modest support for proposition C1, the extent of real changes should not be exaggerated.

Proposition C2 states that *central party elites will retain (or assume) a veto over local membership candidate-selection decisions*. This expectation is more strongly supported by available evidence, though in large part this is because most parties have met it by merely retaining the status quo. As Table 7.1 shows, in most contemporary parties national leaders retain centralized control over use of the party label by would-be candidates. In some cases, this control is exercised early and actively, with central party authorities approving aspirants before other party levels are allowed to endorse them as candidates. Elsewhere, central parties hold a post-facto veto over choices made by local or regional parties. In only a few of these cases do the current controls represent a strengthening of central party powers since the 1960s. Two of the exceptions involve federal countries which traditionally have had relatively weak parties at the national level. One is Canada, where campaign finance laws passed in the 1970s gave national party leaders the right to withhold the party label from candidates; in 1993 the Liberal Party strengthened these provisions to give stronger vetoes to provincial and national party chairs. The second is Australia, where the Labor Party transferred some selection oversight to national party leaders. Meanwhile, in Ireland in 1970 the Fine Gael national leadership gained a more formal veto over candidate nomination, and since this time leaders in both Fianna Fáil and Fine Gael have made increasing use of their powers to veto and impose candidates. During the 1980s the British Labour Party national executive gained enhanced powers to veto candidates, as well as to impose candidates in by-elections.

Given the pre-existing strength of central party veto options—to say nothing of the other disciplinary incentives held by legislative party leaders—it is unsurprising that there has not been much of a move towards greater centralization. In almost all cases national party leaders already possessed at least some powers to exclude unwanted candidates from using the party label. Exceptions include parties in Norway, Sweden, and the United States, as well as the Australian National Party (where regional party leaders control the selection veto). This centralization of final control does not necessarily exclude important involvement by those elsewhere in (or even out of) the party. Indeed, even where national party leaders hold vetoes, most selection decisions may be made at other levels; nevertheless, the fact that such a veto *could* be wielded may represent a substantial constraint on decisions. It is also notable that in recent years there are no instances of parties weakening or eliminating central party vetoes. Clearly, the democratizing moves described above have not been accompanied by decentralization.

In sum, changes in candidate-selection processes provide limited evidence of the kind of procedural transformations predicted in propositions C1 and C2. While these changes are far from universal, they have occurred across a broad range of parties and in a large number of the established democracies.

LEADERSHIP SELECTION

Involvement in the selection of candidates for elective office has traditionally been one of the chief roles which ambitious party activists have enjoyed. Yet, in contemporary liberal democracies they might also aspire to direct participation in the election of party leaders. In the UK, for instance, each of the major nationwide party political organizations has relaxed its long-standing tradition of leadership selection by parliamentary elites to establish a role for grass-roots dues-paying members. The first significant British party to do so was the old SDP in the early 1980s; its successor, the Liberal Democrats, adopted the same practice of leadership election by the mass membership in 1988. In the 1990s, the Labour Party gave a direct vote to its individual members, though these votes only counted as one-third of all those cast in the party's electoral college. After the electoral cataclysm of May 1997, the Conservative Party decided to introduce a direct membership ballot as the second and decisive stage of future leadership contests (Conservative Party 1998). In the USA, of course, changes in party rules and state election laws generated major increases in the role of primary elections in deciding the major parties' presidential nominees after 1968 (Katz and Kolodny 1994: 36).

Just how inclusive are contemporary parties when it comes to deciding who their leaders will be? Table 7.2 attempts to summarize the present situation across sixteen western democracies. One striking feature of the data is how often national patterns emerge; parties that compete and cooperate together seem destined to emulate each other much of the time, at least in the business of leadership selection. Occasionally, this pattern reflects legal constraints; in Germany, for instance, the 1967 party law had the effect of regulating a variety of aspects of internal party life, and this inevitably generated a certain resemblance (Poguntke 1994: 189 ff). However, legal regulations do not offer a universal explanation. Austrian, Finnish, German, Norwegian, Swedish, and US presidential parties all place a high degree of (and often exclusive) leadership-selection power in the hands of a party congress or convention. In contrast, Australian, Danish, Dutch, Irish, and US congressional parties tend to restrict that power to their parliamentary elites. The French left and Italian parties favour a leading role for some type of extra-parliamentary national committees, probably reflecting the influence of the Communist model in each of these countries.

TABLE 7.2: *Party Leadership Selection: National Summaries*

Country	Parliamentary party	National committee	Party congress	Party members/ voter primary
Australia	2			1
Austria		1	4	
Belgium		1	1	5
Canada			2	2
Denmark	6		3	
Finland			6	
France		2	2	5
Germany		1	3	
Ireland	3			1
Italy		3	1	
NL	5		1	1
NZ	1			
Norway			5	
Sweden			6	
UK			1	2
USA (P)			2	2
USA (C)	2			
Total	20	8	37	19

Proposition L1 states that selection of the electoral party leader will generally rest either in the hands of the members of the parliamentary party, or will have passed to the mass membership in some form. Table 7.2 reveals that this statement cannot be straightforwardly substantiated. Some 44 per cent of the cases (37 of 85) for which we have gathered data place the power to decide the leadership in the hands of the party congress or convention, which suggests that—to this limited extent at least—the classic mass party model is not yet entirely obsolete in Western democracies. Nevertheless, closer examination shows that our initial expectations are not completely without foundation. Some forty cases (47 per cent) do give leadership selection power to either the parliamentary elites or the mass membership, which is hardly an insubstantial amount. Moreover, if we interpret 'party elites' more broadly so as to include national executives (not unreasonably given that these are often controlled by, or also sympathetic to, electoral leaderships), we find that 56 per cent of cases conform to the hypothesis. Furthermore, there are a number of party systems which have demonstrated clear trends towards membership selection of leaders in the 1990s, including Belgium, Canada, France, and the UK. Again, these trends tend to confirm the power of diffusion of models of party organization within national contexts. Thus, while it would be an exaggeration to claim that proposition L1 is incontrovertibly sustained by the available evidence, there would seem to be a good deal of truth in it. Overall, the impression is of a mixed pattern whereby the classic mass party model of congress control over leadership selection shares its place with instances of direct control by party elites and the 'paradox' model of membership involvement.

Proposition L2 states that *where the electoral party leader is selected by an electoral college of some kind, party rules will ensure that the majority of the vote is accounted for by the parliamentary elites and/or the mass membership.* Examination of the data reveals that this particular hypothesis has virtually no generalizable force as yet, as the electoral college phenomenon seems to be limited to the case of the British Labour Party. In Labour's case the proposition certainly holds in that the mass membership and the MPs between them now control two-thirds of the vote in the leadership (and deputy-leadership) electoral college.[2] Other parties have flirted with the idea of electoral colleges, though none has introduced them as yet. For instance, Irish Fine Gael launched an internal commission in the early 1990s which proposed leadership selection by a college in which 50 per cent of the votes would be controlled by parliamentarians, 40 per cent by the mass membership, and 10 per cent by local government councillors. Though not implemented at the time of writing, were it to be so this model would clearly conform to proposition L2. Overall, however, while the available data do not contradict this hypothesis, it is of marginal relevance as a model of leadership selection.

POLICY-MAKING

Policy-making is one of the most important functions ascribed to parties. Furthermore, as the research of Klingemann and his colleagues (1994) has shown, parties' election programmes are good predictors of their legislative priorities when in government. Yet, for all the importance of party programmes to democratic theory and practice, we still know very little about where these programmes come from, and particularly about the role of intra-party democracy in the process. Of the three areas of potential membership influence discussed in this chapter, policy-making tends to have been overlooked in comparative studies of party organizational change. For instance, very little attention is paid to this topic in the Katz and Mair data set (1992). Given this lack of attention to policy-making in the party literature, it is very difficult to document the extent to which there has been any change in recent years.[3]

---

[2] This was not the case prior to 1993. When the electoral college initially was introduced in 1981, 70 per cent of the college vote was controlled by those annual conference delegates who represented the local party branches and corporately affiliated organizations (such as the trade unions and socialist societies). This clearly allowed the sub-leader stratum a degree of power which the electoral leadership was ultimately not prepared to tolerate, though it took a significant rebalancing of intra-party power (and a politically fraught struggle) before the necessary rule-change could be made in 1993 (Webb 1995).

[3] In the light of the paucity of hard data on policy formation in parties, much of the discussion in this section is based on feedback received from academic colleagues who specialize in the study of parties in the countries covered by this volume

One good reason for this gap in the literature is the general expectation that we should find little if any change in this dimension. As we have seen, in the processes of organizational reform the bulk of attention has been paid to the dimensions of candidate and leadership selection. According to Mair's 'paradox' these are the areas which facilitate an apparent empowering of the membership while sidelining the factions and the more militant activists. Policy formation is, and arguably has always been, a different matter. Laver and Marsh express this point well with regard to the Irish case: 'While the ordinary member continues to have a real say in candidate-selection, his or her voice may be no more than the faintest of whispers when it comes to deciding the policies on which these candidates fight elections' (Laver and Marsh forthcoming). Party leaderships are anxious to keep a tight rein on policy-making, and this is even more true for electoralist parties.

This concept is encapsulated rather well in R. K. Carty's (n.d.) description of Canadian parties as 'franchise parties', where the members are given a say over candidate and leadership selection in return for which the parliamentary leaders are left with a relatively free hand with regard to setting policy. Dean Jaensch provides a similar description of such a trade-off in his account of the role of members in the Australian Liberal Party: 'The organisation's role is to raise funds, pre-select candidates, campaign, constantly monitor the platform of the party, and to provide every possible support for the party in parliament. Its role is not to make policy, nor to direct members of parliament' (Jaensch 1994: 128).[4]

The extent to which there will be any trends in the policy-making area clearly will depend on how developed internal party democracy was to begin with. The general expectation, as set out in hypothesis P1, is that while party policy generally is supposed to be set forth by the conference, in reality the party leadership is likely to hold greater sway on the policies that matter in an immediate sense (i.e. the party's election programme or manifesto).

The principal focus of this section is the party's election programme, those elements of party policy which are packaged for presentation to voters during an election campaign. Consistent with hypothesis P1, all evidence from the party literature (e.g. Blondel and Cotta 1996; Budge et al. 1987) and feedback from academic specialists points to a common tendency for parliamentary party leaderships to maintain their domination of this process. Generally, the final determination of manifesto content is made by a small group surrounding the electoral leadership which draws up the programme, based in part on underlying party

---

[4] The USA provides an interesting counter-case to the notion of 'franchise' parties. Here the activist members of the party may have little control over candidate nomination, given the role of primaries, but they can often instead impose their demands on the platform, as demonstrated in recent years by the role of Republican party members in setting a far-right agenda which their candidates, many of whom hold more moderate positions, have to accept. Needless to say, however, while the party's platform may appear more extreme in consequence, in a candidate-centred system there is little reason for candidates actually to use it as their campaign platform.

ideology, but also on the leadership's interpretations of what is most marketable (often the party's pollsters provide some input into this process). A typical example was provided by the 1998 Dutch campaign, in which the election programme of the PvdA was drafted by the electoral party leaders.

Naturally, the electoral party leadership does not entirely enjoy carte blanche in drawing up the election programme. As the debacle within the New Zealand Labour Party in the mid-1980s reveals most clearly, there are limits to how far a party leadership can go in setting the election programme before it faces a backlash from its members. In this case, the party leaders 'overturned accepted practices and pursued their own party agenda', much to the dismay of their activist base (Debnam 1994: 55). Certain subjects will always remain taboo; key ideological positions cannot simply be rewritten willy-nilly. For the most part, an electoral party leadership will be able to use the opportunity provided by an election programme to emphasize certain policies which will appeal to the party's voters, and de-emphasize policies which might prove electorally damaging. This strategy is consistent with the ideas behind 'saliency theory' (Budge and Farlie 1983).

The extent to which the electoral party leadership may have flexibility over determining the party's election programme is very much affected by context. For instance, the party leadership has much more influence over the process when they are in government. This point was shown quite clearly in the lead-up to the 1998 German election when Chancellor Helmut Kohl had much greater say than did his challenger, Gerhard Schröder, over their respective party's election programmes.

In general, what evidence we have supports the contention that policy-making remains highly centralized, and as parties continue to professionalize their campaigns it is pretty clear that the process must inevitably become even more centralized. We have already seen how part of the trade-off for this is provided by some move towards a greater say for members over candidate selection and (in a few cases) leadership election, but is there any evidence of some trade-off in terms of efforts to democratize the policy formation process itself? The party leaderships may have retained strong central control over manifesto content, but have they tried to be more inclusive, allowing individual members some influence over policy? This is the question which lies behind the second of our hypotheses for this section.

One potential avenue for exploration here is the party conference, which for many parties has traditionally been the principal decision-making organ of the party. It is through this forum that the party activists have usually been able to hold sway—setting party policy, influencing the party's programme and strategies for forthcoming elections, and bringing influence to bear on the party leadership. Against this, however, is the potential provided by the party conference for the leadership to allow the average member greater input into decision-making on party policy. Consistent with May's Law, therefore, we might expect to find evidence of the party leadership seeking to reduce the role and influence of the activists. A common pattern across a number of parties is for the agenda of the conference to be more tightly controlled by the party leadership. This is particularly noticeable in the (former) mass parties, such as British Labour, where in recent years the conference has become less of a gladiatorial battle between the leadership and the activists and much more of a TV-oriented acclamatory event (Seyd 1999).

In this context hypothesis P3 becomes relevant: *In general, electoral leaderships will seek to curtail the power of party congresses over policy by reducing the frequency with which they are held.* The evidence available from the Katz and Mair data set (1992) is mixed on this point. The general trend across the Scandinavian countries is one of parties increasing the regularity of their national conferences, as evidenced by the Danish Socialist People's Party, the Finnish Left-Wing Alliance, the Norway's Conservative Party, and the Swedish Liberals. Set against these cases, however, are those parties which have reduced the frequency of their conferences: as far back as the 1950s–1960s in the case of the Austrian parties and the German CDU; more recent cases have included Irish Labour, the Belgian Communists, and Flemish People's Union (all in the 1980s).

Another means of assessing the inclusiveness of the policy formation process in parties is to consider the different levels of policy formation. So far we have focused on the development of the parties' election programmes, but what of the underlying ideology or core policies of the party? These are long-term policies which are traditionally set by the party conference, so that a party leadership seeking to change any of them would require a majority vote in the conference. Yet one strategy the party leadership can use is to go over the heads of delegates and open the process up by holding a membership ballot. Once again, the British Labour Party provides a good example, in this case with the membership-wide ballot that culminated the party's 'Clause 4' debate of the mid-1990s (Webb 2000: ch. 7). Though there is not widespread evidence that other parties have used a similar strategy, in the 1990s the German CDU, SPD, and FDP all altered their constitutions to make it possible to substitute a membership vote for a conference vote in policy-making matters; the small FDP even employed such ballots to set party policy in two areas (Scarrow 1999) .

It is also worth examining how parties make decisions about possible coalition arrangements. On one level, there would appear to be an important role for members in deciding on whether in principle the party should go into coalition or not. For instance, with the increased regularity of coalition governments in Ireland from the mid-1980s, the Labour Party rules were changed so that before entering into coalition negotiations the party leaders must seek the agreement of the members in a special conference. By their very nature, coalition negotiations require parties to reconsider some of the issue positions they took prior to the election—policy stances may be changed, positions dropped, priorities reassessed, etc. Such negotiations inevitably reduce the significance of the manifesto, but more importantly it also results in a lesser role for the members in determining the policies of their parties, as the decisions are taken in 'smoke-filled rooms' on the basis of negotiations between party leaders. The findings of Jean Blondel, Maurizio Cotta, and their colleagues (1996) support this notion. Their research of coalition scenarios across western Europe demonstrates clear evidence of a shift in policy-making influence from government to party. However, decision-making has usually remained firmly in the hands of the party leaderships, with only minimal involvement of the mass memberships.

Thus, while there are some hints of democratization in various aspects of parties' policy formation processes, the most significant scope for change is found in the early stages of these processes (in other words, in the development of broad policies which to varying degrees may or may not appear in specific election programmes). This is the stage which entails consultation of the grass-roots members. For instance, in Norway the practice is that the parties take a year to deliberate on the election programme. The grass-roots members are consulted and the draft is debated by party conference, but for the most part the leadership tends to get its way on the main specific policies (Svåsand et al. 1997: 106). An interesting feature of the Norwegian case is how little the members actually debate the details of party policy. As Svåsand and his colleagues report, in the greater majority of cases there is very little discussion of, or disagreement with, party proposals in the local branches.

This point seems generalizable. There is some evidence of party leaderships extending inclusiveness over policy formation as a means of stifling internal debate. For instance, in the early 1990s the British Labour Party established the process of National Policy Forums. The objective appeared laudable enough from a participatory perspective, namely to make the policy process more consensual and inclusive (indeed, non-members are also given the opportunity to have some input). The result has been extremely welcome to the party leadership as these forums have tended to reduce the highly public conflicts at party conferences. Similar tendencies have occurred in a range of other parties, such as the council groups in the Norwegian Labour Party, where the party leadership travels around the country discussing topics with ad hoc groups of members and sympathizers, or knowledge centres in the Dutch PvdA, which have produced a backlash of complaints from party militants in recent years. The German SPD has also made use of policy forums with business and youth.

Two features worth noting about the increasing tendency to open up the policy formation process are (1) the use of new technologies (particularly the internet) to facilitate it, and (2) that in many cases it appears to involve an opportunity for non-members to get involved in the party's internal policy process. As we saw in Chapter 6, all major parties have their own websites, and these are used to varying degrees to allow two-way communication in which the parties may institute discussion groups on specific policy areas. For instance, the Austrian Social Democrats recently made great play of the fact that their 1998 basic party programme was discussed via the internet. In 1997 the Swedish Left Party developed a 'female politics charter' based in part on feedback from an internet discussion group. Of course, by their nature websites are generally accessible to all on-line subscribers, and therefore there are few if any limits on who can seek to influence the party programme.

In summary, while we lack the same kind of hard evidence as provided in the previous sections of this chapter, the secondary and anecdotal evidence is consistent with P1 and P2, while the evidence on P3 is unclear. Overall, the policy-making process inside the parties seems to remain centralized; indeed, if anything it is becoming more centralized. At the same time, there are signs that policy-making is becoming more inclusive, perhaps in part because this helps to emasculate the bothersome activists.

CONCLUSION

Overall, how far does the evidence conform to the hypotheses that we derived from the comparative literature on intra-party power? The answer appears to be that it does to a considerable extent. The main hypotheses on candidate selection (C1/C2) and policy-making (P1/P2) are broadly confirmed, as is the minor hypothesis on leadership selection (L2). The evidence is far more ambiguous with respect to the main proposition about leadership selection (L1) and the minor hypothesis on policy-making (P3), but even here there are more than a few instances where the expectations are born out by the empirical data. In brief, grass-roots party members (and even non-member supporters sometimes) commonly play a significant role in selecting legislative candidates and in legitimizing election programmes, though party elites generally retain vetoes over candidate selection and enjoy considerable autonomy in shaping party policy. In a growing number of cases, moreover, party members are gaining significant rights to elect their leaders. Intra-party decision-making has thus become more inclusive, but not necessarily in a way that restricts the strategic initiatives of leaders. However, it would be an exaggeration to claim that the data conform universally to this pattern of electoralist party organization. The remains of the classic mass party model are especially evident in the significant number of cases in which congress delegates decide on the question of leadership; to this extent, the influence of the sub-leadership stratum has not been completely eroded throughout the advanced industrial democracies. As always, the real world does not provide a perfect fit for any one model of party organization, but it is reasonable to conclude that there are now many instances around the democratic world where party leaders operate a coalition of power in which grass-roots members are significant junior partners.

What are the wider implications of these developments for modern democracies? There are those who would alert us to the dangers of the 'new plebiscitarianism' inherent in a model of intra-party power which threatens to bypass the intermediary representative strata (Lipow and Seyd 1996; Seyd 1999). Nevertheless, for all the manipulative potential of Mair's paradox of democratization as emasculation (of sub-leadership groups), it would be foolish to regard the mass party as some kind of paragon of democratic virtue; Michels pointed out as much early in the twentieth century, and few who witnessed the operation of the British Labour Party's system of delegatory democracy could have deluded themselves in this respect. In any case, if we are to take the notion of cognitive mobilization seriously (see Chapter 1 in this volume), we must give more credit to the potential and actual role played by the ranks of armchair members of modern parties. Many of them may be inactive when it comes to the mundane virtues of attending party meetings and running campaigns, yet they are better placed than most of their predecessors in terms of educational experience and access to independent political information. There are good reasons, therefore, to suppose that they possess the capacity to make informed and rational judgements about matters of candidate and leadership selection, and even party policy. Seen in this light, even the most strategically calculating electoralist leaders may find themselves operating in an authentically democratic context of sorts. At the very least, it would be surprising indeed if party elites generally managed to assume and maintain perfect control of their organizations in the top-down manner which the 'paradox of democratization' interpretation seems to imply. In short, there are still good reasons for supposing that political parties remain vital, if imperfect, mechanisms of linkage in modern democratic societies.

Appendix

Leadership Selectorate Details, by Party

Country	Party	Parliamentary party	National committee	Party congress	Party members/ voter primary
Australia	Labor	x			
	Liberals	x			
	Democrats			x	
Nat. Total		2			1
Austria	SPÖ		x	x	
	ÖVP			x	
	FPÖ			x	
	Green			x	
Nat. Total			1	4	
Belgium	CVP				x
	PSC				x
	BSP				x
	PSB			x	
	VLD				x
	PRL				x
	VU		x		
Nat. Total			1	1	5
Canada	Reform				x
	ND			x	x
	PC			x	
Nat. Total				2	2
Denmark	SF			x	
	SD	x			
	RV	x			
	KRF			x	
	CD	x		x	
	V	x			
	KF	x			
	FRP	x			
Nat. Total		6		3	
Finland	VAS			x	
	SDP			x	
	KESK			x	
	SFP			x	
	KOK			x	
	SKL			x	
Nat.Total				6	

Country	Party	Parliamentary party	National committee	Party congress	Party members/ voter primary
France	PCF		x		
	PS (P)				x
	PS (S)				x
	RPR				x
	FD (CDS)			x	
	DL (PR)				x
	UDF				x
	FN			x	
	Green		x		
Nat. Total			2	2	5
Germany	CDU			x	
	SPD			x	
	FDP			x	
	Greens		x		
Nat. Total			1	3	
Ireland	FF	x			
	FG	x			
	Labour				x
	PD	x			
Nat. Total		3			1
Italy	PDS		x		
	RC		x		
	PPI		x		
	AN			x	
Nat. Total			3	1	
NL	CDA	x			
	PvdA	x		x	
	VVD	x			
	D66	x			x
	CD	x			
Nat. Total		5		1	1
NZ	Labour	x			
Nat. Total		1			
Norway	SV			x	
	DNA			x	
	V			x	
	SP			x	
	KRF			x	
Nat. Total				5	
Sweden	SAP			x	
	C			x	
	FP			x	
	M			x	
	VPK			x	
	MP			x	
Nat. Total				6	

Country	Party	Parliamentary party	National committee	Party congress	Party members/ voter primary
UK	Lab			x	
	C	x			x
	LD				x
Nat. Total		1		1	2
USA (P)	D			x	x
	R			x	x
Nat. Total				2	2
USA (C)	D	x			
	R	x			
Nat. Total		2			

Notes:

1. We have followed the advice of the various country experts published in the sources referred to below in defining 'party leader'. It is not, therefore, always the same office from party to party, but in most cases it seems that it is possible to point to an overall 'real' party leader; sometimes this may be the parliamentary leadership, though sometimes not (for instance, Belgium). It is, however, always the 'electoral' leadership in that it is prominent in election campaigns and responsible for party policy and/or coalition negotiations. In the case of some of the major French parties we have accounted for two separate 'electoral' leaders; clearly presidential nominees qualify, but so do Parti Socialiste first secretaries in so far as these incumbents may well become national prime minister if the party is successful in legislative elections.

2. It is possible for a single party to give a role in leadership selection to more than one of these categories; for instance, the US presidential parties and some of the Canadian parties depend on both voter primaries and national conventions (or 'congresses' in our general terminology here); similarly, the Austrian SPÖ's leader is selected by the national executive but ratified by party congress.

3. 'National committee' refers to any kind of elite level national body of a party; these may vary greatly in size, functions, and power (central committees, political bureaux, national executives, directing committees, etc.).

4. 'Party congress' may refer to a regular conference with a broad remit, or a special electoral convention or college whose main purpose is the selection or endorsement of the party leadership. The British Labour Party uses an electoral college which shares voting rights between parliamentarians, the members of affiliated organizations (e.g. unions) and party members.

5. In the case of some parties included in this table (such as the Green parties of Germany, Sweden and France) the 'leaders' referred to are officially recognized only as 'spokespersons'.

6. USA (P) denotes the the leadership of the 'presidential parties', which is formally concluded at the quadrennial conventions; USA (C) denotes the leadership of the 'congressional' parties in the Senate and House of Representatives.

Sources: Hermet et al, 1998; Katz and Mair 1992; Katz and Mair 1994; Marsh 1993; the various national country experts referred to in the chapter acknowledgement, and the following party officials: Loes Hillenaar (PvdA—NL), Tie Vereecke (BSP—Belgium), Christoph Liedtke (FDP—Germany), Kjell Dahle (SP—Norway), Tom L. Chistensen (KRF—Denmark), Stacey Hanlon (Australian Liberals), David Haure (UDF—France), Yulia Onsman (Australian Democrats), Christian Scheucher (ÖVP—Austria), BjarteTora (KRF—Norway), Tonje Westby (DNA—Norway), Heidi Englund (Miljopartiet—Sweden), Ilpo Kiuru (Kokoomus—Finland), Jennifer Robinson (Canadian Progressive Conservatives).

PART III

Parties in Government

8

Parties in Legislatures:

Two Competing Explanations

Shaun Bowler

FOR Richard Rose 'party cohesion is a means to an end: it ensures the parliamentary endorsement of government measures' (Rose 1983: 283). Parties thus perform a highly important systemic level function in contributing to the formation and, just as important, the maintenance of government. Indeed, it is enormously hard to imagine legislatures without parties (Sinclair 1998: 24). Still, as functional as parties are for parliamentary systems, this does not necessarily explain how parties are functional from the point of view of individual parliamentarians. The fact that parties may perform useful functions inside a legislature does not necessarily explain why individual legislators remain members of the same legislative bloc throughout their careers. And, as the bulk of current writings on legislatures reminds us, it is this individual or micro-level functionality that is all important.

In what follows we look at two broad arguments that help to explain the presence of legislative parties from the point of view of individual legislators. One theory looks to the role of elections and election fighting as the main source of glue that bonds legislators together; the other looks to the need for collective action inside the legislative chamber. This latter argument has become especially influential of late. Influential but not wholly persuasive; and in the last section of the chapter we offer an account in which party organizations provide an important adhesive force and we argue that while 'parties in the electorate' may not provide a sufficient explanation for 'party governmen', 'parties as organizations' may do so.

The chapter then examines evidence that relates to the institutional structures and incentives that benefits political parties within the legislative arena. We examine the formal rules of procedures across the national parliaments in most advanced industrial democracies. Then, we examine the parties' influence on the legislative process and legislative decision-making. The results provide a basis for discussing how in the legislature have reacted to the patterns of change discussed in other chapters of this volume.

TWO COMPETING EXPLANATIONS OF COHESIVE
LEGISLATIVE PARTIES

Two broad arguments have been used to explain the generally cohesive behaviour of party members within legislatures. One approach argues that party behaviour in the legislature arises from actions in the electoral arena, especially the proced-ures for nominating candidates. The origin of this argument lies in the work of Ostrogorskii (1902) on the caucus, and finds modern expression in the work of Downs (1957) and Mayhew (1974). All of these works, as a common theme, emphasize the importance of fighting elections as a factor which shapes the behaviour of politicians. In Mayhew's (1974) term, it is a 'two-arena' model in which incentives in the first electoral arena shape behaviours in the second legislative arena. Parliamentary parties are thus seen as a consequence of the need to fight and win elections. The party organization, label, advice, and finances can help legislators become elected and the impact of this organization ('caucus' for Ostrogorskii) carries through to the legislature. Hence, parties in legislatures develop largely as a consequence of the functional value of parties at election time. The systemic value of parties noted by Rose (1983) results almost as a by-product of organizing for electoral success.

This view implies that as the importance of parties in fighting elections shrinks or changes (as we have seen in previous chapters), we are likely to see changes in the value of remaining a member of a party inside the legislature. For instance, if candidates develop more personalistic bases of electoral appeal, rather than partisan appeals, this may diminish the impact of partisan labels once these candid-ates are elected. Or, if constituency service plays an increasing role in politicians' electoral support (Cain et al. 1987), this may draw candidates to focus on constituency needs in making their political decisions. Consequently, these elect-oral forces may produce changes in the performance of party functions inside legislative chambers.

In contrast, the second approach emphasizes the role of incentives and powers inside the chamber as an explanation for party cohesion and action within legis-latures. We will refer to it as the 'one-arena' model. This argument sees a substan-tially weaker link between the legislative and electoral arenas than Mayhew, Ostrogorskii, and others. Indeed, at an extreme this approach may almost seem to decouple the legislative arena from the electoral arena.

The one-arena approach was a response to formal models of the legislative process which painted a picture of legislatures as comprising entrepreneurial indi-viduals bleached of parties. This new approach, largely due to Gary Cox (Cox 1987; Cox and McCubbins 1993), attempts to 'bring the party back in' to expla-nations of legislative behaviour through a concern for policy. Many of the early formal theories of legislatures were 'policy blind;' legislators were concerned with being elected to the almost complete exclusion of other motivations. While a concern for re election lends itself quite naturally to the 'two-arenas' approach, it also struck some scholars as too simplistic. More recent theories thus allow politicians and parties to have substantive policy interests and preferences (e.g. Laver and Schofield 1990). It is this concern for policy which generates a theory in which parties are seen responding not to the electoral arena, but to incentives within the legislative arena itself.

The incentives that matter under the one-arena argument are those that govern access to policy-making. The simple perks of legislative office—office space, subsidies, secretarial help, and so forth—might be quite nice, but the major resources are procedural advantages which help legislators shape the agenda and the policy outcomes of a legislature. Under this one-arena model, being part of a legislative bloc will give members of that bloc better access to policy-making. Political parties also solve the potential collective action problem within legislatures, by providing an institutional structure to establish policy and ensure compliance of individual legislators (Cox and McCubbins 1993). This implies that paties have a functional value not just from the point of view of the system but also from the point of view of individual members. Parties therefore help further the self-interest of those legislators.

An important implication of this argument, and a point of contrast with the previous model, is that no matter what changes occur in the electoral arena, we should see little if any change in the role of parties inside the chamber. Because incentives to form and maintain cohesive legislative parties are present within the chamber and not the electorate, this insulates parties as organizations within the legislature from changes at the level of the electorate and parties' electoral activities.

As we will argue below neither view on its own offers a complete explanation for the presence of parties inside chambers. However, this discussion suggest a (deceptively) straightforward line of empirical attack. In deciding between the two approaches to explaining party behaviour within legislatures: if we can find some suitable measure of partyness inside a legislature (e.g. roll call voting), then we can simply correlate this with an equivalent measure of parties in the electoral arena (e.g. party organizational structures or declines in party identification). In this way we might be able to see if parties inside the chamber change as partyness declines within the electoral arena.

There are, however, two reasons why this is a difficult line to pursue. First, there is no comprehensive cross-national source of roll call data. Second, and more important, the one-arena model would cast doubt on the value of parcelling out effects due to changes in the electorate as opposed to those due to changes inside the legislature itself. In the 'one-arena' model, roll calls are endogenous to situations inside the chamber, correlations with events outside that chamber may well be spurious. As Sinclair puts it, party leaders can 'sometimes structure the choices members confront so that members in voting their preferences vote in a way that is consistent with the party position' (Sinclair 1998: 6). An especially important means of enforcing loyalty through procedural devices is that of the no

confidence vote (Huber 1996). At the other extreme, 'free votes' take place where
party whips do not even try to impose party discipline in the name of retaining
paty on other roll calls.

The picture muddies even further when we consider the reasons for defection
from the party line. As Rose points out, dissent has often been made 'in the name
of greater partisanship and not in rejection of partisanship.' Hence some deviations from a roll call need not imply a weakening of party *per se* (Rose 1983:
291; see also Crowley 1996: 222). Roll call data, then, make for uncertain inferences about the link between legislative parties and changes in the electorate.

For these reasons, we approach the question of parties within legislatures from
the point of view of the literature that stresses events inside the chamber. Cox's
(1987) own work on the nineteenth-century British parliament to one side, work
on within this literature has mostly been confined to studies of the US Congress.
We need to find evidence that will confirm or disconfirm our two main points.

> *First*, that parties have procedural advantages over individual legislators when
> it comes to access to policy-making inside legislatures. In this way we can
> show that at least some functionality of party exists from the point of view of
> individual legislators.
>
> *Second*, we should see some cohesive party behaviour exist inside a legislative
> chamber even when the electoral connection is extremely weak.

To the extent that I can demonstrate both these points then it can be argued that
the likely impact of changes at the electoral level will be quite limited.

PROCEDURAL ADVANTAGES TO PARTIES WITHIN LEGISLATURES

To explore the one-arena model and the impact of legislative context on legislative behaviour, we begin by examining the possible procedural and policy advantages that political parties may use to generate party agreement and party action.[1]
In other words, we ask whether legislatures create rules or institutional structures
that are designed to strengthen party cohesion in the legislature.

One such advantage is whether officially recognized party groups receive special
privileges and resources within the chamber (a *Fraktion* status). A minimum size

---

[1] The *ad hoc* nature of the list is more or less a product of the state of the literature to date.
There does not seem to be a well-known, theoretically derived, lexicographically ordered set of
procedural advantages. On the basis of the topics of interest of stludies of legislatures, we do
seem to know that committees are important, that who sets the agenda is important and that a
number of other features—how to change the rules of procedures and who constitutes a legit-
imate actor (parties or individuals) are probably important. However, it is far from clear which
features is more important than the other. While the following section thus has something of of
an *ad hoc* air, the procedures listed in the following tables are ones identified in legislative studies as relevant ones.

requirement for Fraktionen provides a further hurdle to individual freedom of action. In addition, in some legislatures Fraktion status is a prerequisite to chairing committees, serving on administrative bodies, and even gaining staff and other legislative resources.

Another important feature is the committee structure of the legislature. Committees are important venues for shaping legislation. This is especially the case for mainland Europe (and the United States) where enormous scope may be delegated to committees. An extreme example is the case of Italian committees which may adopt *leggine* (little laws) without further legislative review. Many other European states have powerful committee structures (Strøm 1990*b*). Committees are especially important where legislation, and detailed examination of it, originates in committees and is then submitted to the floor in terms of a Report rather than a bill being initiated in the larger body (or by a government agency) and then referred to committee. The latter procedure seems limited to Anglo-Irish experience and, possibly, Denmark (Campion and Lidderdale 1953: 21). Committees under the Report system, however, are much more central players since many of the detailed objections have already been dealt with. 'Amendments proposed to a bill' under such a system, 'are as far as possible considered and disposed of by the committee to which the bill is referred' (Campion and Lidderdale 1953: 11). This suggests more limited scope of amendment from the floor in the non-Anglo system and, hence, even greater importance attached to being a committee member.

An important series of procedures benefiting parties, then, involves how legislators are appointed to or removed from committees. It is theoretically possible for legislatures to use non-party-based allocation of committee positions. For example, the legislature could be divided into sections by lot, and sections then examine legislation pending before the chamber. This procedure is employed in the Belgian legislature and in the past in the Netherlands; it clearly takes influence over committee assignment away from parties even as it assures proportional representation of party strengths. If representation on committees is made according to party group, then this is consistent with the argument that party group membership confers advantageous access to policy-making.

A similar argument applies to being removed from committees. Once appointed, committee members could begin to exercise their judgement independent of party counsel. Having a procedure by which parties can remove and/or reassign individual committee members would give parties an important stick as a companion to the carrot of appointment. By the same token, making party the basis of access to the governing body of the legislature grants the party some influence over the agenda of the legislature as a whole. A point we return to in greater detail below.

Table 8.1 displays some evidence that demonstrates that parties—as actors—are given procedural advantages inside legislatures. Across these different systems, that first column of the table shows that in ten of the seventeen countries

TABLE 8.1 Formal Position of Parties in Democratic Legislatures

	Committee appointments on party group basis?	Committee members may be removed	Unattached members same rights as party groups?	Rules on Fraktion C=constitution R=Rules of legislature; S=statute	Minimum size for party grop y=yes n=no or 1 (one)	Minimum size as % of chamber (number)
Australia	yes	yes	yes	no	yes	(5)
Austria	yes	yes	no	R	yes	2.7 (5)
Belgium	no	yes	yes	R	yes	3.7 (8)
Canada	yes	yes	no	(12)	no	
Denmark	yes	yes	yes	R	no	
Finland	yes	no	yes	no	yes	5 (30)
France	yes	yes	no	R	yes	5
Germany	–	yes	no?	R	yes	5
Iceland	yes	no	?	no	yes	
Ireland	yes	no	s	S	yes	4 (7)
Italy	yes	no	s	C R	yes	3.1 20
Japan	yes	yes		no	yes	
Luxembourg	yes	yes	no	R	yes	7.8 (5)
Netherlands	–	yes	yes	R	no	
New Zealand	yes	?	yes	no		
Norway	yes	no	no	C		
Sweden	no	no	no		no	
UK	yes	no	yes	no		

Source: Interparliamentary Union: Doring 1995.

listed, the legislature has some rule-based recognition of party groups or Fraktionen within the chamber. Only three nations have no minimum size requirement for the formation of a party group. Half the countries in this sample have a minimum size requirement for Fraktion status within the chamber. For the remainder, party groups need between 4 and 5 per cent of seats within the legislature to gain Fraktion recognition. Other rules indicate the advantage position of parties even in gaining status. While parties can gain the resources (money, office space, and so forth) consequent on being called a Fraktion with as few as two seats, independent members need twenty-five seats.[2] Eight nations go so far as to explicitly state that the rights of unattached members will not be the same as those who belong to party groups.

While noteworthy, the material rewards of office space, secretarial help, and the like that come with Fraktion status matter less than access to policy-making. As we noted above, the importance of party groups as organizations which shape the incentives of individual legislators lies not so much in the way they allocate material rewards and incentives to groups but in the way in which they allocate procedural and policy-making resources to parties and the way the Rules of Procedure or Standing Orders actively discriminate against individuals.

The structure of committee is thus a useful measure in judging the importance of parties for the policy-making process. In thirteen nations committee appointments are made on the basis of party allocations (column 1 of Table 8.1). In addition, the next column in the table shows that committee members may be removed from a committee by their respective party in eight of the seventeen nations. Party groups have either the carrot of appointment or the stick of removal (or both) in all but two nations.

Restraints on Individual Legislators

The ultimate question is whether there is more direct evidence of procedural advantages that parties possess in the explicit process of policy-making. If the main assumption is that access to policy-making is the key resource at stake, then if parties have meaningful procedural advantages we should expect to see a series of procedures that restrict individuals and privilege parties when it comes to proposing bills and making legislation

The most stringent kind of limit would be to insist that amendments or proposals can only come from recognized political parties or only come from committees (to which parties control access). Seemingly, no legislature imposes restrictions this strict, although some can require a minimum number of legislators to sign a motion before it is moved (e.g. Luxembourg). This does not mean

---

[2] At the very least the rules deal with the 'unattached' or 'mixed' as a group in and of themselves.

TABLE 8.2 *The Weakness of Individual Legislators in Democratic Legislatures*

	Money bills a gov't prerogative yes=yes	Numerical restrictions on private members' bills	Time restrictions on private members' bills	Technical restrictions on private members' bills	Content restrictions on private	Committee veto	Changing the Rules of Procedure
Australia	y	n?	y?	n?	y?	n?	simple majority of those voting
Austria	n	y	n	n	y	y	2/3 vote
Belgium	n	y	n	y	n	y	simple majority of those voting
Canada	y	n?	y?	n?	y?	n?	unanimity to suspend
Denmark	n	n	n	y	n	y	3/4 of those voting
Finland	n	n	y	y	n	y	simple majority of those voting
France	y	n	y	y	y	n	simple majority of those voting
Germany	n	y	n	y	n	n	absolute majority
Iceland	n	n	n	y	n	n	n/a
Ireland	y	n	y	y	y	y	simple majority of those voting
Italy	n	y	y	n	y	y	absolute majority
Luxembourg	n	n	n	n	n	y	absolute majority
Netherlands	n	n	y?	y	y	y	simple majority of those voting
New Zealand	y?	n?	y?	n?	y?	n?	simple majority of those voting
Norway	n	n	n	n	n	n	simple majority of those voting
Sweden	n	n	y	n	n	n	simple majority of those voting
UK	y	n	y	n	y	n	simple majority of those voting

Source: Interparliamentary Union: Doring 1995..

that legislative Rules of Procedure are unimaginative in their use of restrictions. It is possible, for example, to restrict the subject of private members bills by not allowing them to deal with financial matters or, a little less restrictively, require that proposed increases in expenditures proposed by a private members bill be matched by other cuts in expenditure. Other possible restrictions include imposing time limits allowed for consideration of private members' legislation or simply limiting the number they may propose. Other, more technical restrictions can be put in place or committees may essentially be allowed to veto private members legislation.

Table 8.2 reports on this series of restrictions which govern the capacity of individual legislators to propose and make legislation. We find that thirteen of the seventeen nations have two or more of the following restrictions: (1) restrictions on financial legislation, (2) required number of legislators to propose a bill, (3) time, (4) technical, (5) content, or (6) committees. The Norwegian Storting is unique because it lacks any restrictions of this kind on individual legislation, and four more countries having only one restriction. Furthermore, as noted in the last column of the table, changing these restrictions requires at least a simple majority, and in seven cases a super-majority—thus giving the parties policy position a privileged status. Individual legislators who are frustrated by this situation need to find and organize up to several hundred like-minded allies in order to change the rules.

Agenda Control

The general thrust of these limitations on individual legislators can be seen in how the agenda of each legislature is controlled and by whom. We have two ways of illustrating this. The first measure is Herbert Doring's (1995: 225) index of agenda control. Doring's seven-category index is based on descriptive details provided by country experts to Doring. All such indices involve the same kinds of problems in making judgements. And such problems are likely to be felt most strongly in the mid-points of the scale where one might like the scale's distinctions to be clearest. Even with these problems in mind, however, Doring's categorization represents an intuitively plausible and appealing way of thinking about the various ways in which government may—or may not—control the agenda.

Doring's index

I   Government alone determines the plenary agenda

II   In a President's conference [presiding body of the chamber] the govern ment commands a majority larger than its share of the seats in the chamber

III Decision by majority rule at President's conference where party groups are represented proportionally

IV   Consensual agreement of party groups sought in President's conference can be challenged by the chamber)

V   President's decision after consultation of party groups (cannot be challenged by the chamber)

VI   Fragmentation of agenda-setting centres if unanimous vote of party leaders cannot be reached

VII   The chamber itself determines the agenda

The index moves from government solely setting the agenda (I) to sole control by the legislative chamber (VII). This last category presumably would allow the most freedom for individual legislators to influence outcomes. Out of the fifteen countries covered by Doring, legislators in only one country, the Netherlands, had such freedom (Table 8.3). Given that Australian, Canadian, and New Zealand practice accords with that of Britain and Ireland in these matters it is safe to assume that none of these nations would accompany the Netherlands on this scale.

At one end of the scale we see complete domination of he agenda by government, which is typical of the majoritarian states the UK, France, and Ireland.[3] But even proportional parliamentary governments can have substantial influence over the agenda. In Belgium, for example it is, or at least was, possible for the government to move a *motion d'ordre* if it is unhappy with the agenda (Campion and Lidderdale 1953). Remaining states were less majoritarian, but still showed an important role for party, rather than the chamber as a whole. Even under Doring's category VI parties are given veto power; under his category V parties are given control of the agenda that cannot be undone while under IV (the modal category) parties are given power to make the agenda although the floor can alter this proposal.

A second way of looking at agenda control, and one that differs from Doring in approach but not, as we see, in result, is by examining how parties control the presiding body of the legislature. The second column in the table shows that parties are formally represented in the presiding body of the legislature in six of the eighteen nations. Where the presiding body is a single individual—such as a President or Speaker, parties per se have a limited role, typically in electing that person. But where the presiding body is a collective Praesidum, Bureau, or council, party representation becomes much more formal. The Inter-Parliamentary Union categorizes whether the presiding body sets the agenda (see Table 8.3). Even with this different methodology, we arrrive at conclusions that are broadly similar to Doring's. Some legislatures have an individual, rather than a collective governing body (e.g. the Speakership system as distinct from the bureau system). Formal power to set the agendas is vested in either the government or the parties, or often both together.

---

[3] We might also add in Australia, Canada, and New Zealand. Even though these nations were not covered by Doring their close correspondence to the Westminster model does suggest they should be categorized as I in this index.

TABLE 8.3 *Agenda Setting Control of the Parties*

	IPU I Party groups included in presiding body (Bureau)	IPU II Presiding body sets agenda for chamber y=yes n=no	Party or Gov't Central (Based on IPU I and IPU II) P=party G=gov't	Dorling Index
Australia		n	G	(I)
Austria	yes	y	P	IV
Belgium	no	n		IV
Canada		n	G	(I)
Denmark	yes	y	P	V
Finland	no	y	P	V
France	yes	y	P,G	II
Germany	yes	y	P,G	IV
Iceland		y		V
Ireland	no	n	G	I
Italy	no	n		VI
Japan	yes	y	(I)	
Luxembourg	yes	y	P	III
Netherlands	no	n		VII
New Zealand	no	n	G	(I)
Norway	yes	y	P	IV
Sweden	no	n		V
UK	no	n	G	I

Source: Interparlimentarly Union: Doring1995.

Executive Control

An even greater source of legislative power is the ability to remove a government from office. The information in Table 8.4 shows that the removal of a government from office is a collective act that requires legislators to act as a team. In the case of ministerial responsibility, formal procedures are in place which insist on collective, and not just individual, responsibility. This is important in that, in principle, legislatures can—and do—hold individual ministers responsible for their actions, but the requirement of collective responsibility helps to enforce that governments, if they fall, fall as a group. Of course, governments may not just fall but may be pushed by votes of no confidence. Table 8.4 also displays the requirements across nations for a vote of no confidence to be successful. Again we see that the basis for action is collective action.

In terms of the overall concern of this volume, this discussion of procedures inside democratic legislatures shows that even while changes are occurring at the

TABLE 8.4 *The Dominance of Collective Government in Democratic Legislatures*

	Responsibility of ministers c=collective i=individual	Formal basis of ministerial responsibility C=constitution S=statute	Vote of confidence: Prerequisites for invoking procedures	Voting rule
Australia	both	convention	consultation in party room	simple majority of those voting
Austria	both	C art. 76	n/a	n/a
Belgium	both	C art. 88, 101	none	PM's motion carries unless a majority vote no
Canada	both	convention	none	simple majority of those voting
Denmark	both	C art. 13	none	simple majority of those voting
Finland	c	C art. 36	Cabinet approval necessary	simple majority of those voting
France	c	C art. 49,50	Consultation with Cabinet	PM's motion carries unless a majority vote no
Germany	both		none	Chancellor's motion carries unless a majority vote no
Greece	both	C art. 84,85	n/a	n/a
Iceland	i	C art. 14	n/a	n/a
Ireland	c	C art. 28	none	simple majority of those voting
Italy	c	C art. 94	Cabinet approval necessary	simple majority of those voting
Luxembourg	both	C art. 78,80	Cabinet approval necessary	simple majority of those voting
Netherlands	both	convention	Cabinet approval necessary	simple majority of those voting
New Zealand	c	convention	none	simple majority of those voting
Norway	both	convention	none	simple majority of those voting
Sweden	both	C chapter 12, Ch 1 art 6; ch 6 art5	Cabinet approval necessary	simple majority of those voting
UK	both	convention	none	simple majority of those voting

Source: Interparliamentary Union; Huber 1996; Doring 1995.

level of the electorate, there are strong incentives within the legislature which keep parties as central actors. Party groups are important gatekeepers in the production of policy, and those chambers are typically set up to respond as party groups to the initiatives of the government. To some, especially Europeans, eyes, this might seem a fairly long winded way of establishing what we already know: government in most parliamentary democracies is large party government. Except that now we have advanced evidence to show that there are normally formal rules and procedures which help to make this mechanism of party government a reality.

Studying Legislative Behaviour

One consequence of these restrictions is that the legislative agenda of a parliaments is the governments' agenda. Table 8.5 displays descriptive data by country on the introduction and passage of legislation divided into two categories—government bills and private members' bills between the 1970s and 1980s. The figures are further broken down by the portion of legislation introduced as private members' bills and that introduced by the government. There is considerable variation in these figures across these countries. For some countries, the number of private members' bills introduced has increased markedly over the post-war period. In Sweden, for example, in 1960 there were 944 private members' bills, by 1994–5 2,969 were proposed (Kurian 1998: 642). The brief snapshot presented in Table 8.5, then, provides only a partial picture of changes in legislative patterns over the post-war period. But, on average and over the, admittedly brief period covered by this table these figures are very stable. The simple correlation between the percentage of private members' bills in the 1970s and the percentage in the 1980s is 0.85, a correlation which indicates a strong stability in these patterns overall.

But the real consequence of these figures lies in the columns which show how much legislation actually passes. And the pattern here is quite clear-cut: legislators can propose as much legislation as they like, but the legislation which passes is government legislation. Of the bills introduced government bills have a far higher success rate. On average over 80 per cent of the governments' legislation passes, while again on average, 15 per cent of private members' legislation passes. Even where numbers of private members' bills introduced are very large, the bills which pass are government bills. An extreme case here might be the Republic of Ireland where, since 1937, only ten laws which been introduced have been made by private members' legislation since 1937 (Kurian 1998: 368). And even in Sweden it is still the case that 'most bills passed by the Riksdag are government bills' (Kurian 1998: 643) and in Belgium in the 1990s, where, for example, roughly nine in ten bills originate as private members' bills only one in ten are approved (Kurian 1998: 63).

It is also worth noting that the term 'private member's bill' may imply a greater role for individual legislators than might actually be the case. These figures may therefore understate the dominance of governing parties. In some legislatures, for example, only groups of legislators—and not individuals—may propose legislation. In other cases, the term 'private member's bill' may lump together those proposed by parties—most notably opposition parties—and by party groups on committees as well as individual legislators or groups of legislators. In Germany, for example, over the period 1949–4 34 per cent of all bills were non-government bills. However, only 18 per cent of enacted legislation comprised non-government bills. More importantly still, many of these bills were introduced by at least one of the government parties. Between 1990 and 1994 of

TABLE 8.5 *Legislative Agenda of Parliaments*

	Government and private bills introduced and passed (five-year averages)							
	1971–5 % of bills introduced gov't	1981–5 % of bills introduced gov't	1971–5 % of gov't bills passed	1981–5 % of gov't bills passed	1971–5 % of bills introduced by PMS	1981–5 % of bills introduced by PMS	1971–5 % of private bills passed	1981–5 % of private bills passed
Australia	97.6	95.7	90.6	89.5	2.4	4.3	0.0	4.3
Austria	77.5	62.7	86.7	95.9	21.6	33.9	58.7	50.0
Belgium	34.8	22.8	96.8	n/a	65.2	77.2	4.5	7.1
Canada	23.0	20.9	71.0	59.9	77.0	79.1	4.3	2.1
Denmark	87.6	65.8	89.4	88.5	12.4	34.2	3.6	5.6
Finland	7.2	51.6	93.6	97.8	92.8	47.4	1.4	1.2
France	10.6	42.8	71.3	82.2	89.4	57.2	3.3	5.9
Germany	66.0	63.5	69.2	98.8	25.9	22.3	33.3	57.6
Ireland	97.1	91.3	9.1	90.0	1.8	8.7	0.0	10.0
Italy		29.0		51.3		69.7		9.2
Japan	67.4	64	80.0	76	25.4	36	40.8	24
Netherlands	98.2	98.5	99.6	84.7	1.8	1.5	20.0	16.0
New Zealand	82.4	94.2	84.6	97.6	4.9	5.8	0.0	2.0
Norway		90.1		98.9		9.9		12.2
Sweden	9.9	7.7		most	90.1	92.3		1.0
Switzerland	87.9	87.9	93.1	most	12.1	12.1	50.0	9.1
United Kingdom	31.9	36.4	93.2	92.3	38.4	63.6	15.7	9.8
United States	0.0				100.0	100.0	3.6	1.1
Average	54.9	60.3	80.6	86.0	41.3	41.9	15.9	12.7
Average*	58.6	60.3	80.6	86.0	37.4	38.5	16.8	13.4

Notes: Average* indicates averages without US figures.

Source: Interparliamentary Union: Parliaments of the World, 1976, 1986.

the 99 successful non-government laws 97 were introduced by one of the parties in government (Kurian 1998: 273).

Even if the legislative agenda of parliaments is still the governments' legislative agenda it is conceivable that governments may have to rely on different coalitions in order to pass that agenda as party loyalty in the legislature weakens. Rather than being able to rely on solid backbench support, governments may find it necessary to piece together support from parties other than their own in order to offset defections. One way to examine this possibility is by looking at roll call data. As we noted above, roll call data are difficult both to collect and interpret (Saalfeld 1998: 795; and on the latter point see especially Rasch 1999: 134–6). Yet these data provide one way of looking to see if the grip of parties inside the legislature is weakening since decline in party unity would provide some basis for believing that party would somehow matter less.

TABLE 8.6 *Rice Cohesion Indices for France, Germany, Norway, and Switzerland*

(*a*) NORWAY

Main Parties, Election Results (Seats), and Rice Index of Cohesion in Storting and Odelsting Voting, 1979–94.

Session	N Roll-Calls	SV	A	SP	KRF	H	FRP
ELECTION 1977		*(2)*	*(76)*	*(12)*	*(22)*	*(41)*	—
1979–80	285	98.9	98.2	96.9	93.4	96.8	—
1980–81	412	98.8	98.9	95.7	95.3	96.8	—
ELECTION 1981		*(4)*	*(66)*	*(11)*	*(15)*	*(53)*	*(4)*
1981–82	293	98.7	95.8	93.3	94.6	97.5	96.2
1982–83	502	97.2	98.1	97.1	97.0	99.0	98.0
1983–84	375	98.4	97.9	98.1	97.4	99.0	98.2
1984–85	456	98.3	98.7	96.5	98.0	98.9	97.4
ELECTION 1985		*(6)*	*(71)*	*(12)*	*(16)*	*(50)*	*(2)*
1985–86	449	98.0	98.3	98.9	98.0	98.3	98.2
1986–87	329	98.6	97.5	96.4	95.8	96.4	97.2
1987–88	549	98.7	98.3	96.8	94.4	97.3	98.6
1988–89	784	97.0	98.2	95.8	94.2	96.7	99.6
ELECTION 1989		*(17)*	*(63)*	*(11)*	*(14)*	*(37)*	*(22)*
1989–90	1315	98.3	98.9	99.2	98.7	98.4	98.6
1990–91	1711	98.1	98.8	98.6	98.0	98.1	98.4
1991–92	1459	98.0	98.4	97.2	98.1	98.0	98.1
1992–93	1296	96.8	95.9	95.9	95.7	95.9	95.2
ELECTION 1993		*(13)*	*(67)*	*(32)*	*(13)*	*(28)*	*(10)*
1993–94	1178	98.3	99.2	98.1	97.4	98.1	94.1[a]

[a] Including those four representatives leaving the Progress Party (FRP) in April and May of 1994 to serve as independents (they formed their own parliamentary group).

Source: Rausch (1999: 131).

(*b*) GERMANY

Number of Named Votes and Rice Indices of Party Cohesion by Party, 1949–90

Legislative period	# of named votes	Rice index of party cohesion		
		CDU–CSU	SPD	FDP
1949–53	133	86.3	99.7	84
1953–57	169	90	99.3	80.5
1957–61	46	93.6	99.7	95.1
1961–65	37	89.6	98.5	84.9
1965–69	24	89.6	93.1	97.4
1969–72	38	87.3	99.9	97.9
1972–76	51	98.8	98.3	98.9
1976–80	59	93.7	98.4	94.9
1980–83	26	99.2	99.3	95.9
1983–87	343	99.7	96.0	97.7
1987–90	216	98.9	95.7	95.6
1949–90	1142	94.3	97.8	91.4

Source: Saalfeld 1997:50.

(*c*) SWITZERLAND

Rice Index of Party Cohesion in the National Council, 1920–1994

	1920–53	1971–83	1983–7	1987–91	1991–4
Governmental parties					
Radicals	68.9	74.7	73.4	70.5	79.2
Social Democrats	95.4	91.3	89.1	92.9	96.3
Christian Democrats	75.5	63.0	60.1	70.4	68.3
People's Party	80.5	84.4	74.0	77.8	80.7
Non-governmental parties					
Green Party				92.1	94.9
Liberals		78.2	97.9	96.2	90.4
Independents/					
Protestant Party[a]		79.0	79.5	83.1	85.5
Swiss Democrats			69.0		85.5
Automobile Party	98.2				
(N)	(108)	(22)	(56)	(77)	(163)

[a] The Rice index for 1971–83 and 1987–94 is limited to the Independents (not including the Protestant Party).
Notes: No data available for 1953–67

Source: Lanfranchi and Luthi 1999: 109.

(*d*) FRANCE

Rice Indices by party 1946–1973

	Communist	Socialist	Radical Socialist	Centre Left	Christian Democrat	Independ- ents	Gaullists
1946–51	99.9	97.9	79.6	80.5	93.7	73.4	89.6
1951–56	99.9	98.7	79.3	83.9	89.4	84.4	84.7
1956–58	99.9	96.4	68.6	84	94.6	77	77
1958–62	99.8	97.6	63		73.5	60.9	84.2
1962–67	99.8	99.6	91.7		79.5	82.9	96.1
1967–68	99.7	99.8	99.8		89.2	94.7	96.5
1968–73	99.8	99.4	94.7		76.3	86.3	88.9

Source: Wilson and Wiste 1976.

While data on some countries—Australia, Austria, Belgium, Ireland, Italy, and Japan for example—are unavailable or uncollected, roughly comparable data on a handful of countries do exist. Table 8.6 displays the Rice index from four countries: France, Germany, Norway, and Switzerland.

In examining these data a number of patterns are apparent. First, that the rate of legislative activity is not constant either across countries or within the same

TABLE 8.7 *Breaks in Party Line Voting for Denmark and the UK*

(*a*) Denmark 1971–1986

Period	Dissent
1971–72	11.5
1972–73	25.5
1973–74	17.0
1974–75	9.7
1975–76	10.5
1976–77	11.9
1976–77 (2nd)	9.8
1977–78	16.6
1978–79	6.1
1979–80	8.7
1980–81	9.4
1981–82	4.3
1982–83	8.8
1983–84	3.8
1984–85	9.1
1985–86	6.3

Note: Dissent is defined as breaks in party line in final divisions adopting bills as a % of all bills.

Source: 1971–1979 Svensson 1982; 1979–1986 Damgaard and Svensson 1989.

(*b*) UK 1945–1992

Parliament	Dissent
1945–50	7.0
1950–51	2.5
1951–55	3.0
1955–59	2.0
1959–64	13.5
1964–66	0.5
1966–70	9.5
1970–74	20.0
1974	23.0
1974–79	28.0
1979–83	20.0
1983–87	22.0
1987–92	20.0

Note: Dissent is defined as number of divisions witnessing dissenting votes expressed as a % of all divisions.

Source: Norton (1996) Table 8.1.

country across time. In Germany, for example, the post-unification period and the post-war period saw heights of legislative activity while the intervening years were relatively slack. Second, that, just as rates of activity cycle up and down, so too do rates of party loyalty: these indices vary across country, party, and time. But the variation is within an extremely narrow range and, more to the point, shows no sign of any secular downward trend.

The evidence from these countries is backed by more anecdotal evidence from elsewhere. In the Netherlands, for example, Andeweg reports that party discipline 'has increased significantly' although, as he notes 'it is difficult to gauge actual party cohesion in parliamentary votes accurately as roll calls are rare and dissenters therefore are not registered' (Andeweg 1997: 118). A different measure of party loyalty is available for two nations—Denmark and the UK. In looking to see whether there are breaks in party ranks on bills, and if so how many, the Danish data (Table 8.7) show more or less the same pattern as roll data: some cycling up and down in dissent but no sign of any increased level of dissent. Indeed, the simple correlation between these breaks in party unity and time have a correlation of –0.66 (N=16) which means that, if anything, these data show a downward trend in dissent.

Overall, however, the roll call data that there are show little sign of decline in party loyalty—with the one exception of the UK. In light of the emphasis upon Britain as a model of parliamentary discipline, the only one of the parliamentary countries for which systematic data exist which shows a sustained increase in dissent is that of Britain from the 1970s onwards. By and large, however, these data show little evidence that parties within the legislature are falling apart or are even noticeably weaker as compared to any earlier period regardless of electoral trends.

THE CONNECTION BETWEEN LEGISLATURES AND THE ELECTORAL ARENA

One implication of an argument which stresses procedural advantages to parties inside the chamber is that we should find evidence of party activity even when the electoral link is weak. Here we can note an initial example that supports this view. Accounts of the British parliament at the turn of the seventeenth and eighteenth century—well over a century before the expansion of the franchise in the nineteenth century—show rival camps of Whigs and Tories devoting considerable effort to coordinating the actions of members (Holmes 1967). Meetings were held to discuss the political line to be taken and tactics to be followed and a 'whipping of sorts' was in place during 1702–14 along, regional lines, in which members were responsible for colleagues from the same region turning up and voting appropriately (Holmes 1967: 300). To be sure, access to money which enable members to fight elections did figure as a prominent part of these caucus operations; but so too did the inducements of office and of access to social circles, most

TABLE 8.8 *Political Groups' Transnationality and Fractionalization after the 1989 Elections and their Cohesion in the 1989–1994 European Parliament*

Groups	Seats	Party Delegations	IF	IA
PES	180	16	0.858	78.6
EPP	121	16	0.873	88.2
ELDR	49	20	0.917	85.7
EDG	34	2	0.111	92.2
V	29	12	0.837	87.5
EUL	28	4	0.360	92.3
EDA	22	4	0.566	64.5
ER	7	3	0.526	88.9
LU	14	5	0.673	93.8
RB	13	9	0.840	69.5

Notes: PES = Party of the European Socialists; EPP = European People's Party; ELDR = European Liberal, Democrat, and Reformist Party; V = The Greens; EUL = Group of the United European Left; EDA = European Democratic Alliance; ER = Technical Group of the European Right; LU = Left Unity; RB = Rainbow Group. The sizes of the groups underwent much variation during the 1989–94 legislative term. Two groups disappeared altogether, the EDG joining the EPP in May 1992, and the EUL joining the Socialists in January 1993.
Source: Raunio 1999: 198.

notably membership in clubs such as the 'Kit-Kat' club. None of this is to say that such legislative parties were exactly as their disciplined counterparts today.[4] But these caucuses are sufficiently ordered to be able to use Whig and Tory as meaningful terms. Thus, even in a very basic legislative setting in which electoral politics were relatively mute, and in which the legislature itself was still only modestly powerful in the face of monarchical power, we still see forms of party organization.

Further evidence comes from the contemporary European Parliament that shows evidence of party discipline being imposed, even when elections and the need to maintain a government is clearly lacking. The European Parliament is not a parliament in the sense that it maintains the executive, yet party groups within the chamber are quite unified as the evidence presented in Table 8.8 shows. This table shows that, by standard roll call measures, party groups inside the European Parliament cohere even when electoral incentives are weak to non-existent. Therefore incentives provided within the chamber must comprise a large part of any understanding of party group discipline. Given the absence of any meaningful electoral connection these roll call measures seem to represent the impact of incentives within the EP itself.

[4] Holmes, for example, notes that a basic difficulty was trying to get MPs simply to show up. Hence the caucses rarely tried to marshall their full strength (Holmes 1967: 322).

These two cases help to further buttress the point that there may only be limited linkage between changes at the level of 'party in the electorate' and 'party in government' hence there is likely only to be limited impact of changes in one arena upon changes in the other.

CONCLUSION

Forming and, just as important, maintaining governments is vital if legislators are to have access to policy-making in these systems. Again, having parties makes this whole process easier in parliamentary systems. Having a disciplined party bloc can mean that one party may control a majority of votes. From the point of view of the political system, parties are highly functional since the whole process of party government becomes easier if one party controls the government. Indeed, one can say that disciplined parties are a consequence of being in government since indiscipline runs the risk of toppling the government and losing access to policy-making. And the procedural evidence of Tables 8.1 to 8.5 is consistent with the argument that governments control legislatures, and also that parties help control government. This party control is achieved not just by putting in place procedures which weaken the scope for individual action while advantaging parties, it is also in the procedures which make government collective, make a falll collective, and, further, give parties a formal say in whether or not to join government. Government is, in this sense, made accountable to party and not just the legislature. This point to which we return in a moment, was seen to be part of the definition of party government in the APSA Report *Towards a More Responsible Two Party System* (APSA 1950: 7), There party responsibility was defined in part as 'the responsibility of party leaders to the party membership'. As we argue below, this kind of responsibility—and the procedures which help buttress it—may be key in understanding the operation of a party government in the European case, with the emphasis here upon the term 'party'.

All of this discussion has been a way of addressing the debate over the origins of disciplined parties as being either outside or inside legislatures. We showed that even in the presence of a very weak electoral connection we saw parties inside legislative chambers. And in those countries where there is evidence of weakening party attachments at the level of the electorate there seemed little evidence of similar trends inside the legislature. The available data do not show declining party unity scores nor do they show the declining success of government legislative agendas tracking electoral changes. Second we showed evidence that there exist a series of procedures which limit individual ability to shape legislation, privilege parties, and privilege governments even more so. Other procedures mean that the government must be of collective form and, further, that legislative parties have a role in saying who forms the government and whether it will fall. Thus, even while changes occur at the level of the electorate there are strong incentives within the chamber which keep parties as central actors.

But an important issue remains. There is nothing in this discussion so far to prevent turnover in party membership. The procedures show, quite straightforwardly, that acting on one's own—or even in small groups—holds little payoff for legislators. Whatever systemic-level functions parties may perform they are also highly functional from the point of individual legislators. But this does not mean to say that legislators will remain members of the same party over long periods of time. These procedures benefit those acting en bloc, not necessarily those who act as part of the same bloc over an extended period of time. Yet legislative parties do seem remarkably stable. To take but one example, between 1950 and 1996 Cowley listed six examples of 'crossing the floor' (from one party to another); and thirty-one examples of defections from one party to join another (Crowley 1996: 217). And this was in the one setting where we do find some evidence of declining party unity scores. Members of legislatures, or at least the UK parliament, thus seem remarkably loyal to one particular partly. At the very least—given the power of government—one might have expected individually maximizing self-interested legislators to jump from the Opposition party to the party of government in the interests of gaining at least some access to policy-making. After all, the Westminster model is the one least open to those not members of the government and opportunities to influence legislation in debate, committee, or through private members' bills are extremely rare. While theory might lead us to expextg to see such defections in actual practice we see very few.

In developing an understanding of why this should be so we distinguish between the kinds of blocs which are prediced by the theories of legislative scholars such as Cox and McCubbins and the kinds of legislative parties we actually see. Parties have a stability of membership that is not explained by the procedural advantage accruing to collective action alone. In order for stability of membership to be produced, and hence produce the kinds of legislative bloc we think of as parties, we need to develop some other arguments. And we pay particular attention to the power of nomination.

Political science has long known the importance of control over nomination (Schattschneider 1942). Above and beyond providing the resources required to fight elections (money, party label, and advice) political parties typically also control access to these resources by controlling the nomination of candidates. Depending upon how the nomination process is organized, parties have great potential to act as gatekeepers. Nomination procedures may help promote party discipline in various ways. One way is through the construction of relatively homogeneous ideological blocs. Another method is by putting in place procedures which can help limit defections by punishing defectors. We begin by first looking at the contribution nomination procedures can make to producing a bloc of broadly like-minded representatives.

The further apart the party blocs are, in ideological terms, then, it seems less likely that a given individual will gain more preferred policies by jumping ship, everything else being equal. Still, most blocs of legislators will occupy a span, and not just a point, in the policy space; and it seems reasonable to think that legislators at the extreme points on these spans will find it appealing to jump into another bloc. This runs the risk of party blocs being subject to unravelling even if they start from relatively far apart positions; especially in multi-party systems where the underlying policy space is probably multi-dimensional. In a one-dimensional policy space it seems plausible to suggest that any divisions between legislative blocs may be produced by an underlying ideological split which makes it hard for legislators to jump between parties (cf Hirschman 1970: 70). Poole and Rosenthal's (1997) work in the USA, for example, argues that consistent ideo-logical positions explain the bulk of roll call decisions. In multi-party systems, however, there are likely to be many more opportunities for legislators to find suitable partners and, hence, explanations of party discipline grounded in ideo-logical divisions are less satisfactory rivals. Like the whips' organization, then, ideological compatibility—except in its most extreme (degenerately homogen-eous) form—may help parties dominate, but it may not comprise a necessary condition for the party basis of legislative action.

Because of this it seems likely that the contribution of nomination procedures to producing a bloc of like-minded legislators which will, in turn, be sufficient to produce a voting bloc whose membership is stable over a long period of time (ie. a party) is quite limited. A potentially more satisfying answer can be found once we turn to look at who nominates. As Chapter 6 on parties as organizations noted, party Fraktionen typically have no say over their own nomination and ratification of candidates. In only four out of sixty-five listed parties do the party statutes formally grant the Fraktion the ability to nominate candidates. And in none of these cases are party Fraktionen given any power other than nomination: they cannot vote or veto nominations or decide between competing nominations. The procedural power to nominate and to be vetoed lies outside the party groups in the legislature. Typically, the most important powers of nomination and veto rest at the level of regional or national party organization. Part of this obviously reflects the mechanical requirements of putting together a list in those nations which use list PR. The consequence of this is that, so long as nominations are controlled by actors other than the backbench legislators themselves, then power-ful inducements exist to slow down or resist 'island hopping' within the chamber. There are two sides to this issue: the reluctance of an individual to jump into another party, and the reluctance of party members outside the legislature to receive such defectors warmly.

Since rewards to parties inside the chamber are typically allocated proportion-ately, additional members to a Fraktion may be welcome. If control of nomina-tion lay among the club of fellow legislators perhaps it might be possible for individual legislators to change parties quite frequently and accommodate each other out of 'clubbability'. Left to their own devices, then, party blocs inside a legislature may welcome defectors from other parties. However, in moving, defectors may threaten the electoral chances of existing party members, and especially those outside the chamber who help influence nomination. Moreover, any attempt of a current legislator to move from party to party would be to engage in a risky gamble, giving up an existing successful nomination by competing for a new nomination against existing partisans. Little wonder, then, that, at least for the British case, far more defections were seen to new parties rather than to existing ones: new parties will not have a series of rivals ready to repel defectors. Little wonder, too, that while self-nominated American legislators form more or less cohesive blocs they often seem like quite different creatures when compared to their European counterparts. Control over nomination can seriously restrict the ability of members of the legislature to engage in a constant dance of changing partnerships.

The power of nomination, and in particular the way in which power over nomination rests out of the hands of legislators, can be seen to provide an important brake on legislators jumping from one bloc to another and thereby helps to underwrite the stability of membership of legislative blocs. This suggests an amended version of the Ostrogorskii argument. Here we developed a reading of Ostrogorskii's argument which held that the cause of disciplined parties in the legislature lay in the election fighting machines. The party of the phrase 'party in government' was due to the party of 'parties in the electorate'. Here the argument has been amended to be that 'party in government' depends in part on 'parties as organizations.'

Changes in the level of the electorate will not diminish the incentives facing legislators to act collectively inside the chamber and so legislative blocs will retain their functionality from the point of view of individual legislators. What will keep legislative parties (as opposed to blocs) functional from that point of view is the presence of party organizations which control the nomination process.

9

Parties at the Core of Government

Kaare Strøm

POLITICAL parties are the most important organizations in modern politics, and only a small percentage of states do without them. Students of political parties have commonly associated them with democracy itself. David Robertson, for example, observes that 'to talk, today, about democracy, is to talk about a system of competitive political parties. Unless one chooses to reject the representative model that has been the staple of the theory and practice of democracy since the French Revolution, one must come to terms with political parties' (Robertson 1976: 1). Much the same point is made by G. Bingham Powell: 'the competitive electoral context, with several political parties organizing the alternatives that face the voters, is the identifying property of the contemporary democratic process' (Powell 1982: 3). Thus, representative democracy has long been associated with, or even equated with, party government.

The vast scholarly literature on political parties reflects their real-life importance and has developed along with them. The twentieth century has been the century of political parties. At least, that was clearly the trend well beyond the first half of the century. The early days of the twentieth century saw the breakthrough of political parties as the democratic organization par excellence. Parties attained this position both because they were unrivalled in their functions of 'linkage' (Lawson 1980; Lawson and Merkl 1988), 'expression', or 'channelment' (Sartori 1976) and, in particular, because they were the vehicles of previously unenfranchised groups such as workers and peasants. Since the late 1960s, however, doubts have grown concerning the power, functions, and even necessity of political parties, as previous chapters in this volume have pointed out.

Political parties have many facets. They originated as more or less formally organized groups of public office-holders, and this in all likelihood is the arena in which their influence has persisted most comfortably. And although parties have roots in society, they are shaped by the political institutions in which they operate.

I am grateful to the editors for helpful comments, to Arend Lijphart for graciously sharing his data, and to Miki Caul, Priscilla Lambert, Lorelei Moosbrugger, and Scott Kastner for valuable research assistance.

As governments have grown and become differentiated, so have by necessity political parties. If political parties at the turn of the century remain the most important vehicles of mass democracy, then their position should surely be most secure at the level of the central government. And to the extent that parties have lost some of their traditional functions, that loss should be least tangible at the governmental level.

This chapter examines the current status of political parties at the core of government in advanced industrial democracies. Historically, this was the origin of the first modern political parties. The two government branches in which parties originated, and which they have in the twentieth century largely controlled, are the legislature and the executive. Shaun Bowler examines parties in the legislature in Chapter 8. This chapter focuses more, though not exclusively, on the executive branch. We recognize, however, that in the parliamentary regimes these are interdependent branches, which cannot well be understood in mutual isolation. In a limited sense, this interdependence implies that the chief executive (prime minister and cabinet) is accountable to, and can be removed by, the parliamentary majority (Strøm 2000). In a broader sense, it has meant control of both branches by a common party or coalition of parties, which have in fact become the main arena in which government policy is formulated and aggregated.

Studies of executive branch parties typically focus on the core executive, i.e. the cabinet or similar group of politically appointed top decision-makers, as this is clearly the most partisan executive arena. While this will certainly be a central theme in this chapter as well, I shall also examine the position of political parties in less obvious reaches of the government, such as central banks.

WHY POLITICAL PARTIES?

This volume has been organized around V. O. Key's (1964) framework for the analysis of political parties, in which he identified three party levels: (1) the party as a collection of voters, members, and activists (party in the electorate); (2) the party as an extra-parliamentary organization designed in large part to contest elections (party organization); and (3) the party as an organization of public officials (party in government). My concern in this chapter is with the third of these aspects of political parties: the party in government. In order to understand the changing forms and functions of parties in government, I believe that it is useful to ask what purposes they serve in the first place. The fundamental assumption that underlie my analysis of political parties is that parties form and survive when some decisive set of political actors find them useful for their own purposes. Parties were formed because parliamentarians and activists found them useful for whatever tasks they wanted to accomplish. They will decline if they no longer serve these purposes efficiently. It is not sufficient that parties perform some political function if the benefits of this function are not worth the costs to those who sustain the party (Müller 2000; also see Chapters 1 and 11 in this volume).

Political parties are collaborative devices for mutual gain. Thus, I presume that parliamentarians, candidates, activists, and voters create and sustain political parties because each expects to benefit. Political exchange, of course, is not necessarily monetized, which is to say that many different goods can in effect be bartered through the 'contracts' that sustain political parties. Another way in which party politics differs from market exchange is that much of it involves delegation of authority and hierarchical arrangements based on division of labour and specialization, as in all markets, but also on command and authority, as in politics generally.

The Primacy of Parties in Government

Of course, the three facets of parties are mutually interdependent, but in what ways? Can legislative parties prosper irrespective of the fate of parties among the voters, or vice versa? This is ultimately an empirical question, but it appears that we can establish some functional hierarchies among these forms.

In a previous publication with Lars Svåsand, I argued that parties in government are in many ways the critical link, the *sine qua non*, of modern political parties (Strøm and Svåsand 1997). Michael Thies takes much the same position in Chapter 11 of this book. Historically, parties were parties in government before they were anything else, and even today it is difficult to see how extra-parliamentary or electoral parties could prosper in the absence of legislative organization. This hierarchical dependence can most easily be seen for the electoral party. Voters can only rely on the party labels, or in other words delegate policy aggregation to party leaders, if the party possesses some leadership capable of enforcing policy agreement in government. If legislative politics is anarchic, then party labels can be of no use to the voters. Legislative parties are not equally dependent on the existence of electoral parties. True, Gary Cox and Mathew McCubbins (1993) argue that re-election-seeking legislators create cohesive legislative parties in order to benefit from a party record among the voters. But many of the gains that legislators can reap from party organization do not depend on the voters' use of party labels. John Aldrich (1995) identifies three sets of political conditions that may generate incentives for party formation: collective action problems, social choice problems, and political ambition. Legislative parties may help representatives solve many dilemmas of the first two types (collective action and social choice problems within the legislative arena) even if regular citizens are not guided by partisanship in their voting behaviour. In brief, electoral parties more critically depend on parties in government than the other way around.

The relationship between legislative and extra-parliamentary parties is somewhat less hierarchical. Strong legislative parties may not be strictly necessary for extra-parliamentary parties. Members who have little in common in the legislature may still find it advantageous to rely on a common party label for their campaign efforts, as did US Democrats in the 1960s. However, a cohesive and disciplined legislative party may very well fail to develop an extensive and effective extra-parliamentary organization.

Finally, the relationship between the strength of extra-parliamentary and electoral parties is least determinate. Strong extra-parliamentary parties may well coexist with weak electoral parties, as increasingly seems to be the case in many Northern European countries. Conversely, weak extra-parliamentary parties are at least conceivable in systems with strong electoral parties (i.e. strong partisan attachments among the voters). Impressionistically, this pattern seems more prevalent in Southern Europe.

In sum, the viability of political parties hinges most critically on the strength of the party in government. A strong party in government can coexist with either strong or weak extra-parliamentary and electoral parties, whereas effective organization outside parliament or among the voters is much less likely if the party in government is weak. Disintegration of the party in government would therefore be a particularly critical form of party decline.

PARTY GOVERNMENT AND ITS ALTERNATIVES

Party government implies that parties control the recruitment (election and appointment) of government personnel, as well as policy-making within government. As Thies points out in this volume, for party government to be efficient, parties must be the only, or the preferred, way in which legislators realize their main political goals: re-election, political power, and policy objectives. Accordingly, the central functions of parties in government are (1) to control policy-making, (2) to control policy implementation and administration, and (3) to take public responsibility for policy outcomes. The ideal type of party government is one in which a single, cohesive party gains control of the policy-making apparatus through elections and formulates policy that is then faithfully executed. Needless to say, such a polity does not exist. Yet, the ideal type can help us specify dimensions along which the 'partyness' of government may vary. It may also aid us in identifying alternatives to party government.

Like other political institutions, political parties are as attractive as the alternatives permit. Regardless of how well parties serve their purposes, they are unlikely to survive if a better alternative emerges. Conversely, even ineffective parties may linger on if the only alternative is an even less attractive form of political organization. It is therefore impossible to make informed judgements about the viability of political parties without knowing the competition they face.

What, then, are the main alternatives to party government? Richard Katz (1987b) identifies three such alternatives: (1) neocorporatism, in which major policy decisions are made by means of negotiations between directly affected, mainly economic interests; (2) pluralist democracy, in which elected representatives are

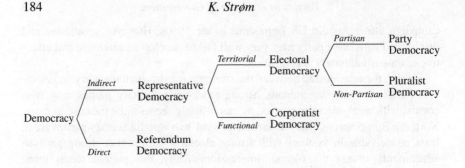

FIG. 9.1. Party Democracy and its Alternatives

directly accountable to their constituencies but little constrained by parties; and (3) referendum democracy, in which the decisions of elected representatives are at all times subject to the direct check of the popular majority.

While these alternative regime forms may seem diverse, it is possible to order them in a hierarchical manner, as illustrated in Figure 9.1. For simplicity, I have confined the schema to various forms of democratic governance, even though parties and corporatist decision-making are clearly compatible with autocratic rule as well. Among democratic regimes, the most fundamental distinction is between direct and representative forms of government. Party government is, of course, a subtype of representative government, whereas referendum democracy is the main alternative under direct governance. Representative government can in turn be sorted according to the use of functional or electoral (territorial-numerical) criteria of representation (Rokkan 1966*b*). Within the rubric of functional representation, corporatism is the most important ideal and real-world model. Finally, electoral forms of representative government can be subdivided according to the role political parties play in structuring the policy process. Hence, the distinction between party government, in which parties play a major coordinating role, and pluralist democracy, in which parties are weaker and each representative more autonomous.

Figure 9.1 illustrates this hierarchy of representation regimes. It also suggests that among the alternatives to party government, pluralist democracy represents the least serious departure, whereas referendum democracy is the most divergent regime form. We might therefore expect shifts between the former two categories to be easier and more frequent than between party and referendum government. The trends and factors that promote one alternative are likely to differ in kind and magnitude from those that foster another. Again, compared to the other two regime alternatives, the structural changes necessary to shift democratic polities from party to pluralist government could probably be relatively more minor.

Challenges to Party Government

Challenges to party government may occur for a number of different reasons and take various forms. Recall that political parties are arrangements that rest, at a minimum, on the cooperation and mutual benefit of legislators, other officials, and the voters. For mass membership parties, we may add the employees and activists of the extra-parliamentary party organization as well. Since parties are also, at least in part, rent-seeking organizations, they have created a variety of institutions which facilitate their success and survival, and from which their members benefit. The sources of party decline, then, may rest in developments that reduce demand for the services that party leaders can provide. As demand for these services declines, we may see erosions in the support of the voters, the cohesion of the legislators, or the continued control of the institutions.

Technological development may undermine the value of the party as a legislative or executive organization. As communication and access to information are revolutionized, individual legislators may free themselves from reliance on party leaders for these purposes. As evidenced in the United States, individual legislators may become proficient at raising funds, communicating with constituents, gaining access to the media, and securing information without the help of their party leaders. As such developments occur, the cohesiveness and discipline of parties in government are likely to decline.

Parties in government are also affected by institutional developments. While many such changes are country specific, there have been major institutional developments across advanced Western democracies that have significantly affected political parties. One particularly important trend is public financing of political parties, their legislative activities, and their campaigns. Public party finance has made their financial basis more secure but at the same time attenuated one purpose of mass membership parties and coordinated fund-raising. Another such trend is the devolution in many countries of authority to sub-national, often regional, levels of government. At the same time, the growing importance of supra-national representative bodies such as the European Parliament has stimulated the formation of embryonic cross-national party families with some coordination and cohesiveness across national boundaries. Ambitious legislators may look to these alternative arenas for career opportunities as well as policy coordination. Many countries have built public and semi-public institutions with authority in such areas as industrial relations, public fund investments, or monetary policy. All of these developments may weaken the hold of national parties in government.

The party in government is thus challenged by changes in organization, technology, and institutions (see also Strøm and Svåsand 1997). These changes may weaken party leaders' ability to provide solutions to the collective action problems that legislators face. Recall that party leaders secure compliance by offering such benefits as campaign funds, information, media access, committee assignments, staffing, and various other perquisites. As new mass media have been developed, individual legislators have become less dependent on party leaders for access. Similarly, the information revolution has reduced party control over information, and public subsidies have weakened some financial incentives.

THE EVIDENCE: DIRECT DEMOCRACY

Let us now empirically examine the status of party government by first considering the alternative models, such as corporatism and direct democracy. There are good reasons to consider the status of these governance regimes. Over the past few decades, the evolution of each of these forms of decision making has in fact been touted as a significant development in advanced industrial democracies. Referendum democracy and other forms of direct popular decision-making are perhaps the most obvious and fundamental challenge to party government. Returning important political decision-making to the citizens themselves dramatically reduces the policy discretion of party leaders. Many recent constitutions allow important issues to be decided by referendum or popular initiative (e.g. France, Italy), and some even require such popular approval for important decisions such as constitutional amendments (e.g. Denmark). Even in countries where direct democracy has no formal recognition in the constitution (e.g. Britain), there seems to be increased public demand for such consultations.

Under many constitutions, referendums are technically only advisory. Yet, it is usually costly for politicians to defy the expressed will of the people. When Norway first considered European Community (EC) membership in the 1960s, Labour Party leader and later Prime Minister Trygve Bratteli long opposed holding a national referendum, as it had no place in the constitution and no such vote had been held for almost fifty years. As other parties came out in support of a referendum, however, it became politically impossible for the Labour Party to resist. And even though the eventual 1972 referendum constitutionally could not bind the parliament, its pro-EC majority did not attempt to thwart the anti-membership popular majority.

The incidence of popular referenda thus appears to be a handy and straightforward inverse measure of the strength of party government: the more extensive the use of direct democracy, the less the 'partyness' of policy-making. To use Thies's framework once again, the more direct democracy is used, the more participatory the decision-making process, and the lower the partyness of policy-making. Yet, a few caveats may be in order. First, referendum democracy need not weaken party government, if parties can and do control the use of such voting occasions. Thus, if referendums are framed and administered by the parties, if they are held only when the parties desire them, and if the voters predictably take their cues from party leaders, then it is not clear that government parties have anything to lose through such mechanisms of decision-making. On the contrary,

TABLE 9.1 *National Referendums, 1950–1995*

Country	1950 -4	1955 -9	1960 -4	1965 -9	1970 -4	1975 -9	1980 -4	1985 9	1990 -4	1995	Total
Australia	1	0	0	2	6	4	2	4	0	0	19
Austria	0	0	0	0	0	1	0	0	1	0	2
Belgium	1	0	0	0	0	0	0	0	0	0	1
Canada	0	0	0	0	0	0	0	0	1	0	1
Denmark	2	0	5	1	1	1	0	1	2	0	13
Finland	0	0	0	0	0	0	0	0	1	0	1
France	0	1	3	1	1	0	0	1	1	0	8
Germany	0	0	0	0	0	0	0	0	0	0	0
Ireland	0	1	0	2	4	2	2	2	4	0	17
Italy	0	0	0	0	1	2	5	7	11	12	38
Japan	0	0	0	0	0	0	0	0	0	0	0
Netherlands	0	0	0	0	0	0	0	0	0	0	0
New Zealand	0	0	0	2	0	0	0	0	4	1	7
Norway	0	0	0	0	1	0	0	0	1	0	2
Sweden	0	2	0	0	0	0	0	0	1	0	3
Switzerland	25	20	16	10	30	56	28	34	57	7	283
Utd Kingdom	0	0	0	0	0	1	0	0	0	0	1
United States	0	0	0	0	0	0	0	0	0	0	0
All Countries	29	24	24	18	44	67	37	49	84	20	396

Sources: Butler and Ranney (1994), *Keesing's Record of World Events, European Journal of Political Research*, various issues.

referendums might conceivably even strengthen their hands. And there is plenty of evidence that in several countries referendums have been manipulated and perhaps even controlled by political parties. After the referendum mechanism came into use in Italy in the 1970s, it was exploited extensively by the Radical Party, and even occasionally by the Christian Democrats. Similarly, the use of direct democracy under French President de Gaulle hardly reflected a challenge to his party, but rather a deliberate attempt by the President himself to strengthen his party and his own grip on French politics. Yet, the conditions under which direct democracy enhances, rather than attenuates, party government, are probably overall the exceptions rather than the rule. Let us therefore consider the incidence of national referendums in advanced industrial democracies after 1950. Table 9.1 breaks them down by country and semi-decade.[1]

Note first that by one simple standard, the incidence of referendums across the OECD countries has increased markedly. Whereas there were only twenty-nine such decisions in all these countries combined in the early 1950s, the number had

[1] Referendum data for the years 1945–93 are from Butler and Ranney (1994) and data for later years from the 1994, 1995, and 1996 editions of the *Political Data Yearbook* published by the *European Journal of Political Research*.

almost tripled, to eighty-four, forty years later. And in the single year of 1995, there were almost as many referendums (20) as the average per half-decade in the 1950s or 1960s. Moreover, the four most recent five-year periods rank first, second, third, and fifth in overall incidence. While these numbers suggest a strong secular increase in the frequency of referendums, they should nevertheless be taken with a grain of salt. A closer inspection of Table 9.1 quickly reveals that more than two-thirds of all national referendums in these countries have in fact occurred in highly atypical Switzerland. And out of the remaining 113 referendums, Italy accounts for 38, whereas four different countries have held only one referendum in the entire post-war era, and three (Japan, the Netherlands, and the United States) none at all. The overall increase in the incidence of referendums is in large part a Swiss phenomenon. Secondarily, it reflects the rapid growth in such votes in Italy after the mechanism was made feasible through a 1970 reform and first used in 1974. Outside of these two countries, the use of referendums has been spotty, and it has followed no clear temporal trend. Australia held a large number of referendums in the 1970s but has since used the institution more sparingly. In Denmark, the decade of referendums was the 1960s, whereas in France the greatest use was made in the early 1960s, reflecting the heyday of Charles de Gaulle's plebiscitary politics. In most other countries, the record is too thin to permit any generalization. Thus, the variation we find in the use of this form of direct democracy is overwhelmingly cross-sectional. The incidence of referendums varies a great deal from one country to the next. It is much less clear that we can observe any meaningful changes cross-nationally over time. Moreover, it is not obvious what implications any such changes might have for the status of party government.

FUNCTIONAL REPRESENTATION AND CORPORATISM

During the 1970s and 1980s, a large literature portrayed corporatism as a significant challenge and alternative to party government. The concept of corporatism has been given a number of meanings, but at least one prominent conception is of direct relevance to the question of governmental party decline. If corporatism is taken to mean concertation, the incorporation of interest groups (particularly those representing economic producer groups) into the process of policy-making, especially in the areas of economic and industrial policy (Schmitter 1982), then corporatism reflects the replacement, or at least weakening, of parties in that governmental role. Indeed, in the heyday of scholarly excitement over corporatism, it was commonly assumed that interest groups were in fact displacing political parties in some policy areas, although it was also noted that well-established practices of corporatism (as, for example, in Austria or Sweden) often coincided with strong political parties (Katzenstein 1985).

Empirical study of the strength of corporatism has been hampered by a lack of consensus on theoretical definitions, as well as by the weakness of the empirical data. Recently, however, Siaroff (1999) has produced a comprehensive time-series study of corporatism—or as he calls it, integration—in twenty-four industrial democracies between the 1960s and the 1990s. Siaroff's scores are aggregations based on multiple indicators, and his sample overlaps in large part with this volume. As Siaroff provides a corporatism score for each country and decade, it is easy to check for evidence for any systematic increase or decrease. Though it is not obvious that increases in corporatism need to imply decreases in party government, it is at least possible that some such inverse relationship may exist. If increased interest group integration in policy-making is observed, then it may well be that parties are relinquishing some of their traditional hold over such decisions. It is also possible, of course, that parties may only deliberately and temporarily delegate such powers, subject to recall at any time that they feel that more direct involvement is worth their efforts.

At any rate, it is not clear that any such development has taken place. Most countries exhibit very little change over the three decades or so of this study. The rank order in the mid-1990s is almost identical to that of the late 1960s, and the mean level of corporatism has changed only marginally. Interestingly, it reached its peak in the 1970s and has since declined somewhat. A small number of countries, notably Finland, Australia, and Italy, appear to exhibit a secular trend toward corporatism. Less plausibly, the same trend is reported for the United States. On the other hand, corporatism has declined, if only ever so slightly, in Belgium and Sweden. Overall, the picture is very stable over time. Other evidence seems to suggest that corporatism has waned in most OECD countries since the 1970s, along with the strength of labour unions. Thus, to the extent that parties in government have suffered over this period, it cannot be due to a significant growth in corporatism.

LEGISLATIVE PARTIES

Political parties are creatures of legislatures. As mentioned above, their ability to reduce transaction costs and solve collective action problems in the legislative arena may be their ultimate rationale and source of strength (Müller 2000). If political parties lose their grip on the parliamentary arena, and particularly their ability to perform these functions, then we might indeed expect them to suffer secular decline. And losing their grip on the legislature should translate into less stable and committal partisan ties among the representatives. Thus, if parties were indeed losing their ability to coordinate legislative behaviour, we should observe at least some of the following phenomena:

1. More deputies are elected without an established partisan label.
2. More deputies change partisan affiliations within an electoral term.
3. Deputies are less constrained by partisan affiliations in their legislative voting.
4. Over time, there is less stability and more fragmentation in the set of parties represented in the legislature.

In this volume, Bowler discusses a number of the institutional features that sustain party organizations in the legislative arena and shows that there is little evidence of any cross-national decline in legislative party cohesion (point 3 above). In this chapter, I shall devote less attention to this institutional framework and more to the structure of party systems as given by the electoral results. As regards party switching (point 2), there are indications that it has increased, at least in several countries that have undergone electoral reform. In Italy, more than 100 deputies changed party affiliations between 1996 and 1999, some of them multiple times. On a smaller scale, such conversions have also taken place in Japan and New Zealand. The current government in New Zealand has promised to introduce legislation to prevent people from changing parties during the term of a parliament, which occurred following the recent reforms of the electoral system. Even the US Congress has witnessed an upturn in the number of party conversions during the 1990s. Thus, after the Republican Party won control of both houses in 1994, two senators and six congressmen defected from the Democrats in fairly short order to join the new majority. In Norway, five members of parliament switched parties in the 1990s, the highest number in any recent decade. In all of these countries, the incidence of partisan conversions seems to have increased. Yet, cross-nationally we know little about such trends. Although this is a fascinating topic, there is no broad and systematic study of the phenomenon, nor do we indeed have reliable cross-national data. In many countries, party-switching is probably fairly rare. While this observation hardly justifies any neglect of the topic, it will have to remain an avenue for future research. In the rest of this section, I shall therefore address myself to points 1 and 4 above.

Point 1 asks whether politicians are increasingly able to win legislative office without a partisan attachment, or at least without being on the slate of any significant national party. Table 9.A in the Appendix reports the percentage of parliamentary seats held by independents, or by parties listed as 'other' in Mackie and Rose's (1991) authoritative survey. Note that non-partisans account for only a tiny share of legislative seats in virtually all countries and periods. The temporal trends are easy to summarize. In no semi-decade prior to 1995 had the proportion of non-partisans cross-nationally averaged even a paltry 1 per cent. The highest incidence, 0.8 per cent, was found shortly after the Second World War, in the early 1950s. By the late 1950s, the record had dropped to less than 0.5 per cent of the seats, where it stayed to the 1980s. Interestingly, however, it has risen noticeably in the 1990s, to a high of 1.2 per cent for the 1995–7 period.

If we consider the country-by-country breakdown, it becomes clear that a small number of countries account for a large proportion of all independent legislators, with Ireland and Japan leading the way. In the early 1950s, almost one Irish legislator in ten was an independent. The incidence then dropped until it bottomed out at 1 per cent in the early 1970s. Since then, it has gradually risen once again, reaching 3.4 per cent for the 1995–7 period. Japan has exhibited a somewhat similar pattern, but with less clear temporal trends. The country witnessed a resurgence of independents in the early 1990s, with the disintegration of the long-dominant Liberal Democratic Party. No other country has a significant and sustained record of non-partisan legislators, though Australia, Finland, Switzerland, and especially Italy have witnessed significant upturns in the 1990s. In sum, although independent legislators are a rare occurrence in contemporary democracies, the figures from the 1990s suggest that they may be on their way to becoming less of an oddity.

Yet the number of independents may be too demanding a standard by which to measure whether the hold of parties on legislative representation is weakening. If such a downturn is on its way, it may manifest itself first in a decline of established parties relative to parties that have played a more marginal role in government. Table 9.B in the Appendix therefore reports the mean percentage of legislative seats won by parties that do not have a significant record as governing parties. Among such parties we count all those that have not held executive office at some point during two different legislative terms (i.e. after two different elections). It is clear that this proportion cross-nationally is much higher than that of independent deputies, overall about 10 per cent. The temporal trend looks similar to the one we observed in the number of non-partisan legislators—a high level immediately after the Second World War, a decline into the 1960s, and a more recent upturn. Yet, with respect to this more inclusive measure, the initial post-war decline is less sharp, whereas the subsequent surge sets in earlier and reaches a higher level. Note that in the late 1990s, these fringe parties had captured more than 20 per cent of all seats cross-nationally, a figure two to three times as high as in the early 1950s.

Fringe parties have been particularly strong in the dominant-party systems of Italy and Japan. This, of course, reflects the inclusion in these numbers of the Italian Communist Party and the Japanese Socialist Party, as well as numerous smaller parties in the same countries. Note, however, that Belgium, Canada, Denmark, Germany, the Netherlands, Norway, Sweden, and Switzerland all post 'respectable' numbers of fringe party legislators. In all of these countries except Denmark and arguably the Netherlands, there has been a significant upturn in the 1990s. Arguably, our measure may inflate these tendencies, as it counts all new parties (those that have not contested at least two general elections) as non-established, even if they have immediately been included in the government (e.g. New Zealand First, or Forza Italia). For countries significantly affected by this counting rule, I therefore report an alternative measure in which all parties in office at the end point of this survey were automatically counted as established parties and thus excluded. As can be seen, this significantly lowers the recent scores for some countries, but it does not (except in Italy) fundamentally change the picture of an upsurge in the 1990s.

Table 9.2 presents country-by-country and pooled regression estimates of the effects of time on the percentage of seats controlled by non-governing parties, using the latter alternative measure. Note that there is only one country for which

TABLE 9.2 Trends in the Percentage of Seats Won by Non-governing Parties (OLS regression estimates)

Country	Constant	Year coefficient	t-statistic	Adjusted R squared	Number of observations
Australia	−0.650	0.000	2.67	0.25	19
Austria	−2.142	0.001	1.18	0.03	14
Belgium	−4.653	0.002	3.63	0.47	15
Canada	−8.198	0.004	2.45	0.26	15
Denmark	−7.676	0.004	3.11	0.32	19
Finland	−4.038	0.002	6.37	0.77	13
France	−0.580	0.000	0.41	−0.08	12
Germany	−3.310	0.002	2.07	0.23	12
Ireland	0.475	−0.000	−0.38	−0.07	15
Italy	−14.629	0.007	2.06	0.25	11
Japan	−16.512	0.008	9.41	0.85	17
Netherlands	−0.991	0.001	0.53	−0.06	13
New Zealand	−5.524	0.003	2.17	0.25	16
Norway	−7.882	0.001	2.82	0.41	11
Sweden	−6.057	0.003	5.15	0.65	15
Switzerland	−4.541	0.002	4.39	0.62	12
United Kingdom	−3.635	0.002	7.14	0.79	14
United States	−0.034	0.000	1.31	0.03	24
All Countries	−4.429	0.002	8.68	0.73	267

Note: Non-governing parties are those that neither participated in the most recent government (end of 1997) nor participated in governments in at least two legislative terms overall. Country dummies not reported for the cross-national analysis. Italy is the excluded category.

Sources: Mackie and Rose (1991); *Electoral Studies*, various issues; *Keesing's Record of World Events;* Woldendorp et al. (1993).

this coefficient is negative, reflecting a secular decline in fringe relative to established parties, namely Ireland. Yet, this relationship is clearly insignificant by conventional statistical standards. Out of the seventeen countries in which the estimated effect is positive, about thirteen are cases in which there has been a significant trend in favour of the fringe parties. In the pooled model, the per annum change coefficient is 0.002, with a robust adjusted R square of 0.73.

These patterns are clearly linked to the pattern of party fragmentation that was discussed in Chapter 3. One of the developments accounting for the growing strength of fringe parties is the increasing fragmentation of many party systems, such as those of Belgium, Canada, Italy, and Norway. Yet, non-governing parties have done well even in countries that have not experienced much net fragmentation, such as Finland, Japan, and Switzerland. There is thus a very strong, cross-national trend toward the strengthening of 'fringe' parties that have not traditionally played any significant role in governing.

The growing strength of fringe parties is thus associated with a trend in many countries toward party system fragmentation. The latter measure may in itself be an important indicator of the strength of party government. As argued above and by Thies in this volume, the purest case of party government is where a single, cohesive party controls government. The more fragmented the party system, the less feasible this form of party control. Thus, party system fragmentation or instability is the fourth indicator of party government decline identified above. Here, I shall examine the evidence on party system fragmentation, using the Laakso and Taagepera (1979) index of the effective number of legislative parties. The larger the effective number of parties, the weaker party government. Table 9.C in the Appendix shows the results for each nation in five-year groupings.[2]

The data show that across the advanced industrial states, the effective number of legislative parties has tended to increase over time. Most of this increase has occurred in two distinct eras. The first period of party proliferation was the early 1970s, when many established parties (particularly Social Democrats and Christian Democrats) began to lose ground to new and nimbler challengers. The second period of such growth was the 1990s, when party system fragmentation rose to the highest post-war levels. Note that in many countries, for example Australia and Finland, the effective number of parties seems to have stabilized at some country-specific level. Yet, the number of countries with a significant temporal trend is larger than those without it. In some countries, notably France, Germany, and Japan, that trend has been a significant decline. But in the majority of cases, party system fragmentation has increased, most notably in Belgium and Italy, but also less remarkably in Austria, Canada, Norway, Sweden, Switzerland, the United Kingdom, and, most recently, New Zealand.

Table 3.2 provided country-specific estimates of the effect of time on legislative fragmentation (the effective number of parties). If one begins the calculations with the first elections of the 1950s, Chapter 3 finds that there is a statistically significant increase in the effective number of parties in fourteen nations. The models report negative coefficients (meaning a secular decline in the number of legislative parties) in only one case (the Netherlands), and this is not statistically significant.[3] When all the nations are pooled, the model yields a strongly positive coefficient for time and a healthy measure of explanatory power (per annum change coefficient = 0.014 with an adjusted R square of 0.67). Thus, on the whole the party systems of advanced industrial democracies have become significantly more fragmented over the past few decades.

[2] The main source of data is Mackie and Rose (1991), adjusted for errors, and updated through data published in *Electoral Studies* and *Keesing's Record of World Events* (previously *Keesing's Contemporary Archives*). Data on the effective number of parties have been graciously provided by Arend Lijphart for the years 1945–90, supplemented by sources mentioned above for more recent elections.

[3] There is somewhat more evidence of decline if the first post-war elections are included in these models, but Table 3.2 excludes these cases because the authors felt that party systems had not stabilized after the disruption of the Second World War until the 1950s.

In sum, these data tell us that the legislative party systems of advanced industrial democracies have been far from static. In general, established parties strengthened their grip on these legislative party systems from the end of the Second World War until the 1960s or even the 1970s. More recently, however, the trend has unequivocally gone toward fragmentation and increasing challenges to the established party system order. These evolutions are least evident in the incidence of independent deputies. In most national legislatures, such representatives still either make up a minuscule proportion of all legislators, or are entirely absent. Yet, the recent trend is unmistakably upward. The same trends, roughly parallel in temporal terms, are much more visible when we consider the strength of fringe and upstart parties relative to the traditional governing parties of the same societies.

EXECUTIVE POLITICS

The executive branches of contemporary polities are sprawling political organizations offering a multitude of enticements to political parties. Yet, in simple terms we can distinguish between three levels of the executive branch for which party control may be more or less salient: (1) the cabinet or core executive, (2) subcabinet appointments under the direct control of the cabinet, (3) autonomous or semi-autonomous agencies empowered to execute public policy with some measure of agency discretion, such as central banks, health agencies, and the like. Executive politics in large part revolves around the decisions of the core executive, or what in many political systems is called the cabinet or council of ministers. As long as modern parties have existed, they have sought to control the core executive. Their control over other aspects of the executive branch has varied a great deal more.

Core Executive

Most studies of parties in the executive branch are concerned centrally with their representation and functions in the core executive (cabinet). The conventional picture of cabinet-level politics is one of total party control. Parties control all cabinet-level appointments, and although non-partisans may occasionally hold cabinet portfolios, they do so rarely and only with party support. Yet, the question with respect to this part of the executive is whether this picture is increasingly inaccurate, whether political parties in fact may be losing their control of the cabinet. If so, this might mean most dramatically that cabinets would be composed increasingly of non-partisans, with no debt or allegiance to any political party.

Although the fine gradations of party attachment may be hard to capture operationally, I have examined the proportion of non-partisan cabinet members in eighteen OECD countries between 1945 and 1997. Table 9.D in the Appendix reports the percentage of non-partisan cabinet members for each country and half-decade (as elsewhere, the most recent time period is truncated to the three years 1995–7 only).[4]

As Table 9.D demonstrates, non-partisan cabinet members are indeed a rare phenomenon. In my sample of advanced industrial democracies, such individuals account for only a couple of percentage points overall. Many countries have no experience with non-partisan cabinet members at all. Indeed, no fewer than seven countries (Australia, Canada, Germany, New Zealand, Norway, Switzerland, and the United Kingdom) fall into this category. What is notable here, of course, is that party control seems particularly entrenched in countries in the Westminster tradition. Of the remaining nations, only three (Finland, France, and Italy) exhibit a proportion of non-partisans greater than 5 per cent overall. The common feature driving these particular systems toward a somewhat higher incidence of non-partisanship may be the polarization of their party systems and the concomitant fragility of their cabinets. Indeed, these are Sartori's (1976) prime examples of polarized pluralism. Also, Finland and France are the premier semi-presidential regimes in Western Europe, and their high incidence of non-partisan ministers may reflect presidential prerogatives and preferences in cabinet appointments.

For our purposes, however, the temporal patterns are of greater interest than these cross-sectional variations. Such temporal patterns are not overwhelmingly strong, yet there appears to be a clear initial trend toward greater partisan control in the early post-war decades, and a reversal of this trend since the early 1980s. After a high incidence of non-partisan cabinet members in the immediate post-war years (not shown), the incidence rapidly receded to a level around 1 per cent and eventually reached a low of a mere 0.5 per cent in the years 1980–4. Since then, non-partisanship has once again taken off, reaching 3.7 per cent in the most recent period, the highest level recorded since 1950. In summary, therefore, the decline of political parties is by this measure only observable in the 1980s and 1990s, whereas the preceding decades represented a period in which political parties strengthened their hold on the core executive.

If we examine these figures more closely on a country-by-country basis, much of the recent trend toward non-partisanship is due to one country, Italy, in which a tradition of *partitocrazia* (partocracy) dramatically collapsed and gave way to a remarkably high incidence of non-partisanship (46 per cent in the most recent period). But Italy is not entirely alone in this trend. There has been a marked, though much less dramatic, increase in non-partisanship in Austria, and a modest return to this practice in Finland. Even France continues to record intermittently high levels of non-partisanship.

---

[4] The main source for the cabinet data is Woldendorp et al. (1993), supplemented for more recent years by information contained in the 1992–6 *Political Data Yearbooks* of the *European Journal of Political Research*, as well as by Müller and Strøm (1997).

TABLE 9.3 Trends in the Percentage of Non-partisan Cabinet Members (OLS regression estimates)

Country	Constant	Year: Coefficient	t-statistic	Adjusted R squared	Number of observations
Australia	n/a	n/a	n/a	n/a	n/a
Austria	−1.809	0.001	1.77	0.11	19
Belgium	1.549	−0.001	−2.75	0.25	21
Canada	n/a	n/a	n/a	n/a	n/a
Denmark	n/a	n/a	n/a	n/a	n/a
Finland	11.603	−0.006	−1.62	0.05	29
France	1.192	−0.001	−0.42	−0.02	32
Germany	n/a	n/a	n/a	n/a	n/a
Ireland	−0.373	0.000	0.62	−0.03	20
Italy	−11.283	0.006	2.95	0.18	37
Japan	−0.666	0.000	1.49	0.04	29
Netherlands	0.924	−0.000	−1.53	0.08	16
New Zealand	n/a	n/a	n/a	n/a	n/a
Norway	n/a	n/a	n/a	n/a	n/a
Sweden	6.470	−0.003	−4.30	0.47	21
Switzerland	n/a	n/a	n/a	n/a	n/a
United Kingdom	n/a	n/a	n/a	n/a	n/a
United States	n/a	n/a	n/a	n/a	n/a
All Countries	0.124	−0.000	−0.09	0.11	387

Note: n/a = not applicable (Missing observations, or no non-zero observations). Country dummies not reported for the cross-national analysis. Italy is the excluded category.

Sources: Mackie and Rose (1991); *Electoral Studies*, various issues; *Keesing's Record of World Events;* Woldendorp et al. (1993).

Table 9.3 presents the regression estimates of the effects of time on the representation of non-partisans cross-nationally. Of course, the complete lack of non-partisans in many countries (notably the Anglo-American democracies) makes these models somewhat less interesting than the ones presented earlier in the chapter. Note, however, that for most of the countries for which we have non-zero observations, the estimated effect of time is negative, which is to say that the trend has been toward lower percentages of non-partisan ministers. The data we have already inspected show us why this is so. These results are driven by the sharp drop-off in non-partisans in the first two decades after the Second World War, which in several countries overwhelms the trends toward greater non-partisanship in more recent years. Overall, a linear model provides a very poor fit, since in most countries the relationship between time and non-partisanship has been curvilinear. Only in Belgium and Sweden, where non-partisanship has not significantly picked up after its initial drop-off, do the national estimates provide good explanatory power. In Italy, where there was no decline in the early post-war years, there is a fairly strong positive relationship between the passing of time and non-partisanship.

We can approach party control of cabinet-level politics more indirectly by examining aspects that are perhaps ultimately more consequential, and at least more immediately dramatic, than the proportion of non-partisan cabinet members. If party control refers to the stability with which specific parties hold the executive, then it may be useful to examine the circumstances under which different cabinets have been terminated. Certain characteristics of transitions from one cabinet to another may reflect the quality of such control. For example, when cabinets are terminated for lack of parliamentary support, or as a consequence of internal dissent, this may indicate less party control than when cabinets resign due to regularly scheduled elections or such non-political (one hopes) events as the death or ill-health of the prime minister.

Thus, in order to assess the stability of party control of cabinet-level politics, I report below the proportions of cabinet resignations that were due to: (1) dissension within government, and (2) lack of support. These causes of resignation are the ones most likely to reflect fragile partisan control—a disequilibrium in the party system. The data are from Woldendorp et al. (1993), with supplements as noted above.[5] Again, the data are reported by country and five-year interval.

Let us first consider the data on internal dissension, as reported in Table 9.4. Clearly, the data here give no indication that party control of cabinet-level politics has been destabilized. Whereas internal dissension was the cause of one-fourth of all cabinet resignations in the late 1940s, the proportion had declined to about one in fifteen by the late 1990s. This is the only period in which such resignations have accounted for less than 10 per cent of the cross-national total. But although the secular trend toward fewer such terminations is clear and strong, it is not monotonic. Indeed, from a low in the early 1960s, the proportion rose sharply to the early 1980s, after which it once again fell markedly. Not surprisingly, internal dissension is most common in countries commonly ruled by broad interparty coalitions, such as Belgium, Italy, and Finland. On the other hand, this cause of cabinet downfall is virtually unknown in the Westminster democracies. Consistently with this cross-national pattern, the rate of such terminations has declined sharply in France, as the party system has become consolidated and depolarized.

Table 9.5 reports similar data for cabinet terminations due to lack of support in parliament. Overall, this is a less common cause of cabinet downfalls. In only one half-decade has this type of resignation accounted for as much as one-fifth of all resignations. That was in the early 1950s, when 18 out of 58 resignations, or 31 per cent, fell into this category. Since then, the lack of parliamentary support

---

[5] Woldendorp et al. report six modes of resignation in all. The remaining categories not reported here are: (1) elections, (2) voluntary resignation of the prime minister, (3) resignation of the prime minister due to health reasons, and (4) intervention by the head of state. While it may be difficult to judge the underlying processes that these codings represent, the two categories reported in the text seem to represent the greatest challenges to party government.

TABLE 9.4 *Cabinet Terminations Due to Internal Dissension, 1950–1997*

Country	1950 –4	1955 –9	1960 –4	1965 –9	1970 –4	1975 –9	1980 –4	1985 –9	1990 –4	1995 –9	Total terminations due to ID
Australia	0	0	0	0	0	0	0	0	0	0	0
Austria	1	1	0	1	0	0	0	0	0	0	3
Belgium	2	0	1	1	2	2	4	2	0	0	14
Canada	0	0	0	0	0	0	0	0	0	0	0
Denmark	0	0	0	0	0	1	1	0	0	0	2
Finland	2	3	2	0	2	2	1	0	2	0	14
France	3	3	0	0	0	1	0	0	0	1	8
Germany	0	2	3	1	0	0	1	0	0	0	7
Ireland	0	0	0	0	0	0	0	1	1	0	2
Italy	3	3	0	1	5	0	2	2	0	0	16
Japan	0	0	0	0	0	0	0	0	2	0	2
Netherlands	0	0	0	1	1	1	2	1	0	0	6
New Zealand	0	0	0	0	0	0	0	0	0	0	0
Norway	0	0	0	0	1	0	0	0	0	0	1
Sweden	0	1	0	0	0	1	1	0	0	0	3
Switzerland	0	0	0	0	0	0	0	0	0	0	0
Utd Kingdom	0	0	0	0	0	0	0	0	0	0	0
All Countries	11	13	6	5	11	8	12	6	5	1	78
All Gov'ts Terminated	58	59	52	50	59	49	56	42	45	15	485
Percentage of Gov'ts Terminated	19.0	22.0	11.5	10.0	18.6	16.3	21.4	14.3	11.1	6.7	

Sources: Woldendorp et al. (1993), Müller and Strøm (1997), *European Journal of Political Research*, various issues.

has remained a numerically modest cause of government terminations. Nor is there any evidence of a secular increase in such events. It is true that 'non-support' terminations reached comparatively high levels in the early 1980s, but they have since fallen back to much more modest levels. In fact, not one of the fifteen resignations in the 1995–7 period has been assigned to this particular cause. Resignations due to lack of parliamentary support have varied much more predictably across countries than over time. Countries such as Denmark, Italy, and Ireland have experienced many such terminations, whereas they have been virtually unknown in the Anglo-American democracies, except for Canada. What this further reflects, quite clearly, is the incidence of minority governments. Not surprisingly, minority cabinets are much more likely than other cabinets to be terminated for lack of parliamentary support, a tendency well documented in previous research (see Strøm 1990*a*).

TABLE 9.5 *Cabinet Terminations Due to Lack of Support, 1950–1997*

Country	1950 –4	1955 –9	1960 –4	1965 –9	1970 –4	1975 –9	1980 –4	1985 –9	1990 –4	1995 –9	Total termin- ations due to LS
Australia	0	0	0	0	0	0	0	0	0	0	0
Austria	0	0	0	0	0	0	0	0	0	0	0
Belgium	1	1	0	0	1	1	1	0	0	0	5
Canada	0	0	1	0	1	0	1	0	0	0	3
Denmark	2	0	0	1	0	2	2	2	1	0	10
Finland	1	2	0	0	0	0	0	0	0	0	3
France	6	1	1	0	0	0	0	0	1	0	9
Germany	0	0	0	0	1	0	1	0	0	0	2
Ireland	2	1	0	0	0	0	1	0	1	0	5
Italy	2	0	3	1	1	3	3	2	1	0	16
Japan	3	0	0	0	0	0	1	0	0	0	4
Netherlands	1	1	0	1	0	0	0	0	0	0	3
New Zealand	0	0	0	0	0	0	0	0	0	0	0
Norway	0	0	2	0	0	0	0	0	1	0	3
Sweden	0	0	0	0	0	0	0	0	1	0	1
Switzerland	0	0	0	0	0	0	0	0	0	0	0
Utd Kingdom	0	0	0	0	0	0	0	0	0	0	0
All Countries	18	6	7	2	4	6	10	4	6	0	64
All Gov'ts Terminated	58	59	52	50	59	49	56	42	45	15	485
Percentage of Gov'ts Terminated	31.0	10.2	13.5	6.0	6.8	12.2	17.9	9.5	13.3	0.0	

Sources: Woldendorp et al. (1993), Müller and Strøm (1997), *European Journal of Political Research*, various issues.

Other Executive Agencies

If it is true that parties are gradually relinquishing their control over the executive branch, we would expect it to show up last in the core executive. Early signs of party decline may be more likely to be found in other executive agencies. Of course, in this respect the various OECD nations start from very different positions, in that partisan control over non-core executive agencies has varied greatly. In some countries, such as Denmark, governments get to make virtually no partisan appointments outside the cabinet. In other countries, such as Italy, tens of thousands of attractive positions in the *sottogoverno* (subgovernment) have traditionally been within the domain of political parties. Most commonly, governments are able to make at least a few subcabinet appointments, such as junior ministers of various ranks and perhaps the directors of some number of executive agencies.

Measuring the 'depth of patronage' across countries and time is very difficult, as institutional differences get in the way of cross-national comparisons, the available data tend to be soft and impressionistic, and formalities of non-partisanship and meritocracy often hide the realities of patronage. Nevertheless, the available evidence suggests that at least in some of the most extreme countries the depth of partisan patronage has diminished. In Belgium, where traditionally cabinet ministers have surrounded themselves with large partisan entourages known as 'personal cabinets', and where large segments of the civil service have been apportioned between the governing parties, partisan patronage has shrunk over the past decade. Since 1988, the governing parties have in their coalition agreements committed themselves to depoliticizing the public sector (De Winter et al. 1997: 423–5). In Italy, the 'first republic' collapsed in the early 1990s amid widespread citizen disgust with the partisan control and abuse of the public sector. Several of the referendums of this period were designed specifically to abolish such partisanship, and later governments have proceeded with privatization efforts and other policies to contain partisan control. In Austria, the spectacular success of the right-wing populist Freedom Party (FPÖ) has derived in large part from its criticism of the cozy 'social partnership' by which Social Democrats (SPÖ) and Christian Democrats (ÖVP) have divided the spoils of government. As the Freedom Party has made inroads, the 'red-black' coalition parties have gradually relinquished partisan control over parts of the public sector.

A specific agency that in many countries has experienced consequential institutional change is the central bank. Central banks are important policy-making agencies found in all modern states (now also the European Union) to coordinate financial policies, control monetary supply, and act as a domestic lender of last resort. The partisan control of central banks varies widely among advanced industrial countries. Until recent years, Germany, Switzerland, and the United States were widely considered to have very autonomous central banks, with weak partisan control. The Westminster systems (Britain, New Zealand, and Australia in particular) and the Nordic countries generally fell at the other extreme, with central banks highly responsive to the governing parties. There was remarkably little change in the institutions of any country over time (Lijphart 1999: 238; Cukierman et al. 1994).

Over the past decade, however, this pattern has clearly changed. Reforms in New Zealand in 1989, Britain in 1994 and 1997, and in Belgium, France, Greece, Italy, Portugal, and Spain between 1992 and 1994 were all designed to enhance central bank autonomy and thus to remove its decisions from short-term political accountability (Maxfield 1997; Lijphart 1999). The creation of a central bank for the integrated currencies of the European Union has exhibited the same pattern: although there was serious dissent over the control of this new institution, the commitment to central bank autonomy was so strong that it was not publicly contested. Thus, during the 1990s the 'partyness' of central banks clearly declined in many advanced industrial democracies. In Thies's terms (Chapter 11), we have

witnessed an evolution toward bureaucratic technocracy, an increase in the autonomy of this key institution of monetary and financial policy-making. The motivation is clearly related to the globalization of the markets for goods and financial
instruments, the related demand for stability and predictability in monetary and
economic policies, and perhaps to a declining trust in the competence and bene-
volence of partisan politicians. In itself, however, the trend toward central bank
independence is hardly a devastating blow to party government.

To summarize, there is relatively little evidence that parties are losing their
control of the core executive in the advanced industrial democracies. It is true that
since the early 1960s, the frequency of non-partisan cabinet ministers has
increased, most notably in the most recent years. Interestingly, this trend has coincided with the rise of independents and smaller parties in legislatures. Yet, the
trend toward non-partisan cabinet members is less cross-nationally robust and is
in fact driven very largely by a few influential countries, such as Italy. Moreover,
the rise in non-partisan cabinet members has had no discernible impact on cabinet stability, as reflected in the causes of cabinet termination. In other agencies
outside the core executive, we can nonetheless observe clear evidence of deliberate challenges to the control exercised by political parties. This is manifested in
reforms to reduce partisan patronage in such countries as Italy, Austria, and
Belgium. Another prominent manifestation lies in the strong cross-national trend
since the late 1980s toward more independent central banks. Thus, political
parties retain strong control of the core executive, whereas their hold on other
executive agencies was waning at the close of the twentieth century.

THE FUTURE OF PARTY GOVERNMENT

Will democratic government in the twenty-first century still mean party government? The evidence we have encountered suggests that political parties remain
well entrenched in the core executives (cabinets) of most advanced capitalist
nations. The farther we move away from this key political institution, the more
clearly we see signs of partisan decay. To some extent, this is visible in the
legislative arena, in which independents have become somewhat more numerous,
and where new and 'fringe' parties in particular have improved their standing.
Impressionistic evidence suggests that party-switching may also have become
more common. Moreover, the decline of partisan control is evident in various
executive agencies below the cabinet level, and most clearly, perhaps, in the status
of central banks. Thus, partisan control has begun to erode toward both ends of
the chain of national policy-making.

Although there may be many factors that have contributed to these developments, it seems reasonable to point to the organizational, technological, and institutional challenges that parties have recently faced. Yet, we should avoid the
assumption that political parties are merely passive victims of large-scale changes

in their environments. Such a portrayal would not only in most cases be inaccurate but it would also ignore one of the most important lessons concerning any political organization. The leaders of parties, like those of other organizations, adapt to changes in their environments and seek above all to perpetuate the organizations from which they benefit (Wilson 1973). Witness, for example, the impressive electoral resilience of religious parties (such as the German Christian Democrats) in a largely secular era, or the ability of Nordic agrarian parties to prosper even as their traditional constituencies have shrunk drastically. Though not always effectively, parties do respond to, and even anticipate, environmental challenges.

Parties may even deliberately manipulate their environments to promote their own success (Selle and Svåsand 1991). We often see such behaviour in the parties in government. For example, through a local government reform, the Danish parties were in the 1970s able to enhance their control of local government, even as their national memberships were declining ominously. Prior to the 1970 mergers of many municipalities, non-partisan candidates had won approximately 40 per cent of all local council seats, mostly in rural areas. After the mergers, this proportion plummeted to 15 per cent, virtually squeezing non-partisan candidates out of office everywhere outside Jutland (Bentzon 1981: 18; Pedersen 1987: 42–3).

Katz and Mair (1995) argue more broadly that the past generation has witnessed the emergence of a new type of political party: the cartel party. The cartel party is characterized by 'the interpenetration of party and state and also by a pattern of inter-party collusion' (Katz and Mair 1995: 17). Such parties cooperate to exploit state resources and authority for their own purposes. Will such opportunistic institutional engineering allow parties to reverse any diminution they have recently suffered? While it is difficult to speculate about the upside potential of political parties, there appear to be limits to the political engineering that they can hope to accomplish. These constraints are most visible in the scepticism that voters show toward reform that seems motivated primarily by a desire to maintain partisan control, or more bluntly, to reap partisan rents. Parties may be most vulnerable precisely when they most clearly control and exploit political rents. The examples of the United States and Italy are particularly telling. American parties have long been decried for their lack of legislative discipline, for their skeletal national organizations, and for their lack of control over ballot access and finances. Yet, the major parties in the United States seem to be relatively successful in dealing with their challenges. Party cohesion in the US Congress is on the increase, party finances have improved, and the weakening of party identification seems to have halted. Despite regular third-party presidential candidates, no third party has managed to contend with the Democrats and the Republicans at the national level.

Post-war Italy, on the other hand, was a classic case of partocracy *(partitocrazia)*. Italian parties existed long before the democratic order, and they shaped its constitution in their image and to their benefit. Over time, they came to extend their tentacles extraordinarily far into Italian business, culture, and social life. One of the most stable electorates in Europe was rooted in strong subcultural communities. Yet, this impressive edifice turned out to be a house of cards, and within a few short years it completely disintegrated. The Christian Democrats, once the very model of a dominant party, no longer exist. Most of their former coalition partners lie in shambles as well. The very success that Italian parties enjoyed in their (admittedly blatant) pursuit of political rents may have been the primary cause of their destruction. While American politicians are certainly also willing and able to chase political rents, their parties have in recent decades become much less useful vehicles for that purpose. Instead, American politicians seek rents individually. Correspondingly, the voters also sanction them as individuals, and the fallout for the parties as organizations is less. In short, parties are most vulnerable when they are most blatantly opportunistic and collusive. Under such circumstances, the road from success to obliteration may be disconcertingly short (see Strøm and Svåsand 1997).

If parties are showing signs of decline, does that mean that we should expect a shift to one of the alternatives identified earlier in this chapter—referendum democracy, corporatism, or pluralist democracy? What are the prospects for these alternatives to party government? Corporatism is a scenario whose time seems to have passed, as economic producer groups have lost much of their cohesiveness and mobilizational capacity. To many citizens, referendum democracy, in which the whole apparatus of representative government would be replaced, or at least checked, by direct popular decision-making, is a more appealing option. Referendum democracy is at the same time the most radical and the least imminent of the alternatives to party government. We may well expect an increase in the use of institutions of direct democracy, particularly as the information revolution facilitates this form of decision-making. Yet, direct decision-making demands time and attention, and its use impedes policy consistency and predictability across issue areas and over time.

The most likely alternative to party government is therefore some form of pluralist democracy, which also represents the least radical departure from the status quo. Pluralist democracy, a form of government closer to that found in the United States, would be feasible in parliamentary systems only if the legislative and governmental parties were to lose much of their cohesiveness. Yet, this is an area in which we do not yet see much evidence of party decline. One of the strengths of party government may therefore lie in the limitations of all the potential alternatives. While parties in government are unlikely to disappear any time soon, they will probably, however, have to share the executive and especially the legislative arena with less established and structured bodies of representatives.

Appendix

TABLE 9.A *Share of Parliamentary Seats Held by Independent or Parties Denoted as 'Other,' 1950–1997*

Country	1950–4	1955–9	1960–4	1965–9	1970–4	1975–9	1980–4	1985–9	1990–4	1995–9	Country mean
Australia	0	0	0	0	0	0	0	0	0.9	2.7	0.3
Austria	0	0	0	0	0	0	0	0	0	0	0.1
Belgium	0	0	0.4	0	0	0	0	0	0.4	0	0.1
Canada	1.9	1.1	0	0.6	0.6	0.3	0.1	0.2	0.1	0.3	0.5
Denmark	0	0	0	0	0	0	0	0	0.1	0.6	0.0
Finland	0	0.2	0	0	0	0	0	0	0.4	1.5	0.2
France	0.4	0	0	0	0	0	0	0	0	0.2	0.1
Germany	0	0	0	0	0	0	0	0	0	0	0.0
Ireland	8.0	4.6	4.4	1.3	1.0	2.2	2.2	1.8	2.9	3.4	3.1
Italy	0.1	0	0	0	0	0.1	0	0	2.0	8.4	0.9
Japan	4.2	2.1	1.8	2.5	3.3	3.9	2.6	2.1	5.7	3.6	3.1
Netherlands	0	0	0	0	0	0	0	0	0	0	0
New Zealand	0	0	0	0	0	0	0	0.1	0.4	0	0.1
Norway	0	0	0	0	0	0	0	0	0	0	0
Sweden	0	0	0	0	0	0	0	0	0	0	0
Switzerland	0	0	0.2	0	0	0.1	0.3	0.3	2.9	1.5	0.5
Utd Kingdom	0.2	0	0	0	0.3	0	0	0	0	0	0.1
United States	0	0	0	0	0	0	0	0	0.2	0.2	0.1
All Countries	0.8	0.4	0.4	0.3	0.3	0.4	0.3	0.3	0.9	1.2	0.5

Note: Entries are percentages, mean values.

Sources: Mackie and Rose (1991), *Electoral Studies*, various issues, *Keesing's Record of World Events*, Woldendorp et al. (1993).

TABLE 9.B *Share of Parliamentary Seats Held by Non-Governing Parties, 1950–1997*

Country	1950–4	1955–9	1960–4	1965–9	1970–4	1975–9	1980–4	1985–9	1990–4	1995–7	Country mean
Australia	0	0	0	0	0	0	0	0	1.0	2.7	0.3
Austria	12.0	5.4	0	0	0	0	0	3.5	7.0	10.4	3.6
Belgium	3.1	1.8	2.9	4.2	9.1	6.7	5.5	5.2	13.9	16.0	6.4
Canada	12.9	11.3	11.1	14.0	15.0	0.8	11.2	12.4	24.5	40.1	17.2
Denmark	11.1	8.9	10.0	10.6	18.9	31.0	25.0	23.5	17.7	17.7	18.4
Finland	0	0.6	1.5	3.1	1.4	5.3	3.9 (3.5)	5.1 (3.5)	9.0 (4.5)	9.5 (5.0)	3.7
France	0	4.0	0.2	0	6.0	4.0	2.2	2.6	1.8	5.3 (4.9)	4.1
Germany	11.7	2.4	0	0	0	0	2.2	7.3	5.4	11.8	3.0
Ireland	11.3	7.9	5.8	1.8	1.0	2.2	3.5	4.1	5.5	6.8	5.1
Italy	30.8	34.9	32.6	40.2	43.3	42.2	41.9	41.1 (39.8)	53.1 (39.6)	98.3	45.5
Japan	13.2	3.0	6.8	13.6	21.4	26.6	25.8	25.8	32.1	45.8	20.4
Netherlands	10.4	7.1	7.2	12.1	18.5	13.1	10.0	7.1	10.1	15.9	10.9
New Zealand	0	0	0	0.8	0	0.4	2.0	0.8	2.2 (1.5)	23 (12.9)	2.8
Norway	0.8	1.2	1.2	1.0	5.4	6.2	4.4	8.9	20.3	14.5	6.3
Sweden	2.7	2.4	2.9	5.1	5.1	5.2	5.7	8.1	17.0	15.8	6.5
Switzerland	13.2	12.2	12.5	15.4	18.6	15.5	16.3	19.6	25.4	19.0	16.8
Utd Kingdom	1.6	1.3	1.2	2.0	3.3	5.8	5.3	7.0	6.9	8.3	4.3
United States	0.2	0.2	0	0	0	0	0	0	0.2	0.2	0.1
All Countries	7.5	5.8	5.3	7.1	9.3	9.7	9.0	10.1	14.1	20.1	9.1
Excluding US	7.9	6.1	5.6	7.5	9.8	10.3	9.6	10.7	14.9	21.2	9.7

Note: Entries are percentages, mean values. Parenthesized entries discount parties in government as of the end of 1997. These numbers are shown only when they differ from the standard measure.

Sources: Mackie and Rose (1991), *Electoral Studies*, various issues, *Keesing's Record of World Events*, Woldendorp et al. (1993).

TABLE 9.C *Effective Number of Parliamentary Parties, 1950–1997*

Country	1950–4	1955–9	1960–4	1965–9	1970–4	1975–9	1980–4	1985–9	1990–4	1995–7	Country Mean
Australia	2.57	2.52	2.59	2.63	2.54	2.46	2.51	2.33	2.36	2.51	2.49
Austria	2.51	2.27	2.20	2.15	2.19	2.21	2.24	2.56	3.14	3.48	2.51
Belgium	2.52	2.56	2.64	4.14	5.42	6.07	7.46	7.08	7.29	8.03	5.28
Canada	1.90	2.04	2.24	2.49	2.54	2.39	2.25	1.95	2.34	2.56	2.42
Denmark	3.85	3.71	3.57	3.98	5.17	5.20	5.26	5.20	4.40	4.54	4.57
Finland	4.72	4.77	5.00	4.99	5.54	5.29	5.18	5.01	5.17	4.89	5.09
France	5.61	4.86	3.44	3.12	3.30	4.39	2.98	3.32	3.03	3.21	3.83
Germany	4.24	3.29	3.10	2.89	2.76	2.84	3.04	3.35	3.23	3.45	3.11
Ireland	3.30	2.84	2.77	2.58	2.51	2.45	2.51	2.76	3.28	3.33	2.79
Italy	2.96	3.50	3.57	3.66	3.54	3.30	3.69	4.05	5.48	7.38	4.46
Japan	3.27	3.00	2.06	2.32	2.61	3.12	2.94	2.71	2.94	3.06	2.84
Netherlands	4.66	4.20	4.29	5.23	6.27	4.79	4.01	3.65	4.08	5.42	4.66
New Zealand	1.91	1.99	1.96	2.00	1.92	1.93	2.05	1.96	1.91	3.23	2.08
Norway	2.84	3.03	3.17	3.44	3.56	3.44	3.15	3.32	4.15	4.04	3.42
Sweden	3.08	3.16	3.14	3.10	3.33	3.44	3.27	3.50	3.99	3.50	3.35
Switzerland	4.87	4.75	4.80	5.07	5.46	5.04	5.21	5.57	6.45	5.60	5.28
Utd Kingdom	2.06	2.02	2.00	2.03	2.11	2.23	2.13	2.14	2.23	2.21	2.11
United States	2.00	1.93	1.89	1.93	1.92	1.82	1.93	1.93	1.94	1.97	1.92
All Countries	3.34	3.21	3.09	3.28	3.57	3.56	3.52	3.56	3.85	4.14	3.35
Excluding US	3.42	3.28	3.16	3.36	3.67	3.65	3.61	3.64	3.95	4.26	3.50

Note: Entries are mean values.

Sources: *Electoral Studies*, various issues, Arend Lijphart, personal communication.

TABLE 9.D *Non-Partisans as Share of all Cabinet Members, 1950–1997*

Country	1950–4	1955–9	1960–4	1965–9	1970–4	1975–9	1980–4	1985–9	1990–4	1995–7	Country Mean
Australia	0	0	0	0	0	0	0	0	0	0	0
Austria	3.6	1.8	0	0	0	0	0	4.0	6.0	6.3	1.8
Belgium	5.0	0	0	0	0	0	0	0	0	0	0.6
Canada	0	0	0	0	0	0	0	0	0	0	0
Denmark	0	0	0	0	0	0	0	0	0	0	0.0
Finland	9.1	23.6	27.3	0	11.4	7.2	2.4	0	0	5.6	13.0
France	1.8	14.9	29.7	18.9	6.5	5.8	1.0	10.9	17.1	2.2	9.2
Germany	0	0	0	0	0	0	0	0	0	0	0
Ireland	2.9	0	0	0	0	0	4.1	2.4	0	0	0.6
Italy	0	0	0	0	0	3.6	0	0	15.7	46.0	5.8
Japan	0	1.0	0	0	0	0	0	0	3.8	3.2	0.3
Netherlands	3.8	0	0	0	0	0	0	0	0	0	0.4
New Zealand	0	0	0	0	0	0	0	0	0	0	0
Norway	0	0	0	0	0	0	0	0	0	0	0
Sweden	14.4	11.4	5.7	0	0	3.1	1.1	0	2.9	0	4.6
Switzerland	0	0	0	0	0	0	0	0	0	0	0
Utd Kingdom	0	0	0	0	0	0	0	0	0	0	0
All Countries	2.4	3.1	3.7	1.1	1.1	1.1	0.5	1.0	2.7	3.7	2.7

Note: Entries are percentages, mean values for cabinets formed in the years indicated.

Sources: Woldendorp et al. (1993); Müller and Strøm (1997); *European Journal of Political Research*, various issues.

10

From Platform Declarations to Policy Outcomes

Changing Party Profiles and Partisan Influence
Over Policy

Miki L. Caul and Mark M. Gray

POLITICAL parties play a vital role in the democratic process, especially when it comes to the making of public policy. Parties structure the policy process by aggregating issues and presenting voters with a package of policies in the form of party programmes. After elections, the winning parties seek to translate their campaign programmes into policies and implement them. In practice, this move from policy presentation to policy implementation provides an integral bridge in the representation process. Conceptually, this translation also represents the link from the role of parties in the electorate to the role of parties in government.

As the preceding chapters demonstrate, there have been considerable changes in terms of parties in the electorate and as organizations, which lead us to question whether there have been changes in how the parties propose and implement public policies. Specifically, a more fluid electorate and an increasing number of new issues may lead to increasingly ambiguous party profiles. Changes in the broader environment of parties such as globalization of the economy may further limit the range of policy choices available to the governing parties. Under these conditions parties may find it more difficult to aggregate issues in a consistent manner, the policies that governing parties enact may become similar, and the partisan character of government may matter less.

This chapter examines whether the role of parties in policy-making has changed substantially since the 1950s. First, we analyse how parties present their policy profiles, and how this has changed over time. Specifically, have parties' ideological positions converged since 1950? If parties' ideological positions are moving closer together, this suggests that it has become more difficult for parties to maintain distinct policy profiles and therefore for voters to perceive differences between parties. Second, as David Farrell and Paul Webb suggest in Chapter 6, parties may have shifted from 'selling' to 'marketing' issues. We extend this idea to examine whether parties have moved from emphasizing a consistent package of ideologically based policies toward marketing an increasingly volatile variety of issues. If parties have become more flexible in terms of the issues that they emphasize, it may be that established parties are moving toward reflecting rather than shaping public opinion, thus relinquishing some of their control over the political agenda.

Finally, we analyse how the party composition of government impacts public policy outputs, and how this has changed over time. If parties' control over policy-making has declined, then this suggests that the role of political parties within the democratic process has fundamentally changed, and the logic of party-based democracy could increasingly be called into question.

THE ARGUMENT FOR PARTISAN CONVERGENCE

Scholars of party competition have long theorized that the major parties would come to resemble one another in their issue positions. Anthony Downs' (1957) spatial theory of party competition predicts that the major left and right parties in two-party systems would move toward one another in pursuit of the median voter. Rational office-seeking parties are expected to change their policy positions to correspond with the majority of voters' preferences, which given a normal distribution typically lies at the centre of the ideological scale.

Even in multi-party systems, analysts have argued that parties are under increasing pressure to converge toward the centre of the political spectrum. For example, Otto Kirchheimer (1966) predicted that the former mass parties would become 'catch-all' parties in an effort to maximize their share of the votes. As the ideological and traditional group bonds that structured party competition diminish in potency, Kirchheimer theorized that parties would integrate an ever greater number of voters drawn from an increasingly disparate set of categories.[1] In other words, the weakened partisan ties we observed in Chapters 2 and 3 should encourage centrist policies in pursuit of the median voter.

Other scholars have suggested that the development of professional media-based campaigns and the rise of candidate-centred politics could prompt convergence toward the lowest common denominator of voter preferences and non-ideological content (Kaid and Holtz-Bacha 1995). Scammell and Semetko (1995: 40) note this radical change in British electioneering in the 1990s, 'There was no real ideological difference between Major's 'caring Conservatives' and Kinnock's 'moderate Labour.' As a marketing rule of thumb, the closer the products, the more important the packaging.'

In fact, many descriptive accounts of political party histories have pointed to

---

[1] We should note that early attempts to operationalize and empirically test Kirchheimer's hypothesis that parties would attempt to broaden their appeal by drawing from a greater number of groups yielded little evidence to support the contention that by the 1970s parties had become more heterogeneous (Rose and Urwin 1969).

ideological convergence. Kirchheimer (1966), for example, described the convergence of the German Christian Democrats and Social Democrats in post-war
Germany. Several analysts of British electoral politics noted the emergence of a
collectivist consensus between Labour and the Conservatives that existed until the
Thatcher era (Norton 1994; Beer 1969), and then the aforementioned move
toward the centre under Major and Blair (Sanders 1998; King et al. 1998). Similarly, the convergence in the party platforms of the major left and right parties in
New Zealand in support of neo-liberal economic reforms in the late 1970s
supposedly planted the seeds of public discontent that culminated in the 1993
electoral system reform (Vowles et al. 1995). Likewise, the space between the
established parties of Finland has steadily shrunk since the 1980s (Pesonen
1999). Similar historical narratives exist in other party systems, but what is
needed is more systematic evidence of partisan change.

The best available data source that allows one to trace party movement in
broad ideological terms over the greatest period of time and number of countries
comes from the Comparative Manifestos Project. Data from party platforms
provide a basis for comparing party images from 1945 to 1987 (Budge et al.
1987; Klingemann et al. 1994). This project shows that through 1987 the major
parties converged toward the centre on the traditional left–right scale. 'To the
extent that there has been any reduction in differentiation, that is, a general
convergence, it happened in all countries at about the same time—during the
1960s and early 1970s—when Western democracies were commonly confronted
with perhaps their greatest recent internal challenge to institutional legitimacy'
(Klingemann et al. 1994: 247).

Using an alternative source of manifesto data, John Thomas (1975; 1979) finds
evidence for a strong trend toward convergence over the same period. On ten major
socio-economic issues from the 1950s to the 1970s, He documents a movement
toward the centre in all ten Western party systems he examines. He theorizes that
this tendency toward consensus arose in the form of an all-party agreement on
economic growth and stability as the primary goals of Western democracies.

Two more recent studies utilize 'expert panels' to place parties on the left–right
ideological continuum. By comparing two surveys of experts from 1982 and
1993, Mair (1995) and Knutsen (1998) trace the movement of parties over this
period. Mair concludes that the distance which separates the major left and right
parties is indeed declining in eleven of thirteen European countries for which the
data is available. As the leading left and right parties move toward the centre, and
the as the range of coalition alternatives increase, Mair argues that individual
parties now find it increasingly difficult to maintain a separate identity. Knutsen
(1998) finds similar movement toward the centre among established parties.
Overall, more parties moved toward the centre (30 per cent) than away from the
centre (14 per cent). This centrist tendency was especially pronounced among
socialist parties—60 per cent moved toward the centre. Offsetting this convergence, however, New Politics parties became more firmly located on the extreme

left and right. Thus, while the major left and right parties have recently moved closer, Knutsen suggests that the entrance of new parties has preserved a broad ideological range in some party systems.

These arguments for convergence have not gone unchallenged. Wagschal (1998) questions the convergence evidence from both the Comparative Manifestos Project and expert judgement data. Wagschal first compares party positions on a continuum of interventionism vs. pro-market tendencies in eighteen countries for two periods—1945–73 and 1974–88. Although Wagschal concludes that parties have not grown closer in the post-1973 period on this issue; only ultra-left parties grew more interventionistic, and moderate leftist and rightist parties both moved in a pro-market direction. Furthermore, Wagschal reveals that party system characteristics may impact on the ideological gap between parties: where there is a low degree of fragmentation, there are smaller ideological differences between the two major parties.

By tracing the movement in parties' ideological positions, we can observe whether there is a pattern of movement towards the centre in advanced industrialized democracies. It is important to examine the long-term process of party movements so that we can see whether recent movements are unique. Further, we are interested in the relative differences between parties within each nation over time, rather than determining the direction of the movement, or the types of parties that have moved.

TESTING FOR CONVERGENCE

To test the convergence hypothesis we draw upon data collected by the Comparative Manifestos Project. The Manifestos project coded the content of election party programmes in fifteen nations for each party from 1950 until 1987. Each programme was coded in terms of the attention it devoted to fifty-four separate themes. In comparison to public opinion surveys or 'expert' judgements, the manifesto data cover the long post-war era and these data represent how the political parties have presented themselves to the public at election time over this period.

Our first goal is to determine whether the ideological positions of the parties have changed over time. Following Klingemann et al. (1994: 40), we added together the percentage of each party's platform devoted to issues with a leftist emphasis and the percentage with a rightist emphasis, and then calculated the difference to create a left–right score for each party in a given election year.[2] Ian

---

[2] The Comparative Manifestos Project coded party platforms for certain issue concerns in terms of emphasis as intended by the Budge et al. (1987) salience theory of party competition, rather than position, as suggested by Downs's (1957) theory. While some categories are clearly coded in terms of ideology, others are only designed to capture policy emphases. Harmel et al. (1995) question the validity of the left/right measure produced by the salience coding of the

Budge (1999) used this same procedure to track the ebb and flow of the left–right images of the British parties over time (also see Hofferbert 1997).

Table 10.1 presents the ideological distance between the major left and right party in each nation from the 1950s to the 1980s.[3] The first column displays the per annum change in the difference between the left–right ideological position of the two parties over the span of the data. We find that the distance between left and right parties decreases in ten of the fifteen nations over time. In short, these results expand and strengthen the conclusions of Budge et al. (1987) and Klingemann et al. (1994).[4]

Majoritarian electoral systems—Britain, Canada, Australia, and New Zealand—are most likely to display ideological convergence. In these nations the converging forces described by Downs presumably combine with the general centralizing tendencies that may affect all party systems. At the same time, ideological convergence is also visible in proportional representation systems such as the Netherlands, Norway, Belgium, Germany, Austria, and Italy.

The American political party system is a notable exception to the general pattern of convergence. As others have shown, the polarization between the Democratic and Republican parties has increased over time (King 1997). The ideological gap at the end of the 1980s was nearly double that of the 1950s. In 1984 there was an unprecedented ideological polarization, corresponding with the 'Conservative Revolution' associated with Reagan's re-election campaign.

---

manifesto data, arguing that ideological position must be coded in terms of positive or negative statements for all categories. In order to best capture left/right ideology with the Manifestos Project data, we replicate the composite left/right scores based on sums of emphases for groups of left and right emphases created in Klingemann et al. (1994), rather than relying on the individual issues. The advantage of the Comparative Manifestos data is that it offers a comparable measure over time, so that we can measure relative movement in left/right emphases over time, rather than calculating absolute issue positions. It is important not to conflate issue emphasis with issue position, and the results must be interpreted with this in mind.

[3] The leading left and right parties in each country are: Swedish Social Democrats and People's Party (1952–64), Centre (1968–79), Moderate Unity (1979–88); Norwegian DNA (Labour) and Hoyre (Conservatives); Danish Social Democrats and Ventsre (Liberals) (1950–68), Conservatives (1971 and 1981–8), and Progress (1973) and Liberals (1975); Belgian Socialists (Francophone 1978–81 and 1987 and Flemish 1985) and CVP; Dutch PvdA (Labour) and KVP (Catholic People's) and CDA from 1981; French Communist (1951–73) and Socialist (1978–88) and Gaullist (1951 and 1958–88) and Conservatives (1956); Italian PCI (Communists) and DC (Christian Democrats); German SPD (Social Democrats) and CDU (Christian Democratic Union); Austrian SPÖ (Socialists) and ÖVP (People's Party); UK Labour and Conservatives; Irish Labour and Fianna Fáil; US Democrats and Republicans, Canadian NDP (Socialist) and Liberals; Australian Labour and Liberals; New Zealand Labour and National.

[4] Our finding that Austria and Germany have some of the strongest patterns of convergence and that France continues to exhibit differences between the two major parties is consistent with Thomas's findings. However, we find that Sweden does not display a pattern toward convergence, while Thomas finds that Sweden is one of the convergence leaders. This discrepancy may be due to different data sources, but most likely is due to the longer time period that our data encompass.

TABLE 10.1 *Ideological Distance between Major Left and Right Party, 1950–1980s*

	Per annum change	Sig.	N	1950s avg.	1980s avg.	Change
Australia	−0.31	0.19	16	20.1	11.2	−8.9
Austria	−1.36	0.37	11	78.7	12.9	−65.8
Belgium	−0.45**	0.03	13	25.2	2.6	−22.6
Canada	−0.55	0.30	13	43.2	7.8	−35.4
Denmark	1.27	0.18	16	42.8	91.5	+48.7
France	0.47	0.54	11	16.7	61.0	+59.3
Germany	−1.02	0.30	10	65.4	15.2	−50.2
Ireland	0.34	0.88	11	14.6	17.1	+2.5
Italy	−0.15	0.28	9	6.6	4.7	−1.9
Netherlands	−0.56*	0.06	10	12.4	1.5	−10.9
New Zealand	−0.59*	0.07	13	32.6	15.4	−17.2
Norway	−0.35***	0.00	9	11.8	1.7	−10.1
Sweden	0.59	0.38	13	27.0	70.7	+43.7
UK	0.24	0.20	11	18.3	5.9	−12.4
US	0.39	0.52	10	51.5	26.5	−25.0

*$p<0.10$, **$p<0.05$, ***$p<0.01$. Per annum change table entries are unstandardized regression coefficients.

After 1984, however, our data show that the polarization falls again, back to the small gap traditionally found in the United States. Parties in both houses of the US legislature have continued to show historically high levels of party line voting into the 1990s (Coleman 1996, Maisel 1998). To the degree that the issues voted on in Congress have ideological meaning it is suffice to say that parties in the United States continue to show growing polarization within government, if not in their campaigns.

Political change by the major left and right parties represents only a portion of the entire party system as Wagschal (1998) argues; other political parties may have responded to this pattern by offering new political choices. Indeed, over this time span many of these party systems have witnessed the emergence of new Green parties, and their eventual entry into several national parliaments (Mueller-Rommel 1989). Similarly, this has been a period during which small New Left parties and centrist parties have often experienced renewed electoral vigour (Mueller-Rommel and Pridham 1991). More recently, New Right parties have forced themselves onto the stage in many party systems, although perhaps too recently to be included in election data from the late 1980s. In sum, even if the major left and right parties have generally converged, the ideological diversity of entire party systems may have followed a different course, with new parties moving into the space vacated by the major parties.

We tested for this possibility by computing the left/right ideological diversity of the entire party system with the party manifesto data. Each political party in the manifesto project was given a summary left/right score, and this ideological score was weighted by the party's share of the votes at each election. Then we computed the standard deviation of weighted party scores for each election. This weighting makes each party's contribution to the diversity score proportional to the voters it represents in the party system. Thus larger parties make a greater contribution to the measure of ideological diversity than do smaller extremist parties, so that the diversity measure accurately reflects the entire distribution of ideology in a party system.

Table 10.2 tracks the changes in the ideological diversity of each party system over time. The first column presents the per annum change in ideological diversity. Of the fifteen countries for which we have data, ideological diversity decreases in eleven (seven are statistically significant even though the number of cases is quite small).[5] In contrast, not one of the positive coefficients is significant. One can also see the general trends by comparing the standard deviation for the first two elections in the 1950 to the last two elections of the 1980s (for which we have data). The change in the average standard deviation shows a decrease in the range of ideology in ten of the fifteen countries since the 1950s.

The individual national data series show that convergence is not a monotonic pattern in many instances. Often a specific election shows a spike (or dramatic convergence) in ideological positions as party strategies change. In Germany convergence focused around the SPD's dramatic move toward the centre with the 1969 Godesberg programme. Ireland, Norway, and Canada showed the sharpest evidence of convergence beginning in the 1970s. In other instances, such as Australia and Italy, there was gradual moderation over time. Nevertheless, although convergence has followed different courses, like water flowing down a mountainside it can follow different routes and still reach the bottom. And the general trend for most advanced industrial democracies is for the major left and right parties, and for the party system as a whole, to display a pattern of ideological convergence over time.

Furthermore, national patterns are generally consistent whether one focuses on only the major parties or the party system as a whole.[6] In contrast, previous research using expert judgements from 1983 to 1992 (Knutsen 1998) suggested that when the major left and right parties moved toward the centre, new parties stepped in on the wings to preserve the overall span of ideologies in the system. Our research does not show this distinction between the major left–right parties

---

[5] We also conducted the same analysis but did not weight each party by its share of the votes. Hence, a small fringe party weighs equally with the largest party. The results are very similar: 12 of the 15 countries yield a negative coefficient, reinforcing the pattern of convergence across the party system.

[6] There are three nations that produce opposing trends. Both Ireland and Sweden show convergence for the two major parties, but not when the entire system is taken into account. Italy shows the opposite: the entire system showed signs of convergence, but the two major parties displayed no movement toward the centre.

TABLE 10.2 *Change in Ideological Dispersion acoss Party Systems, 1950–1980s*

	Per annum change	Sig.	N	1950s avg.	1980s avg.	Change
Australia	−0.45***	0.01	16	24.4	5.7	−18.7
Austria	−0.75	0.30	11	38.9	7.6	−31.3
Belgium	−0.28**	0.02	13	15.9	2.8	−13.1
Canada	−0.28	0.55	13	22.9	24.6	+1.7
Denmark	0.01	0.81	16	35.2	39.7	+4.5
France	0.16	0.42	11	10.9	31.9	+31.0
Germany	−0.80*	0.08	10	20.7	8.2	−12.5
Ireland	−1.13*	0.09	11	36.0	31.7	−4.3
Italy	0.19	0.56	9	8.8	17.5	+8.7
Netherlands	−0.62***	0.00	11	19.5	2.1	−17.4
New Zealand	−0.59*	0.09	13	15.3	7.6	−7.7
Norway	−0.01	0.83	9	8.5	1.3	−7.2
Sweden	−0.22	0.45	13	25.1	27.5	+2.4
UK	−0.14*	0.09	11	9.4	2.6	−6.8
US	0.19	0.95	10	51.4	26.6	−24.8

*$p<0.10$, **$p<0.05$, ***$p<0.01$. Per annum change table entries are unstandardized regression coefficients.

and the party system as a whole. This contrast may be due to the differences in data sources, but it is more likely that the different time periods explains the contrast in results. As we have just noted, much of the party convergence occurred before the 1980s, and thus is missed in more recent analyses of expert judgements.

ISSUE VOLATILITY

Another potential aspect of changing party images involves consistency in party programmes over time. The traditional view of party manifestos treated them as a representation of the party's ideological orientation, updated for the new election. Socialist parties, for example, had a utopian vision of society and saw elections as an opportunity to educate voters in this ideology. Similarly, Christian Democratic and other conservative parties articulated a political philosophy in their manifestos, and this philosophy was an apparent constant across elections. Indeed, as Farrell and Webb point out in Chapter 6, the saliency theory of party competition rests on the assumption that each party focuses on its preferred issues. Similarly, the theory of issue ownership (Petrocik 1996) assumes that parties emphasize issues on which they are advantaged over their opponents, which over time creates the party's reputation. For instance, Labour parties have a natural advantage on the unemployment issue, while conservative parties routinely emphasize the inflation issue. These consistent emphases produce the cues upon which voters base their decision at the polls.

With changes in society and in technology, some scholars argue that the parties' product has become more malleable. For example, contemporary party campaigns have become more dependent on professional advisers, pollsters, and market researchers (Katz and Mair 1995; Farrell 1996). It appears that political parties pay increasing attention to the feedback they gain from public opinion polls and focus group discussions, and adapt their message to suit the interests of the perceived audience. An emphasis on candidate image similarly dilutes the need for fixed ideological appeals. Farrell and Webb (Chapter 6) suggest that parties have shifted from 'selling' an ideology to marketing what will sell. From this we interpret that parties may no longer stress the same issues consistently, but shift their issue profiles at an accelerated pace to match what they expect voters want based on their campaign research.

There are many current examples of this process. Tony Blair's campaign for New Labour in 1997 typified a campaign where the traditional ideology of the Labour Party was lost to a large extent in a campaign rhetoric of vague policy statements and idyllic comments about the future. This led Blair's critics to suggest that instead of the New Labour Party, Blair should have just said the 'New Party'. In the 1998 German elections Gerhard Schröder followed a similar strategy, telling voters that the SPD represented the 'Neue Mitte', while being imprecise about what this actually meant. Both of these campaigns also drew upon Clinton's ability to campaign successfully on the issues that the public seemingly wanted to hear, rather than what the Democratic Party might traditionally emphasize. The question is whether these observations represent a general feature of contemporary political parties.

Another process may also lead to shifts in party profiles. The introduction of new issue concerns increases the number of policy areas that parties confront. On the one hand, scholars such as Richard Hofferbert (1997) conclude that these issues have been integrated into the established party system and the 'discourse in party programmes has come to reflect that transformation to non-economic matters in a manner not likely to be permanently reversed'. Herbert Kitschelt (1994) similarly argues that Social Democratic parties have absorbed many of the New Politics demands as distributive issues of income become intertwined with non-economic issues. On the other hand, Inglehart (1997) finds that New Politics issues constitute their own new dimension. Factions concerned with new issues inside parties may lead to a higher level of intra-party debate. Whether or not established parties take up New Politics issues, the increasingly high number of new issues on the political agenda produces a more fluid environment overall, and this environment may encourage parties to become more flexible programmatically. For instance, the German SPD has vacillated between a centrist and leftist strategy in responding to the new Green party. In 1987 the party tried to attract new votes from the centre and nominated Johannes Rau as chancellor candidate;

in 1990 the party tried to lure Green voters from the left with Lafontaine as their candidate.

Both of these processes imply that there may be increasing volatility between elections in the policy programmes that political parties present to the voters. In their search for votes political parties may be more willing to cater to the public's current interests, responding to voter preferences instead of trying to shape these preferences. In addition, changes in voter preferences, especially the rise of New Politics issues, may press political parties to respond to a more dynamic and diverse set of voter preferences. Of course, parties' emphases are not completely static. Parties can shift their emphases over time, but the amount of shifting is assumed to remain at a steady level. We are interested in determining whether the degree of change in issue emphasis accelerates over time.

TESTING FOR CHANGES IN VOLATILITY

We again turned to the data from the Comparative Manifestos Project to examine volatility in party images over time. Using the twenty-six left–right themes in the manifesto data, we calculated the volatility of campaign platform statements for each major party as the absolute change in attention to these themes across adjacent elections.[7]

We averaged the volatility figures for the parties in each nation in each year and plotted them against time to see if there has been any systematic change in our set of countries in the post-war period. The results are shown in Figure 10.1. In general, the percentage of statements made in these left–right categories in one election is a poor predictor of the percentage made in the next. The total volatility between elections within this set of issues typically ranged between 30 and 50 percentage points for adjacent elections. Thus, it appears that parties commonly change over a third to a half of their thematic emphasis from one election to the next. Indeed, this might be expected if parties are responding to the larger environment in formulating their platforms; for instance, it makes sense to stress unemployment when this is a problem, but then attention shifts when social conditions raise other problems to the fore.

Figure 10.1 also shows that there is no dramatic change in the volatility of

[7] To calculate volatility we selected each party in each nation and isolated the 26 left–right issues. We calculated the percentage of statements made in each category (with the 26 adding up to 100%) and then calculated the absolute value of the change from one election to the next on each issue. At each election the absolute values are summed and divided by two. The volatility trends for the parties are then averaged by nation. We also produced volatility series using the complete set of issues (including 'uncoded' issues) but the overall scores do not differ remarkably from the left–right issue set. We acknowledge that there are always problems with aggregate indicators such as this one. Yet, given that we have a large number of cases, statistical tests by Bartolini and Mair (1990) show that one can consider aggregate volatility as an approximate indicator of individual level volatility.

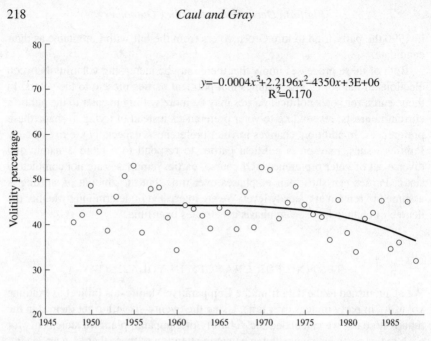

$$y=-0.0004x^3+2.2196x^2-4350x+3E+06$$
$$R^2=0.170$$

FIG. 10.1. Average Volatility of Left-Right Issue Saliency in Party Manifestos, 1948–1988

Note: Y-axis represents volatility percentage. Best-fit curve estimation obtained from Curve Expert 3.01.

party images over time, other than a slight decline in volatility in the 1980s. The decreased volatility in the 1980s may correspond to the ideological convergence we found in a number of these same party systems. However, without observations in the Comparative Manifestos data after 1988 it is difficult to tell if this trend has continued.

On the national level, declines in volatility are easier to identify (see Table 10.3). Five of the sixteen nations analysed here register declining trends that are statistically significant at the 0.05 level and twelve of the sixteen have seen decreased volatility between their first two post-war elections and the last two elections in the 1980s.[8] In five countries the decline is in double digits. The Australian and New Zealand party systems are exceptions to the general pattern, showing increases in volatility over the levels they had experienced in the immediate post-war period.

[8] This is computed by taking the average volatility scores in the second and third post-1948 elections (because the first volatility measure is taken from the difference of the first and second) and comparing them to the volatility scores in the last two elections in the series, which generally occur in the mid-to late 1980s.

TABLE 10.3 *Average Volatility of Left–Right Issue Saliency in Party Platforms,*
1950–1980s

	Per annum change	Sig.	N	1950s avg.	1980s avg.	Change
Australia	0.02	0.84	16	44.1	46.8	+2.7
Austria	−0.06	0.82	11	48.5	43.2	−5.3
Belgium	−0.28**	0.03	14	55.6	43.9	−11.7
Canada	−0.20	0.22	14	42.4	41.3	−1.1
Denmark	−0.25**	0.05	17	58.9	46.5	−12.4
France	−0.39*	0.07	11	36.8	30.3	−6.5
Germany	−0.53***	0.00	10	47.7	32.4	−15.3
Ireland	−0.31	0.21	11	55.6	49.8	−5.8
Italy	0.01	0.93	10	57.8	58.8	+1.0
Netherlands	0.01	0.91	12	28.3	34.5	−6.2
Norway	−0.30***	0.01	10	32.4	21.4	−11.0
New Zealand	0.21	0.22	14	34.7	49.9	+15.2
Sweden	−0.30**	0.04	13	41.8	34.3	−7.5
UK	−0.26	0.28	11	45.1	31.0	−14.1
US	0.08	0.73	10	32.6	27.1	−5.5

$*p<0.10$, $**p<0.05$, $*** p<0.01$. Per annum change table entries are unstandardized regression coefficients.

In sum, between the early 1950s and the late 1980s, there has been a slight tendency for political parties to become more consistent in the attention they give to traditional left/right ideological issues in their platforms. There is no evidence that volatility consistently increased across this set of advanced industrial democracies. In some regards this evidence is consistent with the convergence findings. When parties have converged toward a median position, they may also become more consistent from one election to the next as they focus again and again on a more limited issue space.[9] Certainly the broad comparisons that are possible with the Comparative Manifestos data may mask other elements of changing party images, but these broad comparisons are exactly where change was posited—but not observed.

[9] Kim and Fording (1998) present evidence that the 'voter ideology' in this set of democracies began to move toward the centre and stabilize in the late 1980s. In party systems where voters have moved to the ideological centre and remain we would expect 'Downsian' parties, and indeed the converging systems we have identified (such as Norway, Germany, and Belgium), to eventually show lower levels of inter-election volatility than those that show no convergence. In systems with already compacted issue space, volatility should be low. Page and Shapiro (1992) show that American voters have remained remarkably consistent across the postwar era in their policy preferences and we indeed find that US parties have generally shown the lowest level of volatility throughout the series, eventually showing the second lowest level of volatility in the late 1980s.

THE IMPACT OF PARTY CONTROL ON POLICY OUTPUTS

Few assumptions are more central to democracy than the leap of faith a voter makes at the ballot box. Implicit in electoral choices is the notion that the party or candidate one votes for will somehow be different from and preferable to the competition. The foundation of classical rational choice models of political participation depends on the probability that voters will receive some benefit from helping a party win office.

Ironically, empirical research has often found weak and inconsistent evidence that which party or parties are in government makes a substantial difference in terms of public policy outputs and economic performance. In a comprehensive review of the literature surrounding parties and public policy, Hofferbert and Cingranelli conclude that the last thirty-five years of research 'more often than not, reinforced the cliché that "politics doesn't matter" ' (1996: 594). In contrast, Manfred Schmidt's (1996) review of the literature concludes that parties do offer real choices and that parties have room to steer policy, even economic policy. Variations in time frame, the dependent variable, and methodology can partially explain these conflicting conclusions. Yet, none of these studies has focused on our central research question: has party influence changed over time within countries?

Party Control Does Matter

The original partisan theory, advanced by Douglas Hibbs (1977) and others, simply reasons that parties pursue policies in office that benefit their core political constituencies. As Cayrol and Jaffre (1980: 27) note, 'Parties are expected to represent the social composition of those who mandate them and to respond politically to the demands of their electorate.' For example, leftist parties, whose core constituency has traditionally been labour groups, are expected to increase deficit spending in order to fund the welfare state and to maximize employment, even at the expense of inflation. In contrast, rightist parties, whose core constituency is business and the middle class, are expected to be more fiscally prudent, and to prize low inflation over full employment.

Several empirical studies provide evidence that the partisan character of governing parties does indeed influence the types of policies that result. Frank Castles's (1982) seminal study examines expenditure data from 1960 to the mid-1970s in twenty-one OECD nations. He concludes that party politics is a major determinant of all components of welfare expenditure in this period. The right spends less and the Social Democrats are more generous. Castles's research takes into account both levels and change in expenditure data. While education and health spending are related to the party in control, public income maintenance programmes (ie. Social Security) appear to be unaffected by partisan control of the government.

More recent cross-national evidence also supports the idea that parties influence expenditure priorities. Ian Budge and Hans Keman (1990) analyse change in policy expenditure from 1965 to 1983 and conclude that parties appear to have a stable and important influence over policy. Alexander Hicks and Duane Swank (1992) reach the same conclusion using an alternative form of data analysis, controlling for institutional and other political influences. In a pooled time-series analysis from 1960 to 1982, Hicks and Swank find that centre-left governments tend to increase welfare spending. Further bolstering the 'parties matter' view, the strength of the opposition is influential as well. As right opposition strength increases, left government expansion of welfare efforts decrease.

In addition to policy expenditures, party influence is measured in terms of its impact on macroeconomic outcomes. Changes in the broad economic indicators may reflect the economic policies implemented by the government. Hibbs (1977; 1987) compares rates of unemployment and inflation across a set of industrial democracies over time and finds that party differences in policies and priorities do impact macroeconomic outcomes. He finds that social democratic governments indeed place a higher priority on full employment, at the risks of higher inflation.

Other research maintains that parties matter—but the direction of the relationship may be the reverse of what was previously hypothesized (see Cusack 1999). Although the standard reasoning is that rightist parties spend less than leftist parties and thus produce lower deficits, this assumption has been challenged on several fronts. When right-wing parties expect to fare poorly in the next election, they may engage in deficit spending in order to tie the hands of the incoming left-wing government. David Cameron (1985), for example, established that revenues are lower under rightist governments. Uwe Wagschal (1998) provides evidence from eighteen countries from 1960 to 1992 to show that rightist parties pursue tax-cutting policies designed to benefit their constituency, and collect less revenue so that deficits are subsequently higher than under leftist control. Thus, while we may hypothesize that the partisan composition of the government will influence policy outputs and macroeconomic conditions, there is some debate over the direction of these relationships.

Partisan Control Challenged by Socio-economic Changes

Many analyses of the policy impact of political parties have argued that socio-economic constraints are reducing the importance of partisan control. Several scholars theorize that changes in the international environment, such as the growing influence of the international economy and the Europeanization of policy-making, are limiting both the scope and the discretion of many national governments, and hence the ability of parties in national governments to steer policy has been reduced over time. Parties may be increasingly constrained by the same set of policy parameters and find themselves sharing the same set of policy priorities.

The globalization of the economy since the 1970s has presumably weakened both the economic and political bases for support of the welfare state. With the internationalization of trade, production, and finance, national governments lose some control over economic policy and the national economy is forced to conform to international market forces and compete with other countries that do not provide the same welfare benefits (for a review of literature see Berger and Dore 1996; Keohane and Milner 1996). Consequently, the same market-conforming policies will be implemented no matter whether a social democratic or conservative government is in office. Rather than offering clear alternatives, differences between parties are expected to diminish.

The most recent empirical research supports this thesis of diminishing marginal returns. Although each cross-temporal study utilizes a different set of OECD countries, measures economic policy differently, and employs various control variables, taken together they reveal a pattern of convergence toward tighter economic policies. Thomas Cusack (1999) finds that the impact of partisanship on government spending and on fiscal policy narrowed steadily after 1972. For example, in the earliest period of his study (1961–72), partisan responses to unemployment were strong, as partisan theory suggests. Yet steadily into the 1990s, parties converged in the 'use of fiscal policy as a partisan-based instrument' (Cusack 1999: 480).

Similarly, Keman (1984) found that while left control was particularly important to welfare expenditures, it mattered less across policy areas in the post-Bretton Woods era. Boix's (1998) research indicates that the differences between left and right governments almost disappeared for both fiscal and monetary policy after 1982 (control over public deficits and interest rates, respectively). Garrett and Lange (1991) conclude that while the impact of partisanship of government on fiscal policy is not clear there has been a convergence in monetary policy.

Some earlier research indicates that partisan influence on macro-economic outcomes was attenuated even before the substantial increase in global interdependence. In the same edited volume in which Castles finds that parties matter for expenditures, Schmidt (1982) finds mixed evidence as to whether parties matter for macroeconomic outcomes.[10] The degree of partisan control over macroeconomic outcomes was conditioned in the 1960s and 1970s by the rate of economic growth and extra-parliamentary factors such as the strength of organized labour.[11]

---

[10] Castles (1982) points out that policy areas in which the state has direct competence (expenditure priorities, taxes) are more likely to be affected by overtly political factors than policy areas in which the state has to rely on persuasion of individuals acting within an economic market environment (controlling inflation and unemployment).

[11] Some of the conflicting results regarding the influence of partisan control may be explained partially by the mediating impact of national institutions such as corporatist structures. Social democratic cabinets situated in corporatist economies appear to have asserted more control over fiscal and monetary policy during the 1970s (Boix 1998; Keman 1984). But since we are interested in comparisons over time, and these factors tend to be stable over time, they should have less relevance for our analyses.

In short, existing research is inconclusive regarding degree of party control over policy outcomes and the conditions under which parties can exert their greatest influence. Reviewing the literature on fiscal policy Cusack (1999: 471) states that, 'Evidence has been adduced to show that the left is more fiscally irresponsible that the right, that there is no difference between the left and the right, and that the right is more fiscally irresponsible than the left.'

Although there is a long-standing debate in the comparative public policy literature over the degree to which parties matter for policy, we are ultimately interested in the *changes* in party impact on policy within nations. While most of the previous literature has focused on differences across party systems, we are only interested in whether these effects have changed within countries since the 1960s and 1970s. In addition, it is important to add that the decline of class-based voting across advanced industrial democracies (Franklin et al. 1994) chips away at the tenets of the original partisan theory. This theory rests on a particular conception of the relationship between citizens and the political system. Under this standard conception, clearly demarcated social classes identified with certain parties. Therefore, we could expect to see differences in macroeconomic outcomes because parties pursued economic policies in order to benefit their traditional constituencies. As the historic relationship between the working class and the left becomes weaker, for example, the impetus for leftist parties to deploy economic instruments aimed at full employment at all costs diminishes considerably. Instead, parties may have a greater incentive to choose economic goals that appeal to the median voter.

Systemic changes in the economic system and government budgets may also restrict the parties' potential to control public policy. Most countries around the world are becoming ever more closely knit to global and regional economies where levels of inflation, economic growth, and unemployment are now heavily influenced by events occurring outside their own borders. Secondly, we expect that the growing independence of central banks and the completion of several economic cooperation agreements within our set of nations have together led to a deterioration of the ability of parties in government to influence domestic economic performance.[12] These constraints are part of the development of international economic forces that generally restrict the power of national governments. Finally, we also expect that the growth of non-discretionary budget items has led to a decline in the amount of control parties in government have in spending commitments.

---

[12] Many scholars agree that there has been a general trend towards more independent central banks in Europe over time. Some further argue that as a consequence, parties in government no longer control monetary policy. Elgie (1998) uses Cukierman's (1992) index of central bank independence to look more closely at Britain, France, and Germany over time. Elgie concludes that while the central bank's 'political independence', the ability to make policy decisions without interference from government, has actually decreased, the bank's 'economic independence', the ability to use a full range of monetary policy instruments without restrictions from government, has indeed increased. Because the banks are still politically dependent, Elgie sees no support for a threat to democratic accountability.

TESTING FOR THE IMPACT OF PARTIES ON PUBLIC POLICY

This section empirically examines whether the party composition of government matters less today than it once did. Given the mixed evidence of past research, and our findings on the ideological convergence in some party systems, we expect that if parties ever mattered, they probably matter less today than in the past.

To analyse the impact of parties on policy outputs we first created an indicator of the left–right party composition of government for eighteen OECD nations on an annual basis.[13] We used parliamentary seat share data (Mackie and Rose 1991, *Electoral Studies*, 1990–6) and expert classification of parties (Lane et al. 1997) to define the party composition of the government. The number of seats in parliament held by any party participating in government was used to create a total weighted measure for the left–right strength of a regime.[14] A completely leftist government is scored at –1.0, a pure centrist government at 0.0, and a completely rightist government at 1.0. Any other coalition government of different types of parties can be found somewhere between these 'unanimous' scores.[15]

We then selected six commonly used public policy and economic performance indicators as dependent variables, some of which would be readily available to any voter seeking information from his daily newspaper or evening news. These include annual rates of inflation, unemployment, GDP growth, total government expenditures as a percentage of GDP, welfare spending as a percentage of GDP, and defence spending as a percentage of total government expenditure. Together these are indicators of policy outputs and performance that are the most likely to be affected by the left–right composition of government.[16] These measures are

[13] The nations included are: Austria, Australia, Belgium, Canada, Denmark, Finland, France, Germany, Ireland, Italy, Japan, Netherlands, Norway, New Zealand, Sweden, Switzerland, United Kingdom, and the United States between 1949 and 1995. In years where the composition of parties in government changed we used the score that covered the longest period of time for that year. In bicameral legislatures only the lower house is considered.

[14] Using classifications from Lane, McKay, and Newton (1997), from left to right parties are classified as such: left (Communist, Socialist, Social Democrats), centre (Liberal, Christian Democrat), and right (Conservative, Agrarian, Far-Right). For questionable cases we referred to the ideological position of the party in the Manifestos Project data and other historical expert classifications (Patterson and Thomas 1977, Irving 1979, Stammen 1980, Morgan and Silvestri 1982, Waller and Fennema 1988, Dorfman and Duignan 1991).

[15] For example, a parliament with 400 seats where a government coalition is made up of three parties, one socialist with 50 seats, one liberal with 150 seats, and one agrarian with 25 seats would create a left score of 0.22, centre score of 0.67 and right score of 0.11. Once multiplied and aggregated ((0.22*–1)+(0.67*0)+(0.11*1)) the total ideological score for this government would be –0.12, or slightly left of centre. We have also utilized other variations of party government measures in several models, including dummy variables and disaggregated party scores (three separate weighted seat shares for left, centre, and right parties in government), variables for party control of the presidency (Austria, Finland, France, and the United States)—none attributed additional or improved explanation beyond the results presented.

[16] These indicators are by no means to be considered the only important or relevant measures of policy outputs. Indeed one could code actual legislation or more nuanced economic and government performance indicators. We employ these measures here because they are the most

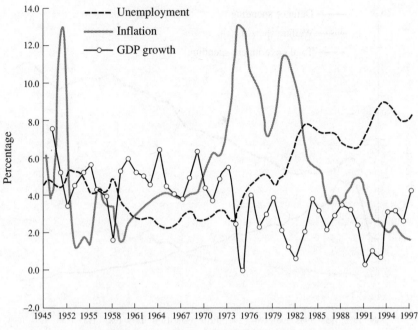

FIG. 10.2. Average GDP Growth, Inflation, and Unemployment, 1949–1997

Note: Y-axis represents percentages.

also useful in that they do not measure what parties want or promise but what actually happens when they are in power.[17] Although these indicators have been criticized for being too aggregated they are employed here because they are the most widely used in political economy and public policy research.[18]

accessible to voters and they are the most commonly used indicators analysed by the media, economists, and political scientists. While admittedly more complex and comprehensive analysis could be done to measure policy outputs they would require more space than could be devoted here to these questions. With that in mind, we have used the most direct and relevant approach and selected the six indicators used here.

[17] This is especially important when one considers that parties may and in many cases do want the same things but do not always get the same results. For instance few parties want high unemployment and inflation and low GDP growth. Thus if one were to do this analysis based on what parties promise and want it would reason that for these indicators there would be perhaps little or no difference between different party regimes. However our data are the objective rates of economic performance and government spending, thus they are measures of what parties can do—and that is certainly the crux of our research question; does the composition of parties in government affect policy outcomes?

[18] The main focus in collecting these data was to find the longest, uninterrupted series for each indicator that had been computed consistently. In some panels, missing data could not be

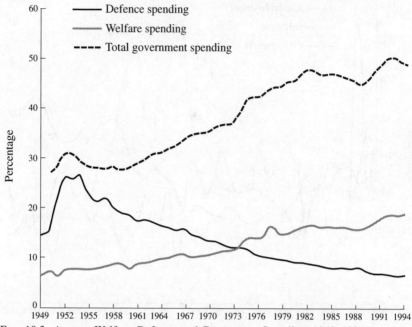

FIG. 10.3. Average Welfare, Defence, and Government Spending, 1949–1995

Note: Y-axis represents percentages. Defence spending is measured as a percentage of total government expenditures. Welfare and Total Government Expenditure are measured as shares of GDP.

Drawing on past research, we expected to find that rightist governments would favour lower rates of inflation and higher rates of unemployment than leftist governments. We also made the assumption that rightist governments would typically support lower levels of government and welfare spending and higher levels of defence spending than leftist governments. From a combination of these policy choices and previous research we expected more rightist governments to show higher levels of GDP growth than those dominated by leftist parties.

Throughout the analysis we take great care to control for the temporal nature of our data. As one can see from Figures 10.2 and 10.3, the aggregated economic performance and spending item trends for all eighteen nations show significant

avoided. In the worst case, neither the OECD nor the World Bank has any data for welfare spending in New Zealand. However this is the only case where data on any indicator is completely or widely missing. The data for the six spending and economic performance indicators was collected from widely used reliable sources: Banks (1998), Flora et al. (1983), Mitchell (1998*a*, 1998*b*, 1998*c*), *OECD Economic Outlook: Historical Statistics* (various years) and *World Bank World Development Indicators* (1999).

TABLE 10.4 *Correlations between Right Party Government and Policy Outputs, 1950–1990s*

	GDP growth	Unemploy-ment	Inflation	Govt. spending	Defence spending	Welfare spending
AUS	0.254	−0.299*	−0.257	−0.422**	0.063	0.002
AUT	0.032	0.154	−0.242	−0.199	0.161	0.092
BEL	−0.254	0.270	0.244	0.191	0.099	0.354*
CAN	−0.319*	0.553**	−0.095	−0.067	0.169	−0.141
DEN	−0.099	0.306*	−0.167	0.100	−0.091	−0.056
FIN	0.103	0.133	−0.144	−0.108	0.409**	0.207
FRA	0.171	−0.531**	−0.104	−0.416**	0.087	−0.267
GER	0.360*	0.577**	−0.462**	−0.342*	−0.363*	−0.355*
IRE	0.151	−0.127	0.153	0.154	−0.242	0.211
ITA	0.248	0.196	−0.188	0.179	0.307*	−0.164
JAP	0.142	0.015	0.025	−0.085	−0.088	−0.113
NET	0.303*	−0.255	−0.265	−0.361*	0.125	−0.039
NOR	0.004	−0.229	0.076	−0.244	0.030	0.034
NZ	0.061	0.187	−0.144	0.018	0.047	—[a]
SWE	−0.414**	0.251	0.252	0.639**	−0.201	0.712**
SWI	0.010	0.590**	−0.383**	−0.108	0.643**	−0.003
UK	0.110	0.256	−0.328*	−0.457**	0.476	−0.146
USA	−0.177	−0.071	−0.197	0.130	0.352*	0.702**

*$p<0.05$, **$p<0.01$. Table entries are Partial correlation coefficients controlling for the year of observation. Right Government variable consists of a measure varying between −1 (left govt.) and +1 (right govt.).

[a] Welfare Spending estimates exclude New Zealand for which there was no comparable data.

changes over time.[19] To avoid spurious relationships in systems where one type of government was in power during the early post-war years and out of government in the latter, we have utilized various methods of time-series analysis and controls to avoid any possibly misleading results.[20]

In our first test of our hypothesis we ran partial correlations between our

---

[19] It is important to note that these are aggregated trends and in many cases vary within individual countries.

[20] For correlations we control for the year of the observation. In regression models we ran both within-nation Prais-Winsten models and pooled cross-sectional models using an OLS fixed-effects method of estimation, again with controls for the year of observation. We also considered using change data (first-differences) yet this method of estimation asks a different question from what we have asked. If the party government variable is converted to first differences then it only changes in years where government changes. This is problematic because we certainly would not want to limit the impact of government on public policy to their first year in government. Logically we would expect the greatest impacts to occur after the initial change. We also employed lagged data in our models to capture the effects of the party composition of government and our control variables at t, $t–1$, and $t–2$, yet these models did not significantly differ from the models only at year t as reported here.

measure of right-wing party government ('right' in that the measure's positive direction represents more right party control over government) and the spending and economic performance measures, controlling for the year of observation. The results are shown in Table 10.4.

We found inconsistent evidence that 'parties matter' in the manner expected by theory. Across the eighteen nations none of the spending or economic performance measures are strongly and generally affected by the party composition of government. If we disaggregate these data and look at separate nations, however, there are several cases where a right-wing government is consistently related to policy outputs.

Germany[21] offers the most convincing case where changes in party government have generally had the predicted impacts on the indicators of economic performance and government spending. When the German government was more heavily controlled by centre or right parties (mainly the CDU) GDP growth and unemployment was higher and inflation, government spending, welfare spending, and defence spending were all lower than when left-of-centre parties were in government (mainly the SPD). All of the relationships are statistically significant at the 0.05 level or less. Few other countries, however, show such a clear pattern. Furthermore, some of the relationships are in the opposite direction to those theorized. Nine of the twenty-eight statistically significant national-level relationships run counter to the hypothesized direction. For example, in Sweden, when the Social Democrats (SAP) either share power or are out of government and a centrist-right coalition controls government, GDP growth is lower and government and welfare spending are higher.[22]

In all, of the 108 partial correlation coefficients for the eighteen nations and six dependent variables over forty-five years only 18 per cent actually attain statistical significance in the hypothesized direction. This is hardly the type of evidence one would expect if the party composition of government has a significant and wide-ranging impact on these primary indicators of economic performance and public policy commitments. Such is the type of empirical evidence that has produced ambiguous conclusions in the literature.

Of course this simple analysis does not directly address the hypothesis that the influence of parties has decreased over time. To determine whether the policy influence of parties is changing, we analysed a variety of pooled cross-sectional models.[23] We also created an additional variable to estimate the changing impact of global and regional forces on government spending and economic performance,

[21] Data for pre-unification Germany is for West Germany only.

[22] These relationships cannot be attributed to the trends in the dependent variables even after controlling for the year of the observations. The Social Democrats have altered their position in government throughout the 45-year time series, being out of or sharing government for parts of four decades (9/51–10/57, 10/76–10/82, 10/91–9/94).

[23] We also produced national-level estimations which in general gave similar results. Where the findings of these estimations were noteworthy we cite them.

consisting of a calculation of the annual OECD average of each dependent variable for all eighteen nations (excluding the country under analysis).[24] The OECD average variables allow us to control for exogenous economic shocks and worldwide trends in spending without using historical dummy or specialized variables.[25] We also introduced a measure of GDP growth as an independent variable into the government spending models to account for domestic recessionary pressures and to control for the fact that total government spending and welfare spending are standardized by the size of GDP.[26]

We used a least squares (OLS) fixed-effects method of estimation to obtain the results for the pooled cross-sectional models for each of the six dependent variables.[27] This allowed us to control for the temporal nature of the data and cross-sectional differences while dealing with any possible autocorrelation problems (Stimson 1985). We also split the analysis into three different periods (1949–65, 1966–80, and 1981–95) to analyse the changing impacts of the independent variables over time. The first period presents the post-war baseline. The second period encompasses the moderation of the growth period in many nations, and the onset of the OPEC price increases of the 1970s. The third period represents the current influence of party governments.

The first of the three models examines the influence of partisan control on economic indicators: GDP growth rates, inflation, and unemployment (Table 10.5). The results show that centrist and rightist governments during the 1949 to 1965 period were more likely to have higher levels of GDP growth. However the effects are not dramatic—about one percentage point is involved. The estimated difference between a socialist government and a liberal government is only 0.62 percentage points, whereas the estimated difference between a socialist government and a conservative government is 1.25 percentage points. In the latter two periods, spanning 1966 to 1995, the impact of the composition of government is not statistically significant.

---

[24] Within each of the eighteen panels a series with the average of the other seventeen countries in the pooled data set for each indicator is used. Thus, Australia has the average of each six dependent variables for the seventeen other countries minus its own observations. This removes any possible endogenous variance.

[25] One of the common dummy variables utilized in public policy models is for the OPEC oil embargo (Hicks and Swank 1992). With the OECD averages the variance attributed to this is captured by the economic changes occurring simultaneously in the seventeen other nations.

[26] This is necessary to delineate cases where the level of spending remains relatively unchanged but GDP does not, thereby creating non-spending related fluctuations in the spending/GDP calculations.

[27] We used the fixed-effects estimation procedure on a stacked-pooled data set of the eighteen countries from 1949 to 1995. Each panel thus contains 46 observations for a total of 828 observations in the complete data set. The software package STATA and its 'xtreg fe' option was used to analyse the data. This method is equivalent to introducing $n-1$ dummy variables for each country and year in the pooled time-series. Models including observations for the independent variables at t, $t-1$, and $t-2$ were not substantially different from those reported here. For unreported results contact the authors.

The OECD GDP growth averages[28] are consistent and statistically significant in each of the three models. Gaining slight strength between periods, this represents a relationship where GDP is likely to grow in any of the countries by approximately 0.77 to 0.88 percentage points when it grows by an average of 1.0 percentage point in the other seventeen nations. This represents evidence that GDP growth within these eighteen nations has been closely interlinked throughout the post-war period.[29]

The model for unemployment in the second panel of the table yields mixed evidence. In two of the three estimations (1949–65 and 1981–95) governments controlled by centre and right parties were more likely to be in power during times with higher levels of unemployment. However, the impact of the party measure is stronger in the earlier period. In general, the difference between a left-dominated government and a right-dominated government during the 1949–65 period was equivalent to a 1.55 percentage point increase in unemployment—again not a dramatic difference and one that decline 1.09 percentage points in the 1981–95 period.

As in the previous models, the OECD unemployment averages are highly significant and of a greater magnitude in each time period. From 1949 to 1980 the relationship is nearly one to one—where an average one percentage point increase in unemployment in the seventeen other nations leads to a domestic increase of approximately one percentage point. The impact of exogenous unemployment changes declines in the post-1981 period to an approximate domestic increase in unemployment of 0.73 percentage points when the average increase in the other seventeen nations is one percentage point.

These estimates provide evidence that the party composition of government has and still does affect unemployment levels but that exogenous economic changes matter as well.[30] Similar estimates regarding the impact of the party composition of government on levels of inflation provide contradictory evidence across the three time periods. While the composition of the government lacks a

---

[28] The OECD average variables for all of the models were excluded to test the possibility that they were 'draining' variance from the party composition of government measure. This was found not to be the case. We also ran models including lags of the OECD averages for t–1 and t–2 but these inclusions did not significantly alter the results presented here.

[29] A similar estimation (unreported) by nation split between pre- and post-1975 showed that GDP growth has been higher under Canadian Liberal Party governments during both periods—2.0 percentage points higher during the pre-1975 period and 2.2 percentage points higher post-1975, while Italian governments containing leftist party participation showed GDP growth of approximately 2.2 percentage points lower in the post-1975 era. In presidential systems, these national-level models included a measure for party control of the presidency, however none obtained statistical significance. In every country, excluding New Zealand, the OECD GDP growth averages were statistically significant.

[30] We also explored models that divided the pooled sample into pre/post-1975 groupings. In some cases these results deviate from the patterns presented here, but we generally felt the three-period model yielded more consistent results. The results of the dichotomous groupings are available from the authors.

TABLE 10.5 *Impact of Right Party in Government on GDP Growth, Unemployment and Inflation, 1950–1990s*

	Economic growth			Unemployment			Inflation		
	1949–65	1966–80	1981–95	1949–65	1966–80	1981–95	1949–65	1966–80	1981–95
Right Party Government	0.624*	0.257	0.179	0.773**	0.102	0.544*	0.393	0.938**	−0.825***
	(0.253)	(0.205)	(0.159)	(0.279)	(0.144)	(0.237)	(0.551)	(0.361)	(0.256)
OECD average	0.773***	0.875***	0.864***	1.079***	1.034***	0.733***	0.902***	0.993***	0.974***
	(0.132)	(0.095)	(0.105)	(0.10)	(0.065)	(0.143)	(0.083)	(0.052)	(0.053)
Constant	1.120	0.508	0.339	0.445	0.049	2.219*	0.418	0.180	0.068
	(0.671)	(0.383)	(0.266)	(0.494)	(0.236)	(1.066)	(0.396)	(0.423)	(0.291)
R-Square	0.158	0.301	0.238	0.198	0.520	0.124	0.291	0.595	0.586
F-test	39.0***	89.3***	68.0***	29.8***	128.3***	17.1***	58.6***	183.6***	175.6***
Number of Obs.	288	270	268	261	256	262	305	270	268

*$p<0.05$, **$p<0.01$, ***$p<0.001$. Dependent Variables are annual rate of GDP growth, unemployment and inflation. Table entries are unstandardized regression coefficients (standard errors are in parenthesis) from fixed-effects pooled time-series models including 18 nations between the specified time periods. Some panels contain missing data. Right Government variable consists of a measure varying between −1 (left govt.) and +1 (right govt.). OECD average includes the OECD average of the dependent variable for the 17 countries in the sample—excluding the nation analyzed in that panel.

statistically significant relationship that is found in 1949–65, there is a positive relationship between right party government and inflation in the 1966–80 period. However this shows a nearly complete reversal in the 1981–95 period where more centre-right dominated governments show the expected lower levels. In each of the later periods the effect is modest, just under 1.9 percentage points.

The results of these three economic indicators thus provide a mixed bag of results. The party composition of government has not had a particularly strong effect on any of the three indicators—as prior research has shown. Furthermore, none of the three sets of models show a consistent impact of changes in government on these indicators across the entire time series. In the post-1980 period, however, rightist governments do show statistically significant effects in the hypothesized direction for unemployment and inflation. Thus, the party composition of government seems to matter more today than it once did—although the effect is weak overall and not as strong or consistent as the influence of international economic changes.

Turning to the impact of parties in government on spending items, we assumed that we might find a stronger and more consistent pattern of relationships than for economic performance data. We began with total government spending (Table 10.6). Even after controlling for cross-sectional differences and the year of observation with the fixed-effects model, the party composition of government did not matter in any of the three time periods. Instead the OECD averages of government spending as a share of GDP were much more successful at predicting changes in domestic levels of spending. Once again the relationships were generally slightly less than one to one percentage point change in each of the three periods.

Also as expected, the GDP growth measure had a negative sign representing the impact of GDP growth on the denominator of the government spending/GDP calculation of the dependent variable. In all three cases growth of GDP seems to outpace growth in spending.[31] This indicator only achieves significance in the 1981–95 period. Similar results were produced in the models for the disaggregated spending items for social welfare and defence.

In both cases, the party composition of government measure did not achieve statistical significance in any of the three time periods. Thus there is consistent evidence that changes in the party profile of government had no measurable

---

[31] Where government spending items are measured as spending/GDP it is necessary to control for changes in the denominator (GDP). For example consider the case where spending remains relatively unchanged from one year to the next while GDP does not. In the case of relatively stationary spending and rapidly increasing GDP it would appear as if spending actually had declined when in fact it may not have (depending on changes in inflation). If GDP grows by 6% in one year and spending increases by 3% that in sum leads to a net slight decline in spending in relation to GDP (depending on the relative size of each). Thus the GDP growth coefficients take the expected negative sign in our models. Controlling for the other influences of the other variables, as GDP increases spending falls when spending is measured as spending/GDP.

TABLE 10.6 *Impact of Right Party in Government on Total Government, Welfare, and Defense Spending, 1950–1990s*

	Total Govt. Spending			Welfare Spending			Defence Spending		
	1949–65	1966–80	1981–95	1949–65	1966–80	1981–95	1949–65	1966–80	1981–95
Right Party	0.248	0.201	0.060	0.051	0.190	0.122	0.468	0.389	0.376
	(0.367)	(0.362)	(0.339)	(0.169)	(0.330)	(0.229)	(0.590)	(0.307)	(0.215)
Government									
OECD average	0.860***	0.977***	0.707***	0.826***	0.825***	0.657***	0.946***	0.975***	0.764***
	(0.101)	(0.043)	(0.116)	(0.056)	(0.064)	(0.177)	(0.075)	(0.017)	(0.126)
GDP growth	0.001	-0.067	-0.478***	-0.024	-0.138	-0.196***	0.200*	-0.057	-0.057
	(0.053)	(0.069)	(0.084)	(0.022)	(0.63)	(0.055)	(0.089)	(0.057)	(0.053)
Constant	4.505	2.273	15.442***	3.518***	3.597***	7.135***	2.898	0.545	2.029*
	(2.853)	(1.699)	(5.258)	(0.358)	(0.852)	(1.890)	(1.608)	(0.857)	(0.984)
R-Square	0.217	0.717	0.245	0.544	0.475	0.192	0.423	0.439	0.144
F-test	24.7***	206.8***	26.5***	73.9***	68.1***	18.2***	62.9***	65.0***	13.8***
Number of Obs.	288	266	266	206	246	250	278	270	267

*$p<0.05$, **$p<0.01$, ***$p<0.001$. Dependent variables are Total Govt. Spending/total govt. spending, Welfare Spending/GDP, Defense Spending/GDP. Table entries are unstandardized regression coefficients (standard errors are in parenthesis) from fixed-effects pooled time-series models including 18 nations between the specified time periods. Right Government variable consists of a measure varying between –1 (left govt.) and +1 (right govt.). OECD average includes the OECD average of the dependent variable for the 17 countries in the sample—excluding the nation analyzed in that panel.

impact during any of the three periods within each of our countries. This is not to say that parties do not change spending priorities or adopt new programmes that are not measurable by the changes in the aggregated measures we have used here.[32] However, we have clearly shown, using these widely analysed indicators, that other influences are at work in the determination of these aggregated spending measures. It is not clear that a shift in the party profile of government in either direction has any impact on the overall size of government, or the scope of the welfare state or defence commitments.

Once again, the OECD spending averages were statistically significant in every estimation and fairly consistent across time with slight decreases in the 1981–95 period for both types of spending. Apparently, spending patterns commonly reflect larger international forces that affect other advanced industrial democracies. For both types of spending the control for GDP growth does take the appropriate sign when statistically significant, yet does so inconsistently across time.

Taken together our results do not differ substantially from the conclusion that 'politics doesn't matter'.[33] The few relationships we did find in the pooled and national-level models compel us to qualify that statement and say, 'politics hasn't mattered—much'. In some countries and during some periods of time, hypothesized relationships were found—albeit at a much weaker and inconsistent level than we had expected. Given this unclear evidence of partisan effects in the first place, it is not surprising that there is not consistent evidence that these relationships have weakened over time. At the same time, the impact of systematic changes within OECD countries, such as the end of the Cold War, the ageing of populations, and global economic interconnectedness—as represented by the OECD average measures—has strongly affected public policy commitments and economic performance.[34] To the extent that this variable is a

[32] A different approach, perhaps using content analysis of legislation passed, could provide different answers to our same question. This alternative could perhaps produce a stronger relationship between the party composition of government and policy outputs defined by the specifics of legislation passed. This would however be a daunting task considering the scope of the research question analysed here, for it would involve coding legislation and its origin for every party in every year since 1950 for eighteen nations. We present this here as a caution that our analysis could obviously be expanded by using a different conceptualization of policy outputs and performance.

[33] We must note that our analysis cannot account for counterfactual scenarios. For example it is plausible that the comparison should be between what Party A did at time *t* and what Party B would have done at time *t*, not between what Party A did at time *t* and what Party B did at time *t*–1. For example, let's say inflation was at 2% under right party government B, and then moved to 5% under left party government A. The real measure of the effect of the switch from right to left is not measurable—it is to compare that 2% with what unemployment would have been had the right party government B stayed in power. Perhaps it would have jumped to 7%. However these counterfactual scenarios are beyond the bounds of empirical analysis and exist in the realm of alternative histories. While such a model cannot be studied it is worth noting the possibility in theory.

[34] It is also important to note that in no case does the OECD average variable 'steal the thunder'

surrogate for external constraints on government, it might be said that the power of parties has been limited.

CONCLUSIONS

In sum, it appears that political parties across advanced industrial democracies increasingly find it difficult to maintain distinct identities. In most countries there has been a general drift towards the centre of the left–right ideological spectrum. At the same time, rather than parties systematically increasingly shifting the issues they emphasize, we find a mixed pattern with an overall general trend towards more stability on left/right issues. However, this stability may simply reflect the major left and right parties focusing on a more limited range of issue space. Contrary to what we hypothesized from research on the changing nature of campaigns, the growing professionalization of parties has not led to a clear pattern of increasing volatility. Professionalization may be linked to institutionalization, making parties less variable over time, at least in terms of the broad manifesto promises intended for all party adherents. Further, in order to be consistent over time we have had to limit the volatility analysis to issues that have been on the agenda since the 1950s—the Old Politics issues. Parties may have grown more volatile in terms of new issues, which are not captured in our analysis. For example, parties may increasingly shift in the amount of attention paid to environmental protection or to minorities as these new issues find their place within the party system.[35]

Yet these mixed volatility findings may also be due to limitations of the Comparative Manifestos Project data. The data only extend to 1987, and the chapters on party identification and voting turnout have noted that partisan changes in these areas have often accelerated in the past decade (see Chapters 2 and 4). In addition, the move from selling to marketing may not be in terms of emphasizing new issues, but instead in terms of the directionality of issues, an occurrence that could not be captured by data that measures the salience of certain issues.

Taken together with the finding of a general pattern of convergence on traditional left–right issues, it may be that after moving towards the centre, parties have become more consistent as range of traditional left–right issues that they address has narrowed. The effects of party composition of government on policy

of the party government measure. We ran models with and without the OECD averages for comparison and found no evidence that the party of control in government mattered systematically. In fact without the OECD averages variable party government was nearly completely ineffective in explaining any remarkable amount of the variance in the public policy output and economic performance measures within countries and in the pooled models.

[35] Although volatility models using the complete set of manifesto issues show no movement toward more volatility, at least to 1987.

are also mixed. Consistent with past literature, we found that the overall impact of parties on policy output is modest. Importantly, this modest impact does not appear to be systematically changing over time within countries.[36] Past research assumed that because parties represent certain constituencies, they pursue policies to benefit those constituencies. Yet parties in government have not consistently followed the goals that scholars had assumed they would. The relationship between partisan control and public policy was not clear in the past and is even murkier today.

The theory that parties matter for policy outputs also relies on the assumption that there were distinct differences in the ideologies of parties. Because we found that these ideological differences in the party platforms are eroding, we cannot expect that parties will have greater impact in the future. At the same time, the erosion of the traditional socio-economic constituencies of parties will add to the lack of a clear partisan impact on economic policy.

Our findings have implications for the link between voters and parties. The absence of clear distinctions between party promises before elections and in party policies and outcomes after elections may greatly affect the way voters think about party politics. The difficulty that parties have in maintaining separate identities in terms of their platforms is probably magnified at the level of the voter. Importantly, if several decades of empirical research cannot determine the impact of parties on policy, then the image that parties project to voters may be even more obscure. If already small differences in partisan control are shrinking even further, then voters' may perceive little difference between a left-wing and a right-wing government.

Taken together, these findings make the model of responsible party government appear increasingly anachronistic. It is clear no modern party system lives up to the Westminster model advocated by scholars in the past, and the model has never applied well to parties in coalition. Yet beyond this classical theoretical assumption, parties have in practice traditionally performed some of these functions to greater and lesser degrees across established democracies. From our findings, we can conclude that parties' role in structuring the vote choice and structuring the policy-making process has weakened. Clear, distinct, and consistent partisan profiles are integral to structuring the voters' choices and to setting the policy agenda. Because party profiles are obscure, it is less likely that once in office parties will have clear and distinct objectives for the policies that they enact. In addition, because parties are growing increasingly similar, parties may no longer simplify the voting choice. And if they do not emphasize issues consistently from one election to the next, then we must question the amount of valuable information that can be provided by parties in government.

If voters are unable to 'feel' and 'see' much difference in the programmatic

---

[36] Which is not to say that party government has not and does not 'matter' in comparisons made across nations instead of within them.

outputs and economic performance of different party governments it becomes more likely that they may no longer see much relevance in going to the polls or even paying attention to politics. In systems where parties look and act more alike the differentiation may increasingly come down to the style and personality characteristics of party leaders and candidates (Wattenberg 1991). The trivialization of party politics may ensue. Although party command over policy and economic outcomes may be constrained by global and social forces beyond their control, it is unlikely that the average voter has been aware of such changes. The focus of public policy will remain on parties—voters and the media expect them to have an impact. However, if the patterns found in our examination of over nearly fifty years of data continue, parties will more than likely persist with a limited capacity to affect aggregate policy outcomes and are likely to continue to struggle to significantly differentiate themselves on policy matters.

11

On the Primacy of Party in Government

Why Legislative Parties Can Survive Party Decline in the Electorate

Michael F. Thies

IT is tempting to view the evidence of declining party identification in the electorates of advanced industrial democracies (Chapters 2–4), and the changing nature of party organizations and campaign activity (Chapters 5–7), and conclude that parties are on their way out as a feature of modern democratic politics. At the same time, the evidence in this section suggests that 'party in government' remains alive and well in the advanced democracies. Parties still dominate the memberships of legislatures and cabinets (Chapter 9). Partisan cabinets still enjoy tremendous procedural advantages over individuals or non-partisan legislative groups. There is no evidence of a secular decline in the cohesiveness of parties in legislative votes (Chapter 8). And partisan shifts in government still produce predictable changes in government policy (Chapter 10).

Is this state of affairs contradictory? Can parties in government survive without parties in the electorate? This essay argues that parties in government can indeed survive, and even prosper, despite what is going on at the voter level. It provides a picture of parties without partisans that is neither paradoxical nor antidemocratic. If parties really are losing their hold on the electorate, it represents a return to their roots as parliamentary organizations. Although 'party decline' at the electoral level might kill off the organizational accoutrements that once aided the core pursuits of professional politicians, it need not strike a death blow to the 'core party', which remains the province of elected officials.

WHY PARTIES?

The first parties were 'parliamentary cliques', long-lived and broad-ranging parliamentary coalitions that pre-dated mass electoral politics. With the advent of mass suffrage, these parliamentary groups used their collective attributes as electoral resources to appeal to voters as 'teams'. Even after the development of mass memberships and complex party organizations, it was always the 'in-government' aspect of parties that provided sustenance to the electoral party and the party organization. Whereas the strength of an electoral party might be measured in terms of its membership or popularity, or by its vote and seat shares, elections are merely a means to an end. Participation in government, or even control of government, is a universal collective goal for parties,[1] and the *raison d'être* for the 'party in the electorate'.

Why Do Legislators Form Parties?

Let us assume that legislators pursue three goals: re-election, policy, and securing powerful institutional posts (Strøm 1990*b*). It follows that legislators will only form or join political parties if parties help them to pursue at least one of these three goals. If partisan affiliation helps a member to be re-elected, to receive a plum committee assignment or cabinet post, or to achieve policy aims, and if the costs of joining a party do not outweigh the benefits obtained, then he or she will join and work within a party. Legislative parties, therefore, are threatened as organizational forms if their usefulness to incumbent members wanes or if the costs of membership increase.

In order to serve as vehicles for their goal-seeking members, parties must control assets and tools that relate to elections, policy-making, and government posts. Parties must perform certain functions for members either exclusively or more efficiently than alternative providers. When the party's ability to perform these functions is compromised or is outstripped by the abilities of alternative providers, it will decline in importance to legislators. This leads us to three questions. First, how is it that parties can serve any function for legislators? Second, what are the central functions of parties in government? Third, what might threaten the party's ability to perform these functions, and thus reduce the party-ness[2] of government?

Parties as Solutions to Collective Dilemmas

Any legislator interested in passing legislation realizes that passing legislation is not as simple as advocating it. She may speechify, arm-twist, cajole, or otherwise advocate or oppose legislation, but passing legislation requires the cooperation of at least a majority of her colleagues, and securing this cooperation will entail costs and risks for herself and for her potential coalition partners. Presumably, many of her potential collaborators are not as interested in her proposal, *per se*, as she is. Thus, she will have to seek out votes, sometimes by promising her support for others' proposals if they support her this time around. Of course,

---

[1] Anti-system parties might be exceptional in this regard.
[2] I borrow the term 'partyness' from Richard Katz (1987*b*).

promises about future behaviour are difficult to enforce, as today's collaborator might worry about becoming tomorrow's patsy. The best solution to this problem might be a logroll, whereby a legislator agrees to attach to her proposal as many proposals by others as are necessary to secure a majority of votes for the total package. However, if every piece of legislation requires intensive logrolling, either enormous resources will have to be expended in the search for the 'minimum winning coalition' or supermajorities will pass omnibus packages that could have been trimmed given better information and enforcement of bargains.[3]

If legislators in a prospective vote coalition decide that they would like to continue to do business together, they need to find a way to control against incentives to renege or defect to rival proto-coalitions dangling better deals. According to Cox and McCubbins (1993), the solution is to hire 'Leviathan': legislators can create structures and procedures that serve to bind the members of the coalition to the straight and narrow. They elect leaders and provide them with discretion over the allocation of selective rewards and punishments that can be used to keep members in line. These leadership tools are effective because they allow leaders to single out potential defectors, and take action constraining only the defector's prospects of attaining his goals. This long-lived, broad-based, highly structured coalition, is precisely a legislative party.[4]

The central functions of parties in government, therefore, are (1) to control policy-making, (2) to control the administrative apparatus of the national government in order to implement those policies, and (3) to take public responsibility for policy outcomes. To understand the centrality of these three party functions, it is useful to refer to the idealized model of party government (sometimes called the 'Westminster' model), in which two homogeneous parties compete for control of government. One party wins a majority of legislative seats and chooses the prime minister and the cabinet. Policy decisions are made within the ruling party and administered faithfully by the government apparatus. At election time, the ruling party runs on its record. Voters base their decisions on their assessment of the performance of the ruling party. The minority party serves in this model as a ruling-party-in-waiting, offering alternative policies and criticizing the performance of the government.[5]

---

[3] Weingast (1979) has argued that the only *structure-free* equilibrium to this problem is a universal logroll, so called because it includes the pet projects of all legislators. The logic is that any minority would have the incentive and the wherewithal to peel off enough members of the majority coalition and form a new majority. Because this is always true, no majority smaller than unanimity is stable. Weingast and Marshall (1988) suggest as an alternative, a *structured* environment, with powerful, self-selected committees. This generates essentially the same outcome: universal logrolls by high-demander committees.

[4] Similar arguments can be found in Schwartz (1989) and Aldrich (1995).

[5] Other activities that are widely perceived to be functions of political parties are not central to their existence. Electioneering tactics such as choosing candidates to endorse, supplying candidates with funding or workers, and mobilizing voters are all activities that a party might choose to undertake, but they are not inherent in the party government model. Similarly, organ-

How do we know the extent to which the ruling party performs the central functions of policy making, administration, and programmatic appeals to voters? Perhaps the easiest way to conceive of appropriate measures is to examine each purported 'function', identify its 'non-partisan' alternative, construct a continuum between the two endpoints of 'partisan' and 'non-partisan', and then attempt to discover the nature of the variable or variables that generate the continuum. If 'partyness' means anything, then each should have clear 'partisan' and 'non-partisan' idealizations as endpoints of a measurable continuum of observable behaviours.

Party-in-Government Function 1: Elections

The simplest of the three party functions to conceptualize is that of taking responsibility for policy outcomes. In the party government model, there are only two parties, and the 'winner' is the party that wins a majority of legislative seats because more voters prefer its vision of policy over that of its rival. If there are more than two parties, and none wins a majority, then all policy proposals will require the support of more than one party. But shared power compromises the ability of a party to campaign, and of voters to vote, on the basis of responsibility for government policy. A party that shares power also shares responsibility, and this obscures accountability. If voters cannot assign responsibility clearly to one party, then they will not know whom to reward or punish, according to their assessment of policy performance. Another threat to partisan elections is the 'personal vote'. In the party government model, the voter's decision is between parties, on the basis of partisan policy platforms. If personalistic factors begin to affect vote choice, or campaign tactics, then the partyness of government is undermined.

The partyness of electioneering is illustrated in Figure 11.1. The two dimensions are the identifiability of government (Lijphart 1984), and the level of the personal vote (Cain et al. 1987; Carey and Shugart 1995). Identifiability refers to the ability of voters to discern what their vote choice implies in terms of partisan control of government. If no party can win sole control over government, then the voter is less able to identify the policy implications of choosing one candidate over another. Since coalition formation takes place after the voter has had his say, the voter knows that there is no longer a one-to-one correspondence between the electoral success of a party and the probability that that party will participate in the government.

izational activities such as building a mass dues-paying membership and otherwise forging links between the legislative party apparatus and voters are possible, but not necessary, paths for parties to take. In the party government model, a party need only present its record to voters, as in a referendum, and voters need only know whether they prefer the programme of the incumbent party or its rival.

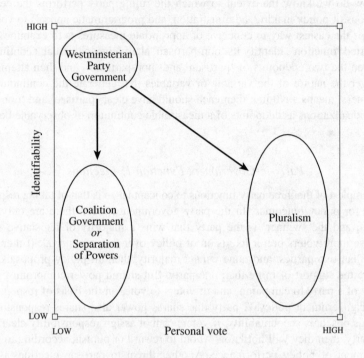

FIG. 11.1. The 'Partyness' of Elections

Note: Any movement away from the top-left corner represents a decline in partyness.

The horizontal dimension in Figure 11.1 measures the level of the personal vote: the extent to which voters cast their ballot on the basis of candidate characteristics instead of partisan characteristics. Note that personal voting can take place even when the identifiability of government is quite high. Thus, even when the other conditions for party government hold, the voters might respond to personal characteristic or personalistic appeals of the district candidate in making their decisions. If candidates compete with personalistic appeals, then the voter might be able to choose a favourite, but it will not be a high partyness vote.

Party-in-Government Function 2: Policy-Making

The Westminster party government model requires that a single majority party decide policy internally and exclusively. Thus, the 'partyness' of government declines when there is a coalition government or separation of powers, or if a ruling minority party must solicit support from other parties. Whenever two or more parties are jointly responsible for all government decisions, no single party can be held solely accountable for outcomes. This clearly violates the strictures of 'party government'.

Alternatively, if a majority party exists but is factionalized along policy lines, it might not be cohesive enough to keep all policy debates in-house, and we might begin to observe policy coalitions that cross party lines. The most extreme form of this state of affairs is what Katz has called legislative 'pluralism', wherein each legislator is an island, and any majority coalition among legislators is equally likely to form from vote to vote.[6] Multi-party coalitions, cartel parties, and legislative pluralism all weaken the partyness of government by increasing the number of parties (or non-partisan individuals) who may *participate* in policy-making.

Another dimension along which the partyness of governmental policy-making might be reduced is *contestation*.[7] The smaller the set of policies that is contestable by the ruling party, the lower the partyness of government. Not all governments are involved in as many aspects of the economy and society as others, and the level of involvement can vary from provider, to regulator, to mediator, to bystander. A government might choose to turn over its right to make policy in certain areas to other groups. An extreme form of this second-level delegation is corporatism, in which the peak associations of important economic interest groups strike bargains over wage, price, employment, and other policies, and then leave it to the government to enforce those pacts. To the extent that policy-making takes place outside the government (and therefore, outside the ruling party), the partyness of government is reduced.[8]

In some countries, by design, all parties represented in the legislature are allocated cabinet portfolios, and participate in top-level decision-making. Every party is partly responsible for all policy outputs, and therefore no party can be held solely accountable for the results of government policies. Many policy issues are

---

[6] Another degenerate form of party-free decision-making might be the 'cartel party' (Katz and Mair 1995) in which all incumbent legislators conspire to perpetuate their (and each other's) tenure in office (official partisan affiliation notwithstanding) by building up 'incumbency advantages'.

[7] I borrow these terms from Dahl's famous *Polyarchy* (1971), although I use the notion of participation differently from him. For Dahl, expansion of participation is about introducing popular sovereignty by removing restrictions on the franchise and expanding civil liberties, where more is 'better'. In the present essay, participation is used to mean the number of legislators (and groups thereof) that participate in policy formation, where more is 'worse' in the sense that it reduces the partyness of government.

[8] Note that corporatism is qualitatively different from deregulation or privatization, in terms of its implications for the party government model. The former retains the government's right to make policy while delegating the actual decision-making. The latter two leave policy up to the market, taking government out of the loop (or at least substantially changing government's role). The partyness of government does not decline simply because the size or activities of government are reduced, as long as whatever governmental responsibilities remain are carried out in as partisan a fashion as before.

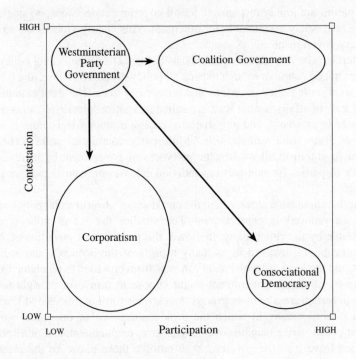

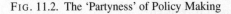

FIG. 11.2. The 'Partyness' of Policy Making

Note: Any movement away from the top-left corner represents a decline in partyness.

'depoliticized' because each party may veto changes to the status quo, or because decision-making is delegated to federal units. This extreme form of policy-making, where contestation is low and participation very high, is called consociational (or consensus) policy-making, and is often designed to reduce the tensions that come from ethnic cleavages in plural societies (Lijphart 1977).

Figure 11.2 illustrates the policy-making function of parties in government. The idealized Westminsterian system, dominated by a single majority party, is located at the top left corner, where all policies are contestable (within the purview of the party) but participation is restricted to the ruling party. Legislators from other parties are relegated to observers' status, and all interest group influence on policy-making must be channelled through the ruling party. As participation expands, due to the advent of coalition governments, or the empowerment of individual legislators at the expense of government control (see Bowler's analysis of legislative procedures in Chapter 8), 'partyness' declines. Partyness also declines when policy issues are taken out of the hands of the ruling party, because of deals made by social or economic groups, as occurs in corporatist systems. Finally, when participation is expanded and the agenda restricted simultaneously, partyness is minimized.[9]

Party-in-Government Function 3: Administration

Even if all government policy decisions are made within a single ruling party, and even if voters vote according to their evaluations of the quality of those policies, the party government model might still be undermined by the party's inability to get the bureaucracy to implement its policies efficiently and faithfully. No legislature, no matter how expert its members, can administer all of its laws and regulations on a daily basis. Moreover, politicians are often not policy experts, and while they might have some idea of the outcome they would like to see in a particular policy area, they do not know what policy will generate that outcome. For these two reasons—division of labour and access to the expertise of specialists—all legislatures and cabinets delegate a good deal of authority to unelected bureaucrats.

As is well known, delegation entails risks. The ruling party must always be concerned that its bureaucratic agents might use the authority and resources they have been granted to move policy in a direction they prefer, but which is dispreferred by the ruling party. Almost by definition, bureaucrats hold an informational advantage over their political 'principals', and they might use that advantage strategically in order to induce the party to act against its own interests. The greater the dangers of such 'agency loss', the more careful the party must be in delegating (McCubbins and Page 1987). The party would do well to control who its agents are, to monitor their activities, to 'check' one agency by delegating simultaneously to a rival agency (Kiewiet and McCubbins 1991), or to mandate administrative procedures that will slow down agency activity and allow third parties to discover and report any non-compliance (McCubbins and Schwartz 1984; Aberbach 1990).

The upshot of the delegation problem for the partyness of government is that the greater the 'slippage' between the policies that the party passes into law and the policies that the bureaucracy ultimately implements, the less the party will be able (or willing) to stand before voters on its record. Just as coalition government obscures the locus of responsibility, the 'intrusion' of autonomous bureaucrats into the policy-making process also weakens the link between partisan control of government and partisan responsibility for governance. Thus, the partyness of government 'declines' to the extent that bureaucratic agents are autonomous.

Figure 11.3 captures the function of administration. The two dimensions here

[9] Note that in this figure, the cohesiveness of parties is assumed to be strong. A third dimension (not shown) might measure cohesiveness directly, with a low score on that measure indicating a move toward pluralization of the policy-making process.

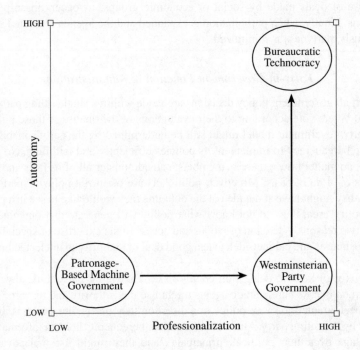

FIG. 11.3. The 'Partyness' of Administration

Note: Any movement away from the bottom-left corner represents a decline in partyness.

are professionalization, which refers to the competence and the insulation of state bureaucrats, and autonomy, which measures bureaucrats' ability to act independ-ently. This time, the partyness of government can be seen to diminish with any move away from the origin (as indicated by the arrows). The professional-ization of the bureaucracy reduces the ability of the ruling party to hire and fire its agents in the bureaucracy, partly because tenure protection and regularized contacts are necessary to attract the best and the brightest to a bureaucratic career. In addition, an increase in the autonomy of bureaucratic agencies decreases the partisan control of the government. This might occur because conflict within the government creates more manœuvring room for agents (McCubbins and Page 1987). Or, political decision-makers might create so-called 'independent agencies', whose activities are insulated from political inter-ference. For both professionalization and autonomy, these developments might represent a net gain for social welfare, but they also indicate a reduction in the partyness of government administration.

THE RELATIONSHIP BETWEEN ELECTORAL PARTY DECLINE AND LEGISLATIVE PARTYNESS: DETECTING CHANGES IN THE PARTY-NESS OF GOVERNMENT

The preceding discussion allows us to consider the measures we might use to determine whether the partyness of government has changed over time in real-world democracies. The task at hand is to identify observable implications of shifts along the horizontal or vertical dimensions illustrated in the figures—to specify what constitutes an increase in participation, bureaucratic autonomy or professionalization, or the personal vote, or a decline in contestation or identifia-bility. Some factors will be institutional; cross-national variation in electoral rules or in the structure of government will produce different maximum levels of party-ness in different countries. Likewise, presidentialism, bicameralism, federalism, and PR electoral systems all tend to increase participation and autonomy (Tsebelis 1995), and to reduce identifiability, no matter what political parties and individual politicians do. Thus, Westminster party government represents no more than an ideal type, an endpoint against which real-world systems can be compared. But it should not be considered an achievable goal unless all West-minsterian political institutions (e.g. a non-federal, unicameral parliamentary system, first-past-the-post elections, nationwide two-party competition, and a docile bureaucracy) are present. It follows that the more fruitful investigative task will be longitudinal in nature—to measure changes in partyness over time, within fixed institutional settings.[10]

THE ELECTORAL VALUE OF GOVERNMENT PARTYNESS

Nowadays, it is difficult to unravel the legislative party from the electoral party. And we have a good theory about how the two feed off each other. The party label serves as a 'short-cut' that helps the candidate and the voter alike to economize in the process of information transfer during a campaign. The voter can use his general knowledge about a party's platform and record as a substitute (or proxy) for specific knowledge about the candidate's stands and preferences that might be unavailable or difficult to obtain (Downs 1957; Campbell et al. 1960). Leaving aside questions of whether or to what extent voters feel some sort of identifica-tion with the party, many clearly believe that party affiliation means something.

Scholars have demonstrated the magnitude of the electoral value of the party label by examining inter-election vote swings to determine how much of a candid-ate's change in vote share from one election to the next is attributable to a local or national swing for (or against) the candidate's party, and how much is particu-lar to the candidate (Stokes 1965). The 'partisan component to the vote' is

---

[10] Appropriately, Part III of this volume is devoted to just these sorts of time-series tests.

substantial in most countries, with cross-national variation the product of institutional differences such as ballot structure and governance structure (Bawn et al. 1998). Good times for the party can be expected to provide a salutary swing for all the party's candidates, while bad times will strike a common blow to their electoral fortunes.

Legislators know that voters look for informational short-cuts. Even if partisan affiliation does not guarantee a sufficient support base for election, it is none the less a valuable asset for party legislators (incumbent and prospective). But if candidates are to put most of their eggs in the partisan basket at election time, they must be assured that it is a hardy basket, with a solid reputation among voters. Thus, we uncover a collective goal for copartisans—all are interested in protecting, even enhancing, the collective reputation of the party, and hence the electoral value of the party label. They might hedge their bets by building a personal following in their districts—a loyal coterie of voters who will support their own candidacies, regardless of the party's reputation (Cain et al. 1987; Cox and Thies 1998). But, all things considered, they would prefer that their party be associated in the minds of most voters with good policies, good practices, and as little corruption as possible.

Unfortunately, the collective good of a favourable party reputation, like most collective goods, can fall victim to incentives for each individual legislative member to free-ride on the public-spirited efforts of others. Such free riding might take the form of each individual legislator grabbing an extra pork-barrel project, the total effect of which would be an over-inflated budget and fiscal deficits. Or, it might involve publicly disavowing party decisions that are unpopular, such as fiscal retrenchment or tax increases. Indeed, the mere public airing of internal party squabbles might be sufficient to bring down the house of cards. If voters become confused as to what the party stands for, the cue of party label will become less meaningful. Or, if voters perceive the party to be fractured by internecine battles, they might worry that the party will never accomplish anything in government. Such damage to the party's reputation would hurt all the party's candidates. In the absence of some sort of mechanism that enforces good behaviour, the incentive to defect will damage the pursuit of the collective goals.

To respond to threats by a member to 'vote her district' (or conscience) instead of the party line, party leaders might counter-threaten to damage the member's re-election prospects, by withdrawing the party nomination, cutting off campaign finance, or stripping the member of her committee posts (among other things). The recalcitrant member, then, is left with a difficult choice. If she calculates that going along with the party on this vote will be enough to doom her career, she might leave the party. If she calculates that the long-term benefits of remaining in the party outweigh the short-term electoral hit she will take for going along, she will succumb to the party whip.

Selective punishments might suffice for isolated incidents of conflicting party and individual incentives, but what about more widespread disenchantment? If a party proposal would damage the electoral prospects of a large group of legislators, then the threat of party discipline would be less credible. Despite the expected benefits that the policy in question might bring the party as a whole, the party is unlikely to relish the idea of cutting off its nose to spite its face.[11] In these cases, the party might prefer to remove the divisive issue from the legislative agenda altogether rather than let it rip the party apart (Rohde 1991; Sinclair 1998). This sort of 'second-best' path is taken all the time; witness the US House Democrats in the 1950s on civil rights issues, the Japanese Liberal Democrats since 1960 on defence issues, and the British Conservatives in the 1980s on questions of European integration.

The catch is that the more issues that are removed from the legislative agenda, the lower the empirical content of the party label becomes. If heterogeneity among parties' legislators leads to public squabbles among copartisans over policy, or if the issue is removed from the legislative agenda (and party platform) in order to hide these problems, voters will become less sure of what the party stands for. For each such issue, partisan affiliation will provide less information for voters about the preferences and likely behaviour of the candidates before them. Thus, even if voters' preferences and candidates' preferences remain stable, the systematic relationship between preference groups in the electorate and party support will decline.

A divergence between the informational content of the party label and the issues of importance to voters might come about for one of two reasons. First, legislative parties might become more heterogeneous for reasons exogenous to the balance of public opinion. For example, two or more parties might decide to merge to enhance their collective legislative strength, but at the cost of increasing heterogeneity. Mixing apples and oranges is fine if you can sell yourselves as the fruit party, but if voters still like apples or oranges, but not both, they will no longer be able to learn much from the 'Fruit Party' label that will help them with their voting decisions. Even if they do like both apples and oranges, it may take some time before they learn that the Fruit Party is still dedicated to their causes.

Second, the relative salience of issues could change within the electorate for exogenous reasons, such that the 'key' issues of the day do not match the 'core' issues for the legislative parties. Examples might include post-materialist issues that cross-cut current party boundaries. A party based on economic conservatism, for instance, might include social conservatives and social progressives. If the most important issue for many voters were to switch from economic ideology to the very social issues that divide the party (or parties), and which the party has steadfastly tried to avoid discussing, voters concerned with social issues would no longer be able to rely on party label when making their voting decisions.

---

[11] Sometimes, the policy might even threaten a *majority* of the party's incumbents, despite its generally beneficial consequences for the party's reputation, in which case leaders are even less likely to use their powers (Thies 1998).

Similarly, voters interested in pushing (or opposing) a post-materialist platform might become disgusted at the current parties' unwillingness to address these issues, and decide to not support any party.

Interestingly, we might find evidence of party decline at the electoral level, but no corresponding decline of partisan ties in the legislature, at least at first. However, if the party component to the vote does indeed diminish due to voters' confusion about the meaning of party cues, then legislative party members will find that the party has less to offer them in their pursuit of re-election. The decline in the importance of the official party endorsement weakens one of the leadership tools for party discipline, but it may or may not be enough to weaken the ties that bind the legislative party together. It is also true that this decline of party-based voting is reversible—if parties make concerted efforts to expand the 'empirical content of the party label', voters will catch on, and start thinking again in partisan terms.[12]

Does Declining Electoral Partyness Doom Parties in Government?

Let us suppose that there really is a sea-change occurring at the electoral level— that parties really are in decline as electoral vehicles, and that voters rely less on partisanship in their decision-making (as argued in Chapters 2–4 above). Must a greater propensity for voters to pay less attention to partisanship lead to declining 'partyness' in the legislature? Why might we expect declining partisanship in the electorate to cause declining legislative partisanship? If Cox and McCubbins are correct, then it is the jointness of electoral fortunes among copartisans that keeps parties together. As they are all in the same electoral boat, a party's MPs share an interest is keeping it afloat. They man the oars and hire a captain and whippers to keep them on an even keel. But what happens if the partisan component of the vote begins to decline? If each individual MP's electoral prospects become more inde-pendent of the prospects of her colleagues, why should she keep rowing? Jumping overboard is considerably less risky once the boat has run aground.

To figure out what would bind legislative parties together in the face of a weakening of the joint electoral connection, we must first dig more deeply into the logic of the Cox–McCubbins (CM) model. For CM, the collective reputation of the party really serves just one role—the jointness of members' electoral fates

---

[12] This logic suggests some testable hypotheses to help determine whether declining part-isanship in the electorate is a result of a decline in the informational content of party labels. If surveys were to reveal increasing disparity among voters concerning their beliefs about party positions on given issues, and if the issues in question were also becoming more salient to voters over time, then we might be able to infer that the problem really is a divergence between 'key issues' for voters and 'core issues' for parties. If *elite* surveys were to reveal intraparty hetero-geneity on issues of increased salience to voters, that inference would be strengthened. Note that in this case, surveys might reveal more than behaviour, because legislative votes that reveal internal party disagreement are unlikely as long as parties are able to keep such issues off the agenda.

makes the party reputation a collective good that all party members have an interest in pursuing. Presumably, this is a powerful motivation precisely because CM base their model—as do many others—on the premise that legislative party members care first and foremost about re-election.

But if legislators care about other things as well, such as policy or government positions, there might be other potential collective goods that could serve the same purpose. Indeed, it seems likely that policy or office is behind the particular choice of party as the re-election vehicle for member-legislators. After all, why is there ever more than one party? Why don't all legislators join together in a universal collective action to maximize incumbency rates?[13]

The answer must be that parties are more than just teams of politicians who have chosen to tie their electoral fates together under the party rubric. They are teams of *like-minded* politicians who join together *to convert their common policy preferences into law*, and who then stand on their joint record at election time. They may not agree on every issue, but they agree on a core set of issues, and it is this core (which need not be a product of the interests of party voters) that defines the party and differentiates it from rival parties.[14] The voter, in turn, uses this information to determine which party has the platform/record closest to his own preferences.

Several inferences follow from this formulation. First, one possible source of disintegration of the legislative party is if the policy core shrinks over time. If more issues divide the party than unite it, and if the issues that unite it are not the most salient, the legislative party is in trouble. All the tools of party discipline that have been delegated to party leaders cannot keep a party together if enough members no longer see a reason to belong. This change might result from changes in the relative salience of issues, which again need not emanate from the electorate. The exogenously determined addition of a highly salient new issue might reveal divisions among party MPs that previously went unnoted, or had been safely buried outside the core. Alternatively, the exogenously determined removal of a highly salient issue—e.g. the end of the Cold War—could rob the party of the core that had held it together.[15]

[13] Katz and Mair's 'cartel party' suggests that this is in fact the future of political parties. But if they are right, the multiplicity of party labels in all electoral democracies remains unexplained (unless their claim is that this is only a temporary state, and that those increasingly meaningless party labels will soon be shed).

[14] The non-core issues are precisely the ones that oblige the party to create structure and organization at the legislative level—to keep intraparty logrolls together on issues for which preferences are heterogeneous.

[15] The recent decline of the Japan Socialist Party is a case in point. From its formation in 1955, most of the JSP's platform was designed to differentiate it from the ruling LDP in the areas of defence and foreign relations. The end of the Cold War seems to have stripped all of these issues of their significance, and in 1994, the JSP's Chairman renounced all of these platform planks, only to see its hard-core supporters abandon it. The LDP, to its fortune, had a much larger core set of issues than Cold War conservatism, so the end of the Cold War has not caused it to melt down as completely as did the JSP.

In the end, to explain why parties hang together, Cox and McCubbins rely on the same sort of collective action problem—a prisoner's dilemma—that makes the formation of the party attractive in the first place. They admit that while party leaders are equipped to deal with isolated cases of defection, the prospect of a pivotal defection (defined as including enough members to cause a majority party to lose its majority) is much more problematic. They contend that party leaders can use their tools to 'divide and conquer' potential defectors. Would-be rebels can be made to back down out of fear that they will be singled out for punishment if they are caught plotting, or if their comrades chicken out at the crucial moment. Since rebellions occasionally do succeed, it seems possible that party rebels could find a way to overcome their own collective action problems just as well as the party did in the first place. The key is that the rebels and the loyalists have different collective goals in mind—they desire different policies on an obviously salient issue dimension.

A second implication of the policy-seeking party model is that a legislative party ought to be able to survive a weakening of the electoral connection. As long as party members continue to agree on what constitutes good public policy, neither universalism nor committee-based mutual deference is likely to be a more attractive organizational principle. What keeps the coalition together is the fact that some policies are not infinitely divisible. If all policy were pork, or if politicians cared only about re-election, then universalism might be the only stable equilibrium. Any 'minimum winning' coalition (Riker 1962) could be broken up by outsiders willing to pay a pivotal group of defectors a premium to switch sides. But if some core issues involve only discrete policy options (if policy is 'lumpy'), then at some point there will be no premium large enough to buy defectors.

A third implication involves an extreme case of 'electoral disconnection', wherein the electoral content of current party labels has shrunk to zero (or, equivalently, if we return to the earliest parties, which formed in the absence of elections—see Holmes 1967). Ironically, the complete absence of partisanship in the electorate, might result in the consolidation of the party system toward two parties. If parties are held together by their common policy goals, and if a majority is needed to pass policy, it is in every party's interest to seek a majority. Comparative politics theories about party systems invariably invoke the electoral connection, due either to rules (Duverger 1954; Riker 1982) or to demographic divisions (Lipset and Rokkan 1967). But if voters ignore the partisan affiliation of candidates, then candidates can join any party they wish, and will attempt to form parties that can provide the things they want. A minimal-winning majority party is more likely to form—a long and broad-based legislative coalition—if legislators are *not* bound by party-based demands from constituents, and if they do not want to share the spoils of victory too widely.

Still, it is difficult to imagine that parties could form around common policy interests and that voters could be completely ignorant of these issue cores. It seems just as unlikely that parties would not form around issues that are salient to voters. Such a mismatch could persist for a while, when relative salience levels change either in the electorate or in the legislature, but eventually some entrepreneurial legislator ought to realize that there is untapped potential for a new party. In the interim, the signs of dealignment among the electorate might appear and grow, but they will not be permanent.

NON-ELECTORAL THREATS TO PARTIES IN GOVERNMENT

If legislators form parties to aid them in pursuit of re-election, policy outputs, and posts, it follows that legislative parties will weaken as their usefulness in these regards wanes. I have already discussed the possibility that the usefulness of parties as electoral vehicles might decline, and that legislative parties could survive this trend as long as they remained useful for the office and policy goals. What might threaten partisan control over the latter two goods?

Posts

Cabinet portfolios, committee seats, and other positions are valuable to legislators for at least three reasons. First, these are plum posts from which to exercise disproportionate influence over particular areas of policy that might be important to the legislator. Second, at election time legislators can 'claim credit' for the areas of policy that went past 'their' desks (see Mayhew 1974: 95), hoping to win extra votes in exchange for the policy benefits accruing to their voters. They can also use these posts as 'bully pulpits' from which to take public positions on policy areas of interest to their constituents (Mayhew 1974: 85). Third, the exclusivity of these posts generates prestige and perquisites (Laver and Schofield 1990: 39–45).

At first glance, the party does not appear to be the only possible organizing principle for the allocation of posts. Certainly, doling out such goodies as a 'privileges of membership' would be an alternative with widespread support, and could substitute for party-based allocation.

However, the key to the value of such posts is that not everyone has all the same ones. Credit claiming would not be very convincing if every member were on every committee. The prestige factor of riding in the ministerial limousine would decline if everyone could do so. Even bringing pork home to the district would be less impressive if pork were simply a privilege of membership, and any challenger could credibly promise the same largesse. Thus, if ever there were a reason for legislators to form minimum-winning coalitions to spread the wealth narrowly, the allocation of posts, perks, and pork would seem to qualify. Universalism would work, but members of a prospective majority coalition would judge it a second-best solution.

Nevertheless, the formation of that majority coalition to divide up intra-legislative spoils would represent the end for party planners, not the means. If there were no other enforcement of the coalitional bargain, any majority coalition would be vulnerable to defections by members offered a better deal to join the current minority. This is the logic that leads Weingast to conclude that universalism would result. Of course, Cox and McCubbins claim that the external enforcement mechanism is the collective reputation of the party at election time, but my purpose is to investigate whether legislative parties can endure when the electoral mechanism fails.

Policy

Downs (1957) asserted that politicians use policy to win elections, and not the other way around. But why do they wish to obtain and retain seats in the legislature in the first place? I have assumed that politicians really do care about enacting policy, at least in some areas. Winning elections is important for instrumental purposes, and the policy outputs of government are the key. Indeed, it might be the case that an individual would not even mind losing an election if contesting it were to induce the victor to modify his policy stance in the loser's direction.[16]

I contend that the bond that holds legislative coalitions together, and simultaneously keeps them from becoming universal, is a commonality of policy interests. I referred earlier to the notion of a party 'core', which I define as the set of common policy interests that are shared by copartisans. This does not imply that every party member's ideal policy for each core issue is identical to every other member's. It simply implies that every member believes that the bundle of compromise party policies on the core issues provides a better net outcome for the member than would result were the member to leave the party.

Of course, if a member were not pivotal—if her defection from her party would not change legislative outcomes—then the member would be indifferent between leaving and staying on policy grounds alone. In this case, what keeps her in the fold is probably the selective benefits (posts, perks, and pork) that her party controls and allocates disproportionately to party members. A second cost of defecting would be the forfeiture of the 'uncollected party-contingent IOUs' (Cox and McCubbins 1993); a member is less likely to defect if she is owed more than she owes in terms of promises about future cooperation.

On the other hand, if a pivotal group were considering a defection, they would compare the net value of the policy stream from their current party's core platform to the expected net policy value emanating from whatever coalition would replace the current majority party. In this case, the party will hang together only as long as all potential pivotal groups calculate that they prefer the former to the latter. A withering of the core, therefore, is dangerous for legislative parties. If

---

[16] This claim recalls Sartori's notion of 'blackmail potential' (Sartori 1976).

internal policy dissension grows over time, the percentage of all issues that constitutes the core shrinks, and the probability that the party will avoid defections also shrinks.

This policy-based notion of legislative party formation and stability implies several hypotheses. First, party splits become more likely as the heterogeneity of parties increases or as differences between parties shrink, other things equal. Second, party splits become more likely as the salience of non-core issues increases. Third, the legislative minority is more likely to reveal shifting coalitions of members (less cohesion and discipline) than the majority, as neither policy benefits nor selective benefits are available to keep minority coalitions together.

VOTERS AS CONSUMERS, NOT STOCKHOLDERS

The discussion above represents only a sketch of what a policy-based theory of legislative political parties might look like, and how it differs from the CM model of legislative party stability as dependent on the 'electoral connection'.[17] The purpose was to suggest that the legislative party does not live by the partisanship of elections alone. To be sure, every legislative party wishes its members to keep winning elections and to add members so that it might enjoy majority control of the legislature, but this does not imply that members have to keep winning on the basis of their partisanship. However they win, as long as they still wish to belong to the party the party is not in danger of crumbling. From the perspective of legislators, the function of the party is to facilitate the production of 'public goods'. One of these is the protection of the electoral value of the party label, but for purposes of legislative party stability, a public good is a public good is a public good. As long as there is a 'core' of policy issues that brings MPs together, there will be a reason to maintain the party. And unless that core is orthogonal to the set of 'key' issues of interest to voters, it seems unlikely that elections will lose their partyness altogether.

Does this mean that the decline of party-in-the-electorate is irrelevant? Not if one is interested in the details of *how* electoral democracy works. But I argue that those who despair that elections without strong partisan identifications bode ill for the future of democracy may be expecting too much of political parties. These characterizations liken voters to stockholders in a partisan firm—owner-operators who 'hire' legislator-managers to run the business for the good of all involved. When the stockholders start selling off their interests in the party and dropping out, the party is in trouble.

---

[17] The difference is more one of emphasis than of type. Cox and McCubbins (1993: 107–135) discuss both 'intralegislative' (posts, perks, unredeemed IOUs) and 'extralegislative' assets (the jointness of electoral fortunes), but they focus on the latter.

By contrast, I characterize party-in-government as primary. Legislators concerned with policy and with their own careers form parties to solve collective dilemmas that crop up in legislative decision-making. At election time, legislators wish to be re-elected, and they have discovered that advertising their partisan affiliation is an efficient way to say a lot by saying a little. Thus, if parties are like firms, then it is party legislators who are the owner-operators and who attempt to sell their products to consumer-voters. In this effort, brand loyalty (party loyalty/party identification) is nice if you can get it, but is not strictly necessary for the health of the firm, which need only keep its sales up, relative to its competitors. I assert, therefore, that party decline in the electorate is best thought of as a tendency away from brand loyalty. The same products exist, still use brand names, and might even signify the same message to buyers as before, but now buyers base their decisions on criteria not covered by the brand-name signal.

CONCLUSION

The evidence of weakening partisanship in the electorate is voluminous; clearly, something is changing in the nature of the relationship between political parties and voters. However, there appears to be no systematic evidence of partisan decline at the level of government. This chapter has considered why this might not be as paradoxical as it seems at first glance.

The gist of my argument has been that V. O. Key's useful classification scheme of party-in-government, party-as-organization, and party-in-the-electorate (Key 1961) does not imply that the three categories are of equal importance. I argue that party in government is logically primary—indeed, the political party is a purposefully designed organization of, by, and for legislators—and that the other two categories are best thought of as indicators or measures of partisan activities on behalf of the core legislative party. Parties existed before elections, but in the age of elections they need to compete for votes in order to retain or enhance their influence in government. They organize local branches, recruit candidates, and advertise their platforms to voters. Over time, different parties have tried out different electoral strategies, resulting in innovations in the nature of party in the electorate and party as organization.

The secular decline in measures of partisan identification, loyalty, and trust among voters might suggest that a further evolution of party strategies is at hand. Or, if the problem is that voters now care most about issues that divide rather than separate parties, it might suggest that current parties in most democracies will give way to new parties, organized around different core issues. To say that parties are top-down organizations does not imply that specific parties cannot be changed or dissolved or replaced as a result of changes in the electorate. It does imply, however, that changes in voter behaviour or perceptions will not necessarily lead to the weakening or instability of the 'partyness' of government.

Finally, while moves away from Westminsterian party government and toward corporatism, pluralism, or bureaucratic government might imply a decline in the partyness of government, they do not imply the inevitable demise of party in government. As long as parties continue to perform *some* indispensable function in the service of even one goal of their members, parties will survive. Moreover, there is no theoretical justification for believing that a decline in the partyness of government is irreversible. Corporatist bargains or consociational mechanisms might prove to be obsolete after a time, and areas of policy previously walled off from partisan politics might again be opened for discussion. New issues might enter the partisan arena, again expanding the proportion of policy-making that carries a partisan tint. Alternatively, issues that divide today's parties might form the basis of a reorganized party system, such that the decline or demise of specific old parties does not in any way imply the decline in the partyness of government, at least in the long run.

Conclusion

12

Partisan Change and the Democratic Process

Russell J. Dalton and Martin P. Wattenberg

THE history of modern representative democracy is deeply intertwined with the development of political parties. We started this book by citing E. E. Schattschneider's (1942: 1) observation that 'modern democracy is unthinkable save in terms of political parties'. This theme has been repeated for decades by scores of political scientists and political analysts. The party government model sees political parties as the key institution linking together various elements of the democratic process and ensuring efficient and effective government (Ranney 1954; Rose 1974; Katz 1987a; Harmel and Janda 1982). Political parties have created political identities, framed electoral choices, recruited candidates, organized elections, defined the structure of legislative politics, and determined the outputs of government. Indeed, to most of us, democracy without political parties is unthinkable.

Nevertheless, political parties recently have been roundly criticized throughout much of the advanced industrialized world. These criticisms often focus on how parties are failing to perform their intended roles within the democratic process (e.g. Lawson and Merkl 1988). These critiques are frequently linked to proposals for institutional reforms to restructure political parties, but without challenging the basic conception of party government as the foundation of representative democracy. In other cases, however, the very concept of party government has come under challenge. Several democratic theorists and political figures have called for democratic reforms that would inevitably diminish the role of political parties (e.g. Barber 1984; Budge 1996). Some analysts also argue that the contemporary role of political parties is inevitably eroding, and thus we should think about a non-partisan future for democracy.

This volume addresses this debate on the role of political parties in advanced industrial democracies. What functions do political parties actually perform today, and how have these changed in the second half of the twentieth century? How has the modernization of these societies led to new forms of political communication and interest representation? Have these changes altered the traditional role of political parties within the democratic process? Other societal trends are transforming the characteristics of contemporary publics. Have these developments affected the relationship between citizens and parties? We considered these questions by assembling an extensive and unmatched body of evidence on the functioning of political parties in advanced industrial democracies.

This chapter begins by reviewing the empirical evidence regarding parties in the electorate, as organizations, and in government. It then examines the consequences of these trends for democratic politics. Finally, we consider the cumulative meaning of these findings for contemporary democracies. If citizens and parties are changing in fundamental ways, what does this mean for the ideals and practice of democracy?

CHANGES IN PARTIES IN THE ELECTORATE

The model of party government begins with the individual voter. Both social psychologists and rational choice theorists agree that partisan ties are a key element in explaining how the average person manages the complexities of politics and makes reasonable political choices. Electoral analysts maintain that partisanship provides a cue to political decision-making—a tool for evaluating political phenomena, a stimulus to political participation, and a source of political loyalties that guide political behaviour in general. Thus it is fair to say that the concept of party identification has been the most important concept in our understanding of individual political behaviour.

In the mid-1980s, however, this pattern began to change. Instead of stressing the stability of partisanship and voting behaviour à la Seymour Lipset and Stein Rokkan's (1967) thesis of frozen party alignments, there was growing evidence of electoral change. Russell Dalton, Scott Flanagan, and Paul Beck (1984: 451) maintained that 'electoral alignments are weakening, and party systems are experiencing increased fragmentation and volatility. . . . Virtually everywhere among the industrial democracies, the old order is crumbling' (also see Crewe and Denver 1985). Still, some scholars argued that little real change had occurred. For example, Peter Mair (1993: 132) concluded that: 'The electoral balance now is not substantially different from that 30 years ago, and, in general electorates are not more volatile than once they were' (also see Klingemann and Fuchs 1995; Bartolini and Mair 1990; Keith et al. 1992). Thus, we began our analyses by examining whether partisan loyalties have endured among democratic publics.

Chapter 2 examined the extent of party identifications with the most complete inventory of data that has ever been compiled for the advanced industrial democracies. Despite the unique political histories and political structures of these nations, there is a broad pattern of weakening partisanship. In seventeen of nineteen nations the percentage of party identifiers has decreased, and in every case the strength of party ties has eroded. For instance, between the 1960s and the 1990s the percentage of strong partisans decreased by 26 per cent in Britain, 15 per cent in Sweden, Austria and Australia, 9 per cent in Norway, and 7 per cent in the United States.

Dalton links these dealignment trends to processes of modernization and cognitive mobilization. The decrease in partisanship generally is greater among the young, the better educated, and the politically sophisticated. These are the new non-partisans who remain interested in the political process, but who are more likely to think of democratic politics in apartisan or even anti-partisan terms. Equally important, dissatisfaction with the functioning of democracy is not systematically related to weakening party ties.

Even if one accepts these trends in partisan identification measures, some scholars have nevertheless questioned their political significance. For example, Bruce Keith et al. (1992) claim that the rise of independents in the United States represents a mere change in labelling without behavioural consequences. More recently, Larry Bartels (2000) maintains that the impact of partisanship on voting has actually increased in American elections over the past two decades. Similarly, other political scientists maintain that claims about partisan change in Europe are based on a myth (Mair 1993; Bartolini and Mair 1990; Zelle 1995).

To address these questions, Chapter 3 examined the behavioural consequences of partisan dealignment. Broadening the set of nations and extending data into the 1990s, we find strong evidence of growing volatility and party fragmentation. For instance, aggregate electoral volatility increased in fifteen of eighteen nations between the 1950s and the 1990s, and the effective number of parties increased in seventeen nations. Moreover, the consequences of partisan dealignment are seen in other aspects of electoral behaviour. Without the reinforcement of habitual party ties, more voters are uncertain about the ultimate voting choice as the campaign begins, and thus make their choice later in the campaign. In countries where ticket-splitting is possible, more voters are dividing their party choices. Candidate-centred politics appears to be on the rise, although this is much more pronounced in presidential than parliamentary systems. And signifying the different style of dealignment politics, while general political interest is broadly increasing in the advanced industrial democracies, actual participation in campaigns and volunteer work for political parties is decreasing. In short, partisan dealignment is transforming the relationship between some voters and political parties—a relationship that was once seen as an essential element in the process of representative democracy.

One of the most important functions of political parties is to mobilize people to go to the polls. As Chapter 4 demonstrates, this is clearly one area where the parties are no longer functioning as effectively as they once did. In seventeen out of the nineteen countries examined, recent turnout figures are lower than those of the early 1950s. The median change from the 1950s is a 10 per cent decline in turnout. Party systems that are notoriously weak have seen the most pronounced drops in electoral participation, whereas the presence of strong political parties appears to have dampened the decline of turnout.

The temporal sequence for turnout decline differs from the decline of party identification. Whereas party identification has withered gradually, turnout decline is mostly a phenomenon of the last dozen years. This difference may simply reflect the fact that party identification is an attitude whereas turnout is a behaviour. While mass attitudes may shift gradually over time, it takes a major shock to impact a habitual behaviour like participation in elections. Chapter 4 presents evidence that recent shake-ups in the party systems of the OECD democracies have provided the necessary jolt to send turnout plummeting.

Wattenberg views the decline of turnout as indicating a broad-based weakening of party systems. He draws an analogy to the market-place for a business product, noting that if the producers of a given product were still making profits but overall sales were down it would be obvious that consumers no longer find as much use for this merchandise. The fact that voter turnout has declined would thus indicate that citizens of advanced industrialized democracies now find less of value in what the political parties have to offer.

To add to all of this, acceptance of political parties is strikingly low among most democratic publics. Data from the 1995–98 World Values Survey describe a pattern that is commonly found in other surveys. Respondents were asked to rate their confidence in a long list of political institutions, and political parties came in a disappointing last (see Table 12.1). Averaged across the eight advanced industrial democracies in the study, only 22 per cent of the public expressed confidence in political parties as institutions.[1] Can political parties successfully be the central institutions of representative democracy with such low public support?

In summary, our findings point to an erosion in partisan loyalties, measured either attitudinally or behaviourally. Moreover, in responding to these trends the political parties may be encouraging further dealignment. As more voters base their electoral choices on the candidates and campaign issues, David Farrell and Paul Webb (Chapter 6) suggest that the parties have become more flexible in their issue programmes, as well as more candidate-centred in their election profiles. Indeed, for all the five countries for which we can track media coverage of campaigns over time (Chapter 3), there is a trend toward more candidate-centred coverage. Personalistic campaigns diminish the heuristic value of partisan cues for even those who continue to label themselves as identifying with a particular party. The labels may still be there for some voters, but there is good reason to suspect that they mean less and less. Thus, the cumulative effect is to further erode partisanship as a tool for decision-making and as a source of political loyalties.

---

[1] Various public opinion surveys suggest that parties routinely fare poorly in such comparisons, so this is not an entirely new phenomenon (e.g. Poguntke and Scarrow 1996). In Chapter 2, however, we cite longitudinal evidence from several nations that indicates that these evaluations have worsened in recent decades.

TABLE 12.1 Confidence in Political Institutions, 1995–1998

Institution	%
Police	77
Armed forces	66
Legal system	59
Ecology movement	58
United Nations	56
Companies	50
Churches	46
Civil service	44
Women's movement	44
Unions	43
National government	38
Parliament	38
European Union	36
Press	32
Political parties	22

Source: 1995–8 World Values Survey in eight OECD nations. Table entries are the percentage expressing 'a great deal' or 'very much' confidence in each institution.

It should be noted that the trends we have described may be reversible. Indeed, as politicians become aware of these changes, they may consciously attempt to restore public confidence in political parties and rekindle party allegiances (Webb et al. 2000). For instance, German President Richard von Weizsäcker (1992) tried to sensitize party leaders to the need for reform when anti-party sentiments rose within the German electorate in the early 1990s. Popular dissatisfaction with partisan politics has apparently stimulated recent attempts at electoral system reform in several of these nations (Shugart and Wattenberg 2000; Norris 1995*b*). Similarly, discussions of party renewal have been a recurring theme in recent American politics, coming from both politicians and political scientists (Price 1984; Sabato 1988; White and Mileur 1992). There are distinct advantages for established political parties to have core adherents who can be depended upon at the next election (see Chapter 11).

Yet, we believe that reversing the dealignment trend within the electorate would be a difficult task. It would require changes in the organization and activities of political parties, changes in the policy core of the parties, and changes in the political context that fosters many of these trends—especially the role of the mass media. Moreover, dealignment is not just a reaction to changes within the parties, but also to changes in the skills and interests of citizens that will probably continue. The breadth of these trends across a diverse set of democracies further suggests that these forces may be difficult for any group of politicians to reverse, and indeed there has not yet been a significant trend reversal among the OECD nations. For instance, partisan dealignment has been clearly documented and openly discussed in American and Swedish politics for more than two decades—yet neither nation has been able to recreate the old partisan order. It simply may be that social and political modernization makes it impossible to return to the more partisan forms of politics which Schattschneider observed. Therefore, partisan dealignment may be an indicator of systematic and enduring change in the relationship between citizens and political parties in contemporary democracies.

CHANGES IN PARTIES AS POLITICAL ORGANIZATIONS

The major message of Chapters 5–7 is that party organizations have evolved and adapted as society has modernized. These chapters generally challenge the notion that parties as organizations are in the process of withering away. Although party organizations have dramatically altered the way they do business in recent decades, they still continue to perform many of their traditional functions, especially those that are more directly linked to the vitality of the parties themselves. At the same time, it is debatable whether the new style of party organization is as effective in producing the desired results for the political system as a whole.

The one aspect of party organizational change that most clearly fits the label of party decline is party membership. Susan Scarrow (Chapter 5) shows that the number of dues-paying members has declined in most established political party systems since the 1960s. Scarrow demonstrates, however, that this is a relatively recent trend. Only five of eighteen countries had well-established membership-based parties on both the left and the right before the Second World War. Thus, most parties actually achieved their peak drawing power for only a brief period in the 1950s and 1960s, following which their membership rolls declined sharply.

Scarrow cautions against interpreting declines in overall party membership as signifying the impending demise of party organizations. The tasks of a party organization do not require that every member be highly active, and the degree of activity among those remaining members has typically increased. Furthermore, she indicates that many parties have dispersed their local organizational units more widely in an attempt to reach beyond their traditional geographic strongholds. Political parties have apparently adapted to a more volatile campaigning environment by broadening their organizational base, even if the foundations of their mass membership are thinner.[2]

Scarrow believes that a significant sustained increase in party membership is

---

[2] At the same time, Whiteley and Seyd (1999) show that the development of local party organizations in Britain has diminished the central party's control over the actions of grass-roots organizations and their memberships. Instead of following the directives of a central party office, they find that local activists display considerable autonomy in their campaign activities. If this observation can be generalized to other party systems, then greater local activity may simultaneously mean less party unity.

unlikely to occur in these nations, although there may be temporary increases as some parties marshal their resources in institution-building efforts. Supply-side factors such as changes in lifestyles and housing patterns make it harder to entice people to join local party organizations. Demand-side changes in political communication and campaign technologies similarly undermine the need for party membership. Whereas once parties relied on their members to get their message out to the wider public, this is hardly necessary in today's media-dominated campaigns.

David Farrell and Paul Webb (Chapter 6) further elaborate on how parties are adapting as campaign organizations to the changing political context. Campaign communication once occurred primarily through canvassing and the party press, and most activity was conducted by volunteers who mobilized each party's traditional social base of support. The arrival of television ushered in the second stage of campaigning, in which parties tried to 'sell' themselves to as many voters as possible, not just traditional supporters. Campaigns changed from exercises in mass mobilization toward professionally managed enterprises that sought to project the best possible image. Parties also developed more standardized messages, focusing increasingly on the party leader. Finally, many parties are shifting toward 'marketing' a more malleable political image. Many parties are not stating what they really advocate, but what they think prospective voters want to hear. Certainly this has been a frequent accusation against the Clinton administration in the United States, but the same has been said of Blair in Britain, Schröder in Germany, or Jospin in France. With the arrival of forums for narrowcasting—cable TV and the Internet—campaign messages can become even more specific and targeted at particular groups with particular interests. More than in previous years, party professionals in the leaders' offices are in charge of what has become known as 'the permanent campaign'.

Chapter 6 also discusses how party organizations have become more centralized. Partially countering the implications of Scarrow's argument of revitalized local party organizations, Farrell and Webb demonstrate the strengthening of national party offices. Resources at the local level have generally declined, while staffing levels at the national party offices have typically increased. Furthermore, the national staff members are more likely to be full-time professionals, possessing a variety of specific technical skills. Farrell and Webb summarize this trend as a change from politics as an art to politics as a science. If parties are now shaping their policies to the market-place based on polling data, then there are likely consequences for the other aspects of party-based democracy. For instance, if parties are no longer loyal to their policy commitments, it is fitting that fewer members of the electorate will be loyal to them, and this should also weaken the bonds between parties and their traditional social group allies.

The use of skilled professionals and new technologies also has upped the costs of party campaigning. In most cases where data are available, central party organizations are spending more money than ever before. It might seem paradoxical that party organizations are able to spend more money at the same time that their dues-paying membership is falling. Farrell and Webb resolve this seeming contradiction by presenting evidence in support of Richard Katz and Peter Mair's (1995) cartel party thesis, which argues that established parties have exploited the state as an alternative source of funding through public financing of campaigns, free television advertising, and other state subsidies. The institutionalization of such resources is another factor that strengthens party organizations and their roles in campaigning.

The most controversial aspect of Farrell and Webb's work is their discussion about how the internet may affect party campaigning. Although they caution that there is disagreement in the scholarly community about this new technology, they clearly see major changes in the offing. They postulate that the internet will lead to more targeted policy appeals by the parties, providing a prominent place for serious discussion of many issues. Furthermore, they believe that citizens will take advantage of this informational resource and will become better informed about the issues that concern them. We are sceptical about claims that the internet will create a democratic utopia (also see Hill and Hughes 1998). Party members who formerly attended a few meetings might take advantage of the communication possibilities offered by the internet, but virtual party membership lacks the educational and social capital attributes that come with in-person participation. In any event, for the foreseeable future only a small portion of campaign information is likely to come from internet sources; the mass media and other traditional communication forms will continue to dominate electoral politics.

Scarrow, Webb, and Farrell examine the changing distribution of political power within modern political parties in Chapter 7. For a number of reasons, political parties have expanded the decision-making process to include a wider range of party supporters; the era of party decision-making in smoke-filled rooms is fading into the past. The chapter documents a trend toward more inclusive decision-making in choosing parliamentary candidates and party leaders, as well as in setting party policy. For instance, in the mid-1980s the British Labour Party gave constituency groups greater weight in selecting candidates for parliament and several parties have explored the use of candidate selection primaries. Yet, these democratizing moves have not been accompanied by decentralization of authority. Party leaders have often retained whatever veto power they held over candidate choice. As such, these trends within party organizations might be better described as moving toward consultative democracy rather than direct democracy.

It is uncertain whether parties have adopted more inclusive decision-making procedures because of pressures from more politically aware members or as an incentive to get people to join in a time of declining membership. In either event, they will find it hard to significantly reverse these trends. Participatory rights, once bestowed, are difficult to revoke, as the democratization of the nominating process in the United States demonstrates.

Our findings about dealignment within the electorate (Chapters 2–4), when coupled with these changes within party organizations (Chapters 5–7), help to deepen our understanding of the contemporary process of partisan change. Party identification and party membership data indicate that the citizenry is distancing itself from political parties. Furthermore, the actions of the parties themselves contribute to these trends. In the modern media age, political parties have reduced their needs for a phalanx of party members who provide information to prospective voters, mobilize people to vote, and provide party financing. As Farrell and Webb suggest, in responding to this more fluid electoral environment, the typical party has shifted from 'selling' an ideological programme to 'marketing' a package of policies suggested by pollsters and professional campaign strategists. This trend further decreases the cue-giving function of parties as a political heuristic, and thereby opens the door to increased volatility.

Declining electoral participation reflects a similar mix of reinforcing forces. Weakening partisanship decreases the number of voters who feel motivated to go to the polls to support 'their' party. As Scarrow points out in Chapter 5, without party members personally appealing to friends, neighbours, and co-workers, even fewer individuals will be mobilized to participate. For example, between 1987 and 1997 the British election studies found that the percentage of respondents who stated that a party canvasser had called at their home declined from 47 to 25 per cent. Similar trends have been observed for the United States (Rosenstone and Hansen 1993). This pattern of decreasing party activity reinforces the dealignment trend.

At the same time, the chapters on parties as organizations maintain that partisan dealignment within the electorate is not matched by a parallel decline of parties as political institutions. Rather, party organizations have adapted to the changes in the electorate and society. Indeed, in some ways the typical political party has become stronger as a political institution by marshalling more resources in the national party office, by hiring more professionalized and technically skilled staffers, and by maintaining the national party office as the locus for political control.

Although these developments may strengthen the party organization, they also change the relationship between the party and the public in troublesome ways. Richard Katz and Peter Mair's (1995) notion of a cartel party or Panebianco's (1988) image of parties as electoral professionals epitomize these patterns—the party organization becomes stronger by insulating itself from the public and by institutionalizing support from government sources. Such a development may be good for party officials and prospective party careerists, but is it good for the public and democracy?

Parties are benefiting themselves (financially and electorally) at the expense of some of the functions that have made them so essential to the democratic process, such as socialization, mobilization, and representation. Although the media and other political actors assume some of these functions, it is quite difficult to substitute for the parties' role in mobilizing voters and in representing their views. Interest groups may be more articulate in expressing citizen interests, but they do not aggregate conflicting interests and execute the policies of government. These key democratic functions may be suffering as a result of the changes in partisan politics that we have been documenting.

Insulating the parties from the public opens the way for a variety of other problems to emerge. An inwardly oriented party leadership may be less responsive to the public, or only responsive in following the undismissable trends in public opinion polls. Even worse, such parties may be more willing to engage in collusion or other undemocratic behaviours. The political logrolling between the SPD and CDU that Erwin and Ute Scheuch (1992) observed for Cologne or the party corruption scandals in Japan and Italy illustrate this possibility. If organizational maintenance becomes a party's primary goal, democracy inevitably will suffer. Michael Thies (Chapter 11) even claims that cartel parties represent a 'degenerate form of party-free decision making'. In addition, without party identities, stable party programmes, and personal contact through party members, the legitimacy of parties and the system of party government may diminish. Thus, political parties may endure as institutions in this new form, but one must certainly wonder whether democracy will benefit as a result of this development.

CHANGES IN PARTIES IN GOVERNMENT

As Michael Thies points out in Chapter 11, the initial reason for political parties was to provide a means of organizing and rationalizing the behaviour of individual parliamentarians. Some scholars claim that parties in government represent the core of political parties, and that the electoral role of parties is secondary. Thus, an important measure of party-based government involves the control that parties exercise within the governing process. Chapters 8 to 11 focused on various features of parties in government.

In Chapter 8, Shaun Bowler examined the role of parties within the legislative arena. As Gary Cox and Mathew McCubbins (1993) would argue, political parties exist to control individuals legislatures and ensure responsible government. To ensure partisan control, Bowler describes how the formal rules of most parliamentary systems give political parties a privileged role in the legislative process, such as control over committee chair selection or the initiation of legislation. Furthermore, most legislatures have implemented rules that limit the rights of individual legislators to introduce bills or offer amendments, which essentially transfers political resources to the leadership of parliamentary parties.

Chapter 8 also assembles cross-national and cross-temporal data on roll call voting that demonstrate the persistence of party cohesion in legislative voting. The available data for Germany, Norway, Switzerland, and Denmark show little change in party cohesion over time, and in some cases there has even been increased party cohesion—the United States is a notable example (Rohde 1991). The British Parliament represents the atypical national legislature where party unity has clearly decreased during the post-war period. These findings lead Bowler to conclude that the parties' continued control over the nomination process, and the functional value of party discipline within legislatures, makes legislative politics relatively immune to the dealignment trends noted in other parts of this study.

Another element of party control involves the executive branch. In Chapter 9 Kaare Strøm examines whether parties have experienced diminishing control over the selection of legislative candidates and cabinet members, as indicated by an increasing number of independents in these offices. He finds evidence that partisan independents are still rare in most democracies.[3] (We would also note from the American experience that the label itself is sometimes less significant than the actual behaviour of political elites.) At the same time, he documents a pattern of increasing fragmentation of party systems and an increased role for 'non-governing' parties within modern parliaments. In addition, Strøm tracks the stability of parliamentary governments over time, which fails to show any systematic increase in the regularity with which governments fall due to internal dissension. Strøm concludes, much like Bowler, that although there are some signs of increasing fluidity in these party systems, parties continue to remain a strong force within the governing process.

Ultimately, the influence of parties on voters, candidate selection, campaigns, policy debates, and government decision-making should culminate in a linkage between parties and public policy. Miki Caul and Mark Gray examine different aspects of this linkage in Chapter 10. They analyse party manifesto data in order to determine if the broad ideological profiles of the political parties have system-atically changed (cf. Budge et al. 1987; Klingemann et al. 1994). As others have shown, the left–right profiles of the major parties have tended to converge over time in most nations. In addition, the overall dispersion of all parties along the left–right dimension has decreased since 1950. This is consistent with the notion that the ideological and political groundings of political parties have weakened as many parties in advanced industrialized democracies have adopted vote maxim-izing strategies that have led toward centrist politics.

As a more explicit and innovative test of this hypothesis, Caul and Gray compare the consistency of party platforms over time. If Farrell and Webb are correct that parties are shifting from 'selling' a specific ideological programme to

---

[3] Another indication of weakening elite partisanship is the switching of parties by elected legislators. This once seemed a relatively rare phenomenon, but it has become more common in some nations at least. For example, as a result of the tumult in the Italian party system the *New York Times* (19 Dec. 1999) reports: 'Since April 1996, 108 members of Parliament have changed parties, 20 have shifted allegiances twice, and one has moved four times.' This pattern was also apparent in Japan and New Zealand following the change in the electoral system in these nations. Legislators may feel the need to have a party affiliation for the reasons that Bowler describes in his chapter, but these affiliations may lack the intensity of past commitments.

'marketing' issues that pollsters and campaign consultants believe will attract potential voters, then we would expect party platforms to become more variable from election to election as the issues that interest voters vary. Caul and Gray's data actually show decreasing volatility in parties' issue agendas in most nations. We treat these findings as exploratory, because one might debate whether the manifesto data can track the type of changes Farrell and Webb outlined.[4] The stabilization of party images also might be a consequence of the professionalized and institutionalized parties that Farrell and Webb describe. We hope these findings encourage further research on this topic.

The last section of the Caul and Gray chapter looks at the correlation between partisan control of government and various measures of policy outputs. The research literature has always found modest partisan effects on policy when analysed with highly aggregated budgetary and economic statistics. Indeed, Caul and Gray find that partisan control is weakly related to the various measures of output, and there has not been a systematic increase or diminution of these influences over time. The strongest predictor in most models is the weighted average of other OECD nations on the dependent variable, suggesting that most of the major policy shifts are produced by broad international conditions rather than the outcome of the last domestic election.

Drawing upon the evidence of Chapters 8–10, Michael Thies describes why parties should continue to play a significant role within the governing process, despite the other evidence of partisan dealignment and partisan change assembled in the other parts of this book. Thies's argument is based on the functions that parties perform—and perhaps only parties can perform—within the governing process. Building on the work of Cox and McCubbins (1993), his chapter contends that cohesive political parties address many of the collective action and responsibility problems that arise in the governing process. For instance, parties evolved as institutions to structure the electoral process because they were very efficient and effective in performing this function. Similarly, cohesive party groups can limit the self-interest of individual legislators so that governments can pursue broader national policy needs. Along with Bowler and Strøm, Thies sees a natural connection between the parties' control of the electoral arena and the legislative process. Thies also presents the theoretical basis for parties as tools for controlling the bureaucracy and the administration of public policy. Party control is one mechanism for addressing the delegation problem in carrying out public policy. Indeed, in a tone that follows in the tradition of political party research, Thies echoes the claim that democracy without parties is unthinkable.

---

[4] Part of the critique is based on questions of whether the broad issue salience measures of the party manifesto data are sufficiently detailed to capture significant political changes; in addition, Caul and Gray only analysed left–right issues, and the rise of new non-economic and cultural issues may be another source of volatility. Finally, Farrell and Webb discuss the shift toward marketing as a new phase of party campaigning, and the manifesto trend data end in 1987.

Linkages between Changes in Parties in the Electorate, as Organizations, and in Government

Certainly, one of the major findings of this project is the variation in partisan change across the three levels we have examined. While there is strong evidence of dealignment within the electorate, parties as political organizations are adapting to these trends, and the evidence suggests that parties are alive and well within the governing process. Before discussing the implications of these variations in party change across levels, we want to consider the argument that parties must inevitably structure the democratic governing process—and thus other elements of party government will eventually conform. We would temper this proposition with three observations.

First, even if there is an unavoidable logic that leads to party-based government, cross-national evidence demonstrates that nations actually vary considerably in their degree of partyness. For example, as can be seen in Table 8.1, some nations, such as Germany, Austria, Denmark, and Luxembourg—give parties a strong formal backing in the legislative rules; but there are few rules supporting parties in Britain, Italy, and Sweden.[5] The locus of control for agenda setting (presumably a surrogate of party-based decision-making) is also quite varied across nations (see Table 8.3). The models of policy impact in Chapter 10 similarly demonstrate considerable variability in the influence of party control of government on policy outcomes. Although it is difficult to determine which dimensions of partyness within government are most important (or how they should be measured), it is clear that democracies function within a considerable range of partyness. American political parties are widely viewed as weak because of their lack of control over candidate selection and their relative lack of legislative discipline; yet, democracy still functions within this weak party system. Thus, nations can move toward the lower end of the partyness range while still dealing with the collective action problems emphasized in the rational actor literature.

Second, the rational actor approach presumes that party cohesion in legislatures is linked to party control of the nomination and campaign processes. Bowler describes this as the 'one-arena' model of party government. If parties select likeminded individuals to run under their banner, and party agreement is effective in assisting re-election and the passage of desirable policy, then party cohesion within the legislature naturally follows according to this line of thinking. Therefore, the evidence that campaigns are changing—candidates are becoming more important for electoral choice, candidate selection is becoming a more open process, and voters are becoming less partisan—should eventually lead to weakening party cohesion within parliaments.

---

[5] The British case illustrates the ambiguity of the rational party approach. Although Thies posits that partyness is greatest in a Westminster system, this is the one parliament where legislative cohesion has clearly decreased over time. Furthermore, Britain scores relatively low on party rules (only one of four possible rules).

Furthermore, the evidence for a relationship between the partyness of elections and the partyness of parliaments remains largely inferential rather than empirically demonstrated. In Chapter 7 Scarrow, Webb, and Farrell present two measures of party control of the candidate selection process: the selection of parliamentary candidates and party leaders. In Chapter 8 Bowler presents multiple measures of how parties are enshrined in legislative rules or the agenda setting process (Doring Index): from this we derived a summary index of each function (see Chapter Appendix). Figure 12.1 displays the relationship between party control of leadership selection and the existence of rules to privilege parties within the parliament. Party control of the selection of elites is only weakly related to the existence of partisan rules within the legislature (r=0.18).[6] Similar analyses of the relationship between selection of MP candidates and party rules in the legislature yields an even weaker correlation (r=0.03). In other words, when parties exercise greater control over the candidate selection process, there is only a weak tendency towards having more parliamentary rules to reinforce the privileged position of parties. We repeated these analysis using the Doring index of party control of the political agenda. Legislative party agenda setting (Doring Index) is weakly correlated with both party control over the selection of legislative candidates (r=0.36) and of party leaders (r=0.17).

These analyses provide some evidence that party control in the electoral arena is related to stronger parties in the legislature. However, the degree of linkage is much weaker than Thies, Bowler, and the parties as Leviathan literature would suggest, and hardly sufficient to substantiate the claim that these two domains really represent 'one arena'. The small size of these relationships indicates considerable separation between what occurs in the electoral arena and what occurs in the legislative arena.

Third, we disagree with the view that political parties are ultimately defined by what happens at the governing level, and other elements of political parties will reflect what occurs at this level. For instance, Michael Thies (Chapter 11) suggests that cohesive legislative parties will eventually generate stronger partisan-based voting among the electorates of the advanced industrialized countries. This implies that electoral dealignment should be a temporary phenomenon. We have argued that the separate levels of party activity may be subject to different political and social forces, and this can sever the connection between the various elements of the party government model. Indeed, the strongest longitudinal evidence comes from the United States, where there is little evidence that the increasing cohesion of legislative parties since the early 1980s has reversed part-

---

[6] Additional analyses, not shown, suggest that the extent of party rules in the legislature may be more a function of the diversity of a party system than the strength of political parties. The number of rules is normally greater in multi-party and PR systems, which might generate a need for more rules to regulate the diverse parties present in the legislature. In contrast, formal rules to privilege parties are actually less common in the British Parliament, despite the general view that party government is epitomized by the British system (e.g. Thies, Ch. 11).

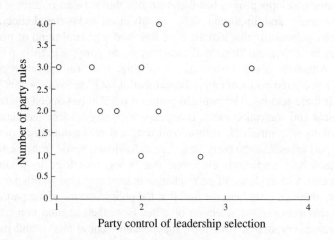

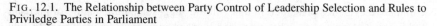

Party control of leadership selection

FIG. 12.1. The Relationship between Party Control of Leadership Selection and Rules to Priviledge Parties in Parliament

Note: The scoring of the party leadership variable was reversed in this figure, so that high values on both variables indicates strong 'partyness.'

Source: See chapter appendix.

isan dealignment among the American public (Coleman 1996; Wattenberg 1998*a*). Thus cohesive legislative parties will not inevitably define voter responses, as other factors are changing the relationship between citizens and parties.

In summary, we think of the general model of party government as a causal chain connecting voters at one end to policy outcomes at the other end of the chain. If this causal chain fails at any point, then the process as a whole may break down. Extra strength in one section of the causal chain (e.g. better financed and more professionalized party organizations) cannot compensate for a gap at another part of the chain. Thus, the chain is as strong as its weakest link, and the weakest link appears to be partisan dealignment among contemporary electorates.

DEMOCRACY IN A DEALIGNED ERA

Should we think what was unthinkable to E. E. Schattschneider? Will contemporary democracies function without political parties? The evidence assembled in this volume, and our own interpretations of these data, suggest that political parties will continue to be a central feature of representative democracy. Indeed, it remains difficult to think of national governments functioning without parties playing a significant role in connecting the various elements of the political process.

At the same time, this project has demonstrated that partisan politics is changing in systematic and important ways in advanced industrial democracies. Contemporary publics in most nations have followed a general trend of partisan dealignment in both their attitudinal attachments to party and their political behaviour. Although many (often most) citizens remained psychologically attached to a preferred political party, the number of such partisans is now lower in almost all these nations. The political parties have also responded to changes in the political and societal context. It appears that party leaders and careerists have created more centralized, institutionalized, and professionalized political parties—in part to insulate the party (and their individual careers) from the whims of a less stable and predictable electorate that is less mobilized by traditional partisan appeals. The evidence of party change is least apparent within parties in government, although even here we find that the policy images of the parties are converging, control over the selection of elites is weakening, and non-partisan forums—such as corporatist structures, independent central banks, and judicial decisions—are becoming a more important part of the governing process. Yet the cumulative evidence presented in this volume suggests that the nature of partisan politics is fundamentally changing in advanced industrial democracies. In this final section we want to discuss some of the likely consequences we envision due to these changes in the democratic process.

The most apparent changes involve the nature of electoral politics. Partisan dealignment means that fewer voters come to each election with standing partisan predispositions, and from this flow multiple effects. Dealignment is producing both the *fragmentation* and the *individualization* of political behaviour. While it was once possible to make reasonable predictions about electoral choice based on simple models of social cleavage voting or partisanship, this is less likely to apply today. Certainly there are still many voters who are motivated by partisan attachments, but there are fewer of those individuals today. Other citizens continue to exist within clearly defined social milieux, and thus social characteristics provide a valid guide to their electoral choices. But there are fewer of these individuals today. These long-term stabilizing influences on electoral politics have generally decreased in influence over time.

As we enter the twenty-first century, citizens are more interested and sophisticated about political matters. A more individualized and inwardly oriented style of political choice should put greater weight on the ebb and flow of events during the campaign. Rather than socially structured and relatively homogeneous personal networks, contemporary publics are more likely to base their decisions on policy preferences, performance judgements, or candidate images.[7]

---

[7] The actions of the political parties also have contributed to these changes. Because of a changing media environment and in response to the lessening of party loyalties, campaigns now more often emphasize the role of leadership, thus contributing to the rise of candidate-centred politics. In short, there has been an interaction between changes in the electorate and changes in the parties that reinforce partisan dealignment.

The fragmentation of politics also displays itself in the increasing heterogeneity of the public's issue interests. Rather than politics being structured by group benefits, which often reflected socially derived cues, citizens now focus on specific issues of immediate or personal importance. The traditional economic issues of the past are now joined by new issues of environmentalism, women's rights, and lifestyle choices (Inglehart 1990, 1997). These new issues often cut across existing partisan alignments. Furthermore, new post-material values often seem antithetical to traditional-style disciplined partisan politics.

The politicization of the issue space by public interest groups, lobbying groups, and other societal interests should reinforce this fragmentation of public interests and the political agenda. Many more organized interests are now represented in Washington, London, Berlin, Paris, Tokyo, and the other capitals of advanced industrial democracies. These interest groups have more ability than ever before to reach and organize their potential members through direct mailings, the mass media, the internet, and other means. The explosion of an interest group society is surely likely to continue as part of the modernization process we have focused on in this volume.

There is considerable room for debate over whether a more fluid pattern of electoral choice will strengthen or weaken the democratic process. The history of electoral research is embedded with questions about the public's decision-making abilities. For example, the classic studies of empirical research doubted whether citizens possessed the knowledge and sophistication to manage the complexities of public policy (e.g. Campbell et al. 1960; Almond and Verba 1963). More recently, Michael Delli Carpini and Scott Keeter (1996) argue that American voters have not demonstrated an increased knowledge of politics; and without political knowledge the ability to make reasoned choices is limited (Luskin 1987). In the absence of party and social group bonds, and with unmediated contact between elites and the public through the electronic media, some voters could be manipulated by unscrupulous elites, swayed by specious policy arguments, or attracted to a demagogic leader. Clinton, Blair, and Schröder all typify the new style of candidate-centred politics, but there is a dark side. The popular appeal of candidates such as LePen, Haider, Berlusconi, and Perot also may arise as a consequence of a dealigned electorate. From this perspective, a more fluid and volatile voting public may undermine the role of elections in determining national priorities, and open the way for ill-informed policy mandates and/or manipulative leaders.

Nevertheless, there is good reason to be relatively sanguine about the ability of the new non-partisans to make reasoned electoral choices. Part of this optimism arises because the new independents are often concentrated among the better educated and the cognitively mobilized. These are not the ill-informed and disinterested independents of the past, who conformed more to Kornhauser's (1959) image of mass society than to the rational citizen of democratic theory. In addition, there is empirical evidence that many citizens can use non-party cues to make reasoned political decisions (Lupia 1994; Popkin 1991; Lupia and McCubbins 1998). A more selective and issue-oriented electorate would imply that citizens are moving closer to the model of independent voter choice that is enshrined in democratic theory.

We cannot resolve these two conflicting visions of dealigned politics within the framework of this project. But it is clear that the nature of electoral politics is changing. Parties used to ensure that elections were judgements on broad policy choices that would guide government action—this function has become less clear as the partisanship of campaigns has diminished, issue interests have become more complex, and other factors influence electoral choice. The ability of mass publics and parties to function responsibility in this new environment holds fundamental implications for the future of democratic electoral politics.

The Impact of the Political Communication Revolution

Changes in political communication have played an especially important role in altering both individual citizens and the general role of political parties in contemporary democracies. It could be argued that one reason why we have seen the least change with regard to parties in government is because this facet of political parties has been least impacted by the changing media environment. For instance, many politicians feared that televising legislative debates would alter the governing process, but in actuality there was little reason to worry because the public has shown no more interest in watching legislation being made than in observing how sausages are made. The exception to the rule occurs during rare moments of high drama and conflict, such as during prime minister's question time in the UK, Australia, and now Japan.[8] But legislative outcomes rarely depend on who wins rhetorical contests on the floor, and the rare moments of drama that catch the public's attention are likely atypical of day-to-day governing.

In contrast, both parties as organizations and parties in the electorate have been profoundly influenced by changes in political communication. As Dautrich and Hartley (1999: 6) have recently written, 'E. E. Schattschneider's (1942) admonition that US elections are ' "unthinkable save in terms of parties" should in the age of contemporary age of US politics be reconsidered. Now, US elections are unthinkable save in terms of the news media.' Although this statement applies more to the US than anywhere else (see Chapter 6), it is evident that the mass media—particularly television—now play a central role in election campaigns in all advanced industrialized countries.

The revolutionary effect of television on political campaigns was evident to

---

[8] One might actually classify these debates as involving campaigns much more than governing, as the object on both sides is typically more about scoring points with the public than about making laws. The televising of parliamentary debates might therefore be considered an element in the development of the so-called 'permanent campaign'.

Hollywood as early as 1958. In the classic movie '*The Last Hurrah* Spencer Tracy's character urges his nephew to follow him along on the campaign trail to witness a traditional campaign while he still can. Tracy's lines go as follows:

It's my guess that the old-fashioned political campaign in a few years will be as extinct as the dodo. It will all be TV . . . Mind you I use the TV sometimes, but I also get out into the wards. I speak in arenas, armories, street corners, anywhere I can get a crowd. I even kiss babies. . . . But there's no use kidding myself—it is on its way out.

While this prediction seems prophetic over four decades later, it also tells us just how clear it was to those who lived through the early years of television that politics was being rapidly transformed. From Tony Blair orchestrating scenic walkabouts, to Helmut Kohl hosting townhall discussions on an RTL television broadcast, the nature of modern partisan politics has been transformed.

The rise of television broadcasting has dramatically altered how politicians present themselves to the public, as well as how the public receives political information. Instead of learning about an election at a campaign rally or from party canvassers, television and newspapers have become the primary sources of campaign information. Parties have thus lost a large part of their role as intermediaries in the information process between the public and elites. Instead of emphasizing the policy content of a campaign, television coverage focuses on a visually appealing backdrop for a speech peppered with short memorable quotes. Ansell and Fish (1999: 289) have observed, 'Neither Gladstone nor Disraeli faced the challenge of '"sound byte" politics,' but this must be the forte of an aspiring politician today. Television-based campaigning also accentuates the personality of the candidates and their videostyle over party ideology or programmatic goals.

Furthermore, the content of the mass media may downplay the importance of political parties, and even adopt an anti-partisan or anti-elite tone. Martin Wattenberg (1998) has shown how the American media have shifted their campaign focus away from the political parties toward the candidates. A similar personalization of campaign coverage has been discussed in many European party systems, often described as the 'Americanization' of electoral politics (Scammell 1997; Panebianco 1988: 266–7). Thus, the media are both replacing parties as sources of political information and possibly diminishing the partisan content of this information.[9] All this undoubtedly contributes to the partisan dealignment that we have observed.

The media's influence can also be linked to many of the institutional changes in party organizations that this project described. Media-based campaigns undoubtedly contributed to the centralization and professionalization of party

---

[9] Just as the media have assumed an information role, a myriad of special-interest groups and single-issue lobbies have assumed some of the parties' roles in representing public interests. These groups can work with political parties as has been the past pattern of labour, business, and other economic interest groups. However, public interest groups and single-issue groups often press their interests without relying on partisan channels.

organizations; political consultants, media analysts, and public opinion specialists became necessary tools in the modern political campaign—not an army of party members. Similarly, parties have focused on ensuring the capital needed to support the technology of modern campaigns, rather than assemble a large pool of cheap labour.

Media-based politics also alters the relationship between citizens and political elites. Politicians are now able to communicate directly with the public, and the public may feel that they 'know' the candidates on a personal basis. On the one hand, this further erodes the role of political parties as information providers, circumventing party structures and activists that once served as intermediaries. On the other hand, it reinforces the emphasis on candidate-centred politics and the personalization of political campaign. The media and the public discuss the candidates personal lives because we come to know them at a personal level, rather than focusing on their policies.

The current communications revolution, epitomized by developments in cable television and the internet, is likely to have a major impact as well. The much-anticipated proliferation of TV channels and websites will offer more information than ever before in an incredible array of formats. Some observers see these developments as offering 'the prospect of a revitalized democracy characterized by a more active and informed citizenry' (Corrado 1996: 29). However, it is questionable whether many citizens will actually take advantage of this new wealth of information. With countless available information sources for a wide variety of specific interests, it will be extremely easy for those at the periphery of politics to avoid the subject altogether. The result could well be a growing inequality of political information, with a small group of committed partisans becoming more knowledgeable while the rest of the public slips further into apathy concerning the parties.

Although much more attention has been paid to the internet than the rise of cable TV, the latter may well have the greatest impact on the future of political parties. One can already see the effect of what Austin Ranney (1990) has dubbed 'narrowcasting' by examining how the spread of cable TV has altered the American political landscape. When CBS, NBC, and ABC dominated the airwaves, their blanket coverage of presidential speeches, political conventions, and presidential debates left little else to watch on TV at those times. As television channels have proliferated, it has become much easier to avoid any exposure to politics, and statistics indicate that exposure has declined.[10] In short, with people given more choices of what to watch, fewer have chosen to watch major

[10] President Nixon got an average rating of 50 for his televised addresses to the nation, whereas President Clinton averaged only about 30 in his first term (Kernell 1997: 132). Political conventions, which once received more TV coverage than the Summer Olympics, have been relegated to an hour per night that draws abysmal ratings. The 1996 presidential debates drew a respectable average rating of 28, but this was only half the typical level of viewers drawn by debates held between 1960 and 1980.

political events. We can expect this pattern to be repeated in other countries as traditional state-run broadcasting networks such as the BBC and ARD/ZDF face new competition from cable stations. One likely result of such a change in television viewing habits is bound to be a decline in overall turnout to support the parties, all else being equal.

Unlike television, the impact of which was evident to Hollywood a mere six years after TV first played a role in the 1952 US presidential campaign, six years after the internet first emerged as a force in the 1994 elections its impact remains unclear. Because people who are already interested in politics are more likely to access political material on the internet, there is good reason to speculate that this medium may have more impact on parties as organizations than parties in the electorate. The remaining activists within the party organizations may find the ease of communication via the internet greatly facilitates their participation in party activities. In particular, the increasing democratization of the decision-making process within party organizations outlined by Scarrow, Webb, and Farrell (see Chapter 7) may be furthered by such communications technology. Small and new parties may also find it easier to organize than ever before. A small group of like-minded individuals who in the past might have been too geographically dispersed to organize a party should find fewer obstacles in the world of the internet, which knows no geographic boundaries. Similarly, new social movements will face fewer organizational start-up costs in an age when people can quickly be brought together through e-mail lists and a website. Governor Jesse Ventura of Minnesota was probably the first successful minor party candidate to create a political organization from scratch almost overnight via the Internet, and no doubt others will follow.

Moving beyond the Electoral Arena

Just as dealignment erodes the partisan basis of electoral politics, so it may affect other elements of democratic politics. For example, the ability to integrate citizens into the democratic process may be lessened. The traditional mass political party involved citizens in politics and legitimized the democratic process through participation in elections and campaigns. Partisan attachments stimulate involvement by the less-educated and the lower-status voters. As these attachments weaken, it is reasonable to expect that these citizens will be left behind in the new political environment.

At the same time that turnout is decreasing, there is evidence that some people are shifting their efforts to other forms of political participation. Participation in unconventional political actions has generally increased in recent years (Topf 1995; Jennings and van Deth 1989). Although there is evidence that engagement in social groups and political groups may be decreasing in the United States (Putnam 2000; but see Ladd 1999 for a counter-argument), such activism is increasing in most other advanced industrial democracies. Contemporary publics are generally more likely to work with others in their community to address a shared problem, to belong to a public interest lobby, and to contact officials directly about their concerns (Dalton 1996*a*, ch. 3–4).

Thus, another consequence of dealignment may be greater public involvement in citizen action groups, social movements, and other forms of direct action. Self-help groups, women's groups, consumer groups, and other citizen movements continue to proliferate. The environmental movement, for instance, has continued to expand its membership base in most of these nations so that its formal membership often exceeds formal party membership. Environmental groups also typify a distinctly non-partisan style of interest representation. Compared to the institutionalized structures of political parties, these citizen groups and social movements are creating a more fluid and varied organizational life for the democratic process.

In many OECD countries citizen groups are now using referendums to involve the public directly in policy-making. Sometimes these forms of direct democracy can be integrated into a partisan framework, but often they are developed as an alternative to partisan politics. Kaare Strøm (Chapter 9) showed that this trend is slowly developing at the national level, but there is even greater pressure for direct democracy at the grass-roots. For instance, the United States and the Federal Republic of Germany have never held a national referendum, but the use of referendums at the state and local level has increased markedly in recent years. Throughout much of the democratic world, referendums have recently been used to decide crucial issues of public policy, such as whether to join the EU and the European common currency, electoral reform in Italy and New Zealand, independence in Quebec, republicanism in Australia, peace in Northern Ireland, etc. Additional discussions about the need for more referendums is common in many nations. This form of direct democracy may further challenge a system of representative democracy based on political parties as the agents of interest aggregation.

Contemporary democracies are undeniably more open to the expression of citizen views, and the political processes are becoming more accessible to the public. However, this opening of the process may come with unintended costs. The classic cross-national study of political participation by Verba, Nie, and Kim (1978) found that social status differences in participation tend to be relatively small for voting, but much larger for direct forms of political action such as participation in citizen groups or protest activities. Lower-income citizens may therefore be disadvantaged in the political process if participation patterns shift toward unconventional, direct-action methods.[11] Increasing inequalities in access

---

[11] Social status differences in participation tend to be relatively small for voting, and much larger for direct forms of political action such as participation in citizen groups or protest activities (Verba et al. 1978; Dalton 1996*a*, chs. 3–4). In addition, the more sophisticated new 'apartisans' favour a more participatory style of democracy and are more likely to be able to manage the complexities of public interest groups, individually initiated citizen contacts, and internet democracy.

to information, as discussed in the previous section, ought to further reinforce this pattern. Widespread participation in elections has long helped integrate citizens into the democratic process and legitimize the process; rising inequality in non-electoral forms of political participation may have exactly the reverse effects.

Parties are also playing a diminishing role as the articulators of political interests. In part this results from the changing nature of interest articulation due to the rise of citizen interest groups and the mass media. Another factor, though, is the parties' changing relationship with society. Attempts to insulate parties from a social clientele, such as in the characteristics of cartel parties, lessen the ability of parties to represent diverse interests and negotiate among members of the party alliance. The shift from 'selling' to 'marketing' parties thus diminishes the parties' function in representing the citizenry. Fortunately, this potential loss of representation is largely counterbalanced by increased roles for other agents of interest articulation. Today, it is much easier for individuals and groups to find some voice with the democratic process, even if voice is not equivalent to policy influence.

Parties differ, however, from interest groups in their advocacy role. Interest groups and citizen groups encourage individuals to think in terms of their specific interests. Each group claims that its desires should be met, and anything short of this is often cast as a failure of the political process. Environmentalists, for instance, criticize the policies of Republican and Democratic administrations, or of Conservative and Labour governments; they are equal opportunity critics of government in their lobbying for additional environmental action. Even the collective decision-making process of elections is diminished, because interest groups often distance themselves from partisan politics and cast aspersions on all political parties. Parties, in contrast, are often advocates for the governing process. The leaders of the victorious parties celebrate election outcomes and proclaim that things will improve, whereas interest groups often challenge the new government regardless of its political orientation. Leaders of the governing parties stress what is right with government, whereas interest groups draw our attention to government's shortcomings.

Regrettably for democracy, the interest aggregation function of political parties has also declined. The lack of stable electoral coalitions, the weakening bonds to social support groups, and the internal changes within political parties are diminishing their ability to assemble diverse political interests into a governing programme. The decline of interest aggregation makes it more difficult for governments to govern, especially if government leaders continue to be guided by the marketing strategy that won them power. Moreover, while interest groups and the media can assume some of the parties' former role in articulating public interests, there is no such ready alternative to parties in terms of interest aggregation.

Thus, we should be concerned that political change may give rise to a pattern of hyper-democracy: we may become more effective in expressing our special interests, while at the same time failing to bring interests together for the common good. Morris Fiorina's (1980: 44) adage that the United States has 'a system that articulates interests superbly but aggregates them poorly' may now well apply quite broadly.

Although many of the challenges to democracy that arise due to modernization forces are beyond the parties' control, it is equally important to recognize that the response of many parties may be exacerbating these problems. The characteristics of cartel parties may especially damage the functioning of the democratic process. When parties make fewer and fewer efforts to mobilize citizens they worsen inequality of participation. Parties that centralize and professionalize their offices in lieu of citizens active as party members might contribute to the demobilization of the public and the diminished understanding and trust in the democratic process. Parties that develop public funding sources in order to insulate themselves from the ebbs and flows of public support will inevitably distance themselves from those they represent. Running elections and governing by marketing principles may be successful in the short term for parties, but this strategy may well undermine the democratic process in the long term.

It is incumbent on democracies and political parties to do more than merely insulate parties and government from the consequences of dealignment. Although the future is always uncertain, we believe that partisan dealignment is now entrenched across the advanced industrial democracies, and that this new reality needs to be accepted and addressed by the parties. Thus we differ with those who argue that the strength of parties in legislatures and the government will inevitably lead to a partisan remobilization of the public. Rather, we see the lack of response by parties in government to the changing realities of dealigned politics as further increasing the gap between the governors and the governed.

Broad cross-national patterns of partisan change thus present new challenges to representative democracy. Dealignment places new demands on the citizenry to make reasonable electoral choices in a new and more complex political setting. The decline of turnout and other forms of political participation through parties creates a new challenge for democracies to involve all of its citizens, especially those with fewer political resources and skills. Democracy's future depends on how citizens, politicians, and political institutions respond to these challenges. The response should not be to look back to a period when political parties were stronger and democracy functioned only through representative institutions. Democracies must adapt to survive, accepting the implications of partisan dealignment. Democracy has progressed in the past by facing such challenges and expanding, and if today's problems are addressed forthrightly we are optimistic that this can continue to be the case.

Appendix

Nation	Electoral System	MP nomination[a]	Leader nomination[b]	Index of Doring party rules[c]	Index[d]
Australia	AV-SSD	3.0	2.0	4	1
Austria	PR-closed list	2.0	2.8	4	4
Belgium	PR-flexible list	2.0	3.6	3	4
Britain	plurality-SSD	2.0	3.0	1	1
Canada	plurality-SSD	1.0	3.5	2	1
Denmark	PR-open list	1.0	1.7	4	5
Finland	PR-open list	2.0	3.0	3	5
France	Majority-plurality-SSD	2.0	3.3	2	2
Germany	MMP-closed list	2.0	2.8	4	4
Ireland	STV-MMD	2.0	1.8	2	4
Italy*	PR-open list	2.0	2.3	1	6
Japan*	SNTV-MMD	1.0	—	3	1
Netherlands	PR-flexible list	2.0	1.7	3	7
New Zealand*	Plurality-SSD	2.0	1.0	—	1
Norway	PR-closed list	3.0	3.0	3	4
Sweden	PR-closed list	3.0	3.0	1	5
United States	Plurality-SSD	4.0	4.0	3	7

* Values for Japan, NZ, and Italy are before electoral reforms passed in 1993–4.

List of abbreviations: SSD = single-seat district; PR = proportional representation; STV = single transferable vote; SNTV = single non-transferable vote; AV = alternative vote; MMD = multi-member district; MMP = mixed-member proportional

[a] The index of MP nomination is based on Table 7.1 and scored: (1) party veto, no local ratification, (2) party veto, local ratification, (3) no party veto, local ratification, (4) primaries or other weak structures.

[b] The index of leader selection is based on Table 7.2 and weighted for the process in different parties; the scale ranges from (1) parliamentary party selects leaders to (4) party members or primaries select leaders.

[c] The index of party rules is a simple count of the existence of four party rules discussed in Chapter 8: committee appointments on party basis, committee members can be removed by parties, party organization has say on joining government coalition, party groups included in the governing body. The index ranges from 0 to 4. Additional nations were coded by the authors.

Values: (1) Strong party control (e.g. PR system with party control of list), (2) strong party control, (3) moderate control, (4) little control by national party.

[d] The Doring index is from Table 8.3, with additional nations coded by the authors.

References

ABERBACH, JOEL. (1990). *Keeping a Watchful Eye: The Politics of Congressional Oversight*. Washington, DC: Brookings.
—— ROBERT PUTNAM, and BERT ROCKMAN (1981). *Bureaucrats and Politicians in Western Democracies*. Cambridge, Mass.: Harvard University Press.
ABRAMOWITZ, ALAN, JOHN MCGLENNON, and RONALD RAPPAPORT (1983). 'The Party Isn't Over: Incentives for Activism in the 1980 Presidential Nominating Campaign', *Journal of Politics*, 45: 1006–15.
ABRAMSON, J., F. C. ARTERTON, and GARY ORREN (1988). *The Electronic Commonwealth*. New York: Basic Books.
ABRAMSON, PAUL, JOHN ALDRICH, and DAVID ROHDE (1998). *Change and Continuity in the 1996 Elections*. Washington, DC: Congressional Quarterly Press.
AITKIN, DON, BRIAN JINKS, GWYNNETH SINGLETON, and JOHN WARHURST (1996). *Australian Political Institutions*. South Melbourne: Addison Wesley Longman.
ALDRICH, JOHN (1995). *Why Parties? The Origin and Transformation of Political Parties in America*. Chicago: University of Chicago Press.
ALLARDT, ERIK, and PERTTI PESONEN (1960). 'Citizen Participation in Political Life: Finland', *International Social Science Journal*, 12: 27–39.
ALMOND, GABRIEL A., and SIDNEY VERBA (1963). *The Civic Culture*. Boston: Little Brown.
—— G. BINGHAM POWELL, and ROBERT MUNDT (1993). *Comparative Politics: A Theoretical Framework*. New York: HarperCollins.
ALT, JAMES (1984). 'Dealignment and the Dynamics of Partisanship in Britain', in Russell Dalton, Scott Flanagan, and Paul Beck (eds.), *Electoral Change in Advanced Industrial Democracies*. Princeton: Princeton University Press.
ANDERSON, CHRISTOPHER, and CARSTEN ZELLE (1995). 'Helmut Kohl and the CDU Victory', *German Politics and Society*, 13: 12–35.
ANDEWEG RUDY (1997). 'Role Specialization or Role Switching? Dutch MPS between Electorate and Executive', in Wolfgang Mueller and Thomas Saalfeld (eds.), *Members of Parliament in Western Europe*. London: Frank Cass
ANGELL, ALAN, M. D'ALVA KINZO and D. URBANEJA (1992). 'Latin America', in David Butler and Austin Ranney (eds.), *Electioneering*. Oxford: Clarendon.
ANSELL, CHRISTOPHER, and STEVEN FISH (1999). 'The Art of Being Indispensable: Noncharismatic Personalism in Contemporary Political Parties' *Comparative Political Studies*, 32: 283–312.
APSA—American Political Science Association Committee on Political Parties (1950). *Towards a More Responsible Two Party System*. New York: Rinehart.
BAKER, KENDALL, RUSSELL DALTON, and KAI HILDEBRANDT (1981). *Germany Transformed: Political Culture and the New Politics*. Cambridge, Mass.: Harvard University Press.
BANFIELD, EDWARD, and JAMES WILSON (1963). *City Politics*. Cambridge, Mass.: Harvard University Press.

BANKS, ARTHUR (1998). *Cross-national Times Series Data* [computer file]. Binghamton: Computer Solutions Unlimited.

BARBER, BENJAMIN (1984). *Strong Democracy*. Berkeley and Los Angeles: University of California Press.

BARDI, LUCIANO (1996). 'Anti-party Sentiment and Party System Change in Italy', *European Journal of Political Research*, 29: 345–63.

—— and L. MORLINO (1994). 'Italy: Tracing the Roots of the Great Transformation', in Richard Katz and Peter Mair (eds.), *How Parties Organize*. London: Sage.

—— and MARTIN RHODES (eds.) (1998). *Politica in Italia 1998*. Bologna: Il Mulino.

BARDONNET, DANIEL (1960). *Évolution de la Structure du Parti Radical*. Paris: Éditions Monchrestien.

BARNES, SAMUEl, MAX KAASE, et al. (1979). *Political Action: Mass Participation in Five Western Democracies*. Thousand Oaks, Calif.: Sage.

BARTELS, LARRY (1992). 'The Impact of Electioneering in the United States', in David Butler and Austin Ranney (eds.), *Electioneering*. Oxford: Clarendon.

—— (2000). 'Partisanship and Voting Behavior, 1952–1996', *American Journal of Political Science*, 44: 35–50.

BARTOLINI, STEFANO (1983). 'The Membership of Mass Parties: The Social Democratic Experience, 1889–1978', in Hans Daalder and Peter Mair (eds), *Western European Party Systems*. London: Sage.

—— and PETER MAIR (1990). *Identity, Competition and Electoral Availability*. Cambridge: Cambridge University Press.

BAWN, KATHLEEN, GARY COX and FRANCES ROSENBLUTH (1999). 'Measuring the Ties that Bind: Electoral Cohesiveness in Four Democracies', in Bernard Grofman, Sung-Chull Lee, Edward Winckler, and Brian Woodall (eds.), *Elections in Japan, Korea, and Taiwan under the Single Non-Transferable Vote*. Ann Arbor: University of Michigan Press.

BEAN, CLIVE (1996). 'Partisanship and Electoral Behaviour in Comparative Perspective', in Marian Simms (ed.), *The Paradox of Parties: Australian Political Parties in the 1990s*. Sydney: Allen & Unwin.

—— and ANTHONY MUGHAN (1989). 'Leadership Effects in Parliamentary Elections in Australia and Britain', *American Political Science Review*, 83: 1165–79.

BEARD, CHARLES (1910). *American Government and Politics*. New York: Macmillan.

BECK, PAUL (1974). 'A Socialization Theory of Partisan Realignment', in Richard Niemi et al., *The Politics of Future Citizens*, San Francisco: Jossey-Bass.

—— (1984). 'The Dealignment Era in America', in Russell Dalton, Scott Flanagan, and Paul Beck (eds.), *Electoral Change in Advanced Industrial Democracies*. Princeton: Princeton University Press.

—— et al. (1997). 'Presidential Campaigns at the Grass Roots', *Journal of Politics*, 59: 1264–75.

BECKER, HORST et al. (1983). *Die SPD von Innen*. Bonn: Verlag Neue Gesellschaft.

BEER, SAMUEL (1969). *Modern British Politics*. London: Faber.

BELLOC, HILAIRE and CECIL CHESTERTON (1911). *The Party System*. London: Stephen Swift.

BENTZON, K. H. (1981). *Kommunalpolitikerne*. Copenhagen: Samfundsvidenskabeligt Forlag.

BERELSON, BERNARD, PAUL LAZARSFELD, and WILLIAM MCPHEE (1954). *Voting*. Chicago: University of Chicago Press.

BERGER, SUZANNE, and RONALD DORE (eds.) (1996). *National Diversity and Global Capitalism*. Ithaca, NY: Cornell University Press.

BERNIER, ROBERT, and DENIS MONIÈRE (1991). 'The Organization of Televised Leaders Debates in the United States, Europe, Australia and Canada', in F. Fletcher (ed.,) *Media and Voters in Canadian Election Campaigns*. Toronto: Dundurn Press.

BERTON, PETER (1991). 'The Japanese Communist Party: The Lovable Party', in Ronald Hrebenar (ed.), *The Japanese Party System,* 2nd edn. Boulder, Colo.: Westview Press.

BILLE, LARS, JØRGEN ELKLIT, and MIKAEL V. JAKOBSEN (1992). 'Denmark: The 1900 Campaign', in Shaun Bowler and David M. Farrell (eds.), *Electoral Strategies and Political Marketing*. Houndmills: Macmillan.

BLONDEL, JEAN, and MAURIZIO COTTA (eds.) (1996). *Party and Government: An Inquiry into the Relationship between Governments and Supporting Parties in Liberal Democracies*. London: Macmillan.

BOIX, CARLES (1998). *Partisan Governments and Macroeconomic Policies in OECD Economies*. Working Paper, Centro de Estudios Avanzados en Ciencias Sociales: Instituto Juan March de Estudios e Investigaciones.

BOK, DEREK (1997). *The State of the Nation*. Cambridge, Mass.: Harvard University Press.

BONCHEK, MARK (1997). 'From Broadcast to Netcast: The Internet and the Flow of Political Information'. Ph.D. Thesis, Harvard University, <http://www.ai.mit.edu/people/msb/thesis/title.html> .

BONE, HUGH (1949). *American Political Parties and the Party System*. New York: McGraw-Hill.

BORRE, OLE, and JORGEN GOUL ANDERSEN (1997). *Voting and Political Attitudes in Denmark*. Aarhus: Aarhus University Press.

—— and DANIEL KATZ (1973). 'Party Identification and its Motivational Base in a Multiparty System', *Scandinavian Political Studies,* 8: 69–111.

BOWLER, SHAUN, and DAVID FARRELL (eds.) (1992). *Electoral Strategies and Political Marketing*. Houndmills, Basingstoke: Macmillan.

—— —— and RICHARD KATZ (1998). *Party Cohesion, Party Discipline and the Organization of Parliaments*. Columbus, Oh.: Ohio State University Press.

BRODER, DAVID (1972). *The Party's Over: The Failure of Politics in America*. New York: Harper & Row.

BRODY, RICHARD (1978). 'The Puzzle of Political Participation in America', in Anthony King (ed.), *The New American Political System*. Washington, DC: American Enterprise Institute.

BRUCE, PETER (1997). 'How the Experts Got Voter Turnout Wrong Last Year', *Public Perspective,* 8: 39–43.

BRYCE, JAMES (1889). *The American Commonwealth*. London: Macmillan & Co.

—— (1982). 'Preface', in Mosei Ostrogorski, *Democracy and the Organization of Political Parties*, vol. ii, (ed.) Seymour M. Lipset. New Brunswick: Transaction Books. First published 1902.

BUDGE, IAN (1996). *The New Challenge of Direct Democracy*. Oxford: Polity Press.

—— (1999). 'Party Policy and Ideology: Reverting to the 1950s?', in Geoffrey Evans and Pippa Norris (eds.), *Critical Elections: British Parties and Voters in Long-Term Perspective*. London: Sage.

—— IVOR CREWE, and DENNIS FARLIE (eds.) (1976). *Party Identification and Beyond*. New York: John Wiley.

—— and DENNIS FARLIE (1983). *Explaining and Predicting Elections: Issue Effects and Party Strategies in Twenty-Three Democracies.* London: Allen & Unwin.

—— and HANS KEMAN (1990). *Parties and Democracy: Coalition Formation and Government Functioning in 20 States.* Oxford: Oxford University Press.

—— DAVID ROBERTSON and DEREK HEARL (eds.) (1987). *Ideology, Strategy and Party Change: Spatial Analysis of Postwar Election Programmes in 19 Democracies.* Cambridge: Cambridge University Press.

BURNHAM, WALTER DEAN (1970). *Critical Elections and the Mainsprings of American Politics.* New York: Norton.

BUTLER, DAVID, and DENNIS KAVANAGH (1988). *The British Election Campaign of 1987.* Houndmills, Basingstoke: Macmillan.

—— —— (1997). *The British General Election of 1997.* Houndmills, Basingstoke: Macmillan.

—— and AUSTIN RANNEY (eds.) (1992). *Electioneering.* Oxford: Clarendon.

—— —— (1994). *Referendums around the World: The Growing Use of Democracy?* Washington, DC: American Enterprise Institute.

—— and DONALD STOKES (1969). *Political Change in Britain.* New York: St. Martin's Press.

—— (1974). *Political Change in Britain*, 2nd edn. New York: St Martin's Press.

CAIN, BRUCE, JOHN FEREJOHN, and MORRIS FIORINA (1987). *The Personal Vote: Constituency Service and Electoral Independence.* Cambridge, Mass.: Harvard University Press.

CAMERON, DAVID (1985). 'Does Government Cause Inflation? Taxes, Spending, and Deficits', in Leon N. Lindberg and Charles S. Maier (eds.), *The Politics of Inflation and Economic Stagnation.* Washington, DC: Brookings Institution.

CAMPBELL, ANGUS, PHILIP CONVERSE, WARREN MILLER, and DONALD STOKES (1960). *The American Voter.* New York: Wiley.

—— —— —— —— (1966). *Elections and the Political Order.* New York: Wiley.

—— GERALD GURIN, and WARREN MILLER (1954). *The Voter Decides.* Evanston, Ill.: Row, Peterson.

CAMPION, GILBERT, and D. LIDDERDALE (1953). *European Parliamentary Procedure: A Comparative Handbook.* London: Allen & Unwin.

CAREY, JOHN, and MATTHEW SOBERG SHUGART (1995). 'Incentives to Cultivate the Personal Vote', *Electoral Studies,* 14: 417–40.

CARMINES, EDWARD, and JAMES STIMSON (1989). *Issue Evolution.* Princeton, NJ: Princeton University Press.

CARTY, R. KENNETH. (n.d.). 'Canadian Parties as Membership Organizations'. Mimeo.

—— (1991). *Canadian Political Parties in the Constituencies.* Toronto: Dundurn Press.

—— and Donald E. Blake (1999). 'The Adoption of Membership Votes for Choosing Party Leaders: The Experience of Canadian Parties', *Party Politics,* 5: 211–24.

CASTLES, FRANCIS G. (1982). 'The Impact of Parties on Public Expenditure', in Francis Castles (ed.), *The Impact of Parties.* London: Sage.

—— and PETER MAIR (1984). 'Left-Right Political Scales: Some Expert Judgments', *European Journal of Political Research,* 12: 73–88.

CAYROL, ROLAND, and JEROME JAFFRE (1980). 'Party Linkages in France: Socialist Leaders, Followers, and Voters', in Kay Lawson, (ed.), *Political Parties and Linkage.* New Haven: Yale University Press.

CHAMBERS, WILLIAM NISBET (1963). *Political Parties in a New Nation.* New York: Oxford University Press.

—— (1975). 'Party Development and the American Mainstream', in W. N. Chambers and Walter Dean Burnham, *The American Party System*, 2nd edn. New York: Oxford University Press.

CHAPMAN, R. M., W.K. JACKSON and A.V. Mitchell (1962). *New Zealand Politics in Action.* London: Oxford University Press.

CHUBB, BASIL (1970). *The Government and Politics of Ireland.* Stanford, Calif.: Stanford University Press.

CLARKE, HAROLD, NITISH DUTT, and ALLAN KORNBERG (1993). 'The Political Economy of Attitudes toward Polity and Society in Western European Democracies', *Journal of Politics,* 55: 998–1021.

CLARKE, HAROLD, and ALLAN KORNBERG (1993). 'Evaluations and Evolution: Public Attitudes toward Canada's Federal Political Parties, 1965–1991', *Canadian Journal of Political Science,* 26: 287–311.

—— —— (1996). 'Partisan Dealignment, Electoral Choice, and Party-system Change in Canada', *Party Politics,* 2: 455–78.

—— —— and PETER WEARING (2000). *A Polity on the Edge: Canada and the Politics of Fragmentation.* Toronto: Broadview Press.

—— and MARIANNE STEWART (1998). 'The Decline of Parties in the Minds of Citizens', *Annual Review of Political Science,* 1: 357–78.

—— et al. (1996). *Absent Mandate: Canadian Electoral Politics in an Era of Restructuring.* Toronto: Gage.

COLE, ALLAN, GEORGE TOTTEN, and CECIL UYEHARA (1966). *Socialist Parties in Postwar Japan.* New Haven: Yale University Press.

COLEMAN, JOHN (1996). 'Resurgent or Just Busy? Party Organizations in Contemporary America', in Daniel Shea and John Green (eds.), *The State of Parties*, 2nd edn. Lanham, Md.: Rowman & Littlefield.

COLEMAN, JOHN (1996). *Party Decline in America.* Princeton: Princeton University Press.

CONSERVATIVE PARTY (1998). *Fresh Future.* London: Conservative Party.

CONVERSE, PHILIP (1966). 'The Concept of the Normal Vote', in Angus Campbell et al., *Elections and the Political Order.* New York: Wiley.

—— (1969). 'Of Time and Partisan Stability', *Comparative Political Studies*, 2: 139–71.

—— (1972). 'Change in the American Electorate', in Angus Campbell and Philip Converse (eds.), *The Human Meaning of Social Change.* New York: Russell Sage.

—— (1976). *The Dynamics of Party Support: Cohort-Analyzing Party Identification.* Beverly Hills, Calif.: Sage Publications.

—— and GEORGES DUPUEX (1962). 'Politicization of the Electorate in France and the United States', *Public Opinion Quarterly,* 26: 1–23.

CORRADO, ANTHONY (1996). 'Elections in Cyberspace: Prospects and Problems', in Anthony Corrado and C. Firestone (eds.), *Elections in Cyberspace: Toward a New Era in American Politics.* Washington, DC: The Aspen Institute.

CORRADO, A. and C. FIRESTONE (eds.) (1996). *Elections in Cyberspace: Toward a New Era in American Politics.* Washington, DC: The Aspen Institute.

COX, GARY (1987). *The Efficient Secret: The Cabinet and the Development of Political Parties in Victorian England.* Cambridge: Cambridge University Press.

—— (1997). *Making Votes Count: Strategic Coordination in the World's Electoral Systems.* New York: Cambridge University Press.

—— and MATHEW MCCUBBINS (1993). *Legislative Leviathan: Party Government in the House.* Berkeley and Los Angeles: University of California Press.

—— —— (1994). 'Bonding, Structure, and the Stability of Political Parties: Party Government in the House', *Legislative Studies Quarterly,* 19: 215–31.

—— and MICHAEL THIES (1998). 'The Cost of Intraparty Competition: The Single, Nontransferable Vote and Money Politics in Japan', *Comparative Political Studies,* 31: 267–91.

CREE, NATHAN (1892). *Direct Legislation by the People.* Chicago: A. C. McClurg.

CREWE, IVOR (1983). 'The Electorate: Partisan Dealignment Ten years On', *West European Politics,* 6: 183–215.

—— and DAVID DENVER (eds.) (1985). *Electoral Change in Western Democracies.* London: Croom Helm.

—— ANTHONY FOX and NEIL DAY (1995). *The British Electorate, 1963–92.* Cambridge: Cambridge University Press.

—— and ANTHONY KING (1995). *SDP: The Birth, Life and Death of the Social Democratic Party.* Oxford: Oxford University Press.

CROLY, HERBERT (1914). *Progressive Democracy.* New York: Macmillan.

CROWLEY, PHILIP (1996). 'Crossing the Floor: Representative Theory and Practice in Britain', *Public Law,* 214–24.

CROZIER, MICHEL, et al. (1975). *The Crisis of Democracy.* New York: New York University Press.

CUKIERMAN, ALEX (1992). *Central Bank Strategy, Credibility, and Independence: Theory and Evidence.* Cambridge, Mass.: MIT Press.

—— Steven Webb, and Bilin Neyapti (1994). *Measuring Central Bank Independence and Its Effect on Policy Outcomes.* San Francisco: ICS.

CURTICE, JOHN, and ROGER JOWELL (1995). 'The Skeptical Electorate', in Roger Jowell et al. (eds.), *British Social Attitudes—the 12th Report.* Brookfield, Vt.: Dartmouth.

CURTIS, G. (1988). *The Japanese Way of Politics.* New York: Columbia University Press.

CUSACK, THOMAS (1999). 'Partisan Politics and Fiscal Policy', *Comparative Political Studies,* 32: 464–86.

CZUDNOWSKI, MOSHE (1975). 'Political Recruitment', in Fred Greenstein and Nelson Polsby (eds.), *Handbook of Political Science.* Reading, Mass.: Addison-Wesley Publishing Co.

DAALDER, HANS (ed.) (1987). *Party Systems in Denmark, Austria, Switzerland, the Netherlands, and Belgium.* London: Frances Pinter.

—— and PETER MAIR (eds.) (1983). *Western European Party Systems: Continuity and Change.* Beverly Hills, Calif.: Sage.

DACHS, HERBERT, et al. (1997). *Handbuch des politischen Systems Österreichs,.* 3rd edn. Vienna: Manzsche-Verlags und Universitätsbuchhandlung.

DAHL, ROBERT (1961). *Who Governs?* New Haven: Yale University Press.

—— (1966). *Political Opposition in Western Democracies.* New Haven: Yale University Press.

—— (1971). *Polyarchy: Participation and Opposition.* New Haven: Yale University Press.

DALTON, RUSSELL (1984). 'Cognitive Mobilization and Partisan Dealignment in Advanced Industrial Democracies', *Journal of Politics,* 46: 264–84.

—— (1988). *Citizen Politics in Western Democracies.* Chatham, NJ: Chatham House.

—— (1994). *The Green Rainbow: Environmental Interest Groups in Western Europe.* New Haven: Yale University Press.

—— (1996a). *Citizen Politics: Public Opinion and Political Parties in Advanced Industrial Democracies,* 2nd edn Chatham, NJ: Chatham House.

—— (1996b). 'A Divided Electorate?', in Gordon Smith et al. (eds.), *Developments in German Politics.* London: Macmillan.

—— SCOTT FLANAGAN, and PAUL BECK (eds.) (1984). *Electoral Change in Advanced Industrial Democracies.* Princeton: Princeton University Press.

—— and MANFRED KUECHLER (eds.) (1990). *Challenging the Political Order: New Social and Political Movements in Western Democracies.* New York: Oxford University Press.

—— and ROBERT ROHRSCHNEIDER (1990). 'Wählerwandel und die Abschwächung der Parteineigungen von 1972 bis 1987', in Max Kaase and Hans-Dieter Klingemann (eds.),*Wahlen und politischer Prozess.* Opladen: Westdeutscher Verlag.

—— and Martin Wattenberg (1993). 'The Not so Simple Act of Voting?', in Ada Finifter (ed.), *The State of the Discipline II.* Washington, DC: American Political Science Association.

DAMGAARD, ERIK, and PALLE SVENSSON (1989). 'Who Governs? Parties and Politics in Denmark', *European Journal of Political Research,* 17.

DAUTRICH, KENNETH and THOMAS H. HARTLEY (1999). *How the News Media Fail American Voters.* New York: Columbia University Press.

DAY, ALAN, and HENRY DEGENHARDT (1980). *Political Parties of the World.* Detroit: Gale Research.

DEBNAM, GEOFFREY (1994). 'Overcoming the Iron Law? The Role of the Policy Committees of the New Zealand Labour Party', in Kay Lawson (ed.), *How Political Parties Work: Perspectives from Within.* Westport, Conn.: Praeger.

DELLI CARPINI, MICHAEL, and SCOTT KEETER (1996). *What Americans Know about Politics and Whether it Matters.* New Haven: Yale University Press.

DESCHOUWER, KRIS (1996). 'Political Parties and Democracy: A Mutual Murder?' *European Journal of Political Research.* 29: 263–78.

DE WINTER, LIEVEN, ARCO TIMMERMANS, and PATRICK DUMONT (1997). 'Belgien: Über Regierungsabkommen, Evangelisten, Gläubige, und Häretiker', in Wolfgang C. Müller and Kaare Strøm (eds), *Koalitionsregierungen in Westeuropa.* Vienna: Signum Verlag.

DIONNE, E. J. (1976). 'What Technology Has Not Changed', in L. Maisel (ed.), *Changing Campaign Techniques.* Beverly Hills, Calif.: Sage.

DORFMAN, GERALD, and PETER DUIGNAN (1991). *Politics in Western Europe.* Stanford, Calif.: Hoover Institution Press.

DORING, HERBERT (1995). 'Time as a Scare Resource', in Herbert Doring (ed.), *Parliament and Majority Rule in Western Europe* Frankfurt/New York: Campus Verlag/St Martin's Press.

DOWNS, ANTHONY (1957). *An Economic Theory of Democracy.* New York: Wiley.

DUNLEAVY, P. and H. WARD (1981). 'Exogenous Voter Preferences and Parties with State Power: Some Internal Problems of Economic Models of Party Competition', *British Journal of Political Science,* 11: 351–80.

DUVERGER, MAURICE (1954). *Political Parties.* New York: Wiley. First French edition.

—— (1963). *Political Parties,* Science Edition. New York: Wiley.

The Economist (1997). 'Decrepit', 3 Apr.

ELGIE, ROBERT (1998). 'Democratic Accountablility and Central Bank Independence: Historical and Contemporary, National and European Perspectives', *West European Politics*, 21: 53–76.

EPSTEIN, LEON (1967). 'Political Parties in Western Democratic Systems', in Roy Macrieurdis (ed.), *Political Parties: Contemporary Trends and Ideas*. New York: Harper & Row.

—— (1980). *Political Parties in Western Democracies*. New Brunswick, NJ: Transaction Publishers. First published 1967.

—— (1986). *Political Parties in the American Mold*. Madison: University of Wisconsin Press.

ERICKSON, LYNDA (1997). 'Canada', in Pippa Norris (ed.), *Passages to Power*. Cambridge: Cambridge University Press.

EVANS, GEOFFREY, and PIPPA NORRIS (eds.) (1999). *Critical Elections: British Parties and Voters in Long-term Perspective*. Thousand Oaks, Calif.: Sage.

FALKE, WOLFGANG (1982). *Die Mitglieder der CDU*. Berlin: Duncker & Humblot.

FARNETI, PAOLO (1985). *The Italian Party System*. London: Frances Pinter.

FARRELL, DAVID (1994). 'Ireland: Centralization, Professionalization and Competitive Pressures', in Richard Katz and Peter Mair (eds.), *How Parties Organize*. London: Sage.

—— (1996). 'Campaign Strategies and Tactics', in Lawrence LeDuc, Richard Niemi, and Pippa Norris (eds.), *Comparing Democracies*. Thousand Oaks, Calif.: Sage.

—— (1998). 'Political Consultancy Overseas: The Internationalization of Campaign Consultancy', *PS: Political Science and Politics*, 31: 171–76.

—— ROBIN KOLODNY, STEPHEN MEDVIC (1998). 'The Political Consultant/Political Party Relationship: A Health Warning for Representative Democracy or a Welcome Advance?' Paper presented at the American Political Science Association annual meeting, Boston, 3–6 Sept.

FAUCHEUX, RON (1998). 'How Campaigns are Using the Internet: An Exclusive Nationwide Survey', *Campaigns & Elections* (Sept.), 22–5.

FIORINA, MORRIS P. (1980). 'The Decline of Collective Responsibility in American Politics', *Daedalus*, 109: 25–45.

—— (1981). *Retrospective Voting in American National Elections*. New Haven: Yale University Press.

—— (1990). 'Information and Rationality in Elections', in John Ferejohn and James Kuklinski (eds.), *Information and Democratic Processes*. Urbana: University of Illinois Press.

—— (1992). *Divided Government*. New York: Macmillan.

FLANAGAN, SCOTT et al. (1991). *The Japanese Voter*. New Haven: Yale University Press.

FLORA, PETER et al. (1983). *State, Economy and Society in Western Europe 1815–1975*. Frankfurt: Campus Verlag.

FRANKLIN, MARK, TOM MACKIE, HENRY VALEN et al. (1992). *Electoral Change: Responses to Evolving Social and Attitudinal Structures in Western Countries*. New York: Cambridge University Press.

FRYE, BRUCE (1985). *Liberal Democrats in the Weimar Republic*. Carbondale: Southern Illinois University Press.

FUKUI, HARUHIRO (1997). 'Japan', in Pippa Norris (ed.), *Passages to Power*. Cambridge: Cambridge University Press.

GALLAGHER, MICHAEL (1988). 'Conclusion', in Michael Gallagher and Michael Marsh (eds.), *Candidate-selection in Comparative Perspective*. London: Sage Publications.

—— and Michael Marsh (eds.), (1988). *Candidate-Selection in Comparative Perspective*. London: Sage Publications.

GALLI, GIORGIO, and ALFONSO PRANDI (1970). *Patterns of Political Participation in Italy*. New Haven: Yale University Press

GALLIGAN, BRIAN, IAN MCALLISTER, and JOHN RAVENHILL (eds.) (1998). *New Developments in Australian Politics*. South Melbourne: Macmillan.

GARRETT, GEOFFREY (1996). 'Capital Mobility, Trade and the Domestic Politics of Economic Policy', in Robert Keohane and Helen Milner (eds.), *Internationalization and Domestic Politics*. New York: Cambridge University Press.

—— and PETER LANGE (1991). 'Political Responses to Interdependence: What's Left for the Left?', *International Organization*, 45: 539–64.

GESER, HANS (1991). 'Dealignment oder neue Integrationsbereitschaft? Aktuelle Entwicklungstendenzen im Anhängerbestand schweizerischer Kommunalparteien', *Schweizerische Zeitschrift für Soziologie* , 2: 233–72.

—— et al. (1994). *Die Schweizer Lokalparteien*. Zurich: Seismo Verlag.

GIBSON, RACHEL, and STEPHEN WARD (1998). 'U.K. Political Parties and the Internet: Politics as Usual in the New Media?', *Press/Politics*, 3: 14–38.

GLUCHNOWSKI, PETER (1983). 'Wahlererfahrung und Parteiidentifikation', in Max Kaase and Hans-Dieter Klingemann (eds.), *Wahlen und politisches System*. Opladen: Westdeutscher Verlag.

GORDON, AUSTIN (1999). 'Election News in Comparative Perspective', University of California, Irvine, Doctoral Dissertation.

GRAY, MARK, and MIKI CAUL (2000). 'Declining Voter Turnout in Advanced Industrial Democracies 1950–1997', *Comparative Political Studies*.

GROSSMAN, L. (1995). *The Electronic Republic*. New York: Penguin.

GRUNER, ERICH (1975). *Die Parteien in der Schweiz*, 2nd edn. Berne: Francke Verlag.

GUNLICKS, ARTHUR (1986). *Local Government in the German Federal System*. Durham, NC: Duke University Press.

HAEGEL, FLORENCE (1993). 'Partisan Ties', in Daniel Boy and Nonna Mayer (eds.), *The French Voter Decides*. Ann Arbor: University of Michigan Press.

—— (1998). 'Conflict and Change in the Rassemblement pour la République', in Piero Ignazi and Colette Ysmal (eds.), *The Organization of Political Parties in Southern Europe*. Westport, Conn.: Praeger.

HARDARSON, OLAFUR TH. (1995). *Parties and Voters in Iceland: A Study of the 1983 and 1987 Elections*. Reykjavik: Social Science Research Institute-University Press, University of Iceland.

HARMEL, ROBERT, and KENNETH JANDA (1982). *Parties and their Environments*. New York: Longman.

—— —— and ALEXANDER TAN (1995). 'Substance vs. Packaging', Paper presented at the annual meeting of the Midwest Political Science Association, Chicago.

HASBACH, WILHELM (1912). *Die Moderne Demokratie*. Jena: Gustav Fischer Verlag.

HAUSS, CHARLES, and L. SANDY MAISEL (1986). 'Extremist Delegates: Myth and Reality', in Ronald Rapoport, Alan Abramowitz, and John McGlennon (eds.), *The Life of the Parties*. Lexington: University of Kentucky Press.

HAZAN, REUVEN (1997). 'Executive-Legislative Relations in an Era of Accelerated

Reform: Reshaping Government in Israel', *Legislative Studies Quarterly,* 23: 329–50.

HEIDAR, KNUT (1994). 'The Polymorphic Nature of Party Membership', *European Journal of Political Research,* 25: 61–86.

HELANDER, VOITO (1997). 'Finland', in Pippa Norris (ed.), *Passages to Power.* Cambridge: Cambridge University Press.

HENIG, STANLEY (ed.) (1979). *Political Parties in the European Community.* London: Allen & Unwin.

—— and JOHN PINDER (eds.) (1969). *European Political Parties.* Allen & Unwin.

HERMET, GUY, JULIAN THOMAS HOTTINGER, and DANIEL-LOUIS SEILER (1998). *Les Parties politiques en Europe de l' Ouest.* Paris: Economica.

HERRING, E. PENDLETON (1940). *The Politics of Democracy: American Parties in Action.* New York: W. W. Norton & Company.

HERRNSON, PAUL (1988). *Party Campaigning in the 1980s.* Cambridge, Mass.: Harvard University Press.

HIBBS, DOUGLAS (1977). 'Political Parties and Macroeconomic Policy', *American Political Science Review',* 71: 1467–87.

—— (1987). *The Political Economy of Industrialized Democracies.* Cambridge, Mass.: Harvard University Press.

HICKS, ALEXANDER, and DUANE SWANK (1992). 'Politics, Institutions, and Welfare Spending in Industrialized Democracies, 1960–82, *American Political Science Review,* 86: 658.

HILL, KEVIN, and JOHN HUGHES (1998). *Cyberpolitics: Citizen Activism in the Age of the Internet.* Lanham, Md.: Rowman & Littlefield.

HIRSCHMAN, ALBERT (1970). *Exit, Voice and Loyalty.* Cambridge, Mass.: Harvard University Press.

HMSO (Her Majesty's Stationery Office) Command 9798 (1986). *Conduct of Local Authority Business, Vol.* i: *The Political Organisation of Local Authorities.* London: HMSO.

HOFFERBERT, RICHARD (1997). 'The Patterns of Party Concerns in Modern Democracies'. Paper presented at the Workshop on Change in the Relationship between Parties and Democracy, Texas A & M University, Collge Station, Tex., 4–6 Apr.

—— and DAVID CINGRANELLI (1996). 'Public Policy and Administration: Comparative Policy Analysis', in Robert Goodin and Hans-Dieter Klingeman (eds.), *The New Handbook of Political Science.* Oxford: Oxford University Press.

HOFSTADTER, RICHARD (1972). *The Idea of a Party System.* Berkeley, and Los Angeles: University of California Press.

HOLMBERG, SÖREN (1994). 'Party Identification Compared across the Atlantic', in M. Kent Jennings and Thomas Mann (eds.), *Elections at Home and Abroad.* Ann Arbor: University of Michigan Press.

HOLMES GEOFFREY (1967). *British Politics in the Age of Anne.* London: Macmillan.

HOLTMANN, EVERHARD (1996). 'Die Organisation der Sozialdemokratie in der Ersten Republik, 1918–34', in Wolfgang Maderthaner and Wolfgang Müller (eds.), *Die Organisation der Österreichischen Sozialdemokratie 1889–1995.* Vienna: Löcker Verlag.

HUBER JOHN (1996). 'The Vote of Confidence in Parliamentary Democracies', *American Political Science Review,* 90: 269–82.

HUMES, SAMUEL, and EILEEN MARTIN (1961). *The Structure of Local Governments throughout the World.* The Hague: Martinus Nijhoff.

HUNTINGTON, SAMUEL (1981). *American Politics: The Promise of Disharmony.* Cambridge, Mass.: Harvard University Press.

INGLEHART, RONALD (1990). *Culture Shift in Advanced Industrial Society.* Princeton: Princeton University Press.

—— (1997). *Modernization and Postmodernization.* Princeton, NJ: Princeton University Press.

International Institute for Democracy and Electoral Assistance (1997). *Voter Turnout from 1945 to 1997: A Global Report.* Stockholm: International IDEA.

IPOS (1995). *Einstellung zur Aktuelle Frage.* Mannheim, Germany: IPOS.

IRVING, RONALD (1979). *The Christian Democratic Parties of Western Europe.* London: George Allen & Unwin Publishers.

JACOBS, FRANCIS (ed.) (1989). *Western European Political Parties: A Comprehensive Guide.* Harlow: Longman.

JAENSCH, DEAN (1994). *Power Politics: Australia's Party System*, 3rd edn. Sydney: Allen & Unwin.

JAKUBOWICZ, K. (1996). 'Television and Elections in Post-1989 Poland', in David Swanson and Paolo Mancini (eds.), *Politics, Media, and Modern Democracy.* Westport, Conn.: Praeger.

JENNINGS, M. KENT, and JAN VAN DETH (eds.) (1989). *Continuities in Political Action.* Berlin: DeGruyter.

JENSSEN, ANDERS (1999). 'All That is Solid Melts into Air', *Scandinavian Political Studies*, 22: 1–27.

JONES, NICHOLAS (1996). *Soundbites and Spin Doctors: How Politicians Manipulate the Media and Vice Versa.* London: Indigo.

JUPP, JAMES (1964). *Australian Party Politics.* London: Melbourne University Press.

—— (1982). *Party Politics: Australia 1966–1981.* Sydney: George Allen & Unwin.

JUST, MARION (1997). 'Candidate Strategies and the Media Campaign', in Gerald Pomper et al. (eds.), *The Election of 1996.* Chatham, NJ: Chatham House.

KAID, LYNDA, and CHRISTINA HOLTZ-BACHA (1995). 'Political Advertising across Cultures', in Lynda Kaid and Christina Holtz-Bacha (eds.), *Political Advertising in Western Democracies.* London: Sage Publications.

—— J. GERSTLÉ, K. SANDERS (eds.) (1991). *Mediated Politics in Two Cultures: Presidential Campaigning in the United States and France.* New York: Praeger.

KATZ, RICHARD (1985). 'Measuring Party Identification with Eurobarometer Data: A Warning Note', *West European Politics*, 8: 104–8.

—— (ed.) (1987a). *Party Government: European and American Experiences.* Berlin: De Gruyter.

—— (1987b). 'Party Government and Its Alternatives', in Richard Katz (ed.), *Party Governments: European and American Experiences*, Vol. ii. Berlin: De Gruyter.

—— (1988). 'Party as Linkage: A Vestigial function?', *European Journal of Political Research*, 18: 143–61.

—— and ROBIN KOLODNY (1994). 'Party Organization as an Empty Vessel: Parties in American Politics', in Richard Katz and Peter Mair (eds.), *How Parties Organize.* London: Sage.

—— and PETER MAIR (eds.) (1992). *Party Organizations: A Data Handbook on Party Organizations in Western Democracies, 1960–90.* Newbury Park, Calif.: Sage.

—— —— (1994). *How Parties Organize.* London: Sage.

—— —— (1995). 'Changing Models of Party Organization and Party Democracy: The Emergence of the Cartel Party', *Party Politics*, 1: 5–28.

—— —— (et al.) (1992). 'The Membership of Political Parties in European Democracies, 1960–90', *European Journal of Political Research*, 22: 329–45.

KATZENSTEIN, PETER (1985). *Small States in World Markets*. Ithaca, NY: Cornell University Press.

KAVANAGH, DENNIS (1995). *Election Campaigning*. Oxford: Blackwell.

Keesing's Record of World Events, various years.

KEITH, BRUCE et al. (1992). *The Myth of the Independent Voter*. Berkeley and Los Angeles: University of California Press.

KEMAN, HANS (1984). 'Politics, Policies, and Consequences: A Cross-National Analysis of Public Policy Formation in Advanced Capitalist Democracies', *European Journal of Political Research*, 12: 147–70.

KEOHANE, ROBERT, and HELEN MILNER (1996). *Internationalization and Domestic Politics*. New York: Cambridge University Press.

KEY, V. O. (1961). *Public Opinion and American Democracy*. New York: Knopf.

—— (1964). *Politics, Parties and Pressure Groups*, 5th edn. New York: Crowell.

KIEWIET, D. RODERICK, and MATHEW McCUBBINS (1991). *The Logic of Delegation: Congressional Parties and the Appropriations Process*. Chicago: University of Chicago Press.

KIM, HEEMIN, and RICHARD FORDING (1998). 'Voter Ideology in Western Democracies', *European Journal of Political Research*, 33: 73–97.

KING, ANTHONY et al. (eds.) (1998). *New Labour Triumphs: Britain at the Polls*. Chatham, NJ: Chatham House.

KING, DAVID (1997). 'The Polarization of American Parties and Mistrust of Government', in Joseph Nye, Philip Zelikow and David King (eds.), *Why People Don't Trust Government*. Cambridge, Mass.: Harvard University Press.

KIRCHHEIMER, OTTO (1966). 'The Transformation of the Western European Party Systems', in Joseph LaPalombara and Myron Weiner (eds.), *Political Parties and Political Development*. Princeton: Princeton University Press.

KIRCHNER, EMIL (1988). *Liberal Parties in Western Europe*. Cambridge: Cambridge University Press.

KITSCHELT, HERBERT (1994). *The Transformation of European Social Democracy*. Cambridge: Cambridge University Press.

KLINGEMANN, HANS-DIETER, and DIETER FUCHS (eds.) (1995). *Citizens and the State*. Oxford: Oxford University Press.

—— RICHARD HOFFERBERT, and IAN BUDGE (1994). *Parties, Policies and Democracy*. Boulder, Colo.: Westview Press.

KNUTSEN, ODDBJORN (1998). 'Expert Judgements of the Left-Right Location of Political Parties: A Comparative Longitudinal Study', *West European Politics*, 21: 63–94.

KOBACH, KRIS (1994). 'Switzerland', in David Butler and Austin Ranney (eds.), *Referendums around the World*. Washington, DC: American Enterprise Institute.

KOGAN, MAURICE, and DAVID KOGAN (1982). *The Battle for the Labour Party*. London: Fontana.

KOLODNY, R., and RICHARD KATZ (1992). 'The United States', in Richard Katz and Peter Mair (eds.), *Party Organizations*. London: Sage.

KOOLE, RUUD (1994). 'The Vulnerability of the Modern Cadre Party in the Netherlands', in Richard Katz and Peter Mair (eds.), *How Parties Organize.* London: Sage.

KORNHAUSER, WILLIAM (1959). *The Politics of Mass Society.* Glencoe, Ill.: Free Press.

KURIAN, GEORGE (ed.) (1998). *World Encyclopedia of Parliaments and Legislatures.* Washington, DC: CQ Press.

LAAKSO, MARKKU, and REIN TAAGEPERA (1979). 'Effective Number of Parties: A Measure with Applications to West Europe', *Comparative Political Studies,* 12: 3–27.

LADD, EVERETT CARL (1999). *The Ladd Report.* New York: Free Press.

LANE, JAN-ERIK, and SVANTE ERSSON (1987). *Politics and Society in Western Europe.* London: Sage.

—— DAVID MCKAY, and KENNETH NEWTON (1997). *Political Data Handbook OECD Countries.* Oxford: Oxford University Press.

LANFRANCHI, PRSICI, and RUTH LUTHI (1999). 'Cohesion of Party Groups and Interparty Conflict in the Swiss Parliament: Roll Call Voting in the National Council', in Shaun Bowler, David Farrell, and Richard Katz (eds.) *Party Discipline and Parliamentary Government,* Columbus Oh.: Ohio State University Press.

LAPALOMBARA, JOSEPH, and MYRON WEINER (eds.) (1966). *Political Parties and Political Development.* Princeton: Princeton University Press.

LAVER, MICHAEL (1997). *Private Desires, Political Action: An Invitation to the Politics of Rational Choice.* Thousand Oaks, Calif.: Sage.

—— and W. BEN HUNT (1992). *Policy and Party Competition.* NY: Routledge.

—— and MICHAEL MARSH (1999). 'Parties and Voters', in John Coakley and Michael Gallagher (eds.) *Politics in the Republic of Ireland.* 3rd edn. London and New York: Routledge/PSAI Press.

—— and NORMAN SCHOFIELD (1990). *Multiparty Government: The Politics of Coalition in Europe.* Oxford: Oxford University Press.

—— and KENNETH SHEPSLE (1996). *Making and Breaking Governments.* Cambridge: Cambridge University Press.

LAWSON, KAY (ed.) (1980). *Political Parties and Linkage: A Comparative Perspective.* New Haven: Yale University Press.

—— and PETER MERKL (eds.) (1988). *When Parties Fail: Emerging Alternative Organizations.* Princeton N.J.: Princeton University Press.

—— and COLETTE YSMAL (1992). 'France: The 1988 Presidential Campaign', in Shaun Bowler, David Farrell, and Richard Katz (eds.), *Electoral Strategies and Political Marketing.* Houndmills, Basingstoke: Macmillan.

LAZARSFELD, PAUL, BERNARD BERELSON, and HELEN GAUDET (1948). *The People's Choice.* New York: Columbia University Press.

LEDUC, LAWRENCE, RICHARD NIEMI, and PIPPA NORRIS (eds.) (1996). *Comparing Democracies.* Thousand Oaks, Calif.: Sage.

LEVINE, STEPHEN (1979). *The New Zealand Political System.* Sydney: George Allen & Unwin.

—— and NIGEL ROBERTS (1992). 'A Sore Labour's Bath? The Paradox of Party Identification in New Zealand', in Margaret Clark (ed)., *The Labour Party after 75 Years.* Wellington: Victoria University Department of Politics.

LEWIS-BECK, MICHAEL (1984). 'France: The Stalled Electorate', in Russell Dalton, Scott Flanagan and Paul Beck, (eds.), *Electoral Change in Advanced Industrial Democracies.* Princeton: Princeton University Press.

LIJPHART, AREND (1977). *Democracy in Plural Societies: A Comparative Exploration*. New Haven: Yale University Press.

—— (1984). *Democracies: Patterns of Majoritarian and Consensus Government in Twenty-One Countries*. New Haven: Yale University Press.

—— (1994). *Electoral Systems and Party Systems: A Study of Twenty-Seven Democracies, 1945–1990*. New York: Oxford University Press.

—— (1997). 'Unequal Participation: Democracy's Unresolved Dilemma', *American Political Science Review*, 91: 1–14.

—— (1999). *Patterns of Democracy: Government Forms and Performance in Thirty-Six Countries*. New Haven: Yale University Press.

LIPOW, ARTHUR, and PATRICK SEYD (1996). 'The Politics of Anti-partyism'. *Parliamentary Affairs*, 49: 273–84.

LIPSET, SEYMOUR MARTIN (1963). *Political Man*. New York: Doubleday.

—— and STEIN ROKKAN (eds.) (1967). *Party Systems and Voter Alignments: Cross-National Perspectives*. New York: Free Press.

LÖFGREN, KARL (1998). 'Scandinavian Political Parties on the Internet', *ECPR News* 10: 9–11.

LONGCHAMP, CLAUDE (1991). 'Politisch-kultureller Wandel in der Schweiz.', in Fritz Plasser and Peter Ulram (eds.) *Staatsbürger oder Untertanen? Politische Kultur Deutschlands, Österreichs und der Schweiz im Vergleich*. Frankfurt: Lang.

LUNTZ, FRANK (1988). *Candidates, Consultants and Campaigns*. Oxford: Blackwell.

LUPIA, ARTHUR (1994). 'Shortcuts versus Encyclopedias', *American Political Science Review*, 88: 63–76.

—— and MATHEW MCCUBBINS (1998). *The Democratic Dilemma: Can Citizens Learn What they Need to Know?* Cambridge: Cambridge University Press.

LUSKIN, ROBERT (1987). 'Measuring Political Sophistication', *American Journal of Political Science*, 31: 856–99.

MCALLISTER, IAN (1992). *Political Behavior*. Melbourne: Longman Cheshire.

—— (1996). 'Leaders', in Lawrence LeDuc, Richard Niemi, and Pippa Norris (eds.), *Comparing Democracies*. Thousand Oaks, Calif.: Sage.

MCCORMICK, RICHARD (1975). 'Political Development and the Second Party System', in William Nisbet Chambers and Walter Dean Burnham (eds.), *The American Party Systems*, 2nd edn. New York: Oxford University Press.

MCCUBBINS, MATHEW, and TALBOT PAGE (1987). 'A Theory of Congressional Delegation', in Mathew McCubbins and Terry Sullivan (eds.), *Congress: Structure and Policy*. New York: Cambridge University Press.

—— and THOMAS SCHWARTZ (1984). 'Congressional Oversight Overlooked: Police Patrols Versus Fire Alarms', *American Journal of Political Science*, 28: 165–79.

MACHIN, HOWARD (1996). 'The 1995 Presidential Election Campaign', in Robert Elgie (ed.), *Electing the French President: The 1995 Presidential Election*. Houndmills, Basingstoke: Macmillan.

MACKIE, THOMAS, and RICHARD ROSE (1991). *The International Almanac of Electoral History.*, 3rd. edn. Washington, DC: Congressional Quarterly Press.

MACRAE, JR., DUNCAN (1967). *Parliament, Parties and Society 1946–1958*. New York: St Martin's.

MADERTHANER, WOLFGANG, and WOLFGANG MÜLLER (eds.) (1996). *Die Organisation der Österreichischen Sozialdemokratie 1889–1995* (Vienna: Löcker Verlag).

MAINE, HENRY SUMNER (1886). *Popular Government.* New York: Henry Holt & Company.

MAIR, PETER (1993). 'Myths of Electoral Change and the Survival of Traditional Parties', *European Journal of Political Research,* 24: 121–33.

—— (1994). 'Party Organizations: From Civil Society to the State', in Richard Katz and Peter Mair (eds.), *How Parties Organize.* London: Sage.

—— (1995). 'Political Parties, Popular Legitimacy, and Public Privilege', *West European Politics,* 18: 40–57.

—— (1997). *Party System Change.* Oxford: Clarendon Press.

MAISEL, L. SANDY (1998). *The Parties Respond: Changes in American Parties and Campaigns.* Boulder, Col.: Westview Press.

MARGOLIS, M., D. RESNICK, and CHIN-CHANG TU (1997). 'Campaigning on the Internet: Parties and Candidates on the World Wide Web in the 1996 Primary Season', *Press/Politics,* 2: 59–78.

MARSH, MICHAEL (1993). 'Selecting the Party Leader', *European Journal of Political Research,* 24: 229–31.

MAXFIELD, SYLVIA (1997). *Gatekeepers of Growth: The International Political Economy of Central Banking in Developing Countries.* Princeton: Princeton University Press.

MAY, JOHN (1973). 'Opinion Structure of Political Parties: The Special Law of Curvilinear Disparity', *Political Studies,* 21: 135–51.

MAYER, HENRY (ed.) (1973). *Australia's Political Pattern.* Melbourne: Cheshire.

MAYHEW, DAVID R. (1974). *Congress: The Electoral Connection.* New Haven: Yale University Press.

MAZZOLONI, GIANPIETRO (1996). 'Patterns and Effects of Recent Changes in Electoral Campaigning in Italy', in David Swanson and Paolo Mancini (eds.), *Politics, Media, and Modern Democracy.* Westport, Conn.: Praeger.

MÉNY, YVES, and ANDREW KNAPP (1998). *Government and Politics in Western Europe,* 3rd edn. Oxford: Oxford University Press.

MICHELS, ROBERT (1959). *Political Parties: A Sociological Study of the Oligarchical Tendencies of Modern Democracy,* trans. Eden and Cedar Paul. New York: Dover Publications. First published 1915.

MICKIEWICZ, E. and A. RICHTER (1996) 'Television, Campaigning, and Elections in the Soviet Union and Post-Soviet Russia', in David Swanson and Paolo Mancini (eds.), *Politics, Media, and Modern Democracy.* Westport, Conn.: Praeger.

MILLER, ARTHUR, and OLA LISTHAUG (1990). 'Political Parties and Confidence in Government', *British Journal of Political Science,* 29: 357–86.

—— et al. (1976). 'A Majority Party in Disarray: Policy Polarization in the 1972 Election', *American Political Science Review,* 70: 753–78.

MILLER, WARREN (1976). 'The Cross-national Use of Party Identification as a Stimulus to Political Inquiry', in Ian Budge, Ivor Crewe, and Dennis Farlie (eds.), *Party Identification and Beyond.* New York: Wiley.

—— and M. KENT JENNINGS (1986). *Parties in Transition.* New York: Russell Sage Foundation.

—— and J. MERRILL SHANKS (1996). *The New American Voter.* Cambridge, Mass.: Harvard University Press.

MILLER, WILLIAM, HAROLD CLARKE, MARTIN HARROP, LAWRENCE LEDUC, and PAUL WHITELEY (1990). *How Voters Change.* Oxford: Oxford University Press.

MILNE, R. S. (1966). *Political Parties in New Zealand.* Oxford: Clarendon Press.

MITCHELL, B. R. (1998*a*). *International Historical Statistics: Africa, Asia & Oceania, 1750–1993*. New York: Stockton Press.

—— (1998*b*). *International Historical Statistics: The Americas, 1750–1993*. New York: Stockton Press.

—— (1998*c*). *International Historical Statistics: Europe, 1750–1993*. New York: Stockton Press.

MORGAN, ROGER, and STEFANO SILVESTRI (1982). *Moderates and Conservatives in Western Europe*. London: Heinemann Educational Books.

MORSEY, RUDOLF (1966). *Deutsche Zentrums Partei*. Düsseldorf: Droste Verlag.

MUELLER-ROMMEL, FERDINAND (1985). 'New Social Movements and Smaller Parties: A Comparative Perspective', *West European Politics*, 8: 41–54.

—— (1989). *New Politics in Western Europe*. Boulder, Colo.: Westview Press.

—— and GEOFFREY PRIDHAM (1991). *Small Parties in Western Europe*. London: Sage.

MUGHAN, ANTHONY (1993). 'Party Leaders and Presidentialism in the 1992 British Election: A Postwar Perspective', in David Denver, Pippa Norris, David Broughton, and Colin Rallings (eds.), *British Elections and Parties Yearbook*. London: Harvester Wheatsheaf.

—— (1995). 'Television and Presidentialism: Australian and U.S. Legislative Elections Compared', *Political Communication*, 12: 327–42.

MULGAN, RICHARD (1994). *Politics in New Zealand*. Auckland: Auckland University Press.

MÜLLER, WOLFGANG (1996). 'Die Organisation der SPÖ, 1945–95', in Wolfgang Maderthaner and Wolfgang Müller (eds.), *Die Organisation der Österreichischen Sozialdemokratie 1889–1995*. Vienna: Löcker Verlag.

—— (2000). 'Political Parties in Parliamentary Democracies: Making Delegation and Accountability Work', *European Journal of Political Research*, 37 (forthcoming).

—— and FRITZ PLASSER (1992). 'Austria: The 1990 Campaign', in Shaun Bowler and David Farrell (eds)., *Electoral Strategies and Political Marketing*. Houndmills, Basingstoke: Macmillan.

—— and KAARE STRØM (eds.) (1997). *Koalitionsregierungen in Westeuropa*. Vienna: Signum Verlag.

—— and PETER ULRAM (1999). 'Schwaeche als Vorteil: Staerke als Nachteil', in Peter Mair, Wolfgang Müller, and Fritz Plasser (eds.), *Parteien auf komplexen Waehlermaerkten*. Vienna: Signum Verlag.

NABHOLZ, RUTH. (1998). 'Das Waehlerverhalten in der Schweiz: Stabilitaet oder Wandel? Eine Trendanalyse von 1971–95', in Hanspeter Kriesi, Wolf Linder and Ulrich Kloeti (eds.), *Schweizer Wahlen*. Berne: Haupt.

NEGRINE, RALPH, and S. PAPATHANASSOPOULOS (1996). 'The Americanization of Political Communication: A Critique', *Press/Politics*, 1: 45–62.

NEILL, LORD (1998). *Report of the Committee on Standards in Public Life on the Funding of Political Parties in the UK*. London: The Stationery Office.

NEUMAN, W. R. (1991). *The Future of the Mass Audience*. Cambridge: Cambridge University Press.

NEUMANN, SIGMUND (1956). 'Toward a Comparative Study of Political Parties', in Sigmund Neumann (ed.), *Modern Political Parties*. Chicago: University of Chicago Press.

—— (1965). *Die Parteien der Weimarer Republik*. Stuttgart: W. Kohlhammer Verlag. First published 1932.

NIE, NORMAN, SIDNEY VERBA and JOHN PETROCIK (1976). *The Changing American Voter.* Cambridge, Mass.: Harvard University Press

NIEMI, RICHARD, and JOEL BARKAN (1987). 'Age and Turnout in New Electorates and Peasant Societies', *American Political Science Review,* 81: 583–88.

—— RICHARD KATZ, and David Newman (1980). 'Reconstructing Past Partisanship', *American Journal of Political Science,* 44: 633–51.

NORPOTH, HELMUT (1983). 'The Making of a More Partisan Electorate in West Germany', *British Journal of Political Science,* 14: 53–71.

NORRIS, PIPPA (1995*a*). 'May's Law of Curvilinear Disparity Revisited: Leaders, Officers, Members and Voters in British Political Parties', *Party Politics,* 1: 29–47.

—— (1995*b*). 'Politics of Electoral Reform', *International Political Science Review,* 16: 65–78.

—— (1996). 'Legislative Recruitment', in Lawrence LeDuc, Richard Niemi, and Pippa Norris (eds.), *Comparing Democracies.* Thousand Oaks, Calif.: Sage.

—— (1997*a*). *Pathways to Power: Legislative Recruitment in Advanced Democracies.* Cambridge: Cambridge University Press.

—— (1997*b*). *Electoral Change in Britain Since 1945.* Oxford: Blackwell.

—— (ed.) (1999). *Critical Citizens: Global Support for Democratic Governance.* Oxford: Oxford University Press.

NORTON, ALAN (1994). *International Handbook of Local and Regional Government.* Aldershot: Edward Elgar.

NORTON, PHILIP (1978). *Conservative Dissidents.* Temple Smith.

—— (1994). *The British Polity.,* 3rd edn. New York: Longman.

—— (1996). *The Conservative Party.* London: Prentice Hall.

NOUSIAINEN, JAAKKO (1971). *The Finnish Political System.* Cambridge, Mass.: Harvard University Press.

NYE, JOSEPH, PHILIP ZELIKOW, and DAVID KING (eds.) (1997). *Why People Don't Trust Government.* Cambridge: Harvard University Press.

OECD Economic Outlook: Historical Statistics. Various issues.

OFFE, CLAUS (1984). *Contradictions of the Welfare State.* Cambridge, Mass.: MIT Press.

O'SHAUGHNESSY, N. J. (1990). *The Phenomenon of Political Marketing.* London: Macmillan.

OSTROGORSKI, MOSEI (1902). *Democracy and the Organizaton of Political Parties.* New York: Macmillan.

—— (1982). *Democracy and the Organization of Political Parties,* vol.ii, ed. Seymour Lipset. New Brunswick, NJ: Transaction Books. First published 1902.

OVERACKER, LOUISE (1952). *The Australian Party System.* New Haven: Yale University Press.

PAGE, BENJAMIN, and ROBERT SHAPIRO (1992). *The Rational Public: Fifty Years of Trends in American Policy Preferences.* Chicago: University of Chicago Press.

PANEBIANCO, ANGELO (1988). *Political Parties: Organization and Power.* Cambridge: Cambridge University Press. First published 1902.

PARRY, GERAINT, GEORGE MOYSER and NEIL DAY (1992). *Political Participation and Democracy in Britain.* Cambridge: Cambridge University Press.

PATTERSON, THOMAS (1994). *Out of Order.* New York: Vintage.

PATERSON, WILLIAM, and ALISTAIR THOMAS (1977). *Social Democratic Parties in Western Europe.* New York: St Martin's Press.

PEDERSEN, MOGENS (1979). 'The Dynamics of European Party Systems', *European Journal of Political Research*, 7: 1–26.

—— (1987). 'The Danish "Working Multiparty System": Breakdown or Adaptation?', in Hans Daalder (ed.), *Party Systems in Denmark, Austria, Switzerland, the Netherlands, and Belgium*. New York: St Martin's.

PERSSON, T., and SVENSSON, L. (1989). 'Why a Stubborn Conservative Would Run a Deficit: Policy with Time-Inconsistent Preferences', *Quarterly Review of Economics*, 104: 324–45.

PESONEN, PERTTI (1999). 'Politics in Finland', in W. Philipps Shively (ed.), *Comparative Governance*. McGraw-Hill.

PETROCIK, JOHN (1996). 'Issue Ownership in Presidential Elections: With a 1980 Case Study', *American Journal of Political Science*, 40: 825–50.

Pew Research Center (1996). 'One-in-Ten Voters Online for Campaign '96: News Attracts Most Internet Users'. Washington, DC: Pew Research Centre.

PHARR, SUSAN, and ROBERT PUTNAM (eds.) (2000). *Disaffected Democracies: What's Troubling the Trilateral Democracies*. Princeton: Princeton University Press.

PIERCE, ROY (1995). *Choosing the Chief: Presidential Elections in France and the United States*. Ann Arbor: University of Michigan Press.

PISSORNO, ALESSANDRO (1981). 'Interests and Parties in Pluralism', in Suzanne Berger, (ed.), *Organizing Interests in Western Europe*. Cambridge: Cambridge University Press.

PLASSER, FRITZ, and PETER ULRAM (eds.) (1996). *Staatsbürger oder Untertanen? Politische Kultur Deutschlands, Österreichs und der Schweiz im Vergleich*. Frankfurt: Lang.

—— —— (1997). 'Dealignment und Neustrukturierung des politischen Wettbewerbs in Österreich', Paper presented at the international conference Demokratiewandel: Befunde der Einstellungsforschung in Deutschland und Österreich im Vergleich. Innsbruck.

—— —— and GÜNTHER OGRIS (eds.) (1996). *Wahlkampf und Wählerentscheidung: Analyzen zur Nationalsratswahl 1995*. Vienna: Signum.

POGUNTKE, THOMAS (1994). 'Parties in a Legalistic Culture: The Case of Germany', in Richard Katz and Peter Mair (eds.), *How Parties Organize*. London: Sage.

—— (1996). 'Anti-party Sentiment: Conceptual Thoughts and Empirical Evidence: Explorations into a Minefield', *European Journal of Political Research*, 29: 319–44.

—— (1998). 'Party Organizations', in Jan van Deth (ed.), *Comparative Politics: The Problem of Equivalence*. London: Routledge.

—— and SUSAN SCARROW (1996). Special issue on the theme of anti-party sentiment, *European Journal of Political Research*, 29.

PODE, KEITH, and H. ROSENTHAL (1991). 'Patterns of Congressional Voting', *American Journal of Political Science*, 35/1: 228–78.

POPKIN, SAMUEL (1991). *The Reasoning Voter*. Chicago: University of Chicago Press.

POWELL, G. BINGHAM, JR. (1982). *Contemporary Democracies*. Cambridge, Mass.: Harvard University Press.

—— (1986). 'American Voter Turnout in Comparative Perspective', *American Political Science Review*, 80: 17–44.

PRICE, DAVID E. (1984). *Bringing back the Parties*. Washington, DC: Congressional Quarterly Press.

PROCHART, HELMUT (1996). 'Personalisierung und Kandidatenzentrierung in Österreichischen Wahlkampfen'. Master's Thesis: University of Vienna.

PUTNAM, ROBERT (1995). 'Bowling Alone', *Journal of Democracy,* 6: 65–78.

—— (2000) *Bowling Along.* New York: Simon and Shuster.

QUAGLIARIELLO, GAETANO (1996). *Politics without Parties.* Aldershot: Avebury.

RANNEY, AUSTIN (1954). *The Doctrine of Responsible Party Government, its Origin and Present State.* Urbana, Ill.: University of Illinois Press.

—— (1981). 'Candidate Selection', in Austin Ranney and David Butler (eds.), *Democracy at the Polls.* Washington: American Enterprise Institute.

—— (1990). 'Broadcasting, Narrowcasting, and Politics', in Anthony King (ed.), *The New American Political System*, 2nd version. Washington, DC: Congressional Quarterly Press.

RASCH, BJORN ERIK (1999). 'Electoral Systems, Parliamentary Committees, and Party Discipline: The Norwegian Storting in Comparative Perspective', in Shaun Bowler, David Farrell, and Richard Katz (eds.), *Party Discipline and Parliamentary Government.* Columbus, Oh.: Ohio State University Press.

RAUNIO, TAPIO (1999). 'The Challenge of Diversity: Party Cohesion in the European Parliament', in Shaun Bowler, David Farrell, and Richard Katz (eds.), *Party Discipline and Parliamentary Government*, Columbus, Oh.: Ohio State University Press.

RICHARDSON, BRADLEY (1997). *Japanese Democracy: Power, Coordination, and Performance.* New Haven: Yale University Press.

—— (1991). 'European Party Loyalty Revisited', *American Political Science Review,* 85: 751–75.

RIDDELL, PETER (1996). *Honest Opportunism: How We Get the Politicians We Deserve.* London: Indigo.

RIEGER, GUENTHER (1994). ' "Parteienverdrossenheit" und "Parteienkritik" in der Bundesrepublik Deutschland', *Zeitschrift fuer Parlamentsfragen*, 25: 459–71.

RIKER, WILLIAM (1962). *The Theory of Political Coalitions.* New Haven: Yale University Press.

—— (1982). 'The Two-Party System and Duverger's Law: An Essay on the History of Political Science', *American Political Science Review,* 76: 753–66.

—— and PETER ORDESHOOK (1968). 'A Theory of the Calculus of Voting', *American Political Science Review,* 62: 25–43.

ROBERTSON, DAVID (1976). *A Theory of Party Competition.* London: John Wiley.

ROHDE, David W. (1991). *Parties and Leaders in the Postreform House.* Chicago: University of Chicago Press.

ROKKAN, STEIN (1966a). 'Electoral Mobilization, Party Competition, and National Integration', in Joseph LaPalombara and Myron Weiner (eds.), *Political Parties and Political Development.* Princeton: Princeton University Press.

—— (1966b). 'Norway: Numerical Democracy and Corporate Pluralism', in Robert A. Dahl (ed.), *Political Oppositions in Western Democracies.* New Haven: Yale University Press.

—— and ANGUS CAMPBELL (1960). 'Citizen Participation in Political Life: Norway', *International Social Science Journal,* 12: 69–99.

ROSE, RICHARD (1967). *Influencing Voters.* New York: St Martin's.

—— (1974). *The Problem of Party Government.* London: Macmillan.

—— (1983). 'Still the Era of Party Government', *Parliamentary Affairs,* 36: 280–91.

—— and THOMAS T. MACKIE (1988). 'Do Parties Persist or Fail? The Big Trade-Off Facing Organizations', in Kay Lawson and Peter Merkl (eds.), *When Parties Fail*. Princeton, NJ: Princeton University Press.

—— and DEREK URWIN (1969). 'Social Cohesion, Political Parties, and Strains in Regimes', *Comparative Political Studies,* 2: 7–67.

ROSENSTONE, STEVEN, and JOHN HANSEN (1993). *Mobilization, Participation and Democracy in America*. New York: Macmillan.

ROSPIR, JUAN (1996). 'Political Communication and Electoral Campaigns in the Young Spanish Democracy', in David Swanson and Paolo Mancini (eds.), *Politics, Media, and Modern Democracy*. Westport, Conn.: Praeger.

SAALFELD THOMAS (1997). 'Professionalization of Parliamentary Roles in Germany: An Aggregate Level Analysis 1949–1994', in Wolfgang Mueller and Thomas Saalfeld (eds.), *Members of Parliament in Western Europe,* London: Frank Cass.

—— (1998). 'Legislative Voting Behavior', in George Kurian (ed.), *1998 World Encyclopedia of Parliaments and Legislatures*. Washington, DC: CQ Press.

SABATO, LARRY J. (1988). *The Party's Just Begun: Shaping Political Parties for America's Future*. Glenview, Ill.: Scott Foresman.

SANDERS, DAVID (1998). 'The New Electoral Battleground', in Anthony King et al. (eds.), *New Labour Triumphs: Britain at the Polls*. Chatham, NJ.: Chatham House.

SARTORI, GIOVANNI (1976). *Parties and Party Systems: A Framework for Analysis*. New York: Cambridge University Press.

SCAMMELL, MARGARET (1995). *Designer Politics: How Elections are Won*. Houndmills, Basingstoke: Macmillan.

—— (1997). 'The Wisdom of the War Room: U.S. Campaigning and Americanization'. Shorenstein Center Research Paper R-17.

—— and HOLLI A. SEMETKO (1995). 'Political Advertising on Television: The British Experience', in Lynda Kaid and Christina Holtz-Bacha (eds.), *Political Advertising in Western Democracies*. London: Sage Publications.

SCARROW, SUSAN (1993). 'Does Local Party Organisation Make a Difference? Political Parties and Local Government Elections in Germany', *German Politics,* 2: 377–92.

—— (1996). *Parties and their Members: Organizing for Victory in Britain and Germany*. Oxford: Oxford University Press.

—— (1999). 'Parties and the Expansion of Direct Democracy: Who Benefits?', *Party Politics,* 5: 343–67.

SCHATTSCHNEIDER, E. E. (1942). *Party Government*. New York: Rinehart.

SCHEUCH, ERWIN, and UTE SCHEUCH (1992). *Cliquen, Klüngel und Karrieren*. Reinbeck: Rowolt.

SCHMIDT, MANFRED (1982). 'The Role of the Parties in Shaping Macroeconomic Policy', in Francis Castles (ed.), *The Impact of Parties*. London: Sage.

—— (1996). 'When Parties Matter: A Review of the Possibilities and Limits of Partisan Influence on Public Policy', *European Journal of Political Research,* 30: 155–83.

SCHMITT, HERMANN (1989). 'On Party Attachment in Western Europe and the Utility of the Eurobarometer Data', *West European Politics,* 12: 122–39.

—— and SÖREN HOLMBERG (1995). 'Political Parties in Decline?', in Hans-Dieter Klingemann and Dieter Fuchs (eds.), *Citizens and the State*. Oxford: Oxford University Press.

SCHMITTER, PHILIPPE (1982). 'Reflections on where the Theory of Neo-Corporatism Has

Gone and where the Praxis of Neo-Corporatism May Be Going', in Gerhard Lehmbruch and Philippe Schmitter (eds.), *Patterns of Corporatist Policy-Making*. London: Sage.

SCHUMPETER, JOSEPH (1942). *Capitalism, Socialism and Democracy*. New York: Harper & Row.

SCHWARTZ, THOMAS (1989). 'Why Parties?', Research Memorandum, Department of Political Science, University of California, Los Angeles.

SEGATTI, PAOLO, PAOLO BELLUCCI, and MARCO MARAFFI (1999). 'Stable Voters in an Unstable Party Environment: Continuity and Change in Italian Electoral Behavior'. Madrid: Working Paper of the Instituto Juan March de Estudios e Investigaciones (1999/139).

SELLE, PER, and LARS SVÅSAND (1983). 'The Local Party Organization and Its Members: Between Randomness and Rationality', *Scandinavian Political Studies*, 6: 211–29.

—— (1991). 'Membership in Party Organizations and the Problem of Decline of Parties', *Comparative Political Studies*, 23: 459–77.

SEMETKO, HOLLI, et al. (1991). *The Formation of Campaign Agendas*. Hillsdale, NJ: Lawrence Erlbaum.

SEYD, PATRICK (1999). 'New Parties, New Politics: A Case-Study of the British Labour Party', *Party Politics*, 5: 387–409.

—— and PAUL WHITELEY (1991). *Labour's Grass Roots: The Politics of Labour Party Membership*. Oxford: Clarendon Press.

—— —— (1992) *Labour's Grass Roots*. Oxford: Clarendon Press.

SHAMA, A. (1976). 'Marketing the Political Candidate', *Journal of the Academy of Marketing Science*, 4.

SHEPPARD, SIMON (1998). 'The Struggle for the Agenda: New Zealand Labour Party Candidate Selections 1987–93', *Political Science*, 49: 198–228.

SHEPSLE, KENNETH, and BARRY WEINGAST (1987). 'The Institutional Foundations of Committee Power', *American Political Science Review*, 81: 85–104.

SHIVELEY, W. PHILIPS (1979). 'The Development of Party Identification among Adults', *American Political Science Review*, 73: 1039–54.

SHUGART, MATTHEW SOBERG, and JOHN M. CAREY (1992). *Presidents and Assemblies: Constitutional Design and Electoral Dynamics*. New York: Cambridge University Press.

—— and MARTIN WATTENBERG (eds.) (2000). *Mixed-Member Electoral Systems: The Best of Both Worlds?* Oxford: Oxford University Press.

SIAROFF, ALAN (1999). 'Corporatism in 24 Industrial Democracies: Meaning and Measurement', *European Journal of Political Research*, 36: 175–205.

SIMMS, MARIAN (1996). *The Paradox of Parties: Australian Political Parties in the 1990s*. Sydney: Allen & Unwin.

SINCLAIR, BARBARA (1998). 'Do Parties Matter?', Paper prepared for delivery at the 56th Annual Meetings of the Midwest Political Science Association, 24–5 Apr. 1998, Chicago.

SMITH, ANTHONY (1981). 'Mass Communications', in D. Butler, H. Penniman, and A. Ranney (eds.), *Democracy at the Polls*. Washington, DC: American Enterprise Institute.

SMITH, GOLDWIN (1892). 'Party Government on its Trial', *North American Review*, 154: 582–95.

SMITH, M. R., and L. MARX (eds.) (1994). *Does Technology Drive History?* Cambridge, Mass.: MIT Press.

SPD (1995). *Anlagen zum Abschlussbericht der Arbeitsgruppe Mitgliederentwicklung.* Bonn: Sozialdemokratische Partei Deutschlands.

STAMMEN, THEO (1980). *Political Parties in Europe.* London: John Martin.

STICKNEY, ALBERT (1906). *Organized Democracy.* Boston: Houghton, Mifflin.

STIMSON, JAMES (1985). 'Regression across Time and Space', *American Journal of Political Science,* 29: 914–47.

STOKES, DONALD (1965). 'A Variance Components Model of Political Effects', in John Claunch (ed)., *Mathematical Applications in the Political Science.* Dallas: Southern Methodist University Press.

STÖSS, RICHARD (ed) .(1983), *Parteien-Handbuch.* Opladen: Westdeutscher Verlag.

STRØM, KAARE (1990*a*). *Minority Government and Majority Rule.* Cambridge: Cambridge University Press.

—— (1990*b*). 'A Behavioral Theory of Competitive Political Parties', *American Journal of Political Science,* 34: 565–98.

—— (1997). 'Democracy, Accountability, and Coalition Bargaining', *European Journal of Political Research,* 31: 42–62.

—— (2000). 'Delegation and Accountability in Parliamentary Democracies', *European Journal of Political Research,* 37.

—— and LARS SVÅSAND (eds.) (1997). *Challenges to Political Parties: The Case of Norway.* Ann Arbor: University of Michigan Press.

SUNDBERG, JAN (1996). *Partier och Partisystem i Finland.* Saarijärvi: Schildts Förlags.

—— and S. HÖGNABBA (1992). 'Finland: The 1991 Campaign', in Shaun Bowler and David Farrell (eds.), *Electoral Strategies and Political Marketing.* Houndmills, Basingstoke: Macmillan.

SVÅSAND, LARS (1997). 'Opportunities for Participation in Political Parties', Paper prepared for Conference on Democracy and Political Parties, College Station, Tex, 4–6 Apr.

—— KAARE STRØM and B. E. RASCH (1997). 'Change and Adaptation in Party Organization', in Kaare Strøm and Lars Svåsand (eds.), *Challenges to Political Parties: The Case of Norway.* Ann Arbor: University of Michigan Press.

SVENSSON PALLE (1982). 'Party Cohesion in the Danish Parliament in the 1970s', *Scandinavian Political Studies,* 5.

SWANSON, DAVID and PAOLO MANCINI (eds.) (1996*a*). 'Introduction', in David Swanson and Paolo Mancini (eds.), *Politics, Media, and Modern Democracy.* Westport, Conn: Praeger.

—— —— (eds.) (1996*b*). *Politics, Media, and Modern Democracy.* Westport, CT: Praeger.

TANAKA, AIJI. (1998). 'Two Faces of the Japanese Electorate: The Organized Voters vs. the Unorganized Voters on the Process of Partisan Realignment/Dealignment', Paper delivered at the 1998 Annual Meeting of the Americian Political Science Association, Boston, 3–6 Sept.

TEIXEIRA, RUY (1992). *The Disappearing American Voter.* Washington, DC: Brookings Institution.

THIÉBAULT, JEAN-LOIUS (1998). 'France: The Impact of Electoral System Change', in Michael Gallagher and Michael Marsh (eds.), *Candidate-Selection in Comparative Perspective.* London: Sage Publications.

THIES, MICHAEL (1998). 'When Will Pork Leave the Farm? Institutional Bias in Japan and the United States', *Legislative Studies Quarterly,* 23: 467–92.

THOMAS, JOHN CLAYTON (1975). *The Decline of Ideology in Western Political Parties.* London: Sage.

—— (1979). 'The Changing Nature of Partisan Divisions in the West: Trends in Domestic Policy Orientations in Ten Party Systems', *European Journal of Political Research,* 7: 397–413.

TOGEBY, LISE (1992). 'The Nature of Declining Party Membership in Denmark: Causes and Consequences', *Scandinavian Political Studies,* 15: 1–19.

TOPF, RICHARD (1995a). 'Electoral Participation', in Hans-Dieter Klingemann and Dieter Fuchs (eds.), *Citizens and the State.* Oxford: Oxford University Press.

—— (1995b). 'Beyond Electoral Participation', in Hans-Dieter Klingemann and Dieter Fuchs (eds.), *Citizens and the State.* Oxford: Oxford University Press.

TSEBELIS, GEORGE (1995). 'Decision Making in Political Systems: Veto Players in Presidentialism, Parliamentarism, Multicameralism, and Multipartism', *British Journal of Political Science* 25: 289–325.

TULLOCK, GORDON (1967). *Toward a Mathematics of Politics.* Ann Arbor: University of Michigan Press.

ULRAM, PETER (1994). 'Political Culture and Party System in the Kreisky Era', in Günther Bischof and Anton Pelinka (eds.), *The Kreisky Era in Austria.* New Brunswick, NJ: Transaction Publishers.

VALEN, HENRY, and DANIEL KATZ (1964). *Political Parties in Norway.* London: Tavistock Publications.

VEEN, HANS-JOACHIM, and VIOLA NEU (1995). *Politische Beteiligung in der Volkspartei.* St Augustin: Konrad-Adenuaer-Stiftung.

VERBA, SIDNEY, and NORMAN NIE (1972). *Participation in America.* Chicago: University of Chicago Press.

—— —— and JAE-ON KIM (1978). *Participation and Political Equality.* Cambridge: Cambridge University Press.

—— KAY SCHLOZMAN, and HENRY BRADY (1995). *Voice and Equality: Civic Volunteerism in American Politics.* Cambridge, Mass.: Harvard University Press.

VON BEYME, KLAUS (1985). *Political Parties in Western Democracies.* Aldershot: Gower.

VOWLES, JACK and PETER AIMER (1993). *Voters' Vengeance: The 1990 Election in New Zealand and the Fate of the Fourth Labour Government.* Auckland: Auckland University Press.

—— —— (eds.) (1994). *Double Decision: The 1993 Election and Referendum in New Zealand.* Wellington: Department of Politics, Victoria University of Wellington.

—— et al. (1995). *Towards Consensus.* Auckland: Auckland University Press.

WAGSCHAL, UWE (1998). 'Parties, Party Systems, and Policy Effects', in Paul Pennings and Jan-Erik Lane (eds.), *Comparing Party System Change.* London: Routledge.

WALLER, MICHAEL, and MEINDERT FENNEMA (1988). *Communist Parties in Western Europe.* Oxford: Basil Blackwell.

WARE, ALAN (1987a). *Political Parties: Electoral Change and Structural Response.* Oxford: Blackwell.

—— (1987b). *Citizens, Parties, and the State: A Reappraisal.* Princeton: Princeton University Press.

WATTENBERG, MARTIN (1991). *The Rise of Candidate Centered Politics*. Cambridge, Mass.: Harvard University Press.

—— (1998*a*). *The Decline of American Political Parties 1952–1996*. Cambridge, Mass.: Harvard University Press.

—— (1998*b*).'Should Election Day Be a Holiday?', *Atlantic Monthly*, (Oct.), 42–6.

—— and HANS-DIETER KLINGEMANN (1992). 'Decaying Versus Declining Party Systems: A Comparison of Party Images in the United States and West Germany', *British Journal of Political Science*, 22: 131–49.

WEBB, PAUL (1992). 'Britain: The 1987 Campaign', in Shaun Bowler and David Farrel (eds)., *Electoral Strategies and Political Marketing*. London: Macmillan.

—— (1995). 'Reforming the Labour Party–Trade Union Link: An Assessment', in David Broughton, David Farrell, David Denver, and Colin Rallings (eds.), *British Elections & Parties Yearbook 1994*. London: Frank Cass.

—— (1996). 'Antipartisanship and Anti-party Sentiment in the UK: Correlates and Constraints', *European Journal of Political Research*, 29: 365–82.

—— (2000). *The Modern British Party System*. London: Sage.

—— et al. (ed.) (2000). *Political Parties at the Millennium: Emergence, Adaptation and Decline in Democratic Societies*. Oxford: Oxford University Press.

WEINER, MYRON and JOSEPH LAPALOMBARA (1966). 'The Impact of Parties on Political Development', in Joseph LaPalombara and Myron Weiner (eds.), *Political Parties and Political Development*. Princeton: Princeton University Press.

WEINGAST, BARRY (1979). 'A Rational Choice Perspective on Congressional Norms', *American Journal of Political Science*, 23: 245–62.

—— and WILLIAM MARSHALL (1988). 'The Industrial Organization of Congress', *Journal of Political Economy*, 96: 132–63.

WEISBERG, HERBERT (1980). 'A Multidimensional Conceptualization of Party Identification', *Political Behavior*, 2: 33–60.

WEIZSÄCKER, RICHARD VON (1992). *Richard von Weizsäcker im Gesprach mit Gunter Hofmann und Werner Perger*. Frankfurt: Eichborn.

WESTEN, TRACY (1996). '2004: A Digital Election Scenario', in A. Corrado, and C. Firestone (eds.), *Elections in Cyberspace: Toward a New Era in American Politics*. Queenstown, Md.: The Aspen Institute.

WEYL, WALTER (1912). *The New Democracy: An Essay on Certain Political and Economic Tendencies in the United States*. New York: Macmillan Company.

WHITE, JOHN KENNETH and JEROME M. MILEUR (eds.) (1992). *Challenges to Party Government*. Carbondale, Ill.: Southern Illinois University Press.

WHITELEY, PAUL and PATRICK SEYD (1999). 'How to Win a Landslide By Really Trying: The Effects of Local Campaigning on Voting in the British General Election of 1997', Paper presented at the annual meetings of the American Political Science Association, Atlanta.

—— —— and JEREMY RICHARDSON (1994). *True Blues: The Politics of Conservative Party Membership*. Oxford: Clarendon Press.

WIDFELDT, ANDERS (1995). 'Party Membership and Party Representativeness', in Hans-Dieter Klingemann and Dieter Fuchs (eds.), *Citizens and the State*. Oxford: Oxford University Press.

—— (1999). *Linking Parties with People? Party Membership in Sweden 1960–1997*. London: Ashgate.

WILSON, JAMES Q. (1973). *Political Organizations*. New York: Basic Books.

WOLDENDORP, JAAP, HANS KEMAN, and IAN BUDGE (eds.) (1993). 'Political Data 1945–1990: Party Government in 20 Democracies', *European Journal of Political Research,* 24: 1–119.

World Development Indicators [computer file] (1999.) Washington DC: World Bank.

WRIGHT, WILLIAM (1971). *A Comparative Study of Party Organization*. Columbus, Oh.: Charles Merrill.

WRING, DOMINIC (1996a). 'From Mass Propaganda to Political Marketing', in C. Rallings, David Farrell, David Denver, and D. Broughton (eds.), *British Elections and Parties Yearbook 1995*. London: Cass.

—— (1996b). 'Political Marketing and Party Development in Britain', *European Journal of Marketing,* 30: 100–11.

YSMAL, COLETTE (1994). 'Transformations du militantisme et declin des partis', in Pascall Perrineau (ed.), *L'Engagement politique: declin ou mutation?* Paris: Presses de la Fondation Nationale des Sciences Politiques.

ZELLE, CARSTEN (1995). 'Social Dealignment vs. Political Frustration: Contrasting Explanations of the Floating Vote in Germany', *European Journal of Political Research,* 27: 319–45.

Index